Children in Agony

About the Author

Sibnath Deb is the Faculty Member in the Department of Applied Psychology, Calcutta University, Kolkata. Also, he is a Visiting Faculty at ISPCAN Global Institute, USA and the School of Management, Tripura University. He underwent an intensive course on HIV/AIDS and Qualitative Research in the Community Health Research Training Unit, the University of Western Australia in 1994.

Dr. Deb has authored a book, entitled *Contemporary Social Problems in India*, and has edited two books viz. *Child Abuse and Neglect: South Asian Scenario* and *Child Protection: Socio-legal Measures in India*. Dr. Deb has published 50 research papers in national and international journals of repute. In his 16 years research and academic career he has handled more than 35 large-scale qualitative and quantitative studies on various issues like reproductive and child health including HIV/AIDS, child maltreatment, social and clinical psychology in addition to evaluation of different intervention, programmes for national and international agencies. He is Hony. Founder Secretary of MIDSW an NGO, Council Member of the International Society for Prevention of Child Abuse and Neglect, USA, and founder Vice President of the Indian National Society for Prevention of Child Abuse and Neglect. Currently he is associated with ITPI (Training) and ICMR Task Force Research Project as well.

Children in Agony
A Source Book

Dr. Sibnath Deb

Department of Applied Psychology
Calcutta University
Kolkata

CONCEPT PUBLISHING COMPANY, NEW DELHI-110059

Cataloging in Publication Data—DK
Courtesy: D.K. Agencies (P) Ltd. <docinfo@dkagencies.com>

Deb, Sibnath.
Children in agony : a source book / Sibnath Deb.
p. cm.
With special reference to India.
Includes bibliographical references.
Includes index.
ISBN 8180693252

1. Children—Crimes against. 2. Children—Crimes against—India. I. Title.

DDC 362.880 83 22

ISBN 81-8069-325-2

First Published 2006

Published and Printed by
Ashok Kumar Mittal
Concept Publishing Company
A/15-16, Commercial Block, Mohan Garden
New Delhi-110059 (India)
Phones: 25351460, 25351794
Fax: 091-11-25357103
E-mail: publishing@conceptpub.com

Dedicated to my parents

Late Sushil Chandra Deb, B.Sc.,B.T.,B.L

&

Shandhya Deb

Foreword

Child Abuse and Neglect are worldwide problems; they are part of the lifecycle of violence that afflicts many individuals and is a scourge for society. In 2002 the World Health Organization published its *World Report on Violence and Health** as a response to the 1996 World Health Assembly resolution to address violence as a public health priority. In this report, which is cited by Dr. Deb, the incidence of violence is estimated for various nations and various ages. The report showed the homicide rate for young men 15 to 29 years of age to be 19.4 per 100,000, or about 4.5 times that of their female counterparts. The suicide rate in this age group is cited as 13.9. In children 5 to 14 years of age the suicide and homicide rates are each reported as approximately 2 per 100,000. The homicide rate in children under 5 years is 2.5 times higher at 5.3, while their suicide rate is, thankfully, zero. As high as these figures are, they probably underestimate the true magnitude of the problem. Even in developed countries where child maltreatment has been addressed systematically for several decades even the worst form of maltreatment, which results in death can be missed. In developing countries where such statistics are not yet being gathered systematically and where there is a not a systematic approach to child abuse prevention, the true incidence is likely to be significantly higher.

---

*Krug EG, Dahlberg LL, Mercy JA, Zwi AB, Lozano Re. World report on violence and health. Geneva: World Health Organization; 2002. Available in pdf format at: http://www.who.int/violence_injury_prevention/violence/world_report/wrvh1/en/ It can also be obtained by writing Marketing and Dissemination, World Health Organization, 1211 Geneva 27, Switzerland.

The World Report through a review of the world literature identifies a number of stressors that render children more vulnerable to abuse either because of their own characteristics or because of those of their caregivers or those of the society that surround them. Among these are poverty, overcrowding, instability, availability of arms and illicit drugs, and previous history of violence. Poverty predisposes to abuse mainly through the children's diminished social capital. Into the lower social strata migrate people with lower cognitive ability, mental illness or substance abuse. Poor housing is often overcrowded and its occupants more subject to eviction and frequent relocations. In these circumstances children are less likely to be cared for adequately by their parents and less likely to find others to offer nurture and shelter. They are less likely to receive the education they need to get out of poverty and more likely to be socialized into violent or deviant lifestyles. This cycle is costly for the child who loses his potential for happiness and fulfilment for the family who loses a loving, productive member and for the society that loses a valuable contributor.

Dr. Sibnath Deb has undertaken to paint a picture of the condition of children and their maltreatment around the world with special attention to India, where poverty is widespread, and where children can be considered their parents' property to treat as they will. The issues that are covered in this source book, Children in Agony, include family violence and its impact on children, child abuse and neglect, child labour, child trafficking and prostitution, street children, and juvenile delinquency. Dr. Deb illustrates the lengths to which parents and teachers go to push their children to excel in education and that is to the point of causing injury or even suicide. Some children are forced to work, exploited sexually, sometimes with the mistaken belief that this will cure sexually transmitted diseases in adults, and even sacrificed to appease the gods. In a Kolkata based study carried out by the author, five aggravating factors for parents' cruelty and sociopathic family environment were revealed and these were illiteracy, unemployment, conjugal discord, lack of attachment and history of victimization in the early life of parents.

Dr. Deb is courageous: there is a great deal of pressure to hide the problem of child maltreatment in one's own home, in one's one culture and in one's own country. His book is as disturbing as it is honest, as distressing as it is inspirational in its call to action to prevent child maltreatment. One might well ask, "The problem is so big, where can we to start" and the answer is, 'Anywhere'? Child maltreatment can be prevented by providing all children with the nurture they need to achieve their potential. Children are entitled to this nurture as is decreed by the Convention on the Rights of the Child, to which India like virtually all nations of the world is a signatory. Working with parents to improve child-rearing practices would be a helpful step. Children who are particularly vulnerable to abuse need to be identified and their circumstance improved so that the abuse is never realized. Children who have been maltreated need to be rescued from their noxious environment, either by improving that environment or my removing them to a better situation.

In each of the phases of prevention there is work enough for all disciplines and for all members of society. The multidisciplinary approach is recommended by Dr. Deb who urges improved services and training especially for health professionals and law enforcement agencies. He mentions particularly the National Initiative for Child Protection (NICP), which is a campaign initiated by the Ministry of Social Justice and Empowerment, Government of India, through the National Institute of Social Defence and CHILDLINE India Foundation. It is intended to build partnerships with all responsible sectors and the general population and aims to foster child protection and promote the rights of children by creating a child friendly environment. Dr. Deb also urges community awareness programmes. He has provided some suggestions on how all members of Indian society can take part in addressing this issue and eradicating child abuse.

At a time when globalization can provide greater economic opportunities as well as possible added hazards, India and its economic and political allies would be well served to view its young population as a valuable natural resource and invest in its well-being and their collective future. Children in Agony can serve as a useful source book to assist child rights activists, researchers and policy makers in their task of meeting the needs of children. Would it not be wonderful if the next edition of this book found that its title had to be changed because it was no longer applicable? It is my hope that in reading this book you too will be inspired to do your part and make it so.

Dr. Marcellina Mian, M.D.
Former President of ISPCAN
Professor, Department of Paediatrics
University of Toronto, Canada

Preface

This book addresses the problems encountered by the children in general and disadvantaged children in particular. Efforts have been made to address their problems globally with special reference to India. The issues, which were covered in this book, include family violence and its impact on children, child abuse and neglect, child labour, child trafficking and prostitution, street children, and juvenile delinquency. All these problems are interrelated and have a direct link with poverty, lack of parental guidance and care and family violence. The author has been working on different dimensions of the problem of children and adolescents for the last 15 years as a researcher and social activist. While working in these fields author realized that it is utmost importance to sensitize the larger society, irrespective of social strata, about the problems of children and adolescents with a view to creating more child friendly environment.

Although it is commonly stated that children are the most valuable resources or assets of the society, their rights are largely ignored across the world. However, the U.N. Convention on the Rights of the Child is providing an important foundation to sensitize the larger society about specific rights a child should enjoy and to adopt legislation in different countries in the light of their socio-economic and cultural scenario.

But unfortunately right from mother's womb and infancy stage a large number of children are subjected to various forms of discrimination, maltreatment, abuse and neglect, which affect their normal physical and mental development and as a result the nation loses a good amount of potential human resource. There is no accurate estimation about the magnitude and extent of the problems of children with regard to different issues addressed in this book. However, various national and international agencies have given some estimation, which is sufficient to have some idea about the severity of the problems children face throughout the world especially in the developing countries. There is no doubt that these estimations are not accurate and/or underreported.

Child labour and trafficking in children are the simple examples of deep-rooted problem of a society which has failed to protect and care for its children, a community that is either ignorant of the exploitation or does not feel shame in trading its children for gain.

There are a number of legislations in India to safeguard the rights of the children. Some of the legislations also have some shortcomings and some new legislations should be adopted to address specific problems like boys' sexual abuse and to stop cultural practices, which causes harm to children's career, and social and personality development. But if one prioritizes the problems faced by the huge number of children in the developing countries, the issue of child abuse and neglect does not figure in the top five priority areas. The support which is required for a large number of children in the developing countries like India include adequate nutrition, immunization, other health care facilities, education and safe shelter. Hence, most governmental and non-government agencies give first priority to address the above issues. There is very little awareness, both in the general public and among welfare service providers, regarding the extent and severity of maltreatment and/or abuse of children in India. Furthermore, cultural beliefs and practices have aggravated the problems of children. Most of the child abuse cases occur within the family first and perpetrators are the parents and/or close family members. But owing to lack of consciousness about the issue, lack of implementing machineries and also lack of political will perpetrators are not punished. In order to address the problems of children and adolescent, joint and coordinated effort is required both at the local, regional, national and international level. Otherwise, one day social stability will be at stake if a small portion of abused and neglected children drift into a negative direction.

However, the scenario with regard to problems of children has changed little despite continuous efforts made by the national and international agencies. Moreover, more and more serious steps should be taken in the developing countries to combat problems of children like child abuse and neglect in general and child trafficking, child prostitution, child labour, problems of street children in particular. As Prof. David Finkelhor of the University of New Hampshire, USA reports in the 1996 ISPCAN Report on the State of Child Abuse, Neglect and Exploitation World-wide, 'Child abuse awareness and prevention activities continue in an upward trend, revealing many exciting developments and possibilities. Perhaps most importantly, our knowledge base about the problem is expanding at a rapid rate. Journals are filled with reports about new treatment approaches and insights about the causes and consequences of abuse. The foundation of the professional expertise grows broader and stronger every year. More and more practitioners from different disciplinary backgrounds have been trained and developed specialization in the field. And this knowledge and awareness is expanding across international boundaries at a rapid pace. Every year new places in the world add concern about child abuse to their social and political agendas, including places that at one time seemed very remote from the discussion of these issues. International awareness is also reflected in recent involvement by international organizations in the cause'. With regard to prevention of child maltreatment and abuse the role of UNICEF, ILO, ECPAT, World Vision, ISPCAN and other international agencies is remarkable.

The perception of Prof. David Finkelhor with regard to success in combating child abuse and neglect, perhaps, is partially correct in case of progress in the developing countries. In the developing countries problems are totally different and deep-rooted than that of the industrial countries. In the developing countries a large number of people live below the poverty line and an about one-third population are illiterate. This apart, deep-rooted cultural beliefs and practices and social as well as wide class differences in terms of level of income are the root causes of all these problems of children like child labour, child trafficking and prostitution, helpless condition of street children. It is very difficult to bring overnight change in the situation or to improve the economic condition of the population neither it is possible to eradicate the cultural belief and practices in regard to various issues which affect children like child marriage, sexual abuse of children, and corporal punishment. It requires continuous, planned, sincere and honest efforts to improve the situation, only after a long time one can see the changes in outlook and attitude of elderly people towards children and there could be a child friendly environment. However, over the past one two decades some positive development has been observed in the developing countries too owing to active role of government and non-government organizations. Some of the local NGOs are really working well while some still suffer from lack of professional outlook and proper planning to address the problems of children. At the same time a strong emphasis on documentation and dissemination of their invaluable experience is needed for the purpose of strengthening cooperation and coordination among NGOs with the higher aim of delivering effective services within the limited resources available.

National and international funding agencies should develop some mechanism to monitor the project activities sponsored by them for optimum and effective utilization of resources. There is a wrong notion about the term evaluation as if somebody is coming from outside to find out their faults. In fact, monitoring and evaluation help to understand the shortcomings and gaps in service delivery and in turn it guides the respective organization to take course corrective measures.

The broad objective of this book is to share the first hand experience of the author with regard to different dimensions of the problems of children and to sensitize the social activists, academicians, social and health researchers and policy makers about those issues. The specialty of this book is that apart from the discussion of theoretical and practical knowledge, selective latest study findings, which were reported in the index journals across the globe are provided in this book which will be of immense help for future researchers, academicians, social activists and policy makers.

Efforts have been made to ensure that there is no error and/or printing mistake in the book. However, if there is any mistake and/ or error the same is regretted. The author welcomes any suggestion and guidance, which can be addressed and incorporated in the next edition of this book.

Dr. Sibnath Deb

Faculty Member, Department of Applied Psychology
University College of Science and Technology
University of Calcutta
92, A.P.C. Road, Kolkata -700 009, India
E-mail: sibnath@vsnl.net/sibnath23@rediffmail.com

Acknowledgements

This book is the product of my long field and research experience. The task of writing this book has further been facilitated by discussions, feedbacks and inputs with the personnel of child welfare organisations, academicians, lawyers, pediatricians and my teachers and colleagues in the Department of Applied Psychology, University of Calcutta. In fact, my academic background in Psychology has helped me a lot to understand the problems of children addressed in this book and to complete this task sucessfully. I am grateful to my first teacher in Psychology Shri Salil Chakraborty who motivated me to study this subject. Thereafter, I had good orientation in the Department of Psychology, M.B.B. College, Agartala. My acknowledgement is due to all my teachers in the said Department. I wish to express my deep gratitude and indebtedness to Prof. Sukumar Bose for his judicious guidance in completing my doctoral thesis successfully. Truly speaking, broad outlook of Prof. Sukumar Bose and his style of work addicted me to stick to research. I am also grateful to my other teachers and colleagues in the Department of Applied Psychology, Calcutta University for their valuable inputs in writing the book.

My work experience in one of the leading NGOs in West Bengal called CINI (Child In Need Institute) was an eye opener in my career in the development sector especially in the field of mother and child welfare as well as community-based intervention programmes. During this period I have been exposed to various intervention programmes meant for street and slum children and for the children of commercial sex workers. I was actively involved with a long-term action research project aimed at rehabilitating street children and the children of commercial sex workers through institute and community based rehabilitation programmes. The said project taught me a lot of lessons. I am grateful to Dr. Samir Narayan

Choudhury, Director of CINI, Lakshmi Chatterjee and Dr. Shishir Senapati for giving me the opportunity to work with them and to learn more about the problems of disadvantaged children and community life.

The real break in my career was in TNS MODE—one of the leading and largest multidisciplinary professional research companies in India. I will remain grateful to D.P. Basu, Managing Director of MODE MODELERS Pvt. Ltd. for giving me the opportunity to work in the company. Whatever professional outlook I have developed and/or confidence I have today, for the same, credit goes to D.P. Basu. In fact, I consider him as my professional role model.

I have been associated with the International Society for the Prevention of Child Abuse and Neglect (ISPCAN), USA for the last eight years. I have learnt a lot attending international and regional conferences on child abuse and neglect organised by ISPCAN and also from personal interaction with the authority figures in the field of child abuse and neglect. I am a grateful to Prof. Mercellina Mian, former President of ISPCAN for reviewing my book and writing foreword for the same despite her busy schedule. I am also grateful to Prof. Barbara Bonner, President of ISPCAN, Dr. Danya Glaser, President-Elect, Prof. Harendra de Silva, Prof. Mohd. Shyam Bin Kasim, Prof. Jon Conte, Dr. Kim Oates, Prof. Tilman Furniss, Dr. Irene Intebi, Kimberly Svevo and all other Council Members and staff of ISPCAN for their continuous support and cooperation for sharing of information. In fact, ISPCAN is a resourceful platform for the professionals for sharing and exchanging knowledge in the field of child maltreatment.

In addition, personal interaction with the authority figures in the field of corporal punishment and sexual abuse like Prof. Murray Straus, Prof. David Finklehor and Prof. Games Garbarino in different international programmes enlightened me in this field, which in turn helped me in writing this book. I must record my gratitude to all of them, respectively.

I am also grateful to UNICEF, New York for giving me scholarship for attending the ISPCAN International Congress in Denver in 2002. Encouragement, support and guidance of Gopalan

Balagopal, Senior Adviser, Child Protection Programme of UNICEF, New York deserves due respect.

I am thankful to disadvantaged children of our country for giving me time and sharing valuable information while carrying out study on different dimensions of their problems. In am grateful to Kathakali Mitra, Dipal De, Dr. Gautam Sengupta and Purba Paul for editing my book. I am also thankful to Dr. Dipty Jain, Associate Professor of the Government Medical College, Nagpur, Dr. Deepti Pagare of the Maulana Azad Medical College, New Delhi and to NGO personnel in West Bengal, Mumbai, Delhi and Nagpur for sharing their experience and study findings with me which I have incorporated in this book with due acknowledgement.

It would be an incomplete task if I do not acknowledge and honour the contribution of my beloved father Late Sushil Chandra Deb in my life in developing academic outlook and for coming in academic field. My father is no more but his outlook, visions, honesty, sincerity and value in life still inspire me to work for the disadvantaged population in general and disadvantaged children in particular. Encouragement from my father-in-law Hon'ble Justice D. Biswas further motivated me to complete this book. I must record his continuous encouragement with due respect. It would have been an impossible task for me to complete this book had I not been received cooperation and support from my family. In the last one year I could not give adequate time to my family on account of my commitment in writing this book. I am thankful to my children Shayana Deb and Ayushmann Deb and wife for bearing with me and for extending their cooperation for writing this book. I am also thankful to Ananya Deb and Diptaraj Deb for their continuous support. Finally, I would like to extend my gratitude to all my siblings and other family members for their contribution and support in my career.

Dr. Sibnath Deb

Contents

[1]

Family Violence and Its Impact on Children

Introduction

By the common consent of the enlightened public opinion, 'family' is the oldest social institution that has been acting as a rendezvous of human soul, mind, body, a repository of all human values, beliefs, faiths, wisdom, knowledge and experience. Family is the most protective and intimate place on earth. Family, the atomic unit of society, has always exerted a sobering, civilizing, humanizing influence on the generations of children the world over. But for the institution of family the world would have been something else than what it is today. In short, family has played the greatest role as shaper, builder and architect of human civilization.

The American Home Economics Association and the American Association of Family and Consumer Science define the family unit as:

> *"Two or more persons who share resources, share responsibility for decisions, share values and goals, and have commitment to one another over time. The family is that climate that one comes home to and it is this network of sharing and commitments that most accurately describes the family unit, regardless of blood, legal ties, adoption, or marriage."*

In the truest sense, family is a place to be considered as warm, safe, personal, and peaceful. But it does not always happen. Violence between members of family has a historical tradition that goes back centuries and cuts across continents. However, until the 1960s, most people considered family violence a rare phenomenon. Traditionally family violence was viewed as a private family matter. But by now family violence has been recognized as a significant social and public health problem for both the developed and developing countries. Lia-Hoagberg *et al.* (2001) and Weiss *et al.* (2000) stated that currently family violence has become a major social and health problem in the United States. In India family violence is a very common phenomenon, which causes major problems in the family and affects the process of development of mind and future career of the children. However, this issue is yet to be recognized as a social and public health problem in India.

According to *National Crime Victimization Survey Report* of 1999 conducted by the Department of Justice, every 90 seconds, a person over the age of 12 is sexually assaulted. That translates to 40 an hour, 960 per day, and 350,000 per year. A 1992 study conducted by the National Victim Centre, found the incidence almost twice as high (Kilpatrick *et al.*, 1992).

The National Violence Against Women Survey found that rape is a crime committed primarily against youth. Of the women who reported being raped, 21.6 per cent were below 12, 32.4 per cent were between 2 to 17, 29 per cent were between 8 to 24, and 16.6 per cent were over 25 years. Thus, 54.0 per cent of women victims were below 18 years at the time of the first rape and 83.0 per cent were below the age of 25 (Tjaden *et al.*, 1998). According to the U.S. Department of Justice, nearly 6 out of 10 rape/sexual assault incidents are reported by victims to have occurred in their own home or at the home of a friend, relative, or neighbour (Administration for Children and Families, 1995).

Definition of Family Violence

There is no unanimous definition of family violence. In fact, it is very difficult to define the term family violence. The term family violence and domestic violence is used interchangeably in different literatures. The meaning of both the terminologies is same. Different researchers used different definitions and different terminologies in their studies. Some of the definitions are given below which are used by different researchers and academicians:

One definition views violence as 'an act carried out with the intention or perceived intention of causing physical pain or injury to another person. The physical pain can range from slight pain i.e. a slap to murder.'

Another author defined 'domestic/family violence' 'as a systematic pattern of abusive behaviour occurring over a period of time, that may become more frequent and severe and are done for the purpose of control, domination, and/or coercion. Such behaviour may include verbal abuse and threats; physical, psychological and sexual abuse; and destruction of property and pets. The batterer frequently accomplishes the abuses in an environment of his own creation that ultimately traps the victim in a state of fear, isolation, deprivation and confusion' (Schornstein, 1997).

Barbara Hart, a nationally recognized expert on family violence, defines family/domestic violence as 'family/domestic violence involves a continuum of behaviours ranging from degrading remarks to cruel jokes, economic exploitation, punches and kicks, false imprisonment, sexual abuse, suffocating actions, maiming assaults and homicide. Unchecked, domestic violence usually increases in frequency and severity. Many victims suffer all forms of abuse. Verbal and emotional abuse may be subtler than physical harm, but this does not mean that it is less destructive to victims. Many have said that the emotional scars take much longer to heal than the broken bones.'

According to *Texas Family Code* (Section 71.004) 'Family Violence' is defined as:

An act by a member of a family or household against another member of the family or household that is intended to result in physical harm, bodily injury, assault or sexual assault or that is a threat that reasonably places the member in fear of imminent physical harm, bodily injury, assault or sexual assault, but does not include defensive measures to protect-oneself;

Abuse by a member of a family or household towards a child of the family-or-household; or

Dating violence as defined by Section 71.0021.

'Dating Violence' is defined in the *Texas Family Code* (Section 71.0021) as:

'Dating violence' means an act by an individual that is against another individual with whom that person has or has had a dating relationship and that is intended to result in physical harm, bodily injury, assault or sexual assault or that is a threat that reasonably places the individual in fear of imminent physical harm, bodily injury, assault or sexual assault, but does not include defensive measures to protect oneself.

For the purposes of this title, 'dating relationship' means a relationship between individuals who have or have had a continuing relationship of a romantic or intimate nature. The existence of such a relationship shall be determined based on consideration of the length of the relationship; the nature of the relationship; and the frequency and type of interaction between the persons involved in the relationship.

A casual acquaintanceship or ordinary fraternization in a business or social context does not constitute a 'dating relationship' under Sub-section (b).

Texas Council on Family Violence (TCFV) defines battering as:

A pattern of coercive controls are those which one person exercises over another. Battering is a behaviour that physically harms, arouses fear, prevents a woman from doing what she wishes or forces her to behave in ways she does not want. Battering includes the use of physical and sexual violence, threats and intimidation, emotional abuse and economic deprivation.

The Texas Council on Family Violence (TCFV) has been a leader in the effort to end violence against women in USA. It was established in 1978.

TCFV is one of the largest domestic violence coalitions in the nation. The broad objective of TCFV is to allow women and their families to live violence-free. Activities of TCFV include:

- Assists Texas battered women's shelters, battering intervention and prevention programmes and other family violence service providers,
- Provides prompt answers to thousands of technical assistance questions each year,

- Maintains extensive resource files and a lending library of books, manuals, reports, audio tapes and video tapes on domestic violence and related issues,
- Develops and facilitates training for professionals working with victims and perpetrators of domestic violence,
- Advocates for laws and policies that affect battered women and their children,
- Operates the National Domestic Violence Hotline, a 24-hour hotline for women in crisis and their families.

Domestic violence episodes are not random acts of violence or incidents of mere loss of temper. Rather, such episodes are part of a complex, continuing pattern of behaviour, of which the violence is but one dynamic. The perpetrator of such abuses is one who currently is or has been involved with the victims in an intimate relationship (*Source*: American Medical Association, 1992).

However, family violence can be divided into two broad categories, viz. normal and abusive violence.

Normal Violence: The slaps, pushes, shoves, and spankings that are frequently considered as normal or acceptable part while rearing children or interacting with a spouse.

Abusive Violence: These acts are defined as the acts that have the high potential for injuring the person by the following means, i.e. punches, kicks, bites, choking, beatings, shootings, stabbing (intentional or unintentional).

This apart, a prominent category of family violence in India results from dowry cases between inter-casts and love marriages.

Incidence of Family Violence

Family violence is a serious social and health problem in the developed countries. In the developing countries the situation is no way better than that of developed countries. In the developing countries like India the situation is in suppressed state and that is why it is not visible. On the other hand, there is no data on this issue based on large sample. A tip of the iceberg is reported in the developing countries owing to factors like lack of economic independence of Indian women, male dominated society, social status/stigma, and strong social network. However, from the reported information in the daily newspapers it may be stated that the rate of family violence and thereby the rate of divorce is increasing in the developing countries especially among middle and upper middle class educated families.

Current research findings indicate that family violence occurs all over America and around the world regardless of ethnic, racial, socio-economic, gender and age groups (*Source*: Massachusetts Coalition of Battered Women Service Groups, 1990). Since in the developed countries, documentation of information in regard to any issue is very systematic and up-dated, we have some figures on this.

Prevalence of Family Violence in USA

- Approximately 1.5 million women are raped and/or physically assaulted by an intimate partner each year in the United States (*Source*: National Institute of Justice, July 2000).
- The National Domestic Violence Hotline (NDVH) has received more than 747,000 calls since February 1996 (*Source*: NDVH, April 2002).
- Estimates range from 960,000 incidents of violence against a current or former spouse, boyfriend, or girlfriend per year to 4 million women who are physically abused by their husbands or live-in partners per year (Source: Violence by Intimates: Analysis of Data on Crimes by Current or Former Spouses, Boyfriends and Girlfriends, U.S. Department of Justice, March, 1998).
- While women are less likely than men to be victims of violent crimes overall, women are 5 to 8 times more likely than men to be victimized by an intimate partner (*Source*: Violence by Intimates: Analysis of Data on Crimes by Current or Former Spouses, Boyfriends and Girlfriends, U.S. Department of Justice, March, 1998).
- Violence by an intimate accounts for about 21 per cent of violent crime experienced by women and about 2 per cent of the violence experienced by men (*Source*: Violence by

Intimates: Analysis of Data on Crimes by Current or Former Spouses, Boyfriends and Girlfriends, U.S. Department of Justice, March, 1998).

- In 1994, women separated from their spouses had a victimization rate 1½ times higher than separated men, divorced men, or divorced women (*Source*: Sex Differences in Violent Victimization, 1994, U.S. Department of Justice, September, 1997).

Homicide

- On an average, more than three women are murdered by their husbands or boyfriends in US everyday. In 1998, approximately 1,830 murders were attributed to intimates; nearly three out of four of the murder victims (1,320 total) were women (*Source*: U.S. Department of Justice, Intimate Partner Violence, May 2000).
- In 1996, among all female murder victims in the U.S., 30 per cent were slain by their husbands or boyfriends (*Source*: Uniform Crime Reports of the U.S. 1996, Federal Bureau of Investigation, 1996).
- 31,260 women were murdered by an intimate from 1976-1996 (*Source*: Violence by Intimates: Analysis of Data on Crimes by Current or Former Spouses, Boyfriends, and Girlfriends, U.S. Department of Justice, March 1998).

Children

- When children are killed during a domestic dispute, 90 per cent are under the age of 10; 56 per cent are under age of two (*Source*: Florida Governor's Task Force on Domestic and Sexual Violence, Florida Mortality Review Project, 1997, p. 51, Table 28).
- Studies show that child abuse occurs in 30-60 per cent of family violence cases that involve families with children (*Source*: 'The overlap between child maltreatment and woman battering.' J.L. Edleson, Violence Against Women, February, 1999).

- A child's exposure to the father abusing the mother is the strongest risk factor for transmitting violent behaviour from one generation to the next (*Source*: Report of the American Psychological Association Presidential Task Force on Violence and the Family, APA, 1996).
- Forty per cent of teenage girls age 14 to 17 reports knowing someone their age that has been hit or beaten by a boyfriend (*Source*: Children Now/Kaiser Permanente poll, December, 1995).
- Each year, an estimated 3.3 million children are exposed to violence by family members against their mothers or female caretakers (*Source*: American Psychological Association, Violence and the Family: Report of the American Psychological Association Presidential Task Force on Violence and the Family, 1996, p. 11).
- In homes where partner abuse occurs, children are 1,500 times more likely to be abused (*Source*: Department of Justice, Bureau of Justice Assistance, Family Violence: Interventions for the Justice System, 1993).
- In a national survey of more than 2,000 American families, approximately 50 per cent of the men who frequently assaulted their wives also frequently abused their children (*Source*: Murray A. Straus and Richard J. Gelles, Physical Violence in American Families, 1990).

Dating Violence

- One in five adolescent girls physically and/or sexually abused in a dating relationship (*Source*: Dating Violence Against Adolescent Girls and Associated Substance Abuse, Unhealthy Weight Control, Sexual Risk Behaviour, Pregnancy and Suicide; *Journal of the American Medical Association*, August 2001).
- Physical and sexual abuse against adolescent girls in dating relationships increases the likelihood that the girl will abuse drugs and/or alcohol, develop an eating disorder, consider and/or attempt suicide, engage in risky sexual behaviour and/or become pregnant (*Source*: Dating Violence Against

Adolescent Girls and Associated Substance Abuse, Unhealthy Weight Control, Sexual Risk Behaviour, Pregnancy and Suicide; *Journal of the American Medical Association,* August 2001).

Stalking

- It is estimated that 503,485 women are stalked by an intimate partner each year in the United States (*Source*: National Institute of Justice, July 2000).
- Seventy-eight per cent of stalking victims are women. Women are significantly more likely than men (60 per cent and 30 per cent, respectively) to be stalked by intimate partners (*Source*: Center for Policy Research, Stalking in America, July 1997).

Domestic Violence and the Workplace

- Family violence costs the nation from $5 to $10 billion annually in medical expenses, police and court costs, shelters and foster care, sick leave, absenteeism, and non-productivity (*Source*: Medical News, American Medical Association, January 1992).
- Husbands and boyfriends commit 13,000 acts of violence against women in the workplace every year (Source: Violence and Theft in the Workplace, U.S. Department of Justice, July 1994).
- The majority of welfare recipients have experienced domestic abuse in their adult lives and a high percentage is currently abused (*Source*: Trapped by Poverty, Trapped by Abuse: New Evidence Documenting the Relationship Between Domestic Violence and Welfare, The Taylor Institute, April 1997).
- National Sample Survey carried out among 400,000 women in USA revealed the following findings (*Source*: U.S. Department of Justice, 1994):
  - More than 2.5 million women experience violent crime victimization annually.

— Women are about equally likely to experience violent crime perpetrated by a relative, an intimate, an acquaintance, or a stranger.
— About one in four attacks on females involve the use of a weapon by the offender.
— About one three attacks on females involve a firearm.
— About one-third of female victims of violent crime are injured as a result of the crime.

Table 1.1: Family Violence Incidents in Texas

Family Violence	*2002*	*2001*	*2000*	*1999*	*1998*	*1997*
Family violence incidents	183,440	180,385	175,282	177,176	175,725	181,773
Women killed by intimate male partners	117	113	104	99	110	102

Source: Texas Department of Public Safety reports on a calendar year basis, January 1 - December 31, 1997.

***Some Statistics of Family Violence in Texas** (Source: Texas Department of Public Safety, 2000):*

- Batterers between the ages of 20 and 24 accounted for the highest number of family violence incidents in Texas in 2000, with the second highest being batterers between the ages of 25 and 29.
- The majority of victims of family violence in Texas in 2000 were between the ages of 20 and 24.
- In 2000, there were more than 615 Texas law enforcement officers assaulted during the course of reported family violence incidents.
- The most common weapon involved in family violence cases in 2000 in Texas was physical force through the use of hands, feet and fists. That accounted for 77 per cent of the incidents.

- Of all the women killed in 1997 in Texas, 35 per cent were murdered by their intimate male partners. This is higher than the national average of 28 per cent reported by the FBI.

But unfortunately in the developing countries as in India, there is no system of maintaining a record of family violence for prediction of incidence and magnitude of the problem. Sometimes in local police stations these sorts of cases are reported which go fully underreported. Family violence and/or wife beating cases are not reported because of a number of reasons like lack of inaction on the part of police, lack of NGOs working in this field, lack of social/family network, low level of education, economic dependence, and lack of social awareness.

Myths and Misconceptions about Family Violence

In every society there are some myths and misconceptions about family violence among a large number of population, which has developed over a period of time. These myths and misconceptions play a significant role in developing wrong attitude towards family violence victims. Myths and belief are not based on facts, which can negatively influence treatment and ensure intervention of the victims. Proper understanding about the truth in regard to family violence is necessary to intervene in such case. There are numerous myths about family violence. Some of the popular myths and misconceptions are given below for having proper understanding about this issue:

Chart I: Myths and Misconceptions about Family Violence

1.	Myth: Fact:	The victims caused the violence. She 'asked for it'. The battered caused the violence; he is responsible for his actions.
2.	Myth: Fact:	The victims enjoy the abuse. This is often combined with another myth: If she didn't enjoy it, she would leave him. No one enjoys being beaten.
3.	Myth: Fact:	Family violence is a family or private matter. Family violence is a crime against the victim and against society.
4.	Myth: Fact:	The incidence of family violence is overstated. It is not that much of a problem. Regardless of the exact statistics, family violence is a significant problem across the country.
5.	Myth: Fact:	If the victim left the batterer, the violence would stop. Most victims are in greater danger of increased violence after they leave the abuser.
6.	Myth: Fact:	Family violence only occurs in lower socio-economic groups. Family violence occurs in all socio-economic groups.
7.	Myth: Fact:	Women are just as violent as men. Men make up the overwhelming percentage of family violence perpetrators.
8.	Myth: Fact:	The assault is an isolated incident, unlikely to happen again. Battering is part of a complex pattern of domination and control.
9.	Myth: Fact:	If he beat her up, he must be mentally ill. Mental illness is not a prerequisite for family violence.

(*Source:* Schornstein, 1997)

Causes of Family Violence

Causes behind family violence are numerous, which also vary from society to society and culture to culture. In the developing countries, poor financial condition, lack of education, personality factors, addiction, stress and leading a disruptive life are the major factors behind family violence. Even within the developing countries like India causes of family violence are different among different social strata. In general, it may be stated that family violence occurs more in the lower and upper social strata and the precipitating and predisposing factors are also different in case of these two different social strata. In lower social strata, lack of education, alcoholism, poor financial condition, poor housing and some familial situations are the factors behind family violence while in the upper social strata leading a disruptive social life, alcoholism, stress and strain in daily social life, ego-clash are the main reasons behind it. Researchers across the globe carried out a number of studies on this issue. Findings of some of the studies are presented below:

Weiss *et al.* (2000) stated that family violence affects millions of women in the United States each year. National Research Council (1993) revealed that children whose fathers are unemployed or work part-time are more likely to be abused compared with children of fathers with full-time jobs. National Research Council further indicated that low-income families have the highest rates of physical abuse and are the most likely to be reported. Those in the lowest income groups have 2 or 3 time greater rates of abuse than upper-income group of families. Again, it is important to remember that abuse does occur in all economic groups, but it is most likely to happen among the poor or disadvantaged population.

Given that poverty and unemployment are linked to violence towards children, it is also assumed that other forms of personal and family stress are associated with violence and abuse. A number of researchers have found that overall levels of stressful events in a family and particular stressful events, such as birth of a new baby, presence of a handicapped person in the home, illness, death of a family member, and child are problems linked to higher rates of abuse and violence (Egeland *et al.*, 1980).

There is a saying that family violence is confined to mentally disturbed or sick people. But the Sociologist Murray Straus (1980) claims that mental illness or psychiatric disorders cause fewer than 10 per cent of all instances of family violence.

Although there is an increased awareness about the extent of family violence and the fact that violence is not always caused by mental illness or psychopathology, many people still believe that violence in general, and family violence in particular, is confined to lower social strata and among families having racial and ethnic minorities. This myth is correct as a good number of researchers found out more violence and abuse among the lower class (Gelles 1992, 1995). It is also true that most forms of family violence do not occur with equal frequency across social groups. Social factors are relevant in explaining family violence. Indeed, offenders and victims of family violence originate from every level of the society.

In addition, it is important to point out the dynamic nature of social factors. Changes in social circumstances, such as becoming unemployed or encountering economic problems, can accelerate the risk of abuse and violence in a family or in any close/intimate relationship. In a number of studies it was found that the parents who were abused as children abuse their own children.

Alcohol and drug abuses are the real cause of family violence in the home of the developed and developing countries. A lot of studies found a considerable association between drinking and violence (Fagan, 1990, Gelles, 1974 and Guttmacher, 1995). In case of spousal violence, both the offender and the victim have frequently been drinking before the violence. Perhaps as many as half the instances of violence and abuse involve some influence of alcohol or drugs—a very strong association. But do drugs or alcohol themselves cause people to be violent? Would solving the drug or drinking problem eliminate the violence? Most of the people would say 'Yes'. But findings of some research say 'No'. MacAndrew and Edgerton (1969) observed those peoples' reaction to drinking as varying from culture to culture. In some cultures, people drink and become violent; in others, people drink and remain passive.

Social stress and isolation are also strongly correlated to family violence. Sexual difficulties, low job satisfaction, large family size and poor housing conditions are all related to marital divorce. The more socially isolated a family is, the higher the risk that there will be wife abuse (Fagan and Browne, 1994).

Lown and Vega (2001) determined the lifetime prevalence of physical abuse by a current partner among women of Mexican origin and assessed factors associated with abuse. The self-reported prevalence of physical abuse by a current partner was 10.7 per cent. In a multivariate analysis, factors associated with physical abuse included US birthplace, young age, urban residence, and having four or more children. Social support and regular church attendance were found to be protective.

So far as the after effect of family violence and abuse of women are concerned Constantino *et al.* (2000) carried out a study and found that abused women having a higher number of medically unexplained somatic symptoms, more functional disability, a lower self-rating of general health, and higher health care utilization when compared to non-abused women. The authors' purpose in this study was to examine differences in the occurrences of negative life experiences, level of depression and T-cell function between abused and non-abused women. Significant differences were found between the groups for negative life experiences, level of depression, and T-cell function. The study shows that abused women reported more negative life experiences, experienced higher levels of depression, and experienced lower T-cell function when compared with non-abused women.

Impact of Family Violence on Children

Family violence has a significant impact on the all round development of the children. The immediate effect of family violence on children includes disturbance in education, lack of attention in studies, adjustment problems in school and locality and undercurrent tension at home (Davies and Cummings, 1994; Zimet and Jacob, 2001). Additionally, when children and adolescents witness violence at home, they may come to accept this as a normal and acceptable part of family life. This apart, they suffer from an array of behavioural, emotional and cognitive problems (Fantuzzo and Lindquist, 1989; Jaffe *et al*., 1990). In addition, children also suffer from the following psychological problems (*Source*: NAPCAN Australia and Bec Pierce Australia, 2002):

- Disturbed sleep and nightmares
- Developmental delays
- Regressed behaviour, e.g. a child wetting or soiling where they were once toilet trained
- Anxious or fearful behaviour
- Nervous or withdrawn behaviour
- A change in their demeanour, e.g. now they are quiet whereas they were previously happy and outgoing
- Psychosomatic illnesses, e.g. headaches, stomach aches, stuttering

- Cruelty to animals
- Behavioural problems such as running away from home
- Aggressive behaviour and language at home and/or school

Following quotation is a burning example of family violence that induced mental disturbances in children:

> *'Children worry that their mothers will get seriously hurt or their fathers will go to jail. These thoughts weigh most heavily on a child's mind during school hours, when the child is not home. This constant anxiety does not allow them to pay attention to their studies. Children who live with domestic violence may also have a difficult time relating to their peers. In some cases where the battered mother is isolated, socializing has not been modelled at home. It is not uncommon for children to feel guilty for having fun. Many children do not want to leave their battered mother alone. If intervention does not occur, these children's feelings of anxiety, accountability, guilt, grief and embarrassment will begin to take command of their lives' (Source:* Understanding Children of Domestic Violence by Karen McGuckin).

Of children who witness their mothers being abused by their fathers, 40 per cent suffer anxiety, 48 per cent suffer depression, 53 per cent act out with their parents and 60 per cent act out with siblings (*Source*: Pflout, Schopler & Henley, Forgotten Victims of Family Violence, Social Work, July 1982).

Studies have also found that a child witnessing family violence has less social competence (Wolfe *et al.*, 1986). These children were found to show more anxiety, more aggression, more temperamental problems, more depression, less empathy, less self-esteem, and lower verbal, cognitive and motor abilities than that of children who did not witness violence at home (Hughes, 1988, Westra and Martin, 1981, Holden and Ritchie, 1991).

The worst consequence of family violence on the children is child abuse and neglect, which was first, defined by C. Henry Kempe and his colleagues (Kempe *et al.*, 1962) in their article "The Battered Child Syndrome". Kempe, a physician, defined child abuse as a clinical condition having to do with those who have been deliberately injured by physical assault.

The following cases will describe the consequences of family violence and maladjustment between parents on children. Case studies have been developed on the basis of author's firsthand experience in dealing with such cases in a Mental Health Clinic in Kolkata as Clinical Psychologist. For confidentiality of information real name of the following subjects were changed.

> ***Case 1 (academic performance of child deteriorated):*** *Partha, 15 years, male, studying in class IX was a very good student until last year. He used to stand first or second in the class. Unfortunately in the last year's examination he could not retain his earlier position in the class. School teachers were worried because of his deteriorating academic performance. On probing it was found that for the last two years his family environment had deteriorated on account of regular fighting between his parents who were highly educated and working in good position. Partha has one younger sister. Her academic performance has also been affected. Everyday there was an unhappy situation and it was very difficult for them to study at home. The relationship of parents had deteriorated to such an extent that they could not tolerate the presence of each other. Such a continual disruption of their family environment had left their mark on them, one incidence of it being their loss of interest in studies.*
>
> ***Case 2 (child ran away from home and became alcoholic):*** *Asim, 15 years, male, second child of his parents, a school dropout was loitering in the Sealdah Station, Kolkata. After his inclusion under a welfare programme of an NGO detailed information about his family background was collected. It was found that*

his father was a Diploma Engineer and was working in a Steel Plant. Asim's father was an alcoholic. Everyday he returned home from office in a drunken state and beat his wife and children without any fail. He was totally indifferent about the studies of his children. Due to such prolonged maltreatment Asim's mother got married to somebody and left the house. Gradually Asim and his elder sister started escaping school for films. And finally both of them stopped attending school and Asim became a dependent on alcohol. He developed the habit of drinking alcohol gradually. Initially he had tested the same from a bottle brought by his father and thereafter almost everyday he used to have one or two pegs from his father's alcohol bottle kept at home. One day Asim got into a local train and came to Sealdah Station.

Case 3 (developed anxiety among second daughter the child): *Anita, female, 11 years, a student of class V, middle daughter out of three siblings, attended a Mental Health Clinic with complaints like poor academic performance, lack of attention in studies and a feeling of irrational fear as reported by her mother. After four sittings with the child and collecting detailed information about the family it was found that there is a major problem in interpersonal relationship of parents. Although parents live under the same roof along with the children, they hardly have any communication. Rather they used to fight with each other in connection with minor issues like who will take the children to school and who will purchase dresses and other essential items for the children. Fortunately the academic performance of the other two children was not affected much as their coping capacity was stronger than that of this child. The subject used to suffer from high anxiety especially during the evening, i.e. normally when parents used to fight among themselves after returning from office* *and as a result she could not concentrate on her studies. Unfortunately this was regarded as a minor problem. Before attending the clinic both the highly educated parents did not realize that the problem had developed in the child owing to their problem. However, counselling helped the child to increase her level of concentration in studies and thereby academic performance improved and parents were asked not to create any scene in the family especially in front of their children in future.*

Case 4 (deviation from the mainstream of the society and involvement in immoral activities): *Aparna, 14 years, female, studying in class VIII of a very good school in Kolkata was the only child of her parents. Both the parents were highly educated. There was no financial problem in the family as both the parents were working. Lack of understanding between her parents and a continuous under current tension was the regular feature in the family. Everyday after returning from school she stayed alone with a maidservant, her parents often came back home late after attending parties. There were sometimes instances of physical abuse of her mother by her father. All this nurtured a strong feeling of neglect in Aparna as her parents hardly gave her time and made no effort to understand her. Last year she developed friendship with some local boys and she also stated to spend time outside home in the afternoon and used to come back late. Her parents did not realize what damage they were doing to their child. All of a sudden she got high fever, which continued for four/five days. Parents contacted doctor and after knowing all the symptoms of Aparna doctor advised for blood testing for ascertaining HIV status and found positive result. This is the worst example of family violence and lack of understanding within the parents and communication gap with children.*

Extent of Impact of Family Violence on Children

Researchers and clinicians have found that the effect and consequences of emotional and psychological violence are greater and more profound than the consequences of physical victimization alone (Straus and Sweet, 1992). Sexual abuse also has significant harmful consequences (Browne and Finkelhor, 1986). Sufficient data on magnitude of family violence and violence toward children are not available except physical maltreatment of the child. Findings of some of the studies on child physical abuse are presented below:

Physical Abuse

Straus and Gelles conducted two studies on the subject of family violence, using a nationally representative sample of 2,146 individual family members in 1976 and 6,002 family members in 1985. One part of the study focused on the homes where children under the age of 18 resided. Parents of these homes were asked to report on their own 'conflict management tactics' with their children. Among the list of conflict tactics were nine items that dealt with physical violence. These items ranged from pushing and shoving to the use of a knife or gun. The milder forms of violence were, of course, the most common. However, even with the severe forms of violence, the rates were surprisingly high:

Table 1.2: Frequency of Parental Violence toward Children

Violent Behaviour	*% of occurrences in the past year*			*Total*	*% of occurrences reported*
	Once	*Twice*	*More than twice*		
Threw something at child	1.5	0.7	0.9	3.1	4.5
Pushed, grabbed, or shoved child	5.8	7.5	14.9	28.2	33.6
Slapped or spanked child	8.1	8.5	39.1	55.7	74.6
Kicked, beat, or hit with fist	0.7	0.5	0.3	1.5	2.1
Hit or tried to hit child with something	2.4	2.0	5.3	9.7	14.4
Beat up child	0.3	0.1	0.2	0.6	1.0
Burned or scolded child	0.2	0.1	0.1	0.4	0.6
Threatened child with knife or gun	0.1	0.1	0	0.2	0.2
Used a knife or gun	0.1	0.1	0	0.2	0.2

Source: Based on data from Straus and Gelles, 1988.

- Of the parents surveyed, 1.5 per cent reported that they kick, bite, or punch their child each year, and 2.0 per cent of those surveyed said they have done these acts at least once while the child was growing up.
- A little less than 1 per cent of the parents said they beat their child at least once a year, and 1 per cent said they had beaten their child.
- Out of 1,000, two children faced a parent who threatened by using a gun or a knife during the survey year.
- Out of 1,000, three children were threatened with a weapon by a parent while growing up. The same percentages held for children whose parents reported actually using a weapon.

Straus and Gelles (1988) also estimated the extent of abusive violence. Abusive violence was defined as acts that had a high probability of injuring the child. These included kicking, biting, punching, hitting or trying to hit a child with an object, beating up a child, burning or scolding, and threatening or using a gun or a knife:

- Slightly more than 20 parents out of 1,000 (2.3%) engaged themselves in one act of abusive violence during the year prior to the survey.
- Seven children out of 1,000 were hurt as a result of an act of violence directed at them by a parent in the previous year.

Straus and Gelles' (1988) study on violence towards children confirmed previous findings that violence does not end even when children grow up.

In India few studies have been carried out on child physical abuse. Segal and Ashtekar (1994) found that 60 per cent of the children ran away from home to avoid physical abuse. In another study Segal (1995) observed that 42 per cent of middle class families considered violence as punishment and 2.9 per cent of these families considered violence in an extreme form. Deb and Senapati (1993)

When parental discipline is characterized by harsh corporal punishment, children have every reason to feel unloved and unwanted. Even worse, they live in constant dread of abuse from the people who take care of them. Under such conditions, even brief periods of happiness are infrequent (Hurlock, 1968).

In addition, violent behaviour that is learnt early in life may become the types of behaviours that children come to expect and copy when they are adults. Hence, violent behaviour can be passed on across generations. Many people responsible for violence in their personal relationships have witnessed family violence or experienced abuse as children. Some boys and girls may behave as their parents did, following the role model of their same sex parents (*Source*: NAPCAN Australia and Bec Pierce Australia, 2002).

It is also important to note that all the children exposed to violence in the home do not necessarily become violent themselves.

Prevention

Although family violence and child maltreatment have been recognized as social and public health problems in both the developed and developing countries, very few measures/policies have been taken to stop all forms of family violence and cruelty towards children in the developing countries. In fact, it is very difficult to offer a single solution to curb family violence and cruelty towards children. Moreover the cases of family violence and child maltreatment/physical abuse are not reported in the developing countries. Even if it is reported very few actions have been taken.

However, in recent years, a considerable number of legislation has been enacted to curb family violence in India. The Criminal Law (Second Amendment) Act, 1983 introduced the new offence of cruelty under section 498A. Section 174 of the Criminal Procedure Code was inserted in the Indian Evidence Act and the new section 304B relating to dowry death was incorporated in the Indian Penal Code. But all these sections do not cover the other forms of domestic violence in India like deceiving parents, especially widowed mothers, unmarried sisters or women relatives. Hence, the need for a separate form of legislation is urgently needed in India (Roy Dutta, 2001).

In order to prevent family violence educational approaches for enlightenment is needed that help professionals and communities to develop more effective skills to work with families and communities.

Individual and family counselling is also necessary in case of family violence. However, in case of intervention, underreporting is one of the main problems. A good number of cases are not reported. In some places, especially in the developing countries very few agencies or NGOs deal with such cases. Hence, the question of reporting or intervention does not arise. In some cases especially in the developing countries, community intervention helps a lot to solve familial problems.

In addition the following steps should be implemented for prevention of violence in the family (Klein *et al.*, 1997):

- Early intervention - encouraging the arrest and punishment of male member who abuse their counterpart
- Mandatory arrests
- Civil suits against the abuser
- Laws requiring hospitals to identify and report incidents
- Mandatory 48 hours of confinement to separate victim from abuser
- Mandatory treatment for abusers
- Reduce the amount of violence on television
- Education course for young boys and girls about sex roles and how to resolve conflicts
- Getting more money into the criminal justice system to prosecute offenders
- Getting more money into shelters to help battered women

Proposed Measures for Prevention of Cruelty Towards Children

For prevention of child abuse and neglect, which result from family violence and/or intra-parental conflicts some legal provisions are there. For example, there are some directives in the Article 24 (prohibition of employment of children), 39 (F) (principals to be followed by the State Governments for the welfare of the children) and 45 (free and compulsory education for the children) of the Constitution of India to protect the rights and interest of the children.

Section 317 of IPC says that parents will be punished for abandoning the child. This apart, there are some other measures like Child Labour (Prohibition and Regulation) Act, 1986 and Juvenile Justice (Care and Protection of Children) Act, 2000. In the Juvenile Justice (Care and Protection of Children) Act, 2000 there are some provisions to penalize perpetrators who will abuse, torture and/or neglect juveniles like Sections 23, 24, 25 26, 27 and 28.

However, only legal measures cannot solve any social problem. Public awareness is needed. Public awareness about child abuse, sexual abuse, wife abuse and elder abuse should be fueled by a combination of public awareness campaigns with a view to educating the public about the dangers of and costs of family violence. More and more NGO should come forward to create social awareness about the consequences of family violence and child maltreatment. The programme, which NGOs can take up, includes community and institute based intervention programmes.

Intervention

It is important to identify the families having problems for a long time through survey and bring them under the purview of intervention programme. In this regard NGO should take initiative with the help from government and local youth clubs. In each and every locality network with the local community organizations and youth clubs should be developed for resolving the crises in the family.

This apart, it is important to carry out study on different dimensions of family violence and document the information in regard to intervention programmes so that learning experience can be shared with similar organizations for effective implementation of future programmes to curb the incidence of family violence.

So far as intervention in regard to a child victim is concerned, the first step is to identify abused children in need of services. Even if volunteers do not identify them, a direct telephone online service should be implemented for registering the complaints made by the children themselves only and for taking immediate action against the perpetrator. Consequently, considerable effort should be made so that proper welfare and medical services can be provided.

Family and individual counselling are found to be very beneficial to resolve the problems of family violence. Hence, family and individual counselling services should be made available to the target groups. In case of counselling it is important to maintain confidentiality of the information. Therefore, the concerned agency should ensure the confidentiality of the information. It is expected that counselling services will benefit a large number families and thereby the children.

How to Help Children?

The children who witness violence at home suffer from severe mental disturbances like a feeling of helplessness. During this period they require your support and encouragement to cope with the stressful situations. Hence,

- Encourage children to talk about anything that might be worrying them. Remember, children are not usually encouraged to talk openly about violence at home and no one is supposed to talk about it outside the family. Children's needs are often not recognized because of this.
- Make sure the child knows the violence at home is not his or her fault.
- Tell the child s/he is a very special person and that the child is not alone.
- Give them permission to talk about the violence at home.
- Help them to make a safety plan, which they can follow.
- Let them know that other children have also had similar experiences.
- Provide information as to where all members of the family can get help.

There are people who care like relatives, neighbours, teachers, and counsellors etc. Encourage children to have a support network (*Source:* NAPCAN, 2002).

Problems in Intervention

In the developed countries few professionals explained that they do not report such cases because reporting would expose them.

Reporting to specific authority about such cases mean that they would have to leave work to testify in court, or they would feel uncomfortable while dealing with the family in future if they file a child abuse report. Some professionals said that they did not know how to make a report or would not make one because it would breach confidentiality. Thus, there are those working on the issue of child maltreatment who believe that child abuse is still underreported and that mandatory implementation of laws and public education campaigns still need to be supported.

Unfortunately, in the developing countries very few agencies work on this issue and there is no system of maintaining data in regard to family violence. As a result, the issue of intervention in the developing countries is in a very sorry state. As a result, problems in family become very serious which badly affect the children. Another problem in case of intervention is the denial of the problem, i.e., for the protection of social image a large number of family members do not admit the problem and are reluctant to take help of a counsellor to solve the problem. In order to overcome these problems widespread social awareness about the negative impact of family violence is required and in this regard NGOs should come forward and take the lead role.

Latest Selective Study Findings

Koenig *et al.* (2003) explored the determinants of domestic violence in two rural areas of Bangladesh and found increased education, higher socio-economic status, non-Muslim religion, and extended family residence to be associated with lower risks of violence. The effect of women's status on violence was found to be highly context-specific. In the more culturally conservative area, higher individual-level women's autonomy and short-term membership in savings and credit groups were both associated with significantly elevated risks of violence, and community-level variables were unrelated to violence. In the less culturally conservative area, in contrast, individual-level women's status indicators were unrelated to the risk of violence, and community-level measures of women's status were associated with significantly lower risks of violence, presumably by reinforcing nascent normative changes in gender relations.

Hou *et al.* (2003) explored the post-traumatic responses of abused women to marital violence and examined the correlation between these responses and demographics. This study aimed to raise awareness of post-traumatic responses in abused women among health care providers, who are supposed to pay more attention to this problem. A cross-sectional survey-interview with structured questionnaires was used. Subjects were recruited from the Kaohsiung area. Of the 127 women who participated in this study, 109 (85.8%) completed the questionnaires. The most frequent post-traumatic response was: "I had a strong feeling toward this thing." The least frequent response was: "I felt it seemed that this thing had never happened or it was not true." The standardized mean score of the intrusion subscale (3.12) was higher than that of the avoidance subscale (1.84). The more children an abused woman had, the fewer avoidance responses she exhibited. Of the abused women, 93.6 per cent had a high post-traumatic response score (> or = 19). The results indicate that marital violence leads to post-traumatic responses in abused women in Taiwan. The results can help health care providers to identify post-traumatic responses of abused women at an early stage and can also provide information for planning further treatment strategies for abused women.

Ehrensaft *et al.* (2003) followed an unselected sample of 543 children over 20 years to test the independent effects of parenting, exposure to domestic violence between parents (ETDV), maltreatment, adolescent disruptive behaviour disorders, and emerging adult substance abuse disorders (SUDs) on the risk of violence to and from an adult partner. Conduct disorder (CD) was the strongest risk for perpetrating partner violence for both sexes, followed by ETDV, and power assertive punishment. The effect of child abuse was attributable to these 3 risks. ETDV conferred the greatest risk of receiving partner violence; CD increased the odds of receiving partner violence but did not mediate this effect. Child physical abuse and CD in adolescence were strong independent risks for injury to a partner. SUD mediated the effect of adolescent CD on injury to a partner but not on injury by a partner.

Erlick (2003) stated that violence against women is still rampant in North America. Forty to 51 per cent of women experience some type of violence in their lifetime including child abuse, physical violence, rape and domestic violence. The perpetrator is most likely to be a current or former partner. Such violence stems from historical views of women as property and may flourish because of the public's reluctance to get involved in family matters. The concept of violence has been expanded to include non-traditional types such as sexual harassment, breeches of fiduciary trust and stalking. Treatment of victims of violence must include ensuring their safety, encouraging them to make healthy choices and helping them to understand they are not at fault. Education at all levels is required to change attitudes, which perpetuate violence despite laws, which forbid it.

In Arab and Islamic countries, domestic violence is not yet considered a major concern despite its increasing frequency and serious consequences. Surveys in Egypt, Palestine, Israel and Tunisia show that at least one out of three women is beaten by her husband. The indifference to this type of violence stems from attitudes that domestic violence is a private matter and, usually, a justifiable response to misbehaviour on the part of the wife. Selective excerpts from the Koran are used to prove that men who beat their wives are following God's commandments. These religious justifications, plus the importance of preserving the honour of the family, lead abusers, victims, police and health care professionals to join in a conspiracy of silence rather than disclosing these offences. However, a fair reading of the Koran shows that wife abuse, like genital mutilation and "honour killings" are a result of culture rather than religion (Douki *et al*., 2003).

Singleton *et al.* (2003) assessed domestic violence (DV) exposure, awareness, education, and reporting within a specific geographic region. The goal was to determine what the public perceives as the role of emergency medical services (EMS) in dealing with domestic violence. A prospective, randomized telephone survey with random dialing pattern was used by the institution's Survey Research Laboratory in the Department of Sociology. Households from the region, which was rural with a military subset, were contacted during a four-month study period. Demographic data and opinions about DV exposure and reporting practices were collected. A total of 1,057 individuals completed the survey. A total of 51.3 per cent knew someone who was a DV victim. Although 73 per cent stated they would report DV to law enforcement, 36.2 per cent stated that 9-1-1/EMS providers are the most appropriate contact when reporting DV. Over one third of the people surveyed believed that EMS was the most appropriate contact when reporting DV. Because of the frequency with which EMS professionals may potentially encounter DV, and the fact that they are likely to be the first contact in DV situations, more education may be warranted in the EMS curriculum.

The study of Lown and Vega (2001) revealed the lifetime prevalence of physical abuse by a current partner among women of Mexican origin and assessed factors associated with abuse. The self-reported prevalence of physical abuse by a current partner was 10.7 per cent. In multivariate analysis, factors associated with physical abuse included US birthplace, young age, urban residence, and having four or more children. Social support and regular church attendance were protective.

The study of Constantino *et al.* (2000) found that abuse of women by their intimate partner is a staggering problem in USA. Abused women have a higher number of medically unexplained somatic symptoms, more functional disability, a lower self-rating of general health, and higher health care utilization when compared to non-abused women. The authors' purpose in this study was to examine differences in occurrences of negative life experiences, level of depression, and T-cell function between abused and non-abused women. Significant differences were found between the groups for negative life experiences, level of depression, and T-cell function. The study shows that abused women reported more negative life experiences, experienced higher levels of depression, and experienced lower T-cell function when compared with non-abused-women.

Weiss *et al.* (2000) stated that domestic violence affects millions of women in the United States each year. Physicians are in a unique position to screen for violence in their patients' homes and refer individuals before they are injured or killed. All U.S. medical schools are expected to incorporate partner violence into their curricula.

The MCP Hahnemann School of Medicine has developed and integrated a domestic violence educational intervention program into the existing problem-based medical school curriculum. This educational intervention includes modification of an existing teaching case to include signs and symptoms specific to domestic violence, written learning objectives on domestic violence in the health care setting, relevant resource material, and a 3-hr training program conducted by an interdisciplinary teaching team. Based on quantitative and qualitative data over a 3-year period, this domestic violence education program has been successfully integrated into an existing problem-based curriculum. Overall, the high student exam scores indicate the effectiveness of the teaching program. In addition, the students' evaluation of the program reflects a high level of student satisfaction with the curriculum presented on domestic violence. This article describes both the content of a domestic violence teaching program and the process used to integrate such a program into a medical school curriculum. Although medical schools and their teaching programs are uniquely structured, with slight modifications they are able to accommodate domestic violence teaching programmes.

Raphael (2002) reviews the growing body of research literature on the relationship of domestic violence to welfare. Not only do women on welfare suffer from domestic violence in far greater numbers than women in the general population, but their abusers, threatened by the women's efforts at education, training, or work, also use violence and threats of violence to sabotage these efforts at economic self-sufficiency. For this reason, welfare reform exacerbates domestic violence in the lives of many low-income women. As a result of the federal Family Violence Option, most state welfare plans allow battered women on welfare more time and specialized services before mandating work in order to keep them and their children safe. Recent research and monitoring have shown, however, that the majority of battered women on welfare do not tell their welfare workers about the violence. Ending the isolation of these battered women and helping them with domestic violence services pose difficult challenges. Women's health providers may be in a better position to accomplish this task than welfare department personnel.

Kirisci *et al.* (2001) developed two child self-report scales to measure parental neglect (emotional distance and parental involvement) in a sample of 344 boys between 10 and 12 years of age. Psychometric analyses of the parental emotional distance and involvement scales demonstrated their unidimensionality; construct, concurrent, and predictive validity; and reliability. Cross-sectional analyses indicated that neglect was more severe among boys who had a parent with a DSM-III-R lifetime substance use disorder (SUD) compared to youth whose parents had no Axis I psychiatric disorder. In addition, children reported more severe neglect by the mother than the father. Longitudinal analyses of a sub sample (n = 99) revealed that child neglect at ages 10-12 predicted significant variance on a composite measure of substance use involvement and severity of substance use as well as increased the risk for SUD at the age of 19.

Estes and Tidwell (2002) made an attempt to achieve three objectives in their study, i.e., (i) the influence of a mother's experience of sexual abuse on the sexual abuse behaviours experienced by her child; (ii) to examine child behaviour as it relates to the type of sexual abuse and to gender; and (iii) to explore indicators of family functioning in incestuous and non-incestuous families. Using two self-report assessment measures and a semi-structured intake interview, an intake group design was used with 104 sexually abused children (52 males and 52 females), and their 104 mothers (50 with a history of sexual abuse and 54 without such histories). The incested children displayed significantly more sexualized behaviour than children molested out of the home. Sexually abused males exhibited significantly more sexual behaviour than females. Incested mothers reported significantly more substance abuse on their own part and in their families of origin, and also more physical abuse in these same families. CONCLUSIONS: The findings from this study suggest that incestuous families suffer from a multitude of problems such as intergenerational substance abuse and physical abuse. Also differences between male and female sexually abused children with regard to their sexualized behaviours were clearly noted.

The objective of Coker *et al.* (2001) study was to compare the Women's Experience with Battering Scale (WEB) with the Index of Spouse Abuse-Physical Scale (ISA-P) as screening tools to identify intimate partner violence (IPV). We conducted a large cross-sectional survey of women age 18 to 65 attending one of two family practice clinics from 1997 to 1998. All women completed both the WEB and the ISA-P and a telephone interview. We figured agreement estimates between the two tools, used stratified analysis to evaluate attributes of those more likely to screen as battered or physically assaulted, and compared associations between the WEB and ISA-P and a range of mental and physical health indicators known to be associated with IPV. 18 per cent of 1152 eligible women surveyed had experienced IPV in a current or most recent intimate relationship with a male partner; 17 per cent had been battered (WEB+), and 10 per cent had been physically assaulted (ISA-P+). Had we used the ISA-P alone to assess IPV, we would have missed almost 45 per cent of IPV. As anticipated, the ISA-P was more strongly associated with IPV-associated injuries and number of physician visits in the last year. The WEB was more strongly associated with self-perceived mental health, anxiety, depression, drug abuse, and low social support. Clinician's need validated screening tools to rapidly and reliably screen patients for IPV. Most screening tools assess physical violence and injury without considering the more chronic experience of battering and the psychological terror associated with this violence. The WEB may identify more abused women than tools measuring physical assaults.

Bryant and Spencer (2002) examined the factors that influence nurse practitioners' (NPs) ability to incorporate universal domestic violence screening practices (e.g., asking, identifying, referring and reporting) into their practices. A stratified random survey of certified NPs in New York State was conducted in 1999. There were 118 family, women's health, OB/GYN, and adult NPs in the survey. There were significant differences in the domestic violence screening practices among women's health, OB/GYN, adult, and family NPs. Women's health and OB/GYN NPs were more likely to ask screening questions and identify victims of domestic violence than their other NP counterparts. There is a need to identify strategies that encourage all NPs to incorporate universal domestic violence screening behaviours into their practices.

Since dental personnel are in an excellent position to recognize suspected abuse of dental patients Gutmann and Solomon (2002) conducted a study to determine the extent to which dental hygiene programs have incorporated these family violence topics into the curriculum. Specific data on content, teaching methods, faculty, and resources were collected. Reasons for not including family violence in the curricula, attitudes on mandatory continuing education, and support services available for abuse victims were also examined. A fifteen-item survey was sent to all 229 U.S. accredited dental hygiene programs. Surveys were returned from 173 programs for a response rate of 77.5 per cent. Child abuse was taught in most programs (N=122, 70.5 per cent), while elder abuse (N=95, 54.9 per cent), intimate partner abuse (N=81, 46.8 per cent), and abuse of individuals with disabilities (N=80, 46.2 per cent) was taught in fewer programs. Reasons for not including family violence in the curricula (N=31, 18 per cent) varied. The need is critical for increased curriculum attention in U.S. dental hygiene programs to help stem the epidemic of family violence. Raising dental hygienists' awareness of the problem and potentially increasing the number of reports of and referrals for suspected violence might help more victims.

During 1999 the issue of rape in South Africa was debated at the highest levels. The epidemiology of rape has become an issue of considerable political importance and sensitivity, with President Mbeki demanding an answer to the question: how much rape is there in South Africa? Hence Jewkes and Abrahams (2002) summarise and synthesise the findings of research to provide an overview of the epidemiology of rape of women in South Africa and to show how difficult it is to answer the President's question. The review begins by considering why rape is so difficult to research. Data available shows that rape reported to the police (240 incidents of rape and attempted rape per 100,000 women each year) represents the tip of an iceberg of sexual coercion. Representative community-based surveys have found, for example, that in the 17-48 age group there are 2070 such incidents per 100,000 women per year. Non-consensual sex in marriage and dating relationships is believed to be very common but is usually not well reported in surveys. Forced sexual initiation is reported by almost a third of adolescent girls. In addition coerced consensual sex is a common problem in schools, workplaces and amongst peers. Knowledge of causal and contributory factors influencing the high levels of rape is also discussed. We conclude that the rape statistic for the country is currently elusive but levels of non-consensual and coerced sex are clearly very high. International comparison needs to be approached with caution because most developing countries lack the infrastructure for accurate crime reporting and do not have such a substantial body of survey data.

Laditka *et al.* (2002) examined residents' experiences in a physician home visit program and their attitudes toward working with older patients in a home setting. In-depth personal interviews were conducted with all second and third year residents in a family medicine residency program (n = 17). Most residents expressed positive attitudes about caring for patients in their homes. Residents said home visits allowed them to provide better care, and enhanced their assessment skills and understanding of community services. We identified a lack of coordination and consistency in several areas, including home visit assessments and the role of physician preceptors. The need for formal training to identify and treat elder abuse was also identified. Participation in a home visit program appears to be an effective learning experience for residents, and helps residents to understand the needs of older people living in the community.

Heater *et al.* (2002) examined the emotional and behavioural reactions of 118 predominantly Euro-American, middle-class university students toward an alleged spousal abuse victim. In the context of a decision-making task, participants encountered another male or female student (a confederate) who was supposedly injured in an accident or a spousal abuse incident. Participants completed the Trait Questionnaire, Emotional Reaction Measure, and Social Distancing Measure. Generally, participants felt less sympathy and more anger and ascribed less positive traits to the abuse victim than to the accident victim. In addition, they distanced themselves socially from the abuse victim. Further analyses showed that female participants displayed more negative trait ascriptions and behavioural reactions to the abuse victims than did male participants.

Apsler *et al.* (2002) investigated a broad range of female victims of domestic partner abuse who came to the attention of the police. Ninety-five consecutive victims were interviewed by officers in a police department's domestic violence unit. Twenty-two per cent of the victims matched expectations of women who were both afraid of their abusers and expected future abuse. Surprisingly, 46 per cent of the victims were unafraid of their offenders and believed that future abuse was unlikely. A consistent pattern of findings support the conclusion that a much broader range of victims than expected comes to the attention of the police. These results suggest exploring alternative police responses for different types of victims.

Jewkes *et al.* (2002) undertaken a cross-sectional study of violence against women in three provinces of South Africa in 1998. The objectives were to measure the prevalence of physical, sexual and emotional abuse of women, to identify risk factors and associated health problems and health service use. A multi-stage sampling design was used with clusters sampled with probability proportional to number of households randomly selected from within clusters. One randomly selected woman aged 18-49 years was interviewed in each selected home. Interviews were held with a total 1306 women, the response rate was 90.3 per cent of eligible women. For the risk factor analysis, multiple logistic regression models were fitted from a large pool of candidates of explanatory variables, while allowing for sampling design and interviewer effects. The lifetime prevalence of experiencing physical violence from a current or ex-husband or boyfriend was 24.6 per cent, and 9.5 per cent had been assaulted in the previous year. Domestic violence was significant and positively associated with violence in her childhood, her having no further education, liberal ideas on women's roles, drinking alcohol, having another partner in the year, having a confidant (e), his boy child preference, conflict over his drinking, either partner financially supporting the home, frequent conflict generally, and living outside the Northern Province. No significant associations were found with partners' ages, employment, migrant status, financial disparity, cohabitation, household possessions, urbanisation, marital status, crowding, communication, his having other partners, his education, her attitudes towards violence or her perceptions of cultural norms on women's role. The findings suggest that domestic violence is most strongly related to the status of women in a society and to the normative use of violence in conflict situations or as part of the exercise of power. We conclude by discussing implications for developing theory on causal factors in domestic violence.

The article of Vostanis *et al*. (2001) reports on the prevalence of mental health problems in homeless parents and children who have experienced domestic and neighbourhood violence and their access to social support networks. Three groups of families who had become homeless were compared: those experiencing domestic violence (48 with 75 children), victims of neighbourhood violence (14 with 29 children), and those who became homeless for other reasons (31 with 54 children). Mothers completed a service use semi-structured interview, the Strengths and Difficulties Questionnaire, the General Health Questionnaire, the Family Support Scales, and the SF-36 Health Status Questionnaire. Levels of psychiatric morbidity were high in the group experiencing domestic violence (35.7% in children and 21.9% in mothers) and higher still in those who were victims of neighbourhood violence (52.2% in children and 50% in mothers). Levels of social support were found to be an important factor, particularly in relation to professional support and support from other family members, as they predicted both child and maternal psychopathology. Mental health interventions for victims of domestic and neighbourhood violence should be integrated with community programmes of social reintegration. Mental health professionals should work in close collaboration with Housing Departments, Social Services, Education and the Police.

Onyskiw (2002) obtained baseline data on the health status and use of health services of children exposed to violence in their families. The study used data from the first cycle of the National Longitudinal Survey of Children and Youth (1994-95). According to parental reports, 8.6 per cent of children (n = 1, 648; representing 329,657 children) aged 2 to 11 years witnessed some violence in their families. They were compared to children who were reported to have never witnessed any violence at home. Children exposed to domestic violence had lower health status and more conditions or health problems, which limited their participation in normal age-related activities than children in non-violent families. Despite this, they had no more contacts with family practitioners in the previous year and even fewer contacts with pediatricians than comparison children. They did, however, have more contacts with "other medical doctors," public health nurses, child welfare workers, and other therapists than comparison children. In addition, more child witnesses regularly used prescription medication than children not exposed to violence at home. These baseline findings suggest that exposure to domestic violence has an adverse impact on children's health and use of health services. As future cycles become available, these children will be followed to determine the long-term impact on these outcomes.

Maughan and Cicchetti (2002) examined the unique and interactive effects of child maltreatment and interadult violence on children's developing strategies of emotion regulation and socio-emotional adjustment as well as the mediational role of emotion dysregulation in the link between children's pathogenic relational experiences and behavioural outcome. Person-oriented emotion regulation patterns (EMRPs) were determined based on children's emotional behavioural and self-reported responses to simulated interadult anger. One hundred thirty-nine 4- to 6-year-olds (88 maltreated, 51 non-maltreated) and their mothers served as participants. Maltreatment history predicted children's EMRPs, with approximately 80 per cent of the maltreated pre-schoolers exhibiting dysregulated emotion patterns (i.e., undercontrolled/ambivalent and overcontrolled/unresponsive types) compared with only 37.2 per cent of the non-maltreated controls. Undercontrolled/ambivalent EMRPs were associated with maternal reports of child behavior problems, and were found to mediate the link between maltreatment and children's anxious/depressed symptoms. The present study's findings increase understanding of process relations in pathogenic relational environments, and provide insight into emotion regulation deficits that may impede the development of psychological well-being in maltreated children with varying histories of interadult violence exposure.

Prasad (1999) examined women's experiences in India with health and legal interventions that address domestic violence, dowry-related violence, and rape. By examining the experiences of survivors of abuse with the medico-legal system in New Delhi, it considers the extent to which women are able to access their legal rights within the special protection system constructed specifically for them. The use of primary data highlights the impact of state procedures on women, and it demonstrates how procedure designed to enhance women's access to the law actually inhibit it. Using semi-structured interviews with female survivors of abuse, police officers, case workers, nongovernmental organization leaders, lawyers, physicians, and government officials in a 4-year period, this article examine women's access to state services designed to address violence against women, and raises questions about state tolerance of domestic and sexual violence.

The Supreme Court of India reversed a ruling of the High Court of Punjab and Haryana, which acquitted the defendant of criminal charges for causing the death of his wife by setting her wife on fire. The Supreme Court refused to invalidate the dying declaration of the wife that her husband had set her on fire, despite the fact that it was not recorded by a magistrate. It found the declaration supported by other evidence. In a similar case, the Supreme Court upheld a lower court decision convicting the victim's mother-in-law of murder. It allowed as evidence the statement of the physician who had treated the victim that the victim had told him that her mother-in-law had set her on fire. It also deprecated the failure of the investigating agency to prosecute the victim's husband and brother, who were strongly implicated in the crime. See Lichhamadevi *vs.* State of Rajasthan, 2 August 1988, All India Reporter, Vol. 75, 1988, Supreme Court, p. 1785.

REFERENCES

Administration for Children and Families (1995). *Report on Child Maltreatment,* Department of Health and Human Services, Greenfield, L., Sex Offenses and Offenders, 1997. Washington, D.C.: Bureau of Justice Statistics, U.S. Dept of Justice.

American Medical Association (1992). *Diagnostic And Treatment Guidelines On Domestic Violence* (Pamphlet No.AA 22, 92-406 20M).Chicago: Author.

Apsler, R., Cummins, M.R., and Carl, S. (2002). Fear And Expectations: Differences Among Female Victims Of Domestic Violence Who Come To The Attention Of The Police. *Violence Vict.,* 17(4):445-53.

Browne, A., and Finkelhor, D. (1986). *Initial And Long-Term Effects: A Review Of Research.* In D. Finkelhor And Associates (Eds.), A Source Book On Child Sexual Abuse (Pp. 143 - 179). Beverly Hills, CA: Sage.

Bryant, S.A., and Spencer, G.A. (2002). Domestic Violence: What Do Nurse Practitioners Think? *J Am Acad Nurse Pract.,* 14(9): 421-7.

Constantino, R.E., Sekula, L.K., Rabin, B., and Stone, C. (2000). Negative Life Experiences, Depression, And Immune Function In Abused And Nonabused Women. *Biol Res Nurs 2000 Jan*; 1(3): 190-198.

Coker, A.L., Pope, B.O., Smith, P.H., Sanderson, M., and Hussey, J.R. (2001). Assessment Of Clinical Partner Violence Screening Tools. *J Am Med Womens Assoc.,* 56(1):19-23.

Deb, Sibnath and Senapati Shishir (1993). Safety Needs of Abused Proletarian Bengalee Children (Major Modes of Causal Factors). *Indian Journal of Psychological Issues,* 1(1): 1-9.

Davies, P.T., and Cummings, E.M. (1994). Marital Conflict And Child Adjustment: An Emotional Security Hypothesis. *Psychological Bulletin,* 116(3): 387-411.

Dodge, K.A., Bates, J. E., and Pettit, G.S. (1990). Mechanisms In The Cycle Of Violence. *Science,* 250: 1678-1683.

Douki, S., Nacef, F., Belhadj, A., Bouasker, A., and Ghachem, R. (2003). Violence Against Women In Arab And Islamic Countries. *Arch Women Ment Health,* 6(3):165-71.

Egeland, B., Breitenbucher, M., and Rosenberg, D. (1980). A Prospective Study Of The Significance Of Life Stress In The Etiology Of Child Abuse. *Journal Of Clinical And Consulting Psychology,* 48: 195-205.

Ehrensaft, M.K., Cohen, P., Brown, J., Smailes, E., Chen, H, and Johnson, J.G. (2003). Intergenerational Transmission Of Partner Violence: A 20-Year Prospective *Study. J Consult Clin Psychol.,* 71(4):741-53.

Erlick Robinson, G. (2003). Violence Against Women In North America. *Arch Women Ment Health,* 6(3):185-91.

Estes, L.S., and Tidwell, R. (2002). Sexually Abused Children's Behaviours: Impact Of Gender And Mother's Experience Of Intra- And Extra-*Familial Sexual Abuse. Fam Pract.,* 19(1):36-44.

Fagan, J. A. (1990). *Intoxication And Aggression.* In M. Tonry And J. Q. Wilson (Eds.), Drugs And Crime: Vol.13. Crime And Justice: An Annual Review (Pp.241-320) Chicago: University Of Chicago Press.

Fagan, J.A., and Browne, A. (1994). *Violence Between Spouses And Intimates: Physical Aggression Between Women And Men In Intimate Relationships.* In A. J. Reiss, Jr. And J.A. Roth (Eds.), Understanding And Preventing Violence (3, 115-292). Washington, DC: National Academy Press.

Fantuzzo, J.W., And Lindquist, C. U. (1989). The Effects Of Observing Conjugal Violence On Children: A Review and Analysis Of Research Methodology. *Journal Of Family Violence,* 4: 77-94.

Friederich, W.N. (1988). *Behaviour Problems In Sexually Abused Children.* In G.E. Wyatt and G.J.Powell (Eds.), The Lasting Effects Of Child Sexual Abuse (Pp.171-191). Newbury Park, CA: Sage.

Gelles, R.J. (1974). *The Violent Home.* Beverly Hills, CA: Sage.

Gelles, R.J. (1992). Poverty And Violence Toward Children. *American Behavioural Scientist,* 35: 258-264.

Gelles, R.J. (1995). *Family Violence By Income.* Unpublished Data. Kingston, RI. (Mimeographed).

Gutmann, M.E., and Solomon, E.S. (2002). Family Violence Content In Dental Hygiene Curricula: A National Survey. *J Dent Educ.,* 66(9):999-1005.

Guttmacher, M. (1995). *Forsaking Our Children: Bureaucracy And Reform In The Child Welfare System.* Chicago: Lake View.

Heater, J., Walsh, J., and Sande, G. (2002). Sex And Attributions On Reactions Toward Alleged Spousal Abuse Victims. *Psychol Rep.,* 91(1):243-54.

Holden, G.W., and Ritchie, K.L. (1991). Linking Extreme Marital Divorce, Child Rearing, and Child Behaviour Problems: Evidence From Battered Women. *Child Development,* 62: 311-327.

Hou, W.L., Wang, H.H., and Chung H.H. (2003). Post-Traumatic Responses Of Abused Women To Marital Violence. *Kaohsiung J Med Sci.,* 19(7):352-7.

Hughes, H.M. (1988). Psychological and Behavioural Correlates Of Family Violence In Child Witnesses and Victims. *American Journal of Ortho-Psychiatry,* 58: 77-90.

Hurlock, B.E. (1968). *Developmental Psychology: Life Span Approach.* 5th Edition. Tata Macgraw Hill.

ISPCAN Report (1988). A Cross-Cultural Collaborative Study On Child Physical Abuse.

Jaffe, P., Wolfe, D.A., and Wilson, S. (1990). *Children Of Battered Women. Newbury* Park, CA: Sage.

Jewkes, R., and Abrahams, N. (2002). The Epidemiology Of Rape And Sexual Coercion In South Africa: An Overview. *Soc Sci Med.,* 55(7):1231-44.

Jewkes, R., Levin, J., and Penn-Kekana, L. (2002). Risk Factors For Domestic Violence: Findings From A South African Cross-Sectional Study. *Soc Sci Med.,* 55(9):1603.

Kasim, M.S., Shave, H.M. And Cheetah, I. (1994). Social Factors In Relation To Physical Abuse In Kuala Lumpur, Malaysia. *Child Abuse & Neglect,* 18: 401-409.

Kempe, C. H., Silverman, F.N., Steele, B.F., Droegemueller, W., and Silver, H.K. (1962). The Battered Child Syndrome. *Journal Of The American Medical Association,* 181: 107-112.

Kilpatrick, D.J., Edmunds, C.N., and Seymour, A. (1992). *Rape in America: A Report to the Nation, Arlington,* VA: National Victim Center.

Kirisci, L., Dunn, M.G., Mezzich, A.C., and Tarter, R.E. (2001). Impact Of Parental Substance Use Disorder And Child Neglect Severity On Substance Use Involvement In Male Offspring. *Prev Sci.,* 2(4):241-55.

Klein, E., Campbell, J., Solar, E., and Ghez, M., (1997). *Ending Domestic Violence,* Sage Publications, London.

Koenig, M.A., Ahmed, S., Hossain, M.B., and Khorshed Alam Mozumder, A.B. (2003). Women's Status And Domestic Violence In Rural Bangladesh: Individual- And Community-Level Effects. *Demography,* 40(2):269-88.

Laditka, S.B., Fischer, M., Mathews, K.B., Sadlik, J.M., Warfel, M.E. (2002). There's No Place Like Home: Evaluating Family Medicine Residents' Training In Home Care. *Home Health* Care Serv Q., 21(2):1-17.

Lia-Hoagberg, B., Kragthorpe, C., Schaffer, M., and Hill, D.L. (2001). Community Interdisciplinary Education To Promote Partnerships In Family Violence Prevention. *Family Community Health,* 24(1):15-27.

Lown, E.A., and Vega, W.A, (2001). Prevalence And Predictors Of Physical Partner Abuse Among Mexican American Women. *Am J Public Health,* 91(3): 441-5.

MacAndrew, C., and Edgerton, R.B. (1969). *Drunken Comportment: A Social Explanation.* Chicago: Aldine.

Maughan, A., and Cicchetti, D. (2002). Impact Of Child Maltreatment And Interadult Violence On Children's Emotion Regulation Abilities And Socioemotional Adjustment. *Child Dev.,* 73(5):1525-42.

NAPCAN (2002). Domestic Violence Hurts Children Too? Australia.

National Research Council (1993). Understanding Child Abuse & Neglect. Washington, DC: National Academy Press.

Onyskiw, J.E. (2002). Health And Use Of Health Services Of Children Exposed To Violence In Their Families. *Can J Public Health,* 93(6):416-20.

Prasad, S. (1999). Medicolegal Response To Violence Against Women In India. *Violence Against Women,* 5(5):478-506.

Raphael, J. (2002). Keeping Battered Women Safe During Welfare Reform: New Challenges. J Am Med Womens Assoc., 57(1):32-5.

Roy Dutta, Mala (2001). *Defence For The Offence. Accent* - The Sunday Statesman.

Schornstein, S. L. (1997). *Domestic Violence and Health Care: What Every Professionals Needs To Know.* Sage Publications, London.

Segal, U.A. and Ashtekar, A. (1994). Detection Of Intra-familial Child Abuse: Children At Intake It A Children's Observation Home In India. *Child Abuse & Neglect,* 18: 957-969.

Segal, U.A. (1995). Child Abuse By The Middle Class? A Study Of Professionals In India. *Child Abuse & Neglect,* 19: 217-233.

Singleton, A., Brewer, K.L., and Goodman, P. (2003). Domestic Violence Education And Reporting: Public Attitudes About The Roles Of EMS. *Prehosp Emerg Care,* 7(3):312-5.

Straus, M. A. (1980). *A Sociological Perspective On The Causes Of Family Violence.* In M.R. Green (Ed.), Violence And The Family (pp. 7-31). Boulder, Co., West View.

Straus, M.A. and Gelles, R.J. (1988). *Violence In American Families: How Much Is There And Why Does It Occur?* In E.W. Nunnally, C. Chilman, And F.M.Cox. (Eds.), Troubled Relationships (pp.141-162). Newbury Park, CA: Sage.

Straus, M. A., and Sweet, S. (1992). Verbal Aggression In Couples: Incidence Rates and Relationships To Personal Characteristics. *Journal of Marriage & The Family,* 54: 346-357.

Vostanis, P., Tischler, V., Cumella, S., and Bellerby, T. (2001). Mental Health Problems And Social Supports Among Homeless Mothers And Children Victims Of Domestic And Community Violence. *Int J Soc Psychiatry,*47(4):30-40.

Weiss, L.B., Kripke, E.N., Coonse, H.L., and O'Brien, M.K. (2000). Integrating A Domestic Violence Education Program Into A Medical School Curriculum: Challenges and Strategies. Teach Learn Med, 12(3):133-40.

Westra, B., and Martin, H.P. (1981). Children Of Battered Women. *Maternal Child Nursing Journal,* 10: 41-54.

Wolfe, B.A., Zak, L., Wilson, S., and Jaffe, P. (1986). Child Witnesses To Violence Between Parents: Critical Issues In Behavioural and Social Adjustment. *Journal Of Abnormal Child Psychology,* 14: 95-104.

Zimet, D. M., and Jacob, T. (2001). Influences of Marital Conflict on Child Adjustment: Review of Theory and Research, *Clinical Child Family-Psychological-Review,*4(4):319-35.

2

Child Abuse and Neglect

Introduction

Child abuse and neglect is not only the problem of a particular country or age, it is a universal social problem. In the developing countries like in India it is a minutely recognized social phenomenon regardless of social strata. For example, physical punishment is regarded as one of the methods of behaviour modification of children whereas child marriage is regarded as a part of culture in some parts of India. Sexual abuse of children is not reported much owing to perceived harassment, threat, lack of intervention agencies and social boycott. Deprivation from parental love and affection is not regarded at all as abuse and/or neglect. The worst form of child abuse in India is to sacrifice children in the name of religion. A number of such cases have been highlighted in the newspapers in the recent past. In one such case in rural Orissa in India occurred in 1996, lower court had given a verdict for life imprisonment to father who sacrificed his son before god image being influenced by some religious belief. A good number of minor aged children especially in the rural areas get HIV/AIDS from elderly people. There is a belief that if any elderly people suffering from sexually transmitted diseases have sex with minor aged girl they will be free from the disease. This wrong belief makes a good number of children a victim of sexual abuse and thereby they get HIV/AIDS. Recently in Delhi in India, local Counsellors have taken an initiative to identify the culprits who abuse street/working children sexually with the help of sexually abused children to register criminal cases against them (Source: *Times of India*, Jan.24, 2001). The same initiative is desirable in all the metropolitan cities in India.

A good number of people irrespective of social strata are not aware of the term child abuse and neglect. The causes of child abuse and neglect vary from culture to culture. But in general, physical, mental and sexual abuse is more common among children of lower social strata and/or among disadvantaged group while psychological abuse is more prevalent among the children of upper social strata.

Street/orphan children, the children of commercial sex workers (CSWs) and children living in the urban slum areas are subjected to all form of child abuse and neglect, they hardly get any opportunity for study and have no access to health facilities. In general people of larger society consider them as street urchins and utilize them for their vested interest. The children of CSWs develop an inferiority complex. As a result, a good number of girl children of CSWs accept mother's profession while male children involve themselves in different deviant social activities like alcohol selling, drug peddling, smuggling of goods and selling of tickets in the cinema hall etc in black.

The parents of the rural children with poor economic background have a tendency to send their children to the urban areas for odd jobs. These children come to the urban areas through some channels. Male children are involved in a variety of economic activities like working in tea stalls, grocery shops, garages, working as rag pickers while female children mostly work as maidservants. To their parents the main expectation is that at least their children will get some food and some money at the end of the month, which will supplement their family income, no matter how much they get paid against their services. In this regard Deb (1997) carried out a study-covering maidservants of South Calcutta to understand their condition. The author observed that most of them came from disadvantaged families. They work for about 12 to 14 hours a day against which they get very poor remuneration and mostly leftovers. They are abused physically and mentally for minor mistakes.

In another qualitative study on victimized children of socio-economically disadvantaged families, Deb (1994) found that children were victimized since the early years of their life through a chain of adversities under uncompromising demands of their parents from the children to avoid schooling and to earn money deceitfully. The confession of the children revealed the sequences through which they were gradually drifted into delinquent habits.

From the on-going ever increasing crime scenario in India, it has been observed that most of the crimes are committed by those youths who were neglected, abused and deprived of their basic rights in the formative years of their life. Thilagaraj and Priyamvadha (2000) observed that street children are used as the instruments of professional conmen to evade police and vigilance in a state. To the people of underworld especially those who are involved in organized crime these neglected children are the resources to fulfil their vested interest.

Definition of Child Abuse and Neglect

C. Henry Kempe (Kempe *et al.*, 1962), a physician first drew the attention of larger society and of the researchers about this social problem in his article *The Battered Child Syndrome*:

According to Kempe,

> 'Child abuse as a clinical condition (i.e., with diagnosable medical and physical symptoms) having to do with those who have been deliberately injured by a physical assault'.

This definition restricts abuse to only those acts of physical violence that produce a diagnosable injury.

The National Centre on Child Abuse and Neglect, an agency of the federal government established in 1974, expanded the definition of abuse to include non-physical acts as well. The agency's definition of abuse is:

> 'The physical or mental injury, sexual abuse, negligent treatment, or maltreatment of a child under the age of eighteen by a person who is responsible for the child's welfare under circumstances which indicates that the child's health or welfare is harmed or threatened thereby.'

This definition lumps acts of omission and commission or acts of violence and non-violence together.

Burgess (1979) defined child abuse as:

> 'Any child who receives non-accidental physical and psychological injury as a result of acts and omissions on the part of his parents, guardians or employees.'

According to USA Congress (1986):

> 'Child Abuse and Neglect means the physical or mental injury, sexual abuse and exploitation, negligent treatment, or maltreatment of a child under the age of 18.'

National Institute of Public Cooperation and Child Development (NIPCCD), New Delhi, (1988) defined child abuse and neglect as:

> 'Child abuse and neglect is the intentional non-accidental injury, maltreatment of children by parents/caretakers/individuals employers or others including those individuals representing Government/NGO bodies, which may lead to temporary or permanent impairment of their physical, mental, psycho-social development, disability or death.'

The above definition of NIPCCD is more or less a broad definition, which covers almost all aspects of child abuse and neglect. However, there are a number of definitions of child abuse worldwide. Some definitions focus on the behaviours or actions of adults while others consider abuse to take place if there is harm or the threat of harm to the child (Straus, 1995, 1979; Straus and Hamby, 1997; Straus *et al.*, 1998; Straus and Gelles, 1990).

Recently the International Society for the Prevention of Child Abuse and Neglect (ISPCAN) compared definitions of about from 58 countries and found some commonality in what was considered abusive (Bross *et al.*, 2000). In 1999, the WHO Consultation on Child Abuse Prevention drafted the following definition (Report of the Consultation on Child Abuse Prevention, WHO, Geneva, 1999):

> 'Child abuse and maltreatment constitutes all forms of physical and/or emotional ill-treatment, sexual abuse, neglect or negligent treatment or commercial or other exploitation, resulting in actual or potential harm to the child's health, survival, development or dignity in the context of a relationship of responsibility, trust or power.'

The definition drafted by the WHO Consultation on Child Abuse Prevention covers a broad spectrum of abuse.

Types of Child Abuse and Neglect

Children are being abused, maltreated and neglected in different forms in different communities, social strata and countries. In India children are still regarded as parental property and parents have an expectation that their children will always follow their directives and fulfil their wishes and/or aspirations. Violations of these expectations means children are subjected to abuse, maltreatment and neglect. In a Kolkata based study Deb and Senapati (1993) identified four major modes of mal-handling by the parents, viz., physical torture, wilful negligence, exploitation of innocence and dependency of the child and enticement to accept a disgraceful life.

However, the nature and types of abuse and neglect of children can broadly be divided into following categories like:

- Psychological/emotional abuse
- Physical abuse
- Sexual abuse
- Abuse for commercial purpose
- Neglect

In the following section, each of these types of child abuse and neglect are discussed with its characteristic features:

Psychological/Emotional Abuse

Verbal or non-verbal parent-to-child communications that may be psychologically injurious to the child given the child's age and developmental status.

According to Oates (1996), emotional/psychological abuse means the habitual verbal harassment of a child by disparagement, criticism, threat and ridicule. Emotional or psychological abuse includes behaviour that threatens or intimidates a child. It includes threats, name calling, belittling and shaming.

However, it is very difficult to define psychological/emotional abuse. In this regard, cultural factors play an important role. In some culture one way of dealing with children psychologically is normal while the same style in another culture may be regarded as harmful.

Psychological/emotional abuse can broadly be divided into two categories. First, deprivation from parental love and affection. For example, in urban metropolitan cities where both the parents work they are unable to spend minimum time with their children and look after their studies because of work pressure and other social and family commitments. In that case most of the parents try to supplement their absence by providing materialistic goods to the children as per their demand.

Secondly, mental pressure is exerted by the parents for better academic performance by the children. This is a major problem faced by most of the children in India. It happens because of over competition and limited job opportunities in India. Every parent expects that their children should stand first in the class and/or rank top in the class. This apart, a good number of parents wish to fulfil their unfulfilled dreams through their children. As a result, consciously or unconsciously they always put mental pressure on the children, which causes great academic stress. It has been observed that every year, after publication of secondary and higher secondary results a good number of children attempt to commit suicide and/or run away from the house. This issue needs attention of the education policy makers and school authorities for effective intervention programme. In India there is no system of counselling for the students and parents in school. This concept should be introduced and school authorities should appoint at least two/three student counsellors.

Regarding future career of children most of the parents have a tendency to impose their own ideas. Children's likings are not given priority. As a result, a good number of children gradually lose interest in studies and deteriorate their academic performance. Following is a bright example of over expectation of parents and its consequences:

> **Case 1:** *Sangeeta, female, 17 years, committed suicide out of fear of poor performance held in the examination on June 7, 2003. She was a good student and her*

previous academic result was good. However, on June 4, her one of the examinations did not go too well and she feared that she would not score up to her parent's expectation. After coming back home, she was depressed all evening. She even did not sit for dinner and stayed in her room. That day night her mother heard a thud and went out to look. The neighbours were also attracted by the sound. Sangeeta's family members ran down to find their daughter lying dead on the ground. On a scrap of paper found in her room, she had scribed, 'mother, I could not do better' (Source: The Times of India, Kolkata, June 7, 2003).

There is another form of child abuse. A large number of primary and even the Montessori school teachers who are engaged in private coaching/tuition always have a tendency to complain about the performance of the children to their parents and indirectly ask them to arrange for private coaching. If any parents do not respond to the advice of school teachers their children are subjected to humiliating situations in school, discouragement and even physical punishment for slightest mistakes.

Physical Abuse

Any parent or caregiver act causing non-accidental physical injury or death. According to Oates (1996), physical abuse means non-accidental physical injury as a result of caretaker acts. Physical abuse frequently includes shaking, slapping, punching, beating, kicking, biting and burning.

In India, physical punishment of children has been regarded as a method of behaviour modification. Sometimes the extent of physical punishment crosses the limit and consequences become fatal and/or serious. As a result of unbearable physical punishment every year a good number of children runaway from the family especially in the rural areas. This is the problem across the social strata and culture. The most common form of physical punishment and abuse of children in India include slap, pulling of ear and hair, kick, beatings by cane/bamboo stick, belt and iron rod.

In many countries including India, teachers are still authorized to beat school children with canes or straps and corporal punishment is also used in residential institutions and in children's workplace although school authorities do not admit it. Child physical maltreatment is increasing in the primary and secondary schools to the extent that it has drawn attention of media a number of times. The following case study is another example of physical punishment of children in school and its consequences:

> **Case 2:** *Ramu Abhivan, a class X student of a private school in Chennai (India) committed suicide on June 14, 2003 after he was beaten up by his teacher for not attending a special class. Abhivav had missed the special class after school hours to celebrate his sixteenth birthday. Next day when he went to school he was allegedly beaten by his maths teacher and suffered injuries on his cheek, shoulders and back. Very next day Abhinav hanged himself from the ceiling fan when his family members were away at work leaving a note in which he apologized to his parents and sister for taking the extreme steps as he did not want to go to school. The father alleged that his son was beaten with an iron rod (Source:* Sunday Hindustan Times, *New Delhi, June 15, 2003).*

This is not an isolated case. From personal interaction with the teachers in some schools in Kolkata, it was reported that corporal punishment is very much common and a section of teachers are involved in this act.

The worst form of child abuse is killing a child. The concept of killing a child and offered the sacrifice in front of image of Goddess 'Kali' and alike was practiced in some communities in India long time back. People used to kill small children for betterment of other family members. In the recent past the same incident was reported in a remote village in Orissa.

Sexual Abuse

Sexual abuse refers to sexual exposure or contact by a person older than a child for the purpose of sexual stimulation or exploitation regardless of the use of force or any accompanying physical injury.

According to Oates (1996), sexual abuse of children means involvement of dependent, developmentally immature children and adolescents in sexual activities, which they do not fully comprehend and to which they are unable to give informed consent. Sexual abuse includes touching, fondling and penetration.

Broadly there are two forms of sexual abuse of children i.e., rape and incest. 'Rape' is defined as any sexual behaviour imposed on a child by a stranger, and 'incest' defined as any sexual behaviour imposed on a child by a member of either the immediate or extended family. The extended family includes people whom the child or family has known for a significant length of time and whom they trust, such as fathers, stepfathers, uncles, siblings and other family members, as well as friends, neighbours, teachers, doctors and members of religious communities. Broadening the concept of incest beyond close blood relations is very important. It helps underscore the special harm caused by any sexual activity between a person in a position of status, trust and authority, and a child in a position of dependency. However, sexual abuse can be physical, verbal or emotional (*Source*: ESCAP-HRD, United Nations, 2002).

Physical Sexual Abuse: Touching and fondling of the sexual parts of the child's body (genitals and anus) or touching the breasts of pubescent females; the child's touching the sexual parts of a partner's body; sexual kissing and embraces; penetration, which includes penile, digital and object penetration into the vagina, mouth or anus; masturbating a child or forcing the child to masturbate the perpetrator.

Verbal Sexual Abuse: Sexual language that is inappropriate for the age of the child, used by the perpetrator to generate sexual excitement, including making lured comments about the child's body and making obscene phone calls.

Emotional Sexual Abuse: Use of a child by a parent or adult to fill inappropriate emotional needs, thereby forcing the child to fulfil the role of a spouse.

Exhibitionism and Voyeurism: Having a child pose, undress or perform in a sexual fashion on film or in person (exhibitionism); and 'peeping' into bathrooms or bedrooms to spy on a child (voyeurism); exposing children to adult sexual activity or pornographic movies and photographs.

Abuse may be a single incident, or it may take place over a period of years. Both boys and girls are equally potential to be the victim sexual abuse. Earlier, parents were scared of leaving their little daughters alone, but now even boys are not safe. They are equally vulnerable. But cases of sexually abused boys are rarely reported in India. Disadvantaged boys i.e., children living in slums or on roadsides are more vulnerable to sexual abuse. There is also little recognition of the sexual abuse of boys, which is covered under Section 377 (Sodomy) of the IPC.

There is a misconception among some communities in the rural areas that if any elder person suffering from sexually transmitted diseases (STDs) they will be free from this disease if they have sex with a minor girl. Driven by this wrong notion sometime illiterate people abuse small children sexually and the children become the victim of STDs.

Symptoms of Sexually Abused Children: Sexual abuse may surface through a broad range of physical, behavioural and social symptoms. Indicators, taken separately, may not be symptomatic of sexual abuse. The symptoms that follow are a guide and should be examined in the contest of other behaviours or situational factors which are mentioned below (*Source*: UCDAVIS Children's Hospital):

> ***Disclosure:*** Direct or indirect statement to a parent, friend, teacher or other trusted adult.
>
> ***Physical Symptoms:*** Sexually transmitted disease, genital discharge or infection, physical trauma, pain with urination, general pain, or bleeding.
>
> ***Sexual Behaviours:*** Detailed and age inappropriate understanding of sexual behaviour by younger children; inappropriate or aggressive sexual behaviour with peers or toys; excessive curiosity about sexual matters or genitalia; prostitution of promiscuity.

Behavioural Indicators: Regressive behaviour (wetting/soiling, thumb sucking); psychosomatic complaints (headaches/stomach aches); depression; fears; nightmares or sleep disturbances; repressed anger/hostility; low self-esteem; suicide attempts; poor social skills; rebellious, runaway, or delinquent behaviour; school problems; alcohol/drug abuse.

Is a Medical Examination Really Needed?

Medical examinations are recommended to assess the possibility of injury and physical evidence, to reassure children about the health of their bodies, and to answer questions. Examinations may or may not substantiate whether sexual abuse has occurred.

If the incidence occurred within the past 72 hours, the child should be examined without delay to minimize the loss or deterioration of physical evidence.

When Abuse is Revealed, How Do You Respond?

Some parents are confused about how to react when the incidence of sexual abuse is revealed. Some parents overreact while some remain indifferent. Following are some tips about how to respond when such incidence is reported to parents or guardians:

- Talk to your child in a quiet private place.
- Ask your child to tell you what has happened.
- Assure your child that s/he did the right thing by telling you, that you are sorry for its happening, and that you will do your best to keep him/her safe.
- Make a report to a law enforcement agency or a Child Protective Services.

How You Can Help Your Child Recover?

Sexually abused children undergo severe psychological problems like stress, anxiety, depression, fear and so on. During this period they require mental support and special care to overcome all the psychological problems and in this regard parents and guardians can play a vital role, which is badly needed for a victim child. For Example,

- Believe and support your child. Parental disbelief and withdrawal intensify psychological trauma.
- Assure your child that s/he is all right. Children may develop fears about their physical well-being and safety.
- Respond to questions. Information reduces fear. Keep answers simple.
- Respond to their feelings. Acknowledge emotions and discuss the matter with a calm, reassuring attitude.
- Respect children's privacy. Children have concerns about who knows what has happened. Tell only a select group of people.
- Consider future risk. Provide sex education at home. Describe proper names for body parts. Discuss appropriate and inappropriate behaviour and safety plans.
- Discuss it with siblings. Use general age-appropriate words. Do not discuss details.
- Encourage psychological assessment and counseling for the child and other family members. Traumatic events can affect children's and adolescents' emotional lives and development.
- Report the incident to Child Protective Services.
- Restore regular routines like bedtimes, meals, rules, chores and school attendance.

Myths and Facts about Child Sexual Abuse

There are misconceptions about sexual abuse of children. Following are some examples of misconceptions/myths and the facts, which will be helpful for general population to have a better understanding of this issue:

Chart 2.1: Myths and Facts about Child Sexual Abuse

1.	Myth: Fact:	Children are rarely abused sexually. Children are the most vulnerable section of our society because of their dependence on their elders.
2.	Myth: Fact:	Child sexual abuse occurs mostly in poor, illiterate families. Child sexual abuse occurs in all strata of society because children, irrespective of their family background, are equally vulnerable.
3.	Myth: Fact:	Children should not be allowed to play outside as molestation, sexual assault generally occurs on playgrounds or other public places. Mostly children are sexually abused inside their homes and the abuser is either an acquaintance, relative or family friend.
4.	Myth: Fact:	Generally servants, drivers or strangers abuse children. Family members, acquaintances and relatives who are in a position of power and authority in the family, generally abuse children.
5.	Myth: Fact:	Often precocious children provoke abuse by their seductive behaviour. Children can never invite sexual abuse, as it is an act of violence. Precocity and seductiveness are adult justifications/ misinterpretations.
6.	Myth: Fact:	Children often fantasize about being sexually assaulted. Children are ignorant about sex, so cannot fantasize about being raped sodomised or brutally assaulted.
7.	Myth: Fact:	If there happens to be a case of child sexual abuse, the offender is generally mentally ill. If we know that most of child sexual abuse occurs at home, are we to believe that most homes are infested with psychopaths?
8.	Myth: Fact:	Usually the mother is aware of the fact that her child is sexually abused. Mothers are not aware of the fact that her child is being abused because children are afraid of disclosing their abuse to anyone.
9.	Myth: Fact:	Reporting of child sexual abuse causes more harm than good. If child sexual abuse is not reported, the same abuser may harm other children.
10.	Myth: Fact:	If a child 'consents' it must have liked it, if they don't say 'no' it is not abuse. Sexual abuse is never the fault or responsibility of the child. The offender bears the entire responsibility for the crime, in whatever form it takes, most sexual abuse occurs not by force but by trickery, bribery, manipulation and misuse of authority.

Contd...

Chart 2.1: Contd. ....

11.	Myth: Fact:	Child sexual abuse usually a one time violent act that involves intercourse. Child sexual abuse is the exploitation of a child for sexual stimulation of an adult or any significant older person. It may include obscene phone calls, exposure of genitals or breast, fondling, showing a child pornographic material, masturbation, oral/anal/vaginal intercourse or attempts and exploitation of the child for prostitution/pornography.
12.	Myth: Fact:	Child sexual abuse is a result of western influences/media. Child sexual abuse has always existed in our society.
13.	Myth: Fact:	Girls are sexually abused, not boys. Both boys and girls are sexually abused.
14.	Myth: Fact:	Child marriage protects children from sexual abuse. Child marriage in itself is another form of child abuse.
15.	Myth: Fact:	Infants are not sexually abused. Even 3 months old babies have been sexually abused.
16.	Myth: Fact:	Sex with a virgin can cure sexually transmitted diseases (STD's). Sex with a virgin can never cure STD's. Only medical treatment can cure STD's.

Source: Child Sexual Exploitation and Its Complex Shades: A Compilation, produced by the Forum Against Child Sexual Exploitation

Eight Rules for Safety of Children (Source: Child Sexual Exploitation and Its Complex Shades: A Compilation, produced by the Forum Against Child Sexual Exploitation):

- Before you go anywhere you should always check first with your parents or the person in charge. You tell them where you are going, how you will get there, who will be going with you and when you will be back.
- First you take permission from your parents before getting into a car or leaving with anyone even someone whom you know. You check first before changing plans or accepting money, gifts, or drugs without your parents' knowledge.
- It is safer for you to be with other people when you are going to different places or playing outside. You should always use the 'buddy system'.

- You say 'No' if someone tries to touch you in ways that make you frightened, uncomfortable, or confused. Then you go and tell a grown up you trust what happened.
- You know it is not your fault if someone touches you in a way that is not comfortable. You don't have to keep secrets about those touches.
- You trust your feelings and talk to grown-ups about problems that are too big for you to handle on your own. A lot of people care about you and will listen and believe you. You are not alone.
- It is never too late to ask for help. You can keep asking until you get the help you require.
- You are a special person, and deserve to be safe.

Abuse for Commercial Purpose

When an elderly person for commercial benefit uses a child then this form of abuse is called abuse for commercialized vice.

A good number of children across the globe are abused for commercial purpose. In order to avoid the attention of law enforcement agencies sometimes children are used by anti socials and smugglers as carrier of smuggled goods and for drug peddling. This apart, a large number of girl children with poor economic background are pushed into a negative direction i.e., in flesh trade by some racket.

Neglect

Parent or caregiver fail to provide adequate health care, supervision, home safety and cleanliness, nutrition, personal hygiene, or supervision.

According to Oates (1996), neglect means failure of caretakers to provide for a child's fundamental needs. Although neglect can include children's necessary emotional needs, neglect typically concerns adequate food, housing, clothing, medical care and education.

Disadvantaged children especially the children living in rural areas, in urban slum areas, street and orphan children are deprived from the basic rights i.e., adequate nutrition, education, congenial living environment and health care facilities.

In some communities in India child marriage is regarded as a cultural practice. Children are given marriage at the age of 10 to 12 years and even before that when they are immature in terms of physical and mental development. This sort of cultural practice does not allow a large number of children to go for higher education and their potentials mostly remain underutilized. In the rural areas minor aged girls become mothers of two/three children by the age of 20 years, which is one of the major causes of population explosion in India.

Incidences and Magnitude of Child Abuse and Neglect

It is very difficult to project the incidence rate and magnitude of various forms of child abuse and neglect in India, as there is no system of maintaining record as maintained in the developed countries.

A number of welfare organizations work for the welfare of disadvantaged children but a good number of them are not professionally trained to document the data and write article for publication in the journal for dissemination. As a result, experience of NGOs in this field especially in the developing countries remains unknown to other organizations, academicians and researchers. However, some of the researchers reported their findings in different journals and/or periodicals for dissemination of the same and for creating awareness.

In the following section, findings of some of the reported studies in India are provided to give some idea about the incidence, nature and magnitude of the problems of child abuse and neglect in comparison with findings of selected study carried out in the developed countries.

Sexual Abuse

Reported cases give some idea about various forms of crimes committed against children especially sexual abuse in India during 1992 - 1996 (Table 2.1). In India, cases of sexual abuse/harassment are not reported owing to negligence, perceived harassment in the police department and in the court and threat from the perpetrators. In addition, fear of social discrimination and boycott also inhibit the victim to report the case to police. Hence, the figures in Table 2.1 are definitely an underestimation of actual incidence. Figures in Table 2.1 shows that maximum number of child rape cases was reported followed by kidnapping/abduction and exposure/ abandonment.

Prevalence of sexual abuse varies depending on the definitions used and the method of collecting information. Some researchers collected information directly from the children, others from the adolescents and adults reporting on their childhood while some researchers asked questions to the parents about their children. Figures of reported sexual abuse of children and youth in many countries show that the majority of the victims come from poor

Table 2.1: Incidence of Crime Committed Against Children in India During 1992-1996

Incidence Variation ***Percentage***

Crime Head	1992	1993	1994	1995	1996	1995 over1992	1996 over1995
Child rape (up to 16 years)	3113	3393	3986	4067	4083	31.2	0.4
Kidnapping & Abduction	521	485	864	726	571	9.6	-21.3
Procuration of Minor girls	-	-	206	107	94	-	-21.1
Selling of girls for prostitution	-	-	34	17	6	-	-64.7
Buying of girls for prostitution	-	-	4	19	22	-	15.8
Abetment of Suicide	-	-	7	9	11	-	+22.2
Exposure and Abandonment	-	-	491	570	554	-	-1.8
Infanticide	-	-	131	139	113	-	-18.7
Foeticide	-	-	45	38	39	-	2.6
Child-Marriage Restraint Act	-	-	53	57	89	-	56.1

Source: Crime in India, 1996, p.96 (- Figures not available)

families. In general, rates of the reported cases of sexual abuse of children and youth are higher among girls; however, childcare professionals report that sexual abuse is increasing amongst the boys as well.

In an Indian study carried out by Pagare (2003) in an observation home in Delhi covering 189 boys, sexual abuse was reported in case of 38.1 per cent of children. On clinical examination, among the sexually abused children, (n=72) physical signs were seen in 23.8 per cent and behavioural signs were seen in 16.3 per cent. In case of sexual abuse the most common perpetrators of sexual abuse were strangers. Sexual abuse was found to be significantly associated with domestic violence (p=0.016), solvent/ inhalant use (p=0.0002) and working status (p=0.017). In another study carried out in south Kolkata among migrant child labour. authors found that 11.0 per cent of girl children working as maidservant was subjected to sexual abuse and/or harassment (Deb and Mitra, 2002).

The survey of Romanian families found that 0.1 per cent of parents admitted to having sexually abused their children, while 9.1 per cent of children reported having suffered sexual abuse (Browne, K. *et al.*, 2002). Findings reported in international studies conducted since 1980 reveal a mean lifetime prevalence rate of childhood sexual victimization of 20.0 per cent among women and of 5-10 per cent among men (Finkelhor, 1994). Lifetime prevalence rates for childhood sexual victimization among adult women range from 0.9 per cent (Choquet *et al.*, 1997), using rape as the definition of abuse, to 45.0 per cent with a much wider definition.

In the industrial countries there are systems for maintaining record regarding various forms of child abuse and neglect. Findings vary depending upon methodology, with studies using face-to-face interviews and multiple questions yielding higher rates of sexual abuse. Taking into account the variability in findings, estimates are that, in the general population, between 1 in 3 or 4 women were sexually abused during childhood and between 1 in 6 to 10 men (Friedman, 1998).

In USA over the 20 years information pertaining to child sexual abuse has been reported. It has been observed that the number of cases of child abuse and neglect especially sexually abused cases steadily increased. According to the National Committee for the Prevention of Child Abuse (NCPCA), sexual abuse constitute about 11 per cent of cases reported, in 1995 almost 350,000 cases. Currently, approximately one-third of reports are substantiated after investigation by Child Protection Services (CPS) i.e., about 110,000 cases of sexual abuse annually. Although the number of cases from the CPS report is considerable, a study of 1000 parents conducted by the Gallup Poll in 1995 yielded a projection 10 times larger, of one million children during the previous year.

Physical Abuse

In a recently conducted study in Kolkata in India, it was found that a good number of teachers (26.67% male and 16.67% female) were of the opinion that it is necessary to physically punishing children to make them disciplined and obedient. On the contrary, when it comes to practice, it was found that 33.3 per cent male and 40.0 per cent female teachers used physical punishment although a good number of them did not believe in it. Findings further revealed that 60.0 per cent male and 53.4 per cent female teachers were physically punished during childhood (Deb and Bandyopadhyay, 2003).

In another study conducted in an observation home in Delhi covering 189-boys Pagare (2003) found that about three-fourth (76.7%) of them were physical abused. Majority of the children were runaways (77.8%). On clinical examination, among the physically abused children (n=145) physical signs were seen in 49.7 per cent and behavioural signs were seen in 22.8 per cent. The most common perpetrators of physical abuse were father (55.2%) followed by policemen (29.7%). Author further revealed that physical abuse was significantly associated with domestic violence, substance use in family, stepparent, substance use by child, running away from home and working status.

Segal and Ashtekar (1994) found that 60 per cent of the children ran away from home to avoid physical abuse. In another study Segal (1995) observed that 42 per cent of middle class families considered violence as severe, and 2.9 per cent of these families considered violence in an extreme form. In a recently conducted study on migrant child labour in South Kolkata, it was found that 32.5 per cent of them were abused physically (Deb and Mitra, 2002).

Available data derived from population-based surveys on physical punishment of children indicates that the rates vary considerably. A 1995 population-based survey in the United States asked parents how they disciplined their children. Findings revealed that 40 per 1000 children were abused physically like hitting the child with an object, other than on the buttocks; kicking the child; beating the child; and threatening the child with a knife or gun (Straus *et al.*, 1998). Findings of other studies carried out in other part of the world are given below:

- In Ethiopia, 21.0 per cent of urban and 64.9 per cent of rural school children reported bruises or swellings on their bodies resulting from parental punishment (Ketsela and Kedebe, 1997).
- In a recent study in the Republic of Korea, parents were questioned about their behaviour towards their children. Two-thirds of the parents reported whipping their children and 45.0 per cent confirmed that they had it, kicked or beaten them (Hahm and Guterman, 2001).
- In a cross-sectional survey of children in Egypt, 37.0 per cent reported being beaten or tied up by their parents and 26.0 per cent reported physical injuries such as fractures, loss of consciousness or permanent disability as a result of being beaten or tied up (Youssef *et al.*, 1998).
- In China, the rate of severe violence reported by the children was 22.6 per cent, while in the Republic of Korea it was 51.3 per cent (Kim, *et al.*, 2000).
- Findings of World Studies of Abuse in the Family Environment (World SAFE) project, a cross-national collaborative study clearly revealed that harsh parental punishment is not confined to a few places or a single region of the world. Parents in Egypt, rural areas of India, and the Philippines frequently reported, as a punishment, hitting their children with an object on a part of the body other than the buttocks at least once during the previous 6 months (Wanda *et al.*, 2000).

Out of total 119-reported cases of physical abuse in Kuala Lumpur, Malaysia, 31 per cent were found to be severely abused. Among those severely abused, 18 had intracranial hemorrhage and there were four deaths (Kasim *et al*. 1994). In another study carried out by Farinatti *et al*. (1990) in Brazil also observed that 70 per cent of the children were physically abused.

Zeira *et al*., (2002) found that 29.1 per cent of the students were victims of at least one act of harassment in Jewish and Arab schools. The more common acts were to show offensive pictures or to send obscene letters, to take off or to try to take off part of the student's clothing, and to try to kiss a student. The most vulnerable groups are the Arab boys and 8th grade students. Report rates were the lowest among Arab girls.

Information on the numbers of children who die each year as a result of abuse comes mainly from death registrations or mortality data. Although reliable data are extremely scarce, the WHO estimated that there were 57,000 deaths attributed to homicide among children less than 15 years of age worldwide in 2000. Global estimates of child homicide suggest that infants and very young children are at greatest risk, with rates for the 0-4 year-old age group more than double those of 5-14-year-old (5.2 per 100,000 compared with 2.1 per 100,000) (World Report on Violence and Health, published by the WHO, Oct. 2002). The most common cause of death is head injury, followed by abdominal injuries and intentional suffocation (Kirschner and Wilson, 2001; Alexander *et. al*., 2001; Vock *et al*., 1999).

In most countries worldwide, many children and even babies continue to be subjected to corporal punishment in their homes, with significant numbers suffering death or serious injury. India is not exception to that. Rather in India child physical punishment is regarded as a method of behaviour modification. Owing to unemployment scenario in India and over competition every parent wants their children to stand first in the class and put excessive mental pressure on the children, which becomes intolerable for them. Parents never try to understand that every child has optimum capacity beyond which they cannot perform even if mental pressure is given. If any child is unablé to perform at the level of expectation of parents they are subjected to mental torture and physical punishment. As a result, every year a good number of children run away from home after publication of annual results and/or commit suicide.

Considering the nature and extent of physical punishment of students there is an international movement by social scientists as well as pediatrician to end corporal punishment worldwide. In 1979, Sweden became the first country to prohibit all forms of corporal punishment of students. Since then, at least 10 further states have banned it. Nevertheless, surveys indicate that corporal punishment remains legal in at least 60 countries for juvenile offenders and at least 65 countries in schools and other institutions (*Source:* World Report on Violence and Health, WHO, Oct. 2002).

Psychological/Emotional Abuse

Analysis of qualitative data of Deb and Mitra's study (2002) provided some insight about the issue. Replying to a question when and why they were subjected to mental and physical abuse, most of them stated failure to fulfil unlimited demand of employers and minor mistakes were the main reasons followed by nature and personality of employer especially housewife. For example:

> *'Everyday from morning to till night I perform a lot of activities. One day Boudi (house lady) wanted a glass of water. But I forgot to give her water, which irritated her and for the same reason she used abusive language for a long time.'*
>
> ***—Girl child working as maidservant***

> *'For the last one year and six months I did not visit my home. I was feeling very homesick. I asked my authority to allow me to visit my home for a week. But they did not allow me, rather threatened me to dismiss me from my job if I went home.'*
>
> ***—Boy child working as maidservant***

'One day accidentally broke a glass for which I got two solid slaps as a reward.'

—Girl child working as maidservant

'Whole day I work in tea-stall. In the evening I feel very tired. Sometimes I go to the backside of the stall and sleep and end up being punished for the same.'

—Boy child working in a tea-stall

As per report of the World SAFE study conducted in five countries, the lowest incidence rate of calling children by their names in the previous 6 months was 15.0 per cent. The practice of threatening children with abandonment or with being locked out of the house, however, varied widely among the countries. In the Philippines, for example, mothers frequently reported threats of abandonment as a disciplinary measure (48.0%) while in India 20.0 per cent mothers do so. In Chile, the rate of using such threats was much lower, at about 8.0 per cent (Wanda *et al.*, 2000).

In a study carried out by Benbenishty *et al.* (2002) children reported high rates of victimization by staff members. Almost a quarter of all children participating in this study reported being emotionally maltreated by a staff member, almost a fifth (18.7%) reported being a victim of at least one type of physical forms of maltreatment, and 8.2 per cent reported on at least one sexually inappropriate behaviour by a staff member. The most vulnerable groups for all types of maltreatment were males, children in junior high schools, children in Arab schools, and children in schools with a high concentration of students coming from low-income and low-education families.

Shumba (2002) reported that emotional abuse exists in Zimbabwean primary schools and female teachers appear to be the main perpetrators of this form of child abuse. This form of child abuse may involve one perpetrator and a series of victims.

Abuse for Commercial Purpose

In fact, there is no data on this issue i.e., worldwide how many children are abused for commercial purpose and/or deprived from minimal wage. A large number of children work as bonded labour in the developing countries and/or trafficked for commercial purposes.

Neglect

In India, a large number of children belonging to lower social strata especially in the rural areas are neglected and deprived from their basic rights and a large number of parents are failed to provide protection and care to their children owing to utter poverty, negligent attitude, dependence on alcohol and situational factors. However, there is a no population-based study on this issue in India.

However, recently one study explored the issue of neglect in case of child labour in India from different angles (Deb and Mitra, 2002). First, the study attempted to understand how working children are being treated. Out of a total of 120 children covered in the study 38.3 per cent (46/120) fall sick in the last months. Of them only 19.6 per cent received proper medication while 42.3 per cent were given medicines without consulting the doctor. Fortunately 13 per cent were allowed to take rest. The remaining 26.1 per cent did not receive any medication and remained untreated.

When children are supposed to go to school for study, a large number of children coming from poor socio-economic background are compelled to work for survival. In case of study about 35 per cent (41/120) employers showed their broad outlook allowing the working children to study at home while work pressure is less. This has happed mostly in case of domestic servants. On the other hand, about one-fifth (23.3%) children did not get any cooperation in this regard while 42.5 per cent children were not interested in study (Deb and Mitra, 2002).

About 42 per cent of the working children used to get adequate food while 23.3 per cent never got adequate food. The rest 24.2 per cent got adequate food sometimes. During childhood and adolescence, recreation is necessary for proper mental development. Unfortunately, a large number of the working children were neither allowed to play or gossip with their peer group nor allowed to view recreational programmes on TV which is very much desired by any child. Regarding behaviour of the employers more than one-fourth stated that it was very bad and sometimes it was intolerable (Table 2.2).

Table 2.2: Neglect of Working Children

Neglect	*Boys (N=75)*	*Girls (N=45)*	*Total (N=120)*
Whether fall sick in the last six months:			
• Yes	31 (41.3)	15 (33.3)	46 (38.3)
• No	44 (58.7)	30 (66.7)	74 (61.7)
Whether received treatment in case of illness:			
• Consulted doctor and given medicine	6 (19.4)	3(20.0)	9 (19.6)
• Given medicine without consulting doctor	13 (41.9)	6 (40.0)	19 (41.3)
• Asked to take rest only	4 (12.9)	2 (13.3)	6 (13.0)
• Did not receive any medication or care	8 (25.8)	4 (26.6)	12(26.1)
Whether received cooperation for study:			
• Allowed to study at home	16 (21.3)	7 (15.6)	23 (19.2)
• Allowed to study at home and taken care	10 (13.3)	8 (17.8)	18 (15.0)
• Not allowed to study	18 (24.0)	10 (22.2)	28 (23.3)
• Child did not show any interest for study	31 (41.3)	20 (44.4)	51 (42.5)
Whether get adequate food:			
• Always	32 (42.7)	18 (40.0)	50 (41.7)
• Sometimes	25 (33.3)	17 (37.8)	42 (35.0)
• Never	18 (24.0)	10 (22.2)	28 (23.3)
Whether allowed to play with peer group while working in neighbour's house:			
• Frequently	12 (16.0)	7 (15.6)	19 (15.8)
• Sometimes	20 (26.7)	9 (20.0)	29 (24.2)
• Never	43 (57.3)	29 (64.4)	72 (60.0)
Whether allowed to view TV:			
• Frequently	10 (13.3)	6 (13.3)	16 (13.3)
• Sometimes	42 (56.0)	23 (51.1)	65 (54.2)
• Never	23 (30.7)	16 (35.6)	39 (32.5)
Perceived Behaviour of Employer:			
• Exceptionally good	13 (17.3)	9 (20.0)	21 (17.5)
• Moderately good	17 (22.7)	11 (24.4)	28 (23.3)
• Not so good	25 (33.3)	10 (22.2)	35 (29.2)
• Not at all good	20 (26.7)	15 (33.3)	35 (29.2)

Source: Deb and Mitra (2002)

In Kenya, abandonment and neglect were the most commonly cited aspects of child abuse when adults in the community were questioned on the subject. In this study, 21.9 per cent children reported that their parents had neglected them (*Source:* Nairobi, African Network for the Prevention and Protection against Child Abuse and Neglect, 2000). In Canada, a national study of cases reported to child welfare services found that among the substantiated cases of neglect, 19.0 per cent were involved in physical neglect,

12.0 per cent in abandonment, 11.0 per cent in educational neglect, and 48.0 per cent in physical harm resulting from a parent's failure to provide adequate supervision (Troeme and Wolfe, 2001).

In 2000, nearly three million reports concerning five million children were made in U.S. In almost two-thirds (62 per cent) of these cases, the information provided in the report was sufficient to prompt an investigation. As a result of these investigations, approximately 879,000 children were found to have been victims of abuse or neglect. Nearly two-thirds (63 per cent) of victims experienced neglect, meaning thereby that the caretaker failed to provide for the child's basic needs. Fewer victims were found to have been physically abused (19 per cent) or sexually abused (10 per cent), though these cases are often not likely to be publicized. The smallest number (8 per cent) was found to be victims of emotional abuse, which includes criticizing, rejecting, or refusing to nurture a child. Tragically, an average of three children die everyday as a result of child abuse or neglect in U.S. (*Source:* Child Abuse Prevention Community Resource Packet, 2003, published by the U.S. Dept. of Health and Human Services).

Causes of Child Abuse and Neglect

The causes of child abuse and neglect are numerous and it varies from community to community and country to country. In the developing countries like India the cause of child neglect is mostly poverty, lack of educational and health facilities in the rural areas, wrong perception about the value of education and wrong cultural practice i.e., child marriage. In the rural areas and urban slum areas people with poor economic background have a tendency to opt for a large family to secure their future. As a result, these children are deprived from basic minimal facilities i.e., adequate nutrition, education, health services and care and brought up in hostile and criminogenic environment. Finally, a large number of these children become juvenile delinquents.

In a Kolkata based study Deb and Senapati (1993) revealed mainly the influences of five aggravating factors for parents' cruelty and socio-pathic family environment, viz., illiteracy, unemployment, conjugal discord, lack of attachment and history of victimization in the early life of parents.

Broadly, the causes of child abuse and neglect are as follows:

Individual Factors

Adult Personality

A number of studies established positive correlation between personality and behavioural characteristics of elderly persons and child abuse and neglect. Elderly people who are impulsive, dissatisfied in personal life, perverted, have low self-respect and poor self-esteem found to be abusive (Lindell and Svedin, 2001; Youssef *et al.*, 1998). Parents of the above personality characteristics are unable to plan important things in life like marriage and finding a job. They are also unable to cope with stressful situation in life and develop good social network. In addition, they have unrealistic expectations about child development.

Attitudes and Cognition

These psychological components play major role in abusing children. Elderly people who possess negative attitude towards children are likely to abuse children on account of minor mistakes committed by them. This apart, lack of knowledge of elderly people about child rearing, lack of education, lack of knowledge about the consequence of abuse are the other factors behind child abuse and neglect.

Intergenerational Transmission of Maltreatment

From a number of studies it has been observed that the parents who were abused and/or neglected during childhood have a tendency to abuse and/or neglect their children more than that of parents who were brought up under adequate care (Egeland, 1993; Ertem *et al.*, 2000).

Substance Abuse

The people who are dependent on substance are likely to have less sense of responsibility than people who are not dependent on any substance. There is a positive correlation of child abuse/neglect and substance. In the lower social strata people who are dependent on substance have a tendency to abuse their spouse and children physically and/or psychologically under a drunken state.

Child Special Characteristics

Physically and mentally handicapped children are more prone to abuse and neglect owing to their handicapped conditions. Mentally handicapped children are more vulnerable to sexual abuse while physically handicapped children are subjected to mental torture and abuse. A number of cases have been highlighted by media about sexual abuse of mentally retarded children. It happens because perpetrators feel that mentally handicapped children cannot identify them. Hence, chances of being caught by the family member of mentally handicapped children is less or remote.

Age and Sex

Age and gender are the two important vulnerable factors for child abuse. Fatal case of physical abuse is found largely among young infants (Youssef *et al.*, 1998; Kirschner and Wilson, 2001). The majority of infant deaths in Fiji, Finland, and Germany were less than 2 years of age (Adinkrah, 2000; Vock *et al.*, 1999; Menick, 2000).

Girls are at higher risk of infanticide, sexual abuse, educational, medical and nutritional neglect and forced prostitution. Findings from several international studies show rates of sexual abuse to be 1.5 - 3 times higher among girls than boys (Finkelhor, 1994a).

Family Related Factors

Family Size

The size of the family is one of the important factors of child abuse. From a number of studies it was found that families with four or more children were three times more likely to be violent towards their children than parents with fewer children (Larrain *et al.*, 1997). In addition, household overcrowding increases the risk of child abuse (Youssef *et al.*, 1998).

Family Dynamics/Environment

It plays a major role behind child abuse and neglect. Continuous communication gap and/or maladjustment between parents' results in child abuse and neglect. In addition, in some family step-father/mother have a tendency to neglect the child and/or abuse them on account of small issues. As a result, children in those families feel neglected, rejected and develop a tendency to leave the house.

Meyerson *et al.* (2002) observed that in addition to child sexual abuse and physical abuse, family conflict and cohesion are risk factors for the development of psychological distress and depression in adolescence.

Parenting and Physical Punishment

In India most of the parents still believe that physical punishment is the only method to make a child obedient and/or disciplined. As a result, a good number of children in India become subjected to physical punishment in various forms. Sometimes physical punishment become fatal and/or cause serious injury to child health.

Violence in the Family

Data from across the globe found a strong relationship between intimate partner violence and child abuse and neglect. In a recent study in India, the occurrence of domestic violence in the family doubled the risk of child abuse (Wanda *et al.*, 2000).

Daily Life Events

Stress in Daily Life

Now-a-days especially in the urban areas people live in a very stressful environment. Stress has become a part of daily life. In urban nuclear families where both the parents work to maintain family, they feel very stressed both at home and in office. As a result, most of the urban working parents are unable to give minimum time to their children and to take care of the education of their children. In addition, they lose their temper and patience on slightest provocation, which becomes a cause of family violence. Children are the worst sufferers of this sort of family situation.

Sudden Death of Parents or Main Earning Member in the Family

There are a large number of families in India where most of the family members are dependent on the earnings of one family member only. In case of sudden prolonged illness and/or death of the said sole earning member, minor children have to stop attending school and are compelled to do something to carry on a reasonably comfortable existence. Small children especially males engage themselves in outside economic work while female children take care of all household chores. Sometimes female children indulge themselves in immoral activities i.e., in prostitution. It happens in case of the children whose economic condition and social network is very poor.

Socio-economic, Cultural and Religious Factors

Poor Economic Condition

Poverty is the main cause of child abuse and neglect in the developing countries like India. Because of utter poverty sometimes parents do not mind selling their girl child to a racket of flesh trade even for Rs.2000. There are so many such instances in our society. Involving children in economic activities or taking children by the parents to their work place is a common practice in the rural and urban slum areas.

Early Marriage

In some communities in India, early marriage is a common practice. Children are hardly at an age to be able to judge what is good for them. As a result, their education is badly affected and they are unable to aspire for something good in life. The rate of literacy in those communities is very low especially among female children.

Parental Occupation

The parents who are involved in deviant social activities have a tendency to involve their children with the same activities directly or indirectly. Initially they take assistance from the small children in running their unlawful business and later on given the responsibility of running the business particularly when they are sick and physically handicapped. Such business often relates to alcohol selling and flesh trade.

Cultural Factors

Physical punishment of small children is still regarded as a method of behaviour modification among a large section of people of the society, generation after generation. Sometimes physical torture causes permanent damage or becomes fatal. This is a common practice both in the rural and urban areas.

Another strong cultural belief among rural women is that most of the mothers do not give colostrums to their newly born child out of a feeling that it might cause stomach upset and/or this is something dirty that should not be given to children. Colostrums are very essential to increase the immune system of children and it must be given according to the WHO. However, because of wrong cultural belief colostrums is not given to a large number of children in the rural areas. As a result, children who are deprived from colostrums are prone to childhood diseases more than that of the children who received colostrums.

In some tribal groups in Tamil Nadu adolescent girls are supposed to stay outside home during first menstruation. As long as menstruation continues they will live under the tree or in forest for three/four days and will not have any connection with the family members regardless of season. After three or four days i.e., adolescent girls will be taken back home after bath. During winter or summer, they suffer major problems and some of them fall sick and/or die. However, this is the cultural practice every adolescent girl has to undergo.

On June 18, 2003 a sensational report on child abuse on account of cultural belief was reported in all the leading newspapers in India. A dog is known to be a man's best friend but in some cases can even be a girl's best pet and act as her husband (*Source: The Times of India,* June 18, 2003).

Karnamoni Hasda, a nine-year-old Santhal tribal girl, tied the knot with a street dog in the presence of more than a hundred guests at a marriage ceremony held at Khanyan in West Bengal's

Hooghly district on June 11. Marrying boys and girls with canines is a common practice among Santhals, which is supposed to protect them against any danger. Santhals believe that if the first tooth of a child appears on the upper gum, then there is grave danger to the child's life and only marriage with a dog or bitch can save the infant. There are no restrictions on remarriage of children married to canines. According to Santhal custom, Karnamoni should have been married off when her first tooth appeared, but her father's financial condition did not permit it. Santhals are a backward and extremely poor tribal community found in Jharkhand, especially Chotanagpur and Santhal Pargana regions.

Religious Factors

Sacrificing child before the god is still practiced in the 21st century by some communities in India. Media reported recently two such instances. In one instance, one 2-year-old child was sacrificed before the god out of a feeling that the family will be free from evil forces. Another instance which happened in Arhar village under Vilwara district in Rajasthan on December 7, 2002. Guided by a religious belief, the heart of a five-year old male child was taken away and offered to the God. These are not isolated cases. There are so many such cases, which happen in the interior villages and are often not reported.

Profile of Perpetrators

By definition, perpetrators of child abuse and neglect are the people responsible for the child's safety and well-being and their parents, other relatives and babysitters.

In case of sexual abuse of children especially rape, close family members are mostly responsible and it happens within the family. The rape of a child by a stranger is the rare form of sexual abuse. Young people are most at risk from those living with them, related to them or acquainted with them, such as fathers, stepfathers, uncles, old siblings, boyfriends neighbours and caretakers (Source: ESCAP HRD Course, 2002).

The most common group of people found to be responsible for neglect and physical abuse were mothers acting alone (47 per cent and 32 per cent of victims, respectively). In cases of sexual abuse, non-relatives and fathers acting alone are more likely to be responsible (29 per cent and 22 per cent of victims, respectively) (*Source:* Child Abuse Prevention Community Resource Packet, 2003, published by the US Dept. of Health and Human Services).

Consequences of Child Abuse and Neglect

The consequences of child abuse and neglect can be devastating. Studies highlighted the short-term and long-term psychological damage (Choquet *et al.*, 1997; Wolfe, 1999; Fergusson *et al.*, 1996). Some children have minor symptoms that do not reach clinical levels of concern, or else are at clinical levels but not as high as in children generally seen in clinical settings.

According to WHO, about 40 million children aged 0-14 around the world suffer from abuse and neglect who require health and social care (*Source:* Report of the Consultation on Child Abuse Prevention WHO, Geneva, 29-31 March, 1999).

In brief, the consequences of child abuse and neglect are given below:

- Physical damage can range from death, brain damage, and permanent disabilities.
- The psychological consequences can range from lowered sense of self worth to severe psychiatric disorders, including dissociative states.
- Cognitive problems range from severe organic brain disorders to reduced attention and minor learning disorders.
- Maltreated children's behavioural problems can include violent and criminal behaviour and attempt to commit suicide, aggression, provocative behaviour, or withdrawal that could lead to more abuse.
- Sexually abused children may also develop or learn sexualized behaviours that put them at risk of continued abuse by the same perpetrator or new abuse by different perpetrators (Dodge *et al.*, 1990, Friederich, 1988).

According to WHO, in the long run abused and maltreated children may suffer from developmental effects, disability, eating disorders, sleep disorders, alcohol/drug abuse, depression, anxiety, delinquency, violent behaviour, self-destructiveness, increased probability of becoming an abusing parent, long-term reproductive health outcomes, sexual dysfunction and infertility (*Source:* Report of the Consultation on Child Abuse Prevention WHO, Geneva, 29-31 March, 1999).

Findings reveal that sexually abused children also show higher vulnerability towards re-victimization in life later. Studies report a higher incidence of adult rape among former child sexually abused victims (Fromuth, 1983; Russell, 1984), and some studies showed that they are even more subject to physical abuse by spouses (Russell, 1983). A history of childhood sexual abuse was found in studies of prostitutes (Fields, 1981; Silbert and Pines, 1983), child molesters (Groth and Burgess, 1979), rapists and physically abusing parents (Finkelhor and Browne, A., 1986). Finkelhor reported a connection between homosexuality in male adults and child sexual abuse (Finkelhor, 1984). Steele and Alexander (1981) found that sexually abused individuals generally showed impaired personal and emotional functioning like depression, poor self-esteem, feelings of isolation and stigma, fear of man, hostility towards parent and a higher incidence of eating disorders in their adulthood.

A recent longitudinal cohort study in Christchurch, New Zealand found significant associations between sexual abuse during childhood and subsequent mental health problems such as depression, anxiety disorders and suicidal thoughts and behaviour (Fergusson *et al.*, 1996). This apart, a variety of symptoms, behavioural changes, and diagnosis sometimes occur in sexually abused children (Wolfe, 1999; Briere and Elliott, 1994) like:

- Anxiety symptoms such as fearfulness, phobias, insomnia, difficulty at bath time and bedtime, nightmares that directly portray the abuse, somatic complaints, and post-traumatic stress disorder.
- Dissociative reactions and hysterical symptoms such as period of amnesia, daydreaming, hysterical seizures, and symptoms of dissociative identity disorder.

- Depression manifested by low self-esteem and self-destructive behaviours and self-manipulative behaviours.
- Disturbance in sexual behaviours as an adult including emotional problems related to intimacy, sex guilt and sex anxiety.
- Somatic complaints, such as enuresis, anorexia, obesity, headache and stomachache.

Some of the common health problems affecting children who have been sexually abused that have been identified by health care professions in some Asian countries include: depression, withdrawal, fear, anxiety, vaginal discharge, painful genitalia and pregnancy. Some children also experience psychiatric problems, including running away from home and post-traumatic stress disorder (*Source:* ESCAP HRD Course, 2002).

Cost of Child Abuse and Neglect

It involves a good amount of costs for short-term and long-term care of victim. Included in the calculation are the direct cost associated with treatment, visits to the hospital, doctor, and other health services. In addition, a range of indirect costs are involved in the process. For example, involvement of employed family members in care and supervision of the victim, which reduces productivity of the employed family members. This apart, there are costs borne by the criminal justice system and others institutions like expenditures related to apprehending and prosecuting offenders, the costs to social welfare organizations of investigating reports of maltreatment and protecting children from abuse, costs associated with foster care and so on (*Source:* World Report on Violence and Health, WHO, Geneva, Oct. 2002).

In 1996, the financial cost associated with child abuse and neglect in the United States was estimated at some US$ 12.4 billion (*Source:* WHO Report of the Consultation on Child Abuse Prevention, 1999).

Prevention

Voluminous studies have been carried out across the world on causes and consequences of child abuse and neglect. But very few studies attempted to investigate the efficacy and/or effectiveness of various preventive measures. Hence, it is important to pay more attention on preventive approaches of child abuse and neglect.

Workshop for Parents on Child Development and Healthy Child Rearing Practices

A large number of parents do not have proper knowledge on child development and/or about healthy child rearing practices and as a result, directly or indirectly they abuse and/or maltreat young children. Hence, a good number of countries have taken initiative to educate potential parents on child development and help them improve their skills in managing their children properly and efficiently. Earlier it was viewed that these programmes should cover only high-risk families or those families in which abuse has already occurred. Now the concept has changed. These types of programme should cover all families. For example, in Singapore education and training in parenting begins in secondary schools, with 'preparation for parenthood' classes. Students learn about child-care and development, and gain direct experience by working with young children at preschool and child-care centers (*Source:* WHO Report of the Consultation on Child Abuse Prevention, 1999).

Wolfe *et al.* (1988) evaluated a behavioural intervention to provide training in parenting and found that mothers who received the training in parenting reported fewer behavioural problems with their children and fewer adjustment problems associated with potential maltreatment compared with the mothers in the comparison groups. Furthermore, a follow-up evaluation showed that there was a lower risk of maltreatment by the mothers who had received the training in parenting.

Extending Health Services to Families and Children

Health care professionals can play a very significant role in identifying, treating and referring cases of abuse and neglect and in reporting suspected cases of maltreatment to the concerned authorities for necessary action. It is important to detect the abuse cases as soon as possible to minimize the impact of consequences and to extend necessary remedial services for quick prognosis.

In India there is no system of maintaining any such record. Hence it is important to introduce the system of maintaining record of reported child abuse and neglect cases in both the Government and non-Government health centres. This system will not only help the victim, it will also give some idea about the nature and extent of the problem in the country.

Training for Health Care Professionals

The issue of child abuse and neglect is a very little recognized phenomenon in the developing countries like India. A large number of health care professionals are not aware of the problem and even if some of them are aware of the same they give least importance to this issue. Findings of studies across the world suggest the need for the continuing training for the health care professionals on the detection and reporting of early signs and symptoms of child abuse and neglect (Alpert *et al.*, 1998; Van Haeringen *et al.*, 1998; Vulliamy and Sullivan, 2000). Thereafter, a number of health care organizations have developed training programmes for the same and found it very useful and effective. The WHO, the American Medical Association and the American Academy of Pediatrics have produced diagnostic and treatment guidelines for child maltreatment and sexual abuse (*Source:* American Academy of Pediatrics. Guidelines for the Evaluation of Sexual Abuse of Children: Subject Review, Pediatrics, 1999).

Training for Law Enforcement Agencies Especially for Police Personnel

It is also important to organize training programme for the police personnel to sensitize them about the magnitude and different dimensions of child abuse and neglect and give them clear idea about the laws available in the respective countries for protection of child rights and how these laws could be implemented.

In India, police personnel are supposed to implement thousands and thousands of laws with minimum man power, and poor infrastructure facilities. Given the overall law and order scenario in the country, the issue of child abuse and neglect does not figure out in the priority areas of attention. However, sensitization programme on child abuse and neglect was found to be very effective in developing interest among the police personnel about the issue and ensure their special attention on it.

First time in India, multidisciplinary training programme on child abuse and neglect was conducted in Kolkata in June 2003 by an organization called MIDSW [Metropolitan (Bypass) Institute for Developmental Studies and Welfare] under the leadership of the author of this book and it was possible because of child friendly attitude of the Director General of Police (Training). The training programme was funded by the International Society for the Prevention of Child Abuse and Neglect (ISPCAN), USA. The training programme was highly successful in sensitizing the police personnel about the issue and making them understand about the application of different provisions of existing laws for the protection of child rights in India.

However, it is necessary to organize such type of training programme for the police personnel periodically.

Training for the NGO Personnel

Since NGOs work directly in the field and they have regular connection with the community, it will be beneficial to give them training on child abuse and neglect with a view to sensitizing them about the severity of the problem and to ensure their special attention on the issue. Some of the NGOs are already working in the field of child abuse and neglect. But training will be an opportunity for all of them to share latest information about the issue and to learn from each other and develop partnership. Given the over all scenario of child abuse and neglect, no single agency can combat this problem effectively in the developing countries like India. Both Government and non-government organizations should work together following partnership approach.

In 2003, for first time in India, multidisciplinary training programme on child abuse and neglect was organized in Kolkata and in Nagpur jointly by the MIDSW—an NGO involved in child protection activities in Kolkata and the Government Medical College, Nagpur. The programmes were funded by the ISPCAN. Training programmes were found to be effective and useful in achieving the objectives.

Community Awareness Programme

Public awareness about child abuse especially sexual abuse should be organized with a view to educating the public about the negative effects of child abuse and neglect. In public awareness campaign on legal measures for protecting the rights of the children should be emphasized. In this regard, more and more NGO should come forward to take up community and institute based intervention programmes with the help from Youth Club Members. It is important to select a potential target group for creating awareness about the issue. At the same time it is also important to understand the efficacy and/or impact of awareness programmes through a systematic study from time to time. Awareness campaigns also need to be evaluated for effective implementation of future programmes.

The easiest way to sensitize the people of a cross-section of the society is the media. In this regard media should be active in sensitizing community members about this issue. Documentary films should be made on this issue highlighting the various incidences of child sexual abuse and its long-term impact on children. Media should also highlight the legal measures available in our country for prosecution of the perpetrators and the nature of punishment for various offences with regard to child sexual abuse and/or involvement of children in prostitution.

The author's first hand experience says that a good number of awareness programme conducted in the past on various emerging social and health issues had minimal impact on the society. It could be because of improper planning/coordination and/or haphazard arrangement of the campaigns with poorly developed brochures and posters. Author also feels that supportive information and research findings is necessary while delivering lecture for kindling social awareness on the intended issue.

Educational Programme for the Teachers, and Guardians and Children in School

In some countries physical punishment of children is regarded as a method of behaviour modification. In the developing countries like India physical punishment of children in school and at home is very common. Sensitization programmes on child abuse and neglect and its consequences in school for the teachers and guardians is essential to curb the incidence of physical punishment and to ensure healthy disciplinary measures to correct behaviour of problematic children.

Secondary efforts to prevent sexual abuse could include offering services or educational opportunities to girls and families considered to be at risk for sexual abuse.

Without spooking them to nightmares, children have to know about the dangers of sexual abuse. This will not only give them knowledge to protect themselves but it will also sensitize them to support and help other children from becoming the victim of sexual abuse.

Teach your children the names of different organs and that body is private and not supposed to be touched without their permission. Give them unconditional permission to say 'no' even to a family member. Tell them to tell you if they are asked by anybody to be touched. Make it clear that you are available, open and on their side if an adult ever touches them in such a way that makes them feel uncomfortable and that you will protect them.

School-based Educational Programme for the Children

School-based educational programme should be launched to educate the children especially abuse sexual abuse and its effect, providing them with a sense of empowerment and teaching them how to recognize a situation of potential abuse, to protect themselves and what to do if they experience actual or potential abuse. The lessons, which could be given to children include:

- Learning touch distinctions (i.e., good touch/bad touch;green light touches/red light touches);
- Learning rules about touching;

- Learning children's rights and body boundaries;
- Learning about private parts;
- Learning skills for avoiding abuse, including saying 'no', screaming for help, running away;
- Knowing the difference between 'good secrets' and 'bad secrets';
- Realizing the idea that sexual abuse is never thc child's fault; and
- Knowing the need and ways to report abuse.

Given the nature and extent of corporal/physical punishment in schools in West Bengal the Hon'ble Chief Justice of Calcutta High Court Mr. A.K. Mathur banned the age-old practice of caning or beating students in schools (*Source: The Times of India*, Feb.6, 2004). According to Chief Justice, in the age of scientific teaching, caning or beating—which is contrary to the Universal Declaration of Human rights—cause serious mental trauma. Even after the judgment of High Court a number such cases have been reported in West Bengal. For example, two class I students of a school of Hooghly were locked up in an iron chest by their teacher for allegedly shouting in class. Hence, the relevance of the project is highly justified.

Intervention

So far as intervention aspect is concerned, the first step is to identify the abused children in need of services. Even if volunteers cannot identify them, a direct telephone online service should be implemented for registering the complaints made by the children themselves and for taking immediate action against the perpetrators. Consequently, considerable effort should be made so that proper welfare and medical services can be provided.

Psychological and Medical Services for the Victim

Need-based psychological like individual and family counselling and medical services should be provided to the victim children by sensitive and trained professionals. Counselling of the victim and their family members should be a continuous processes to follow-up the cases.

Services for the Abused and Addicted Parents and Parents with Mental Health Problems

The parents and the family members who were abused and/or suffering from mental health problems and have addiction problem require mental health and medical services. A number of studies have found positive association with the above problems of parents with child abuse and neglect.

Helping Children Who Have a Parent with a Mental Illness

Mental illness of either or both of the parents is one of the main causes of child abuse and neglect. Findings reveal that about 20.0 per cent of the parent population has mental health problems at some time in their lives (*Source:* NAPCAN, 2001). Hence if a parent is suffering from a serious mental problem their ability to care for, nurture and protect their children may be impaired. A parent who is hearing voices, having hallucinations or feeling as if they want to hurt themselves can be very frightening. Children may feel confused and scared. It becomes hard for children to talk about what is happening to their parents and to talk about the effect of the mental illness on everyone in the family. They are worried about what their parent might do. Children can feel very lonely. Some of the children also develop guilt feeling and/or inferiority complex. They also feel shaky and do not feel like to interact with other children in the school or in the community out of a fear of disclosing the information about their parent's mental health problems. These children badly need mental support, which may come from other family members, friends, school-teachers or someone else trustworthy and known to the child.

Unfortunately, in the developing countries like India these children suffer from severe stress on account of social isolation and/or social stigma. The problem is more acute in case of nuclear families especially where there is no third person in the family to give company to a child. Very few agencies deal with the problems of these children and extend them support. However, the concerned adults can extend their support and care services to these helpless children by:

- Explaining that they can ask for help.
- Listening to their feelings, fears and showing compassion. Children need others to understand their mental health problems and this is meant both for the parents as well as for the children.
- Helping them to write a diary or draw about how they feel.
- Helping the child identify and learn to build a network with adults they can feel safe.
- These should be people that the child can ring or contact for help when they find themselves unsupported, afraid or alone.
- Learning strategies to keep themselves safe during crisis. Provide them with emergency medical contact numbers.
- Ensuring that there is a good and reliable person available at short notice to care for the children if their parents are unwell.

Family Intervention

In planning a comprehensive treatment approach for families in which sexual abuse has occurred, certain social factors must be addressed. The social factors in some families significantly contribute to abusive situation while having only minimal relevance in other families. The structure and living style of some families are highly dysfunctional. These families are often described as multi-problem families and may be viewed as high risk for sexual abuse of children.

Families with poor social network should be assisted to increase their social network. This may be done by re-establishing ties with members of the extended family, joining a support group such as Parents Anonymous (Finkelhor and Baron, 1986).

In addition to family activities, the peer relationships of sexual abuse victims need to be carefully assessed as studies have indicated that these children are isolated from their peers (Finkelhor and Baron, 1986). Whether this isolation is a cause or a result of the abuse is not clear, but it does appear that victims need assistance in increasing their social contacts and peer relationships.

Behaviour Modification of Deviant Children with a History of Neglect and Abuse

Owing to continuous exposure to hostile and criminogenic environment some children get themselves involved in deviant social and economic activities for survival under compulsion. These children require support services for changing their outlook and deviant profession.

In an in-depth follow-up case study an attempt was made by Deb *et al.*, (1997) to modify the deviant behaviour of a neglected and abused street child. Findings revealed that supportive counselling and continuous efforts brought some positive change in the outlook of child resulting in moderate improvement in interpersonal relationships and some interest in vocational training. The case study suggests detachment of child from pathogenic parental influence during rehabilitation.

In another longitudinal study, it has been observed that seven out of 10 children were successfully institutionalized and pursuing their studies satisfactorily while the remaining three children were unable to settle down to institution and became dropouts due to certain personal and environmental factors like unfavourable parental influences, pathological and deviant behaviour of either of the parents, low intelligence, organic impairment and uncongenial living environment (Deb, 1996).

Effective Implementation of Law

For effective implementation of law, cooperation from people of all sections of the society is urgently required. In case of child sexual abuse NGOs should come forward and extend their support to the victim by reporting the case to the Police Department to take up the issue in court. In this regard, law enforcement agencies especially the Police Department should take a note of the incident, if any victim approaches them for reporting. While taking a note of the incident assurance should be given to the victim about his/her security. Each and every Police Station should have at least one female Police Officer who will probe the issue and collect detailed information. While collecting information about the incident ethical issues should be taken care of and the victim should be dealt with proper care so that the victim does feel secured and comfortable in sharing the incident.

Research reports suggest that harassment in Police Department and further in the court discourage victims from reporting such cases. The previous study findings could be probed wrong by the Police Department through their participation in social awareness campaign in this regard and giving assurance to public about the justice on the reported child abuse cases.

Recently in Delhi local Counsellors have taken an initiative to identify the culprits who abused street/working children sexually with the help of sexually abused children to register criminal cases against them (*Source: Times of India*, Jan. 24, 2001). The same initiative should be taken in all the metropolitan cities in India.

In fact, no single agency can solve any social problem. Community members should also extend their support and cooperation to the Law Enforcement Agencies providing information about any such incident and act as witness in the court. In this regard, indifferent attitude of people sometimes act as a barrier to give justice to the victims. This common ignorant attitude of the people should be altered for eradication of social problem. In other words, people should raise their voice for justice, irrespective of any caste and banner. Otherwise, the issue of social change and intrusion of justice for victimized population will always remain a topic of discussion.

What Individuals Can Do to Prevent Child Abuse?

In this regard, Prevent Child Abuse America has developed the following 'Five R's,' which can help individuals better understand the role they can play in child abuse prevention (*Source:* Child Abuse Prevention Community Resource Packet, 2003, published by the U.S. Dept. of Health and Human Services).

Raise the Issue

Call or write candidates and elected officials to educate them about issues in your community and the need for child abuse prevention, intervention, and treatment programmes. Contact your local school district and faith community to encourage them to sponsor classes and support programs for new parents.

Read Out to Kids and Parents in Your Community

Anything you do to support kids and parents in your family and extended community help to reduce the likelihood of child abuse and neglect. Be a good neighbour. Offer to baby-sit. Donate your children's used clothing, furniture, and toys for use by another family. Be kind and supportive, particularly to new parents and children.

Remember the Risk Factors

Child abuse and neglect occur in all segments of our society, but the risk factors are greater in families where parents:

- Abuse alcohol or drugs
- Are isolated from their families or communities
- Have difficulty in controlling their anger or stress
- Appear disinterested in the care, nourishment, or safety of their children
- Seem to be having serious economic, housing or other problems

Recognize the Warning Signs

Some of the warning signs that a child might be abused or neglected include:

- Nervousness around adults
- Aggressive toward adults or other children
- Inability to stay awake or to concentrate for extended periods
- Sudden, dramatic changes in personality or activities
- Acting sexually and/or showing interest in sex that is not appropriate for his/her age
- Frequent or unexplained bruises or injuries
- Low self-esteem
- Poor hygiene

Report on Suspected Abuse or Neglect

If you suspect that abuse or neglect is occurring, report it and keep reporting it until something is done. Contact child protective services in your locality or your local police station.

Other Ways You Can Help

Build a Support Network by Getting Involved in Your Neighbourhood

- Develop friendly relationships with your neighbours and their children. Problems often seem less overwhelming when you have support nearby.
- Get involved in your child's school. Join the parent-teacher organization and attend school events.
- Talk to your friends and neighbours about child abuse and how to prevent it.

Take Part in Community Prevention Efforts

- Help local organizations distribute materials on parenting and child abuse prevention.
- Encourage local schools or other community organizations to provide parenting education.
- Request a speaker for in-service training through the child protective services hotline.
- Organize a fundraiser or a food drive to support an organization that helps families in your community.
- Contact your elected officials and ask them to support funding for prevention efforts and policies that support children and families.
- Make a donation to an organization that works to prevent child abuse. You can donate money, or give clothing, food or toys to a social service agency that helps families in your community.
- Start or join a community coalition to prevent child abuse and neglect.

In a cross-cultural study respondents stated that many parents would be capable of providing better care to their children if they were exposed to different ways of disciplining their children and if they better understood the implications of their actions on their child's development. Parenting education efforts, support groups for new parents and public education campaigns all were cited as possible strategies for preventing future abuse. Respondents also felt that community leaders and public officials should take a more visible stand against those elements in the culture that promote or condone acts of aggression towards children (*Source:* Crying Out: Children and Communities Speak on Abuse and Neglect—A Report, published by World Vision, UK, 2002).

Problems in Intervention

Child abuse and neglect cases especially sexual abuse are not reported in the developing countries because of perceived harassment, threat, social boycott and/or stigma. In the developed countries few professionals explained that they do not report such cases because of the perception that reporting would expose them to hostile situation. Reporting to a specific authority about such cases means that they would have to leave work to testify in court, or they would feel uncomfortable while dealing with the family in future if they file a child abuse report. Some professionals said that they did not know how to make a report or would not make one because it would breach confidentiality. Thus, there are those working on the issue of child maltreatment/abuse who believe that child abuse is still underreported and that mandatory implementation of laws and public education campaigns still need to be supported.

National Initiative for Child Protection

National Initiative for Child Protection (NICP) is a campaign initiated by the Ministry of Social Justice and Empowerment, Government of India through the National Institute of Social Defence and CHILDLINE India Foundation.

NICP aims at building partnerships with the Allied Systems such as the police, the health care organisations, the judicial system, the juvenile justice system, the education system, the transport system, the labour department, the media, the department of telecommunications, the corporate sector, elected representatives and general population.

NICP hopes to achieve this by training people who work within the Allied Systems, by using advocacy and creating awareness and by involving children in making decisions that will directly affect their lives.

Vision of NICP

The shared vision of NICP is to build partnerships for child protection and promotion of child rights, by creating a child friendly environment. The best interest of the child will be ensured through training of functionaries of Allied Systems, advocacy and awareness creating, which would result in the development of various programmes and services for child protection. Children's participation is visualized as an integral component of NICP at all levels. The slogan of NICP: '....to every child a childhood' (*Source:* National Initiative for Child Protection: A Resource Book, 2000).

Legal Measures for Prevention of Child Abuse and Neglect

This apart, in India there exist some legal measures for the prevention of cruelty towards children such as The Indian Penal Code, 1860, The Immoral Traffic (Prevention) Act, 1956 and The Juvenile Justice (Care and Protection of Children) Act, 2000.

The Indian Penal Code, 1860

Following are the sections in the Indian Penal Code (1860), which can prosecute the perpetrators who abuse children sexually and for commercialized vices:

> ***Section 366-A: Procuration of Minor Girl***
>
> *Whoever, by any means whatsoever, induces any minor girl under the age of eighteen years to go from any place or to do any act with intent that such girl may be, or knowing that it is likely that she will be, forced or seduced to illicit intercourse with another person shall be*

punishable with imprisonment which may extend to ten years, and shall also be liable to fine.

Section 366-B: Importation of Girl from Foreign Country

Whoever imports into India from any country outside India or from the State of Jummu and Kashmir any girl under the age of twenty one years with intent that she may be or knowing it to be likely that she will be forced or seduced to illicit intercourse with another person, shall be punished with imprisonment which may extend to ten years, and shall also be liable to fine.

Section 372 Selling Minor for Purposes of Prostitution, etc.

Whoever sells, lets to hire, or otherwise disposes of any person under the age of eighteen years with intent that such person shall at any age be employed or used for the purpose of prostitution or illicit intercourse with any person or for any unlawful and immoral purpose, or knowing it to be likely that such person will at any age be employed or used for any such purpose, shall be punished with imprisonment of either description for a term which may extend to ten years, and shall also be liable to fine.

Section 373: Buying Minor for Purpose of Prostitution, etc.

Whoever buys, hires or otherwise obtains possession of any person under the age of eighteen years with intent that such person shall at any age be employed or used for the purpose of prostitution or illicit intercourse with any person or for any unlawful and immoral purpose, or knowing it to be likely that such person will at any age be employed or used for any such purpose, shall be punished with imprisonment of either description for a term which may extend to ten years, and shall also be liable to fine.

Section 376-2C: Punishment for Rape

Whoever, being on the management or on the staff of a jail, remand home or other place of custody established by or under any law for the time being in force or of a woman's or children's institution takes advantage of his official position and commits rape on any inmate of such jail, remand home, place or institution, shall be punished with rigorous imprisonment for a term which shall not be less than ten years but which may be for life and shall also be liable to fine.

The Immoral Traffic (Prevention) Act, 1956

This law provides justice to sexually abused girls of minor age. The sections meant to provide justice to victim girls are quoted below:

Section 5-D: Procuring, inducing or taking person for the sake of prostitution

Any person who (a) procures or attempts to procure a person (women or girl) whether with or without his consent for the purpose of prostitution; or (b) induces a person (women or girl) to go from any place, with the intent that he, may for the purpose of prostitution become the inmate of, or frequent, a brothel; or (c) takes or attempts to take a person (women or girl) or causes a person (women or girl) to be taken, from one place to another with a view to his carrying on, or being brought up to carry on, prostitution; or (d) causes or induces a person (women or girl) to carry on prostitution; shall be punishable on conviction with rigorous imprisonment for a term not less than three years and not more than seven years and also with fine which may extend to two thousand rupees, and if any offence under this sub-section is committed against the will of any person, the punishment of imprisonment for a term of seven years shall extend to imprisonment for a term of fourteen years.

Section 6: Detaining a Person (Women or Girl) in Premises where Prostitution is Carried on

(1) any person who detains any person (women or girl), whether with or without his consent—(a) in any brothel, or (b) in or upon any premises with intent that such person may have sexual intercourse with a person who is not the spouse of such person, shall be punishable on conviction, with imprisonment of either description for a term which shall not be less than seven years but which may be for life or for a term which extend to ten years and shall also be liable to fine.

Section 7: Prostitution in or in the vicinity of Public Places

(1) Any person (women or girl), who carries on prostitution and the person with whom such prostitution is carried on, in any premises—

Sub-section 1A of Section 7

Where an offence committed under sub-section (1) is in respect of a child or minor, the person committing the offence shall be punishable with imprisonment of either description for a term which shall not be less than seven years but which may be for life or for a term which may extend to ten years and shall also be liable to fine.

The Juvenile Justice (Care and Protection of Children) Act, 2000

The above act repealed the previous law meant for juveniles called 'The Juvenile Justice Act', 1986. In this law, the issue of childcare and protection has been given duc importance. The following sections are meant for prevention of cruelty to juveniles:

Section 23: Punishment for Cruelty to Juvenile or Child

Whoever, having the actual charge of, or control over, a juvenile or the child, assaults, abandons, exposes or wilfully neglects the juvenile or causes or procures him to be assaulted, abandoned, exposed or neglected in a manner likely to cause such juvenile or the child unnecessary mental or physical suffering shall be punishable with imprisonment for a term which may extend to six months, or fine, or with both.

Section 24: Employment of Juvenile or Child for Begging

(i) Whoever employs or uses any juvenile or the child for the purpose or causes any juvenile to beg shall be punishable with imprisonment for a term which may extend to three years and shall also be liable to fine.

(ii) Whoever, having the actual charge of, or control over, a juvenile or the child abets the commission of the offence punishable under sub-section (1), shall be punishable with imprisonment for a term which may extend to one year and shall also be liable to fine.

Section 25: Penalty for Giving Intoxicating Liquor or Narcotic Drug or Psychotropic Substance to Juvenile or Child

Whoever gives, or causes to be given, to any juvenile or the child in intoxicating liquor in a public place or any narcotic drug or psychotropic substance except upon the order of duly qualified medical practitioner or in case of sickness shall be punishable with imprisonment for a term which may extend to three years and shall also be liable to fine.

Section 26: Exploitation of Juvenile or Child Employee

Whoever, ostensibly procures a juvenile or the child for the purpose of any hazardous employment keeps him in bondage and withholds his earnings or uses such earning for his own purposes shall bè punishable with imprisonment for a term which may extend to three years and shall also be liable to fine.

The UN Conventions on Rights of the Child

The Convention on the Rights of the Child was adopted by the General Assembly of the United Nations on November 1989. The Government of India acceded to this convention on 11th December, 1992.

Article 1: Definition of a Child

A child is recognized as a person under 18, unless national laws recognize the age of majority earlier.

Article 2: Non-discrimination

All rights apply to all children without exception. It is the state's obligation to protect children from any form of discrimination and to take positive action to promote their rights.

Article 3: Best Interest of the Child

All actions concerning the child shall take full account of his/her best interests. The state shall provide the child with adequate care when parents, or others charged with that responsibility, failed to do so.

Article 4: Implementation of Rights

The State must do all it can to implement the rights contained in the Convention.

Article 5: Parental Guidance and the Child's Evolving Capacities

The State must respect the rights and responsibilities of parents and the extended family to provide guidance which is appropriate to her/her evolving capacities.

Article 6: Survival and Development

Every child has the inherent right to life and the state has an obligation to ensure the child's survival and development.

Article 7: Name and Nationality

The child has the right to a name at birth. The child has also the right to acquire a nationality and, as far as possible, to know her or his parents and be cared for by them.

Article 8: Preservation of Identity

The State has an obligation to protect, and if necessary, reestablish basic aspects of the child's identity. This includes name, nationality and family type.

Article 9: Separation from Parents

The child has a right to live with his/her parents unless this is deemed to be incompatible with the child's best interest. The child also has the right to maintain contact with both parents if separated from one or both.

Article 10: Family Reunification

Children and their parents have the right to leave any country or to enter their own for purposes of reunion or the maintenance of the child-parent relationship.

Article 11 Illicit Transfer and Non-return

The State has an obligation to prevent and remedy the kidnapping or retention of children aboard by a parent or third party.

Article 12: The Child's Opinion

The child has the right to express his/her opinion freely and to have that opinion taken into account in any matter or procedure affecting the child.

Article 13: Freedom of Expression

The child has the right to express his/her views, obtain information, make ideas or information known, regardless of frontiers.

Article 14: Freedom of Thought, Conscience and Religion

The State shall respect the child's right to freedom of thought, conscience and religion, subject to appropriate parental guidance.

Article 15: Freedom of Association

Children have a right to meet others, and to join or form associations.

Article 16: Protection of Privacy

Children have the right to protection from interference with privacy, family, home and correspondence, and from liable or slender.

Article 17: Access to Appropriate Information

The State shall ensure the accessibility of children to information and material from a diversity of sources, and it shall encourage the mass media to disseminate information which is of social and cultural benefit of the child, and take steps to protect him/her from harmful materials.

Article 18: Parental Responsibilities

Parents have primary responsibility for raising the child, and the state shall support them in this. The State shall provide appropriate assistance to parents in child rising.

Article 19: Protection from Abuse and Neglect

The state shall protect the child from all forms of maltreatment by parents or others responsible for the care of the child and establish appropriate programmes for the prevention of abuse and the treatment of victims.

Article 20: Protection of the Child without Family

The state is obliged to provide special protection for a child deprived of the family environment and to ensure that appropriate alternative family care or institutional placement available in such cases. Efforts to meet this obligation shall extend due regard to the child's cultural background.

Article 21: Adoption

In countries where adoption is recognized and/or allowed, it shall only be carried out in the best interests of the child, and only with the authorization of competent authorities ensuring safeguards for the child.

Article 22: Refugee Children

Special protection shall be granted to a refugee child or to child seeking refugee status. It is the state's obligation to cooperate with competent organizations, which provide such protection and assistance.

Article 23: Disabled Children

A disabled child has the right to special care, education and training to help him/her, enjoy a full decent life in dignity and achieve the greatest degree of self reliance and social integration possible.

Article 24: Health and Health Services

The child has a right to the highest standard of health and medical care attainable. State shall place special emphasis on the provision of primary and preventive health care, public health education and the reduction of infant mortality. They shall encourage international cooperation in this regard and strive to see that no child is deprived of access to effective health services.

Article 25: Periodic Review of Placement

A child who is placed by the state for reasons of care, protection or treatment is entitled to have that placement evaluated regularly.

Article 26: Social Security

The child has the right to benefit from social security including social insurance.

Article 27: Standard of Living

Every child has the right to a standard of living adequate for the child's physical, mental, spiritual, moral and social development. Parents have the primary responsibility to ensure that the child has adequate standard of living. The state's duty is to ensure that the responsibility can be fulfilled, and is. State responsibility can include material assistance to parents and their children.

Article 28: Education

The child has a right to education, and the state's duty is to ensure that primary education is free and compulsory, to encourage different forms of secondary education accessible to every child and to make higher education available to all on the basis of capacity. School discipline shall be consistent with the child's right and dignity. The state shall engage in international co-operation to implement the right.

Article 29: Aims of Education

Education shall aim at developing the child's personality, talents, mental and physical abilities to the fullest extent. Education shall prepare the child for an active adult life in a free society and foster respect for the child's parents, his/her own cultural identity, language and values, and for the cultural background and values of others.

Article 30: Children of Minorities and Indigenous Populations

Children of minority communities and indigenous populations have the right to enjoy their own culture and to practice their own religion and language.

Article 31: Leisure, Recreation and Cultural Activities

The child has the right to leisure, play and participation in cultural and artistic activities.

Article 32: Child Labour

The child has the right to be protected from work that threatens his/her health, education and development. The state shall set minimum ages for employment and regulate working conditions.

Article 33: Drug Abuse

Children have the right to protection from the use of narcotic and psychotropic drugs, and from being involved in their production or distribution.

Article 34: Sexual Exploitation

The state shall protect children from sexual harassment and abuse, including prostitution and pornography.

Article 35: Sale, Trafficking and Abduction

It is the state's obligation to make every effort to prevent the sale, trafficking and abduction of children.

Article 36: Other Forms of Exploitation

The child the right to protection from all forms of exploitation to any aspects of the child's welfare not covered in Articles 32, 33, 34 and 35.

Article 37: Torture and Deprivation of Liberty

No child shall be subjected to torture, cruel treatment or punishment, unlawful arrest or deprivation of liberty. Both capital punishment and life imprisonment without the possibility of release are prohibited for offences committed by a person below 18 years. Any child deprived of liberty shall be separated from adults unless it is considered in the child's best interests not to do so. A child who is detained shall have legal and other assistance as well as contact with the family.

Article 38: Armed Conflicts

The State parties shall take all feasible measures to ensure that child below 15 years of age have no direct part in hostilities. No child below 15 shall be recruited into the armed forces. State shall also ensure the protection and care of children who are affected by armed conflict as described in relevant international law.

Article 39: Rehabilitative Care

The State has an obligation to ensure that the child victims of armed conflicts, torture, neglect, maltreatment or exploitation receive appropriate treatment for their recovery and social re-integration.

Article 40: Administration of Juvenile Justice

A child in conflict with the law has the right to treatment which promotes the child's sense of dignity and worth, takes the child's age into account and aims at his or her re-integration into the society. The child is entitled to basic guarantees as well as legal and other assistance for his or her defense. Judicial proceedings and institutional placements shall be avoided whatever possible.

Article 41: Respect for Existing Standards

Whatever standards set in applicable for national international law relevant to the rights of the child are higher than those in the convention, the higher standard shall always apply.

Articles 42—54: Implementation and Entry into Force

The provisions of articles 42—54 notable foresee:

- The State's obligation to make the rights contained in the Convention widely known to both adults and children.
- The setting of a Committee on the rights of the child composed of ten experts, which will consider reports that States parties to the Convention are to submit two years after ratification and every five years thereafter. The Convention enters into force and the Committee would, therefore, be set up—once 20 countries ratified it.
- States parties are to make their reports widely available to the general public.
- The Committee may propose that special studies be undertaken on specific issues relating to the rights of the child, and make its evaluations known to each State Party concerned as well as to the UN General Assembly.

- In order to 'foster the effective implementation of the Convention and to encourage international cooperation', the specialized agency of the UN (such as ILO, WHO and UNESCO) and UNICEF would be able to attend the meetings of the Committee. Together with any other body recognized as 'competent', including NGOs in consultative status with the UN and UN organs such as UNHCR, they can submit pertinent information to the Committee and be asked to advise on the optimal implementation of the Convention.
- A reservation incompatible with the object and purpose of the present Convention shall not be permitted.

Role of International Agencies

United Nations Children's Fund (UNICEF)

Created by the United Nations General Assembly in 1946 to help children after World War II in Europe, UNICEF was first known as the United Nations International Children's Emergency Fund. In 1953, UNICEF became a permanent part of the United Nations system, its task being to help children living in poverty in the developing countries. Its name was shortened to the United Nations Children's Fund, but it retained the acronym "UNICEF," by which it is known to this day.

UNICEF is mandated by the United Nations General Assembly to advocate for the protection of children's rights, to help meet their basic needs and to expand their opportunities to reach their full potential.

UNICEF is guided by the Convention on the Rights of the Child and strives to establish children's rights as enduring ethical principles and international standards of behaviour towards children. UNICEF insists that the survival, protection and development of children are universal development imperatives that are integral to human progress.

UNICEF mobilizes political will and material resources to help countries, particularly developing countries, ensure a "first call for children" and to build their capacity to form appropriate policies and deliver services for children and their families.

UNICEF is committed to ensuring special protection for the most disadvantaged children—victims of war, disasters, extreme poverty, all forms of violence and exploitation and those with disabilities.

UNICEF responds in emergencies to protect the rights of children. In coordination with United Nations partners and humanitarian agencies, UNICEF makes its unique facilities for rapid response available to its partners to relieve the suffering of children and those who provide their care.

UNICEF is non-partisan and its cooperation is free of discrimination. In everything it does, the most disadvantaged children and the countries in greatest need have priority.

UNICEF aims, through its country programmes, to promote the equal rights of women and girls and to support their full participation in the political, social, and economic development of their communities.

UNICEF works with all its partners towards the attainment of the sustainable human development goals adopted by the world community and the realization of the vision of peace and social progress enshrined in the Charter of the United Nations.

Working with national governments, NGOs (non-governmental organizations), other United Nations agencies and private-sector partners, UNICEF protects children and their rights by providing services and supplies and by helping shape policy agendas and budgets in the best interests of children.

The International Society for Prevention of Child Abuse and Neglect (ISPCAN)

The International Society for Prevention of Child Abuse and Neglect, founded in 1977, is the only multidisciplinary international organization that brings together a worldwide cross-section of committed professionals to work towards the prevention and treatment of child abuse, neglect and exploitation globally. ISPCAN's mission is to prevent cruelty to children in every nation, in every form: physical abuse, sexual abuse, neglect, street children, child fatalities, child prostitution, children of war, emotional abuse and child labour. ISPCAN is committed to increasing public awareness of all forms of violence against children, developing activities to prevent such violence, and promoting the rights of children in all regions of the world.

Specific Objectives of ISPCAN

- Increasing awareness of problems, issues, and alternative solutions for child abuse at all levels.
- Facilitating the exchange of knowledge about these problems, issues, and solutions.
- Identifying, sharing, and improving practices and models for detection, treatment, and prevention.
- Designing and facilitating education and training of professionals and concerned volunteers in prevention.
- Promoting and facilitating research and the dissemination of academic and practical materials for exchange of information and action.
- Supporting international efforts to protect the Rights of the Child.

Latest Selective Study Findings

Haskett *et al*. (2003) made an attempt to utilize the cognitive behavioural model of abusive parenting to select and examine risk factors to illuminate the unique and combined influences of social cognitive and affective variables in predicting abuse group membership. Participants included physically abusive parents (n=56) and a closely-matched group of comparison parents (n=62). Social cognitive risk variables measured were (a) parent's expectations for children's abilities and maturity, (b) parental attributions of intentionality of child misbehaviour, and (c) parents' perceptions of their children's adjustment. Affective risk variables included (a) psychopathology and (b) parenting stress. A series of logistic regression models were constructed to test the individual, combined, and interactive effects of risk variables on abuse group membership. The full set of five risk variables was predictive of abuse status; however, not all variables were predictive when considered individually and interactions did not contribute significantly to prediction. A risk composite score computed for each parent based on the five-risk variables significantly predicted abuse status. Wide individual differences in risk across the five variables were apparent within the sample of abusive parents. Findings were generally consistent with a cognitive behavioural model of abuse, with cognitive variables being more salient in predicting abuse status than affective factors. Results point to the importance of considering diversity in characteristics of abusive parents.

Rosenthal *et al.* (2003) investigated age and gender differences in perceived emotional support in children and adolescents who experienced sexual abuse from the time of discovery to 1 year later. Also examined were the relations among sources of support and adjustment and whether support explained resilience, defined as better adjustment over a year's time. One hundred and forty-seven sexually abused youth were interviewed at the time of discovery (T1) and 1 year later (T2). Information gathered included severity of the sexual abuse, satisfaction with support from caregivers, same-sex and other-sex friends, feelings of shame about the abuse, and attribution style. Youth adjustment was measured using reports from the youth themselves, caregivers, and teachers. Children reported the most satisfaction with support from caregivers followed by friends whereas adolescents reported similar levels of support from friends and caregivers. Satisfaction with support was differentially related to adjustment. Youth who reported more satisfaction with caregiver support at T1, reported less depression, better self-esteem but more sexual anxiety 1 year later. More satisfaction with support from friend's predicted lower self-esteem but less sexual anxiety. More satisfaction with initial caregiver support at T1 predicted better parent- and teacher-rated adjustment 1 year later, after controlling for initial adjustment. In general, initial caregiver emotional support at the time of abuse discovery predicted resilience in child and adolescent victims of sexual abuse. Findings suggested that treatment should include a focus on helping caregivers provide appropriate emotional support.

Dong *et al.*, (2003) assessed the relationship of childhood sexual abuse (CSA) to nine other categories of Adverse Childhood Experiences (ACEs), including childhood abuse, neglect, and multiple types of household dysfunction. Retrospective cohort study data were collected from 17,337 adult health plan members who responded to a survey questionnaire. Regression models adjusted for age, race, and education were used to estimate the strength of the association of CSA to each of the other nine ACEs and a graded relationship between measures of the severity of CSA and the number of other ACEs (ACE score). CSA was reported by 25 per cent of women and 16 per cent of men. In comparison with persons who were not exposed to CSA, the likelihood of experiencing each category of ACE increased 2- to 3.4-fold for women and 1.6- to 2.5-fold for men ($p< 0.05$). The adjusted mean ACE score showed a significant positive graded relationship to the severity, duration, and frequency of CSA and an inverse relationship to age at first occurrence of CSA ($p < 0.01$). CSA is strongly associated with experiencing multiple other forms of ACEs. The strength of this association appears to increase as the measures of severity of the CSA increases. The understanding of the interrelatedness of CSA with multiple ACEs should be considered in the design of studies, treatment, and programs to prevent CSA as well as other forms of ACEs.

The objectives of Cheit (2003) study were threefold. First, to determine the extent to which those charged with child molestation receive newspaper coverage; second, to analyze the nature of that coverage; and third, to compare the universe of coverage to the nature of child molestation charges in the criminal justice system as a whole. Two databases were created. The first one identified all defendants charged with child molestation in Rhode Island in 1993. The database was updated after 5 years to include relevant information about case disposition. The second database was created by electronic searching the Providence Journal for every story that mentioned each defendant. Most defendants (56.1%) were not mentioned in the newspaper. Factors associated with a greater chance of coverage include: cases involving first-degree charges, cases with multiple counts, cases involving additional violence or multiple victims, and cases resulting in long prison sentences. The data indicate that the press exaggerates "stranger danger," while intra-familial cases are underreported. Newspaper accounts also minimize the extent to which guilty defendants avoid prison. Generalizing about the nature of child molestation cases in criminal court on the basis of newspaper coverage is inappropriate. The coverage is less extensive than often claimed, and it is skewed in ways that are typical of the mass media.

Sandnabba *et al.* (2003) explored the sexual behaviours of 2 to 7-year-old children through reports of day-care personnel. An overall aim of this exploratory study was to provide information about the frequencies of child sexual behaviours. Also, the aim was to explore any age and gender differences. A representative sample of 364 Finnish children not screened for developmental delay, sexual abuse history or psychiatric problems (181 girls and 183 boys) in 190 day-care centers were studied using the "Day-Care Sexuality Questionnaire" (DCSQ), with 244 sexual and other behaviour items. Age influenced more the extent of the 244 sexual behaviours of boys than of girls. In sexual behaviours increasing with age, girls showed behaviours with a more social character, whereas boys showed more explorative and information-seeking behaviours. Girls had a higher frequency of domestic and gender role exploring behaviours, whereas the boys tended to engage in explorative acting and information-seeking behaviors. The results suggest that child sexual behaviour reported by day-care personnel may provide useful information about the development of children's sexuality. Implications for sexual abuse investigations were discussed.

Adinkrah (2003) explored the nature and extent of paternal filicides in Fiji, a non-Western society, and the social and cultural forces underlying them in order to enhance our knowledge of the phenomenon. Information was obtained from a number of sources, including (a) a police homicide logbook, (b) newspaper reports of homicide, and (c) detailed interviews conducted with criminal justice and medical personnel. Information from these data sources were consolidated to construct case histories of paternal filicides. These cases were then analyzed for dominant themes. Case illustrations are presented in the text. Several of the study's findings are congruent with other studies of paternal filicides: poor, working class fathers were the offenders in all cases. As a corollary, their victims were from low socioeconomic backgrounds. Regarding location, paternal filicides occurred in the home of the offender and victim. The filicides were the culmination of stresses and strains associated with marital disharmony and excessive corporal child-control strategies. The general conclusion of this study is that further research in non-Western societies has the potential to increase our understanding of the social factors and processes involved in paternal child murders. We will then be better positioned to craft effective intervention strategies.

Goodman-Brown *et al.* (2003) investigated variables associated with delay of disclosure of child sexual abuse and tested a model of time to disclosure. Data were obtained for 218 alleged child sexual abuse victims whose cases had been referred to District Attorneys' Offices. Five variables were posited to influence the delay between an abusive event and children's disclosure of that event to a reporting adult: child's age, gender, type of abuse experienced (intrafamilial or extrafamilial), perceived responsibility for the abuse, and fear of negative consequences of disclosure. These variables were used to create a model of factors influencing children's disclosure of sexual abuse. Findings revealed that age, type of abuse, fear of negative consequences, and perceived responsibility all contributed to predicting time to disclosure. There was significant support for the model, suggesting that children who were older, came from incestuous families, felt greater responsibility for the abuse, and feared negative consequences of disclosure took longer to disclose. Children's cognitive appraisal of others' tolerance of disclosure of child sexual abuse, and their own perceptions of responsibility for the abuse, are crucial to the decision to disclose. When evaluating children for possible sexual abuse, developmental, cognitive, and socio-emotional factors need to be taken into consideration.

Walrath *et al.* (2003) examined multiple empirically based perspectives (i.e., child, caregiver, and clinician) of behaviour and functioning as they contribute to the clinical and psychosocial profile of children (aged 5 to 17.5 years) with reported histories of sexual abuse. A large, multi-site data set of children referred into Comprehensive Community Mental Health Services both with and without reported histories of sexual abuse, was examined. Seven hundred and fifty-nine children with a reported history of sexual abuse were compared to 2722 without such a history on caregiver and child reported behaviour, clinician rated functioning, diagnosis, demographic variables, and life challenges. The multiple perspectives contributed unique and specific information to regression models: caregiver-reported behaviour contributed information about externalizing behaviour while child-reported behaviour added information about internalizing behaviour and clinician ratings about self-harmful behaviour. Children with reported histories of sexual abuse were also more likely to be female, Caucasian, and have reported histories of life challenges (e.g., physical abuse, substance use, running away). Child sexual abuse was associated with higher rates of depression and anxiety diagnoses, and lower rates of substance abuse, conduct, and attention deficit disorder diagnoses. The findings indicate that the profile of children entering into Comprehensive Community Mental Health Services with reported histories of sexual abuse, as compared to those without such histories, is complex and best understood via multiple perspectives. Caregiver, child and clinician rated information, when taken together, provide a comprehensive clinical and psychosocial profile around which to plan and implement individualized service plans.

The aim of Collin-Vezina and Cyr study (2003) was to review what is currently understood about intergenerational transmission of child sexual abuse (CSA). CSA transmission is discussed first from the point of view of men CSA survivors who become sexually abusive, and then from the perspective of mothers who survived CSA whose children have been sexually abused. Mechanisms that may help us understand how CSA is transmitted from one generation to another are described. More specifically, focus is given to those mechanisms that might differentiate CSA survivors who break the cycle of abuse from those who perpetuate it. In light of the research reviewed, it seems that the transmission of CSA is far from inevitable, since one-third of sexually abusive men and half of sexually abused children's mothers mentioned having been sexually abused in their childhood. Because of the retrospective method used in many studies, causal links could not be established. However, some mechanisms have been proposed in order to better understand the phenomenon of CSA. Severities of abuse, attachment relationships with parental figures, as well as dissociative symptoms that follow the abuse were identified. Dissociative symptomatology appeared to be a determining factor in understanding the cycle of CSA. More studies on CSA transmission are needed to understand the mechanisms that are involved in that cycle, as well as to develop effective strategies to treat and prevent CSA.

Yanowitz *et al*. (2003) examined the teachers' expectations about the effects of physical and emotional abuse on children's classroom behaviours. Not only do teachers have to decide if a particular child is the victim of abuse, they may also have to contend with changes in that child's classroom behaviour. Teachers generated what they thought were typical outcomes of physical and emotional abuse on children's classroom behaviour. Responses generally fell into the following categories: lowered self-esteem, heightened aggression, academic difficulties, and poor social interaction skills. Teachers who mentioned lowered self-esteem were more likely to generate it as the result of emotional abuse rather than physical abuse. Teachers' expectations generally mirrored research findings as to the actual effects of child abuse. Suggestions are made to incorporate the results in training programs designed to increase teachers' self-confidence in reporting potential cases of child abuse.

Wark *et al*. (2003) made an attempt to demonstrate the relationship between retrospective reports of child neglect, family of origin functioning, and current psychological distress. It was hypothesized that experience of childhood emotional neglect would be associated with lower levels of cohesion and adaptability in participants' family of origin and greater levels of current psychological distress. Gender effects were explored. Retrospective reports of emotional neglect in childhood were quantified by use of a parental bonding measure, specifically by assessing level of perceived parental care. Participants were assigned to one of three groups based on level of care scores: neglect by a primary male caregiver, neglect by a primary female caregiver, and no neglect. These groups were compared on three variables: current psychological functioning, retrospective report of family of origin adaptability, and retrospective report of family of origin cohesiveness. Amount of time left in the care of others was used as a covariate based on attachment theory literature. Data were analyzed for 69 female and 22 male undergraduate students. Participants who reported a childhood experience of emotional neglect by a primary female caregiver described greater current psychological distress than those reporting no neglect or neglect by a primary male caregiver. Participants who experienced emotional neglect by a primary female caregiver, as compared to those reporting emotional neglect by a primary male caregiver and those reporting no neglect, described lower cohesion and adaptability in their family of origin. There were no differences between male and female participants in terms of impact of emotional neglect. This study suggests potential caregiver gender effects, regardless of respondent gender. Perceived neglect by female, but not male caregivers, led to psychological distress in adulthood and was associated with lower cohesion and adaptability in one's family of origin. Future research should attempt to account for the participants' expectations regarding male and female caregiver roles.

Lamb *et al.* (2003) attempted to determine whether child witnesses of sexual abuse were more or less informative about the alleged incidents than alleged victims when interviewed similarly. Twenty-six alleged victims of child sexual abuse (aged 5 to 14 years; M=9.8 years) and 26 children who had witnessed but not experienced similar events were interviewed by experienced youth investigators about the alleged abuse. Children in the two groups were matched with respect to their age, relationships with the alleged perpetrator, and seriousness of the alleged offenses. All children were interviewed using the NICHD investigative interview protocol. Witnesses and victims provided similar amounts of information about the incidents of abuse. Interviewers used more open-ended invitations and elicited more information using open-ended prompts from witnesses than from victims, whereas they used more risky (including suggestive) prompts when interviewing victims. These results confirm that young children can be informative witnesses about events that they have either experienced or witnessed.

Swanston *et al.* (2003) made an effort to understand the psychological adjustment of 103 sexually abused children in Sydney after nine years as compared to non-abused young people of similar age and gender to assess group differences and examine potential risk factors. At intake, data on the nature of the index sexual abuse, demographics and the family environment were collected by clinicians. A comparison group, of similar age and gender, was selected from schools in the catchment area of the CPUs. Six years after presentation for the abuse, records of the statutory child protection authority were checked to determine any further notifications for abuse and/or neglect. Nine years after intake, 49 of the abused young people and 68 of the non-abused young people and/or their parents were interviewed and assessed. The sexually abused young people performed more poorly than non-abused young people on psychometric tests of depression ($p=.001$), self-esteem ($p<.001$), anxiety ($p<.001$), behaviour (Child Behavior Checklist: $p=.01$; Youth Self Report: $p=.01$; Young Adult Self Report: $p<.001$), and despair ($p=.001$). They were also more likely to have a history of bingeing ($p=.002$), self-inducing vomiting ($p=.02$), smoking cigarettes ($p=.01$), and using amphetamines ($p=.002$), ecstasy ($p=.002$) and cocaine ($p=.004$). Potential risk factors were in two groups, family and child. Family factors: family functioning, parental drug/alcohol problems, mother's sexual abuse history, mother's depression and socio-economic status. Child factors: despair and hopefulness, number of negative life events, ratings of their father's care, previous notifications for child sexual abuse and placements in out-of-home care by the statutory child protection authority. In the presence of other risk factors, child sexual abuse was a significant predictor of self-esteem, behaviour and bingeing. Rather than focusing only on the individual's child sexual abuse, treatment may also need to address the family's functioning and the individual's feelings of despair.

Komen (2003) made an attempt to document the changes in the way juvenile judges and judicial child protection workers deal with physical child abuse in the period 1960-1995 in the Netherlands. The study is based on an analysis of files on adolescent and younger children placed by juvenile judges in the Dutch judicial child protection system during the 1960s, 1970s, 1980s, and 1990s. The prevalence of very severe physical violence against children was lower in the recent files than in the older files. Spanking and other minor violence acts were noted more often than in the older files. In the 1960s files, the parents talked still rather openly about the physical punishments they used in child rearing. In spite of the growing attention for and increasing concern about child abuse among professionals, judicial child protection workers intervened less harshly in recent cases of physical child abuse than in the 1960s. The decrease in severe physical child abuse may indicate that physical child abuse is actually becoming a less serious problem in the Dutch judicial child protection system. But that may not be the case because of the increased reluctance of parents to report and changes in intervention practices. Other than expected, the growing sensibility for child abuse did not mean more effective control by judicial child protection workers. Possible reasons for these changes are discussed, including the strengthening of the position of perpetrators in law proceedings and the emancipation of children and women in society.

Tirosh *et al.* (2003) assessed physicians' attitudes towards corporal punishment in childhood and their subsequent actions regarding the reporting of child abuse. 107 physicians (95 pediatricians and 12 family practitioners) who work in hospitals and community clinics in northern Israel were interviewed. Of the participants, 16 per cent were new immigrants. A structured interview was conducted by one of two pediatric residents. Attitudes towards corporal punishment were not influenced by the physicians' sex or specialty. Corporal punishment was approved by 58 per cent of the physicians. A significant difference in attitudes towards corporal punishment between immigrants and Israeli born physicians was found ($p=.004$). Family practitioners and especially senior ones were found significantly less tolerant towards corporal punishment than pediatricians ($p=.04$). While reporting behaviour was not found to be associated with parental status and the past experience of the physicians with child abuse, a significant effect of attitudes towards corporal punishment on reporting behaviour was found ($p=.01$). Corporal punishment is still perceived as an acceptable disciplinary act by a significant proportion of physicians responsible for the health care of children in our area. Attitudes towards corporal punishment are different between immigrants and native born Israeli trained doctors and, unexpectedly, pediatricians were more tolerant of corporal punishment than family practitioners.

Offen *et al*. (2003) tried to determine whether reported childhood sexual abuse is related to the severity of symptoms in patients who experience auditory hallucinations. A sample of 26 adult male and females with psychotic disorders involving auditory hallucinations were interviewed and were asked to complete three self-report measures: the Dissociative Experiences Scale (DES-II and DES-taxon versions); the Beck Depression Inventory (BDI); and the Beliefs About Voices Questionnaire (BAVQ). They were also asked about any history of sexual abuse in childhood. A history of childhood sexual abuse was reported by 10 of the 26 patients (38.5%), and was associated with higher levels of depression and dissociation, as well as being linked to a tendency to regard the voices as more malevolent. The same three features were all associated with the age at first reported abuse, with a younger age of first experience being related to higher levels of psychopathology in all instances. These results require replication and refinement in future research, but indicate a need for greater attention to be paid to the possible role of childhood sexual abuse when understanding and treating auditory hallucinations.

Sobti *et al*. (2000) made an attempt to document the knowledge, attitude and practice of doctors regarding torture. Although, majority of the doctors in India are aware of various national and international human rights institutions, but they seem not to be aware of the human rights of the detainees. It is interesting to note that the doctors are aware of the long term physical and psychological effects of torture and also agreed that physical examination is not sufficient to detect torture sequelae. A large number of doctors have seen cases of torture, and were willing to treat them and felt reasonably competent. A significant number of doctors justified use of coercive technique and manhandling in dealing with detainees by law enforcement agencies. A small number of doctors expressed their unwillingness to get involved in the treatment of the victims of torture due to medico legal consequence. The dissemination of information on human rights and medical ethics and incorporating them into the medical curriculum at undergraduate and postgraduate training was emphasized by majority of the respondents. Respondents expressed almost unanimous view on the importance of the role of medical ethics and the profession's responsibility to its members. An important finding of the study is the need for IMA to help establishing counselling and rehabilitation centres for treatment of torture victims and educate its members. A large number of doctors mentioned the need of initiating community action in case of rape, child abuse, dowry victims and sexual harassment. Further, a majority of respondents expressed the view that the medical association should take the responsibilities of protecting the doctors who fearlessly testify cases of torture besides disciplining doctors who facilitate torture. Respondents felt that the reasons for doctors' participation in torture need further study. It is encouraging that most of the responding physicians are willing to take up training and become counsellor for victims of torture to be able to provide treatment, counselling and rehabilitation.

Hunter *et al.* (2000) tried to determine the type and severity of discipline practices in rural India and to identify risk and protective factors related to these practices. Five hundred mothers, ages 18-50, participated in face-to-face interviews as part of a cross-sectional, population-based survey. One of the mother's children was randomly selected as the referent child. The interview focused primarily on discipline practices and spousal violence. Socio demographic characteristics, neighbour support, residential stability, and husband's drinking behaviour were also assessed. Nearly half of the mothers reported using severe verbal discipline and 42 per cent reported using severe physical discipline. While common, severe discipline practices occurred less frequently than moderate practices and had different risk factors, notably low maternal education and spousal violence. Results suggest that increased formal education for rural women in India may have the added benefit of reducing family violence, including spouse and child abuse.

According to Mehta (1982) child abuse and neglect, though existing in India, has not come to light because of underlying social constraints like poverty, malnutrition and infection. With an intention to study the problem of physical abuse in neglected children, patients admitted to the pediatric wards of our institution, predominantly with some form of physical abuse were specifically looked for from

January 1976 onwards. Over a period of 4 ½ years, 18 such cases were encountered. Most of the babies were less than four weeks of age, were predominantly females, were quite often premature or malnourished, and rarely had a physical deformity. These babies were deserted and later were found by police or social workers in gutters, dustbins, garbage tins, railway platforms, etc. The spectrum of abuse and injuries included newborn babies with intact placenta, at times lacerated, strangling marks on the throat, multiple bruises, bleeding from the umbilicus, avulsion of the scalp with severe bleeding, shock as a result of environmental stress (i.e., hypothermia), evidence of infection, rat bite marks, and fractures. The morbidity was very high, ultimately resulting in 88.9 per cent mortality over varying periods of time, maximum survival being 22 days. The motive behind this abuse always was an unwanted baby.

Sriram *et al.* (1981) reviewed eight cases of the Battered Baby Syndrome, diagnosed in the Orthopaedic Department of a large children's hospital in India during a three year period. Majority of the cases had major fractures due to repetitive child abuse. Most of the children were undernourished and psychoanalysis of the parents revealed that with regard to child abuse, conditions in India do not differ materially from the Western World. This review does not include minor injuries to the children or solitary fractures in children as a result of child abuse. This may indicate that many cases have been missed. The importance of early detection of this condition and multidisciplinary approach in the management has been stressed. This condition has yet to gain wide recognition in Indian.

Shumba (2002) made an attempt to determine the nature, extent and effects of emotional abuse; and who the perpetrators are in Zimbabwean primary schools. In this study, emotional abuse shall refer to constant belittling of a pupil, the absence of a positive emotional atmosphere, verbal abuse, shouting, scolding, use of vulgar language, humiliation and negative labelling of pupils, and terrorizing of pupils by teachers in schools. The study found that the majority of teacher trainees and teachers believe that shouting, scolding, use of vulgar language, humiliation and negatively labeling of pupils as stupid, ugly, foolish is mainly done by female teachers in schools. However, 52.7 per cent of the teacher trainees indicated that it is the male teachers who "use vulgar language on pupils". This study found some of the forms of emotional abuse that are perpetrated on pupils by teachers in schools. The findings seem to be consistent with the literature available on the gender of perpetrators associated with this form of child abuse. It is clear that emotional abuse exists in Zimbabwean primary schools and female teachers appear to be the main perpetrators of this form of child abuse. This form of child abuse may involve one perpetrator and a series of victims.

Kendall-Tackett (2002) describes four possible pathways by which childhood abuse relates to health problems in adults. Literature on the long-term effects of childhood abuse is organized in a health psychology framework describing behavioural, social, cognitive, and emotional pathways. Key studies from the health psychology and behavioural medicine literature are included to demonstrate how these pathways relate to health. Childhood abuse puts people at risk of depression and post-traumatic stress disorder, participating in harmful activities, having difficulties in relationships, and having negative beliefs and attitudes towards others. Each of these increases the likelihood of health problems, and they are highly related to each other. Childhood abuse is related to health via a complex matrix of behavioural, emotional, social, and cognitive factors. Health outcomes for adult survivors are unlikely to improve until each of these factors is addressed.

Bentovim (2002) conducted a study to determine whether it is possible to prevent those sexually abused boys who are at risk of abusing other children from doing so, and to assess whether factors associated with an experience of sexual abuse in young people who are offending can be dealt with as a key aspect of therapeutic work alongside treatment of offending behaviour. The author examined cross-sectional and longitudinal research which demonstrates the impact on sexually abused children of living in a climate of violence, suffering physical abuse, exposure to abuse of maternal figures, and suffering disruption and poor quality of care and supervision. These factors are confirmed in prospective research. The application of these findings to therapeutic programmes for boys who are sexually abused is described, including the assessment of care needs as well as the specific therapeutic work with the young person, and work to modify the family context. The specific treatment of victimization experiences in young people who have committed sexual offences is also examined, with recommendations for modification of treatment approaches suggested. It is vital in therapeutic work with boy victims of sexual abuse that the issue of their abusive potential be considered; even if a relatively small proportion of such boys will go on to abuse others. Given that boys who do sexually abuse are likely to have grown up in a climate of violence and poor care, methods of dealing with such victimization experiences need to be developed alongside offending focused-treatments.

Heger *et al.* (2002) compared the rates of positive medical findings in a 5-year prospective study of 2384 children, referred for evaluation of possible sexual abuse, with two decades of research. The prospective study summarizes demographic information, clinical history, relationship of perpetrators, nature of abuse, and clinical findings. The study reports on the results by patterns of referral and the medical examination. There were 2384 children evaluated in a tertiary referral center between 1985 and 1990 for possible sexual abuse. Children were referred after they disclosed sexual abuse, because of behavioural changes or exposure to an abusive environment, and because of possible medical conditions. A total of 96.3 per cent of all children referred for evaluation had a normal medical examination; 95.6 per cent of children reporting abuse were normal, 99.8 per cent who were referred for behavioural changes or exposure to abuse were also normal. Of the 182 children referred for evaluation of medical conditions, 92 per cent were found to be normal at the time of examination by the Child Advocacy Centre. The remaining 15/182 (8%) that were found to be abnormal were diagnosed with sexually transmitted diseases, acute or healed genital injuries, and were 17 per cent (15/88) of the total cases found to have medical findings diagnostic of abuse. Interviews of the children indicated that 68 per cent of the girls and 70 per cent of the boys reported severe abuse, defined as penetration of vagina or anus. Penetration was associated with a higher percentage of abnormal findings in girls

(6%) compared to 1 per cent of the boys. The relationship of the abuser impacted on the severity of the abuse. Research indicates that medical, social, and legal professionals have relied too heavily on the medical examination in diagnosing child sexual abuse. History from the child remains the single most important diagnostic feature in coming to the conclusion that a child has been sexually abused. Only 4 per cent of all children referred for medical evaluation of sexual abuse have abnormal examinations at the time of evaluation. Even with a history of severe abuse such as vaginal or anal penetration, the rate of abnormal medical findings is only 5.5 per cent. Biological parents are less likely to engage in severe abuse than parental substitutes, extended family members, or strangers.

Kelly *et al.* (2002) examined the long-term impact of mother-son incest and positive initial perceptions of sexual abuse experiences on adult male psychosocial functioning. Sixty-seven clinic-referred men with a history of sexual abuse participated. The participants completed self-report measures regarding their current psychosocial functioning and described the nature of their sexual and physical abuse experiences during childhood. Seventeen men reported mother-son incest, and these men endorsed more trauma symptoms than did other sexually abused men, even after controlling for a history of multiple perpetrators and physical abuse. Mother-son incest was likely to be subtle, involving behaviours that may be difficult to distinguish from normal caregiving (e.g., genital touching), despite the potentially serious long-term consequences. Twenty-seven men recalled positive or mixed initial perceptions of the abuse, including about half of the men who had been abused by their mothers. These men reported more adjustment problems than did men who recalled purely negative initial perceptions. Mother-son incest and positive initial perceptions of sexual abuse experiences both appear to be risk factors for more severe psychosocial adjustment problems among clinic-referred men.

Lucas *et al.* (2002) made an attempt to describe the factors related to fatal abuse in three age groups in the United States Air Force (USAF). Records from 32 substantiated cases of fatal child abuse in the USAF were independently reviewed for 60 predefined factors. Perpetrators were predominantly male and the biological fathers of the victims. Infant and young child perpetrators reported childhood abuse histories, while child perpetrators reported the highest frequency of mental health contact. Victims' families reported significant life stressors. Families of young child victims were more likely divorced, separated, or single. Incidents with infants and young children tended to occur without witnesses; incidents with child victims tended to have the victim's sibling(s) and/or mother present. Fatal incidents were more frequent on the weekend, in the home, and initiated by some family disturbance. Differences among groups in factors related to infant and child homicide across age groups may assist in the development of more tailored abuse prevention efforts and may also guide future investigations.

Runyon *et al.* (2002) attempted to examine specific differences in the Post-Traumatic Stress Disorder (PTSD) symptomatology among abused children with and without concurrent depression. PTSD and depressive symptoms were identified that discriminate between 98 children divided into three groups: (1) abused children with PTSD, (2) non-abused children who meet criteria for Major Depressive Disorder (MDD), and (3) abused children with both PTSD and MDD. Analyses revealed that nine items reflecting depressive symptomatology, primarily vegetative symptoms, differentiated the diagnostic groups (PTSD-only, MDD-only, and the combined group). A discriminant analysis revealed that the sum of responses to the nine significant items adequately predicted diagnostic classification for those with PTSD and depression, but did not correctly diagnose any in the combined group. Analyses also revealed that three post-trauma symptoms, including psychological amnesia, flashbacks/reenactments, and sleep difficulties, discriminated between the groups. The PTSD-only group reported more episodes of psychological amnesia while the PTSD and MDD group experienced more flashbacks. For the sample of abused children examined, these results illuminate differences with respect to PTSD symptom presentation for those children with PTSD who have a concurrent depressive disorder and their non-depressed counterparts. Children with PTSD who have a concurrent depression report greater levels of intrusive PTSD-related symptoms.

Tang (2002) aimed to explore the prevalence rate and profiles of abusers and victims of child sexual abuse in a Chinese society. A convenience sample of 2,147 Hong Kong Chinese college students completed questionnaires which included items on definitions of child sexual abuse, recall of sexual abuse experience before age 17, information about the sexual abuse incidents, and personal demographics. The overall prevalence rate for various forms of child sexual abuse was 6 per cent, with the rates being higher for females than for males. The average age of the victims at the time of the sexual abuse was 11 years old, with a majority of them experiencing sexual abuse during their teenage years. The average age of the abusers as estimated by the victims was 24 years old, and only 28 per cent of the abusers were strangers to the victims. Males were about three times more likely than females to be sexually abused by their friends, whereas females were about twice more likely than males to be sexually abused by strangers. Only 39 per cent of the victims reported their sexual victimization to others, and 56 per cent of the reported incidents were not followed up. As compared to Western studies, the present study showed lower rates for more intimate or severe forms of child sexual abuse. The Chinese victims were more reluctant to disclose their sexual victimization than their Western counterparts. Limitations and practical implications of the study are also discussed.

Walsh *et al.* (2002) examined the relationship between a history of parental psychiatric disorder and a history of child abuse in a general population sample of Ontario residents. A representative community sample of 8548 respondents who participated in the Ontario Mental Health Supplement (OHSUP) were interviewed about parental psychiatric history and completed a self-report measure of childhood physical and sexual abuse. Respondents reporting a parental history of depression, mania, or schizophrenia had a two to threefold increase in the rates of physical, sexual, or any abuse. Parental history of antisocial disorder increased the risk of exposure to physical abuse (adjusted odd ratios [OR 6.1] and any abuse [OR 7.5]). There was no statistically significant difference between parental psychiatric disorder and childhood physical or sexual abuse by gender of the respondent. There was a trend for increasing risk associated with father only, mother only, and both parents having any psychiatric disorder. The elevated risk for physical and sexual abuse among respondents reporting a parental history of psychiatric illness highlights the need to examine the mechanism for this association. Such information is important in developing approaches to assist families where the risk of child maltreatment is increased.

REFERENCES

Adinkrah, M. (2000). Maternal Infanticides in Fiji. *Child Abuse and Neglect,* 24: 1543-1555.

Adinkrah, M. (2003). Men Who Kill Their Own Children: Paternal Filicide Incidents In Contemporary Fiji. *Child Abuse & Neglect,* 27(5):557-68.

Alpert, E.J. et al., (1998). Family Violence Curricula in US Medical Schools. *American Journal of Preventive Medicine,* 14: 273-278.

Alexander, R.C., Levitt, C.J., and Smith, W.L. (2001). Abusive Head Trauma. In: Reece R.M., Ludwig S, Eds. *Child Abuse: Medical Diagnosis and Management,* 2nd ed. Philadelphia, PA, Lippincott Williams and Wilkins, 47-80.

American Academy of Pediatrics. Guidelines for the Evaluation of Sexual Abuse of Children: Subject Review, *Pediatrics* (1999), 103: 186-191.

Benbenishty, R., Zeira, A., and Astor, R.A. (2002). Children's Reports Of Emotional, Physical And Sexual Maltreatment By Educational Staff In Israel. *Child Abuse & Neglect,* 26(8): 763-82.

Bentovim, A. (2002). Preventing Sexually Abused Young People From Becoming Abusers, And Treating The Victimization Experiences Of Young People Who Offend Sexually. *Child Abuse & Neglect,* 26(6-7):661-78.

Briere, J.N. and Elliott, D.M. (1994). Immediate and Long-term Impacts of Child Sexual Abuse. The Future of Children, 4, 54-69.

Browne. K. *et al.*, (2002). *Child Abuse and Neglect* in Romanian Families: A National Prevalence Study 2000. Copenhagen, WHO Regional Office for Europe.

Cheit, R.E. (2003). What Hysteria? A Systematic Study Of Newspaper Coverage Of Accused Child Molesters. *Child Abuse & Neglect,* 27(6):607-23.

Choquet, M. *et al.*, (1997). Self-reported Health and Behavioural Problems Among Adolescent Victims of Rape in France: Results of a Cross-sectional Survey. *Child Abuse & Neglect,* 21: 823-832.

Collin-Vezina, D., and Cyr, M. (2003). Current Understanding About Intergenerational Transmission Of Child Sexual Abuse. *Child Abuse & Neglect,*27(5):489-507.

Deb, Sibnath (1994). Victimized Children of Socio-economically Disadvantaged Families: A Calcutta Based Study. *8th International Symposium on Victimology,* organized by the Australian Institute of Criminology, Adelaide, Australia between 21-26 Aug. 1994.

Deb, Sibnath (1997). Harassment of Urban Girl Children Engaged in Domestic Work. Presented in an *International - Interdisciplinary Conference on the Urban Childhood,* Organized by the Institute of Child Research, Trondheim, Norway between 9 -12 June, 1997.

Deb, Sibnath and Bandyopadhyay, Anuradha (2003). Is Corporal Necessary in School? *Social Defence* (accepted).

Deb, Sibnath and Mitra, Kathakali (2002). Nature And Types Of Abuse And Neglect Among Migrant Child Labour: A Qualitative Study. *The 14th International On Child Abuse And Neglect* held in Denver in July 2002.

Deb, Sibnath and Senapati, Shishir (1993). Safety Needs Of Abused Proletarian Bengalee Children (Major Modes Of Causal Factors). *Indian Journal Of Psychological Issues,* 1 (1): 1-9.

Deb, Sibnath, Datta K. and Ghosh M. (1997). Modification Of A Deviant Street Children's Behaviour: An In-Depth Case Study. *Indian Journal Of Criminology,* 25 (1): 15-22.

Deb, Sibnath (1996). Institutionalization Of Abused Street Children: An In-Depth Study. Paper Presented In *The 11th International Congress On Child Abuse & Neglect,* Organised By The University Of Dublin, Ireland Between August 18-21.

Dodge, K.A., Bates, J. E., and Pettit, G.S. (1990). Mechanisms In The Cycle Of Violence. Science, 250: 1678-1683.

Dong, M., Anda, R.F., Dube, S.R., Giles, W.H., and Felitti, V.J. (2003). The Relationship Of Exposure To Childhood Sexual Abuse To Other Forms Of Abuse, Neglect, And Household Dysfunction During *Childhood. Child Abuse & Neglect,* 27(6):625-39.

EASCAP - HRD, United Nations, NY (2002). Training Manual on Psychosocial and Medical Services for Sexually Abused and Sexually Exploited Children and Youth.

Egeland, B. (1993). A History of Abuse is a Major Risk Factor for Abusing the Next Generation. In: Gelles, R.J. Loseke, D.R., eds. *Current Controversies on Family Violence.* Thousand Oaks, CA, Sage, 197-208.

Ertem, I.O., Leventhal, J.m. and Dobbs, S. (2000). Intergenerational Continuty of Child Physical abuse: How Good is the Evidence? *Lancet,* 356: 814-819.

Farinatti FAS, Fonseca NM, Dondonis M and Brugger E (1990). Child Abuse and Neglect in a Developing Country. *Child Abuse & Neglect,* 14: 133- 135.

Fergusson, D.M., Horwood, M.T., and Lynskey, L.J. (1996). Childhood Sexual Abuse and Psychiatric Disorder in Young Adulthood. II: Psychiatric Outcomes of Childhood Sexual Abuse. *Journal of the American Academy of Child and Adolescent Psychiatry,* 35: 1365-1374.

Fields, P.J. (1981). Parent-Child Relationships, Childhood Sexual Abuse, and Adult Interpersonal Behaviour In Female Prostitutes. *Dissertation Abstracts International,* 42, 5: 20536-20546.

Finkelhor, D. (1984). *Child Sexual Abuse: New Theory And Research.* New York: The Free Press.

Finkelhor, D., and Baron, L. (1986). High Risk Children. In D.Finkelhor And Associates (Eds.), *A Sourcebook On Child Sexual Abuse* (Pp. 60-88). Beverly Hills, CA: Sage Publications.

Finkelhor, D., and Browne, A., (1986). Initial And Long-Term Effects: A Conceptual Framework. In D. Finkelhor And Associates (Eds.). A *Sourcebook On Child Sexual Abuse* (Pp.180-198). Beverly Hills, CA: Sage Publications.

Finkelhor, D. (1994). The International Epidemiology of Child Sexual Abuse. *Child Abuse & Neglect,* 18: 409-417.

Friedman, S. Howard (1998). *Encyclopedia Of Mental Health.* Vol.1, Academic Press, London.

Friederich, W.N. (1988). Behaviour Problems In Sexually Abused Children. In G.E. Wyatt and G.J.Powell (Eds.), The Lasting Effects Of Child Sexual Abuse (Pp.171-191). Newbury Park, CA: Sage.

Fromuth, M.E. (1983). *The Long Term Psychological Impact Of Childhood Sexual Abuse.* Unpublished Doctoral Dissertation, Auburn University, Auburn, AL.

Goodman-Brown, T.B., Edelstein, R.S., Goodman, G.S., Jones, D.P., and Gordon, D.S. (2003). Why Children Tell: A Model Of Children's Disclosure Of Sexual Abuse. *Child Abuse & Neglect,* 27(5):525-40.

Groth, A.N. and Burgess, A.W. (1979). Sexual Trauma In The Life Histories Of Rapists And Child Molesters. *Victimology- An International Journal,* 4: 10-16.

Hahm, M. and Guterman, N. (2001). The Emerging Problem of Physical Child Abuse in South Korea. Child Maltreatment, 6, 169-179.

Haskett, M.E., Smith Scott, S., Grant, R., Ward, C.S., and Robinson C. (2003). Child-Related Cognitions And Affective Functioning Of Physically Abusive And Comparison Parents. *Child Abuse & Neglect,* 27(6):663-86.

Heger, A., Ticson, L., Velasquez, O., and Bernier, R. (2002). Children Referred For Possible Sexual Abuse: Medical Findings In 2384 Children. *Child Abuse & Neglect,* 26(6-7):645-59.

Hunter, W.M., Jain, D., Sadowski, L.S., and Sanhueza, A.I. (2000). Risk Factors For Severe Child Discipline Practices In Rural India. *J Pediatr Psychol,* 25(6):435-47.

Kasim, M.S., Shafie, H.M. and Cheah, I. (1994). Social Factors in Relation to Physical Abuse in Kuala Lumpur, Malaysia. *Child Abuse & Neglect,* 18: 401-409.

Kelly, R.J., Wood, J.J., Gonzalez, L.S., MacDonald, V., and Waterman, J. (2002). Effects Of Mother-Son Incest And Positive Perceptions Of Sexual Abuse Experiences On The Psychosocial Adjustment Of Clinic-Referred Men. *Child Abuse & Neglect,* 26(4):425-41.

Kempe, C. H., Silverman, F.N., Steele, B.F., Droegemueller, W., and Silver, H.K. (1962). The Battered Child Syndrome. *Journal Of The American Medical Association,* 181: 107-112.

Kendall-Tackett, K. (2002). The Health Effects Of Childhood Abuse: Four Pathways By Which Abuse Can Influence Health. *Child Abuse & Neglect,* 26(6-7):715-29.

Ketsela, T., and Kedebe, D. (1997). Physical Punishment of Elementary School Children in Urban and rural Communities in Ethiopia, *Ethiopian Medical Journal,* 35: 23-33.

Kim, D.H. *et al.*, (2000). Children's Experience of Violence in China and Korea: A transcultural Study. *Child Abuse & Neglect,* 24: 1163-1173.

Kirschner, R.H., Wilson, H. (2001). Pathology of Fatal Child Abuse. In Reece R.M., Ludwig S. eds. *Child Abuse: Medical Diagnosis and Management,* 2nd ed. Philadelphia, PA, Lippincott Williams and Wilkins, 467-516.

Komen, M. (2003). Physical Child Abuse And Social Change. Judicial Intervention In Families In The Netherlands, 1960-1995. *Child Abuse & Neglect,*27(8):951-65.

Lamb, M.E., Sternberg, K.J., Orbach, Y., Hershkowitz, I., and Horowitz, D. (2003). Differences Between Accounts Provided By Witnesses And Alleged Victims Of Child Sexual Abuse. *Child Abuse & Neglect*, 27(9):1019-31.

Larrain, S., Vega, J. and Delgado, I. (1997). *Family Relations and Child Abuse,* Santiago, UNICEF.

Lindell, C. and Svedin, C.G. (2001). Physical Abuse in Sweden: A Study of Police Reports Between 1986 and 1996. *Social Psychiatry and Psychiatric Epidemiology,* 36, 150-157.

Lucas, D.R., Wezner, K.C., Milner, J.S., McCanne, T.R., Harris, I.N., Monroe-Posey, C., and Nelson, J.P. (2002). Victim, Perpetrator, Family, And Incident Characteristics Of Infant And Child Homicide In The United States Air Force. *Child Abuse & Neglect* ,26(2):167-86.

Mehta, M.N. (1982). Physical Abuse Of Abandoned Children In India. *Child Abuse & Neglect,* 6(2): 171-5.

Meyerson, L.A, Long, P.J, Miranda R. Jr, and Marx B. P. (2002, April). The Influence Of Childhood Sexual Abuse, Physical Abuse, Family Environment, And Gender On The Psychological Adjustment Of Adolescents. *Child Abuse & Neglect,* 26(4): 387-405.

Menick, D.M. (2000). The Psychosocial Features of Infanticide in Black Africa: The Case of Senegal. *Child Abuse & Neglect,* 24: 1557-1565.

NAPCAN (2001). Helping Children Who Have A Parent With A Mental Illness, Australia.

Oates, R. K. (1996). The Spectrum *Of Child Abuse*. See Also Sagatun & Edwards, Supra Note 10.

Offen, L., Waller, G., and Thomas, G. (2003). Is Reported Childhood Sexual Abuse Associated With The Psychopathological Characteristics Of Patients Who Experience Auditory Hallucinations? *Child Abuse & Neglect,* 27(8):919-27.

Pagare, Deepti (2003). A Study Of Physical And Sexual Abuse And Behavioural Problems Amongst Boys From An Observation Home In Delhi. *Unpublished Doctoral Dissertation in Community Medicine,* University of Delhi.

Report of the Consultation on Child Abuse Prevention, 29-31 March 1999, WHO, Geneva (document WHO/HSC/PVI/99.1).

Rosenthal, S., Feiring, C., and Taska, L. (2003). Emotional support and adjustment over a year's time following sexual abuse discovery. *Child Abuse & Neglect,* 27(6):641-61.

Runyon MK, Faust J, Orvaschel H. Differential symptom pattern of post-traumatic stress disorder (PTSD) in maltreated children with and without concurrent depression. *Child Abuse & Neglect* 2002-Jan;26(1):39-53.

Russell, D.E.H. (1983). The Incidence And Prevalence Of Intrafamilial And Extrafamilial Sexual Abuse Of Female Children. *Child Abuse & Neglect,* 7: 133-146.

Russell, D.E.H. (1984). The Prevalence And Seriousness Of Incestuous Abuse: Stepfathers Vs. Biological Fathers. *Child Abuse & Neglect,* 8: 15-22.

Sandnabba, N.K., Santtila, P., Wannas, M., and Krook, K. (2003). Age And Gender Specific Sexual Behaviors In Children. *Child Abuse & Neglect,* 27(6): 579-605.

Segal, U.A. and Ashtekar, A. (1994). Detection Of Intra-familial Child Abuse: Children At Intake It A Children's Observation Home In India. *Child Abuse & Neglect,* 18: 957-969.

Segal, U.A. (1995). Child Abuse By The Middle Class? A Study Of Professionals In India. *Child Abuse & Neglect,* 19: 217-233.

Shumba, A. (2002). The Nature, Extent And Effects Of Emotional Abuse On Primary School Pupils By Teachers In Zimbabwe. *Child Abuse & Neglect,*26(8):783-91.

Sobti, J.C., Chapparawal, B.C., and Holst, E. (2000). Study Of Knowledge, Attitude And Practice Concerning Aspects Of Torture. *J Indian Med Assoc,* 98(6): 334-5:338-9.

Sriram, K., Rathnavel, S., Papakumari, M, and Somasundaram, O. (1981). Battered Baby Syndrome: A Review Of Eight Cases. *Ann Acad Med Singapore,* 10(4):466-71.

Straus, M.A. (1995). *Manual for the Conflict Tactics Scales.* Durham, NH, Family Research Laboratory, University of New Hampshire.

Straus, M.A. (1979). Measuring Intrafamily Conflict and Violence: The Conflict Tactics (CT) Scales. *Journal of Marriage and the Family,* 41, 75-88.

Straus, M.A., Hamby, S.L. (1997). Measuring Physical and Psychological Maltreatment of Children with the Conflict Tactics Scales. In: Kantor et al., eds. *Out of the Darkness: Contemporary Perspectives on Family Violece.* Thousand Oaks, CA, Sage, 119-135.

Straus, M.A. *et al.*, (1998). Identification of Child Maltreatment with the Parent-child Conflict Tactics Scales: Development and Psychometric Data for a National Sample of American Parents. *Child Abuse & Neglect,* 22: 249-270.

Straus, M.A., and Gelles, R.J. (1990). (Eds) *Physical Violence in American Families:* Risk Factors and Adaptations to Violence in 8,145 Families. New Brunswick, NJ, Transaction Publishers.

Steele, B.E., and Alexander, H. (1981). Long-Term Effects Of Sexual Abuse On Childhood. In P.B.Mrazek And C.H.Kempe (Eds.), *Sexually Abused Children And Their Families* (Pp. 223-233). New York: Pergamon Press.

Silbert, M. H., and Pines, A.M. (1983). Early Sexual Exploitation As An Influence In Prostitution. *Social Work,* July-August, 285-289.

Swanston, H.Y., Plunkett, A.M., O'Toole, B.I., Shrimpton, S., Parkinson, P.N., and Oates, R.K. (2003). Nine Years After Child Sexual Abuse. *Child Abuse & Neglect,* 27(8):967-84.

Tang, C.S. (2002). Childhood Experience Of Sexual Abuse Among Hong Kong Chinese College Students. *Child Abuse & Neglect,*26(1):23-37.

Thilagaraj, R. and Priyamvadha, M. (2000). Deviance Among Street Children. *Indian Journal Of Criminology,* 28 (1): 41-44.

Times of India (2001). *Abused Children To Help Trace Culprits.* 7.

Tirosh, E., Offer Shechter, S., Cohen, A., and Jaffe, M. (2003). Attitudes Towards Corporal Punishment And Reporting Of Abuse. *Child Abuse & Neglect,* 27(8):929-37.

Troeme, N.H. and Wolfe, D. (2001). *Child Maltreatment in Canada: Selected Results from the Canadian Incidence Study of Reported Child Abuse and Neglect.* Ottawa, Minister of Public Works and Government Services, Canada.

Van Haeringen, A.R., Dadds, M. and Armstrong, K.L. (1998). The Child Abuse Lottery: Will the doctor Suspect and Report? Physician Attitudes Towards and Reporting of Suspected Child Abuse and Neglect. *Child Abuse & Neglect,* 22: 159-169.

Vulliamy, A.P., and Sullivan, R. (2000). Reporting Child Abuse: Pediatricians's Experiences with the Child Protection system. *Child Abuse & Neglect,* 24: 1461-1470.

Vock, R., *et al.*, (1999). Lethal Child Abuse Through the Use of Physical Force in the German Democratic Republic (1 Jan. 1985 to 2 Oct. 1990): Results of a Multi-centric Study. *Archiv Fur Kriminologie,* 204: 75-87.

Walrath, C., Ybarra, M., Holden, E.W., Liao, Q., Santiago, R., and Leaf, P. (2003). Children With Reported Histories Of Sexual Abuse: Utilizing Multiple Perspectives To Understand Clinical And Psychosocial Profiles. *Child Abuse & Neglect,* 27(5):509-24.

Walsh, C., MacMillan, H., and Jamieson, E. (2002). The Relationship Between Parental Psychiatric Disorder And Child Physical And Sexual Abuse: Findings From The Ontario Health Supplement. *Child Abuse & Neglect,* 26(1):11-22.

Wanda, M. Hunter, Dipty, Jain, Lautra, S. Sadowski, and Antono I. Sanhueza (2000). Risk Factors for Severe Child Discipline Practices in Rural India. *Journal of Pediatric Psychology,* 25,6: 435-447.

Wark, M.J., Kruczek, T., and Boley, A. (2003). Emotional Neglect And Family Structure: Impact On Student Functioning. *Child Abuse & Neglect,* 27(9):1033-43.

Wolfe, D.A. *et al.*, (1988). Early Intrvention for Parents at Risk of Child Abuse and Neglect. *Journal of Consulting and Clinical Psychology,* 56: 40-47.

Wolfe, D.A. (1999). *Child Abuse: Implications for Child Development and Psychopathology,* 2nd ed. Thousand Oaks, CA, Sage.

World Report on Violence and Health, published by the WHO, Geneva (Oct.2002).

Yanowitz, K.L., Monte, E., and Tribble, J.R. (2003). Teachers' beliefs about the effects of child abuse. *Child Abuse & Neglect,* 27(5):483-8.

Youssef, R.M., Attia, M.S., Kamel, M.I. (1998). Children Experience Violence: Parental Use of Corporal Punishment. *Child Abuse & Neglect,* 22: 959-973.

Zeira, A,, Astor R,A, and Benbenishty, R. (2002 Feb). Sexual Harassment In Jewish And Arab Public Schools In Israel. *Child Abuse & Neglect,* 26(2): 149-66.

[3]

Street Children

Introduction

India has the largest number of street children in the world. Proportion of street children is increasing rapidly in all the metropolitan cities in India bearing a history of illegitimate extra-marital sexual act, vagrant parents, maltreatment, family violence, breakdown of rural economy and urbanization.

The issue of street children has become a serious social problem. If proper steps are not taken one day social stability will be at stake. Street children are deprived from basic minimal facilities in life. As a result, they develop a negative attitude towards existing social system and structure. Since they are alienated from the mainstream of the society for survival they are involved in deviant social and economic activities from the very beginning of their life. Since they do not get education, in later age they do find it a difficulty to manage a decent job for survival and lead an aimless and haphazard life. Anti-socials and criminals take the advantage of miserable and helpless condition of the street children and they involve them in deviant activities. Unfortunately, by and large, our society also considers them as problem creator, street urchin, and criminal. A large section of people of high and middle class feel that street children should not be seen on the street, as it looks odd. Change of attitude of larger society towards street children is needed to bring them in to the mainstream of the society.

Definition

The term 'street children' was introduced in the 1980s to refer to children who live or spend significant amount of time on the street or urban areas to fend for themselves and/or their families through 'various occupations'. This also denotes children who inadequately protected, supervised and cared for by responsible adults.

In other word, a 'street child' is understood, as a minor who appears to be without adequate protection in the street. This definition includes, but is not restricted to, a number of those also known under different headings 'abandoned children', 'children at high risk', 'children without families', or even 'children in need of care and protection'. What counts in the description of the target group is apparent need not require the definition. It should be stressed on pavement exigencies.

The definition of 'street children'—those for whom the street has become their home, with no protection, supervision, or direction from responsible adults includes several problematic terms. Attempts to categorize their working and living circumstances have also been difficult.

In general term 'street child' is used to refer to all children found unaccompanied in the environment of the street, the risks that children are exposed to differ significantly, depending on their circumstances. Children's lack of accountability and apathy to parents, elders, teachers, authority etc. contribute to their attitudes, motivation and are manifested in different forms.

According to UNICEF, 'street children' are those for whom the street (in the widest sense of the word, i.e. unoccupied dwellings, wasteland, etc.) more than their family has become their real home, a situation in which there is no protection, supervision, or direction from responsible adults'.

The children commonly called 'street children' are best considered as children living and working in a particular urban environment. They are children out of place in the sense that they do not have what society considers having a correct relationship to major institutions of childhood- the family and education.

Broadly, the street children can be grouped into three categories as follows:

- *Children on the Street:* These children form the largest category that has homes; most return to their families at the end of the day.

- *Children of the Street:* These children are a group who has chosen the street as their home and it is there that they seek shelter, livelihood, and companionship. They have occasional contacts with their families.
- *Abandoned Children:* These children have severed all ties with their families. They are entirely on their own, not only for material survival but also psychologically.

A common expression used more commonly about these street children is 'children out of place' which refers to those children who have apparent dislocation from the places that are commonly regarded as 'normal' in western-like the middle-class children- family homes, schools and clubs.

Children out of place are not what they are said to be; they are more than victims or products of systems/situations. Their situation is complex. Just as there is no single category 'street children' there are no simple answers or quick fixes. Up to now this has not been adequately addressed at any level. Children out of place are not only part of the urban problems; they must also be seen in other contexts, including international and global scenarios. Political causes and consequences must be addressed.

In the last few decades a large number of poor children worldwide have been labelled 'street children' as they struggle to survive by themselves. However, this cannot be considered a new phenomenon. In the past, such children were reported as vagrants wandering on the streets and a threat to society in various countries.

In one study carried out in Rio de Janeiro, Brazil in 1989, street children were into four main categories like (i) family-based street workers, (ii) independent street workers who have tenuous ties with their families and occasionally sleep on the streets, (iii) children who live on the streets and have no contact with their families (children of the streets); and (iv) children of street families (Rizzini *et al.*, 1994).

In the 1990s, some researchers have preferred to use the term 'working children' to refer to children who are generally found on the streets during the day, but who go home to sleep at night (children on the streets) and 'street children' to refer to those children to whom the street is their home (children of the streets). The term 'working children' is used since most of them have street jobs (Rizzini *et al.*, 1994). In an attempt to avoid confusion, Rizzini and others clarified that this was not suggesting that 'street children' never work nor did all working children actually work.

Others such a Blanc *et al.* (1994) have argued that real 'street children' are those that live on their own on the streets and according to their definition, 'street children' are the roofless and rootless who live alone or with children like themselves.

From the available literature, it is clear that the definition of 'street children' is problematic and research has yet to unveil the various categories and sub-groups of children that fall under the general group of 'street children' in different cultural context (*Source*: ESCAP-HRD, United Nations, 2002).

Today there are millions of children in the world, who are forced to seek survival on the streets of cities. They work and live alone without adequate food, shelter, education, affection and social security. Though the physical deprivations faced by them are of very distressing nature, more damaging are the psychological and social deprivations. It is important to understand the problems and needs of street children and to draw them into the mainstream of our society.

Background of Street Children

The phenomenon of street children is rather universal with all cities in the countries of the third world. Owing to various reasons street children are found in the street of cities especially in the metropolitan cities. In general, street children can be divided into the following categories (Ghosh, 1992).

- Children belonging to the families who have migrated permanently;
- Children belonging to the families who have migrated temporarily and would go back to their homes after some time;
- Children who come from suburbs and adjoining villages

of the city in the morning, following some vocations during the day and go back in the evening;

- Children of very poor families lacking care and protection;
- Child workers;
- Unattached children who include orphans, abandoned children, maladjusted children, delinquent children, run-away children, and so on.

Children of Permanently Migrated Families

Normally cities are the big commercial centers with a large number of factories, industries and offices, which allures needy people for finding out the means of life. The potentiality of employment is practically very high. As a result, people from suburbs and from rural areas with inadequate income are attracted by these income prospects.

By and large the issue of street children is closely associated with the process of fast urbanization that has been taking place in the major cities of India after independence. The families that come to city in search of a means of life are driven out from their homes for several reasons. Though the most important and pervasive one is poverty, other reasons like natural calamities, litigation in the family, lack of cultivable land also work as contributing factors. The villages around some cities in India are very prone to floods, which is a common phenomenon every year. The natural calamities often force the people to migrate to the city for a better life.

They come to the city with high expectations and full of hopes that they would easily get jobs there and would be able to live comfortably with their families. But except for the fortunate ones the dream is shattered in the case of many.

These permanent migrants not only come from the suburbs and adjoining villages of cities but also from the neighbouring States. Most of these migrants become permanent residents of cities in India because they do not have any place to go back, even if they wish to go back. Besides, dire poverty and too much over-crowdedness in villages with need for daily workers in the field gradually diminishing with sophistication and mechanization of the cultivation process compel a number of families to come and settle in the city permanently even though they do not get a home there. They either work as daily wage earners at different construction sites or become rickshaw-pullers.

Children of Temporarily Migrated Families

All the cities in India is expanding day by day and thereby because of obvious reasons the number of high-rise buildings, workshops, flyovers, warehouses and the like are being regularly constructed. These avenues also attract job seekers from different rural areas to city. They come with their families and live in temporary hutments erected by them in open space. Almost all members of their families excepting the toddlers work as labour. As they work during a particular period, after the work is over they go back to their native place.

Mobile Children

Another group of children come to the city regularly by train or bus to work as hawker. They come early in the morning and take their place near the stations or in the open space for selling their goods. Some also go on hawking their wares from one place to another. After they sell off whatever they have brought, they go back to their homes. Not only do these children carry the heavy load of their goods and manage to sneak into the train ducking the ticket collectors, they also take the risk of smuggling rice from the suburbs or their villages which act is against the law of the country. As a result they often have to end up in local police lock-ups.

Many such children who do not have wares to sell take to rag picking. Metropolitan cities have a huge dumping ground. This ground provides a very important source of garbage's, which can be sold in the market for producing new products. This source of income often attracts women and children.

Children of Poor Families

The fourth group of children belongs to destitute families who are almost permanent residents of the city, living in the street often for generations. These children are in dire need for care and protection. They do not know of their roots with nothing to look back to. Many of them are born in the street and brought up there. They are half-fed and ill clad. Begging and picking garbage are their main occupations. They are the most vulnerable group who often involve themselves in anti-social activities.

The girl street children belonging to this category are very much prone to be victims of sexual abuse and exploitation. Nobody takes care of them or gives them protection. They are easily lured to the dark world of immoral means of supporting themselves.

Working Children

Majority of the street children are working children. Compelled by their basic need to support themselves and often their families, these children take up many different types of work ranging from casual rag pickers to regular helpers in garages or roadside dhobis, tea stalls or shops. Many children are forced to spend most of the time in the streets because of the nature of the work undertaken by them. The child who works as a helper at a tea stall start working as early as 5 a.m. and by the time he ends up it is almost midnight. With this routine of 30 days a month they have no opportunity for doing anything else, not even to spend a few hours for themselves. With the increase in the number of automobiles and two-wheelers in the city, there has also been a sharp proliferation of workshop for their repair and maintenance. To a large extent these workshops are unlicensed and do not have a regular place of work. So they run their trade on the open streets. These makeshift garages are thriving swiftly in city particularly in residential as well as where transport services operate. Almost all these workshops have at least two to three child workers who work from eight in the morning till the evening, spending 9-10 hours on the road, thus remaining exposed to obvious hazards of the street along with other material hazards that naturally go with such work.

Rag picking is another major occupation, which is taken up by many children living in the street because it does not require an employer nor any capital to run it. Many children living in sheltered houses turn into street children because of this profession taken up by them.

Abandoned and Orphan Children

According to one estimate, there is a staggering 30-80 million children in India today who have been disowned by their parents/relatives because of poverty, destitution, unwanted or pre-marital birth, and death or desertion by one of the parents. Abandoned newborn babies in the hospitals across the country in India are common incidence.

The National Crime Records Bureau figures indicate that abandoned infants have been increasing, particularly in Maharashtra, Madhya Pradesh and Gujarat.

This apart, a large number of children become the victims of unnatural family conditions. Since these children have no place to go, they are compelled to live in the street and they involve themselves in delinquent activities for survival.

Many street children who are orphans or deserted by their parents are often associated with antisocial groups who use them for their vested interest. Many girls have been found to be under the care of elderly women who not only live on their earnings but also engages them in immoral activities in the evening as they reach puberty. These children obviously fall in the category of high-risk children or latchkey children.

Prevalence and Magnitude of Street Children in India

It is very difficult to find out the prevalence and/or magnitude of street children since they are mobile. The emergence of street children has been described as an immense tragedy worldwide.

Regarding the volume of street children there is no reliable data. However, the Anti-Slavery Society—an UK based NGO—estimates that there are about 31 million street children across the globe (Pinto, 1990).

Although an exact estimate of the number of street children in India is not available, a situation analysis of street children conducted in seven cities estimated that there are nearly 100,000 street children in New Delhi including children who live with their families on the street and are engaged in rag picking, vending etc., (Pinto and Nangia, 1988). NGO activists say there are at least

50 girls—the youngest is a six year old—and more than double that number of boys who hang about the railway station, the busiest in the Indian capital. They scavenge for food in the bins on the platforms and trawl the tracks for discarded plastic for recycling. The girls are much fewer, only because most are taken away by touts and sold in brothels. Those who do survive on the platform, provide sex to the gangs of boys and men on the station in return for protection from the police and touts (Patro, 1997).

In India, though there are several research studies and statistics available on working children, information, which may contribute towards the understanding of situations and problems of working children, is very limited. While some statistics place the national figure at a lakh, other studies indicate that there are one-lakh street children in Delhi alone (Nangia, 1988). In Chennai, there are about 27,000 street children (Bosco Institute of Social work, 1989). It has also been estimated that there are approximately 100,000 street children in Kolkata. On the streets of Kolkata there are 50,000 children who have run away from homes (Bose, 1992). Street Children run away from destitute or cruel homes and survive on the street in uncertainty, poverty and fear of abuses (Teuns, 1990).

Data reveal that more than one million children in the Calcutta Metropolitan Area live in slums, of whom about half a million are critically affected by poverty, malnutrition, lack of shelter and sanitation. Whatever be the actual number of street children in Kolkata, their extreme deprivation and living conditions make them a highly visible group calling for immediate attention of policy makers and the city as a whole. The majority of the street children in Kolkata are migrants, whereas in Chennai and Mumbai, more than 77 per cent are non-migrants. More than 90 per cent of the children in Kolkata migrated due to economic reasons (*Source:* CINI-IPER Report, 1994 and IPER Report, 1992). Economic reasons for migration predominate in the other cities as well.

According to one estimate, there is a staggering 30.80 million children in India today, who have been disowned by their parents/ relatives because of poverty, destitution, unwanted or out of marriage birth, and death or desertion of one or both parents. Very recently, alarmed at the increasing number of newborn babies being abandoned at hospitals across the state, the Tamil Nadu Government has decided to demand proof of address before granting admissions to maternity wards in Government hospitals. As many as 11 infants were abandoned in two Chennai hospitals alone in the past one year. According to officials, the cases of abandonment were much higher in the district hospitals. The National Crimes Records Bureau figure indicates that abandonment of infants has been increasing, out of 582 cases reported in 1998; 279 cases particularly were from Maharashtra, 115 from Madhya Pradesh and 107 from Gujarat (*Source:* CHILDLINE India Foundation, Mumbai, 2003).

Living Condition of Street Children

There are thousands of children who live and work in the city streets of India. According to a study conducted among the street children in the city of Chennai, about 90 per cent of them live with their parents in the streets (National Labour Institution—1992). Contrary to the general conception that many street children are delinquents, the study revealed that only 6.6 per cent of the total sample had served time in juvenile homes or correctional institutions. Studies in a few other Indian cities showed that the majority of the street children were doing rag picking for their living. Usually, these children are unable to submit references or pay deposits to their employers to obtain any work (Walolkar, 2003).

Thousand of children can be found working and, sometimes, living on city streets in India. Although they all look alike, a distinction must be made between children actually living on the streets and those who go home in the evening. These two groups have different life histories and prognosis; they differ especially with regard to the risks they face and the protective factors, which are available to them. The knowledge about their psychological development is still sketchy. In fact, living on the streets is harmful because of the exposure to addictions, violence, and exploitation.

Recently, researchers carried out studies on the emotional, cognitive, and social development of street children and found that, although these children are exposed to stressful situations and to great personal and social risks, they develop coping skills that allow them to overcome the hazards of life on the streets. They master strategies to establish social groups that increase safety and improve the odds of surviving. Recently researchers have found that street children and low socio-economic status children present similar levels of depression and of subjective well-being. Nevertheless, alternatives to a nurturing home must be found. The street is not a healthy place for an Bharatin to live, even if it does not cause great psychological harm (Koller and Hutz, 2002).

Usually no facilities are available for the street children, they have to cope with what they can use as 'free' facilities. The abusive conditions at home made these children run away from home. The children usually exercise their choice and remove themselves from the environment. They learn to survive through 'unconventional' means. A place to sleep at night and escape from the hell of abuse is always a cause of worry for these children. While some have a fixed place to sleep, others sleep wherever they find it convenient and safe. Having no permanent place also means that the children cannot store their possessions in a secure place. However, they often have to contend with the police, who would drive them off the road, platform, abandoned building etc.

The spatial distribution of pavement dwellers are as follows-people on the pavement tend to gather in a number of places and sleep in shop verandahs, under bridges, trees, in bus shelters, abandoned buildings or just out in the open, railway station platforms. A minority seeks shelter in public places, on the beach or under trees, construction sites. They are virtually excluded from urban infrastructure and facilities whatsoever and have to rely on roadside amenities for water used for drinking and cooking. Open space serves as sanitary purposes. Medical, educational and other essential services are inaccessible to them.

Almost all street children of Kolkata do not have access to shelter in contrast with Chennai, Mumbai and Bangalore where almost 43 per cent, 38 per cent and 80 per cent of street children respectively, have access to covered shelter at night (*Source:* CINI-IPER Report, 1994 and IPER Report, 1992).

The local police and even the municipal cleaners create great difficulties for the street children in India. For any petty thefts, they are the first ones to be accused by the police. It is observed that the police extort about half the earnings of the rag pickers as commission. The children also had to pay some staff members of the municipality to ease the way for rag picking (*Source:* National Labour Institution, Noida, U.P., 1992).

Chilly winter nights, mosquito bites, regular theft and violence, susceptible to bullying, policemen, local dada's, passerbys, passengers, railway staffs, coolies harassment, accidents, sudden showers, absence of dry place to sleep during monsoons etc. are the constant problems these children face who are out on the streets.

One such problem faced by a street child for the price of protection has been narrated below:

> ***Case 1:*** *The police once took Jamir while he was sleeping under a railway ticket counter. Somebody had stolen steels from the staircase and the police accused him of having stolen it and beat him up. At another time, when they caught him and accused him of stealing something, he told them 'I knew who had stolen it'. He gave them a name and ran away from the police station as soon as he could. At the station there were dada's (big bully) who would demand regular protection money. They would take away whatever money was in Jamir's pocket. Therefore it was useless for him to keep money. So if he had money he used to spend it on movies. The dada's would keep blade in their fingers, and as they walk past children like him, they slash either the face or hands/legs.*

A large number of children are found today living on a railway station in every corner of the country. Life on a railway station has its own rhythm—mostly characterized by trains whistling in and out and the movement of large numbers of people with trains arriving and departing. Within this floating population are some people who are constant features—vendors selling various eateries/drinks, book sellers, others like the railway staff and of course coolies (porters). It is in this environment that children on the platforms eke out their existence: washing, bathing, earning, eating food, playing and sleeping. While some on the platform live with their family or other relations, many live on their own.

Like all street children the ones living at the railway stations are mobile groups and often do not stay in one place for long.

The following case narrates how a 7-8 year old boy, not by any choice, landed up at a Kolkata railway station:

> ***Case 2:*** *Shubhashish was 7-8 years old when he ran away to his mashi (mother's sister) place. He stayed there for about a week. His mashi insisted that he return. So one day he caught a train and came to Sealdah. Everyone was getting down at Sealdah so he also got down. After some time he caught another train to go back. But that train did not go to Dumdum (mashi's place). It stopped at another station. He got down and walked out of the station. He took another train and came back to Sealdah. After that he did not go back to his mash's place or to his home. He came to Sealdah and stayed there. There was no reason for coming to Sealdah, it happened only because the train stopped at this station (terminal point).*

Living condition on street encounters innumerable problems. Most of the time the street/pavements are left with waste disposals on which the makeshift houses of the street dwellers are constructed. The offensive stench often spread outs almost blocking normal breathing. In such unhygienic and unhealthy environments children of the homeless usually dwell without having any other alternative choice. The improper sanitation system on the street affects miserably the health of the street child and their families dwelling with them. Moreover, the environmental pollution emitted by the vehicles encircles the air and makes them prone to innumerable diseases.

In some places in the city, children on the streets sometimes share the common bathrooms and latrines, share the living areas, cook and eat in the open because of lack of kitchen space, makes their living claustrophobic and deprives the residents of any sort of privacy. Though there is no water shortage in those areas where they live but many water sources are located near public toilets or garbage dumps. This increases the chances of water contamination.

Defecation in the open and in public places deteriorates further their health conditions. The violence and aggressions are everyday occurrences and happen at any time of the day and night. Gang wars between two areas take place almost regularly on every street.

Inadequate food, unhygienic living conditions and the strain of work affects the health of working street children. From a number of studies it has been reported that the majority of the children fall prey to physical weakness, fatigue, backache and muscle pain. Also children are affected by respiratory tract infections, tuberculosis, diarrhea, and skin diseases, worm infestations.

About 88 per cent of street children on an average in Kolkata, Chennai, Mumbai and Bangalore lack basic sanitation facilities. Access to recreational facilities, sports and games and socio-cultural activities is also very poor. Eighty-three per cent of street children in Kolkata suffer from exposure to the weather. 83 per cent of the children in Kolkata about 87 per cent in both Chennai and Mumbai and 99 per cent in Bangalore suffer from exposure to filth and smoke. Twelve per cent of the street children work with hazardous materials and 8.7 per cent with hazardous machines. Only 8.6 per cent of girl street children enjoy good health, while 58.5 per cent have very bad health. About 48 per cent do not have access to any medical facility and though 49.7 per cent do have access to medical facilities provided by government, these are rarely availed owing to the hostile attitude of doctors and hospital staff and public attitude towards them. Only 2.4 per cent of girl street children were treated by private medical practitioners when ill. Preventive health also seems lacking—as many as 96.8 per cent of street children surveyed were not fully immunized. More than 90 per cent of street children in Kolkata are undernourished and suffer from moderate to excessive protein and vitamin deficiency. Only 7 per cent of Kolkata's street children (as compared to an average of 17 per cent for other Indian cities) are adequately nourished. In Kolkata, 18 per cent of street children live on one meal a day while the remaining 82 per cent get two meals. In Chennai, Bangalore and Mumbai, 20.7 per cent, 15.9 per cent and 1.8 per cent children respectively live on a single meal per day. More street children suffer from excessive protein deficiency in Kolkata (64%) than in other cities. More than 70 per cent of Kolkata's street children have an unsatisfactory age-height ratio (CINI-IPER Report, 1994).

Now though the conditions might have improved through various intervention programmes rendered by several NGOs and welfare organizations, still the situation in India is grave.

The children identify violence on the street and home as a danger that they and other children face most often. On the streets, frequent bullying occurs while at home beating/thrashing, mostly by fathers or by the mothers, clients, poses a risk to them. Often the mothers of these children as well as their mother's clients entice the children in exchange of a small remuneration to buy liquor, pan, cigarettes or drugs for their clients. This exposes the children to the risk of being tempted to try these out.

Most problems of urban childhood have their roots in a country's rural sector. This is especially true for countries like India where thousands of children are forced to migrate from villages to cities to ultimately end up in extremely exploitative situations.

Thanks to empirical research, there is now a greater understanding of the characteristics of street children in general and the nature of their daily lives. It is commonly accepted that these children constitute a fundamentally different category of children to street living children. The majority of studies on street children have focused exclusively on the street living child, leaving our understanding of the psychological characteristics of street children.

Many street children end up by settling in the city street, marrying and having a family. In this manner the street influences in propagating their generation.

Problems Encountered by the Street Children

In everyday life they encounter numerous problems like neglect, abuse, exploitation and so on. In this regard, Glauser (1990) stated that street children are always in anticipation that any moment they might be woken up by a policeman's boot or stick or may be drenched by a jet of cold water from truck, car, bus lined up for a street wash. They spend the nights anywhere in the streets, stay up late, get little sleep, and are exposed to passers-by as abandoned, homeless, tramps, thieves or juvenile delinquents. However, a brief description of the major problems encountered by the street children is given below:

Lack of Safe Shelter

This is the basic problem they face. Wherever they stay and wherever they go, there is practically no safe shelter for street children. Everywhere they are at high risk of exploitation, sexual abuse and harassment. Nowadays a good number of NGOs started working for the welfare and rehabilitation of the street children in different parts of the country. A good number of fortunate children enjoy this facility, which is more needed for a girl child.

Inadequate Food

For earning money for bread and butter whole day they work hard as no body is there to ensure two meals a day for them. Since most of them are illiterate and have no skill they are mostly involved in casual work against very low wage. Sometimes some of them are involved in deviant social activities knowingly or unknowingly as influenced by the anti-socials for which these innocent children are not responsible. In fact, our social system and structure is responsible for pushing/compelling innocent children in negative direction.

Lack of Medical and Educational Facilities

In case of any health problem, most of the street children remain unattended, except few lucky children who are under the intervention programme of NGOs. Sometimes they visit nearby/local Govt. Health Centers for treatment and get free medicine. Since no body is there to follow up whether they are taking medicine on time or not, and since there is no secured and safe place to preserve medicines after one or two days they do not take the medicine regularly. Hence, a large number of street children suffer from different health problems through out the year.

Most of them do not get the opportunity to study. As a result, in future when they become older they do not get better job. Whole life they work as unskilled labourers.

Physical and Mental Health Problems

Homeless youth are at alarmingly high risk for a myriad of physical and psychological problems as a result of both the circumstances that preceded their homelessness, and as a direct consequence of life on the streets. Most of these children have nobody to look after them and most of them have no knowledge of medical facilities, which they could avail of. As a result, in case of any health problem mostly they remain unattended. Nowadays a number of NGOs are extending health services to the disadvantaged children. But their services are inadequate and follow-up is also very poor.

Sexually transmitted infections (STIs), pregnancy, trauma, tuberculosis, uncontrolled asthma, and dermatologic infestations are a few of the health problems, which are commonly present among street children. These somatic problems are compounded by high rates of drug and alcohol abuse as well as depression and suicide. Despite the obvious need for medical services, homeless youth often do not receive appropriate medical care due to numerous individual and systems barriers impeding health care access by this population. In addition to the barriers experienced by the adult homeless population, homeless adolescents confront further hurdles stemming from their age and developmental stage. Some of these impediments include a lack of knowledge of clinic sites, fear of not being taken seriously, concerns about confidentiality, and fears of police or social services involvement. Improved access to appropriate health care is necessary if we are to better support and care for this population of young people. To effectively manage and treat homeless youth, individual providers must be aware of the diagnoses associated with homelessness, as well as the community resources available to these youth. Finally, providers need to be the voices advocating for improved services for this disadvantaged and silent population (Feldmann and Middleman, 2003).

Street children are most vulnerable to HIV/AIDS as most of the female child and a good number of male children are sexually abused. In a small sample study covering 14 street children in 1994, two cases were found HIV positive while two others tested were infected with hepatitis B and syphilis. The two boys who tested positive for the AIDS virus were completely shattered after they came to know of it, according to the doctor. They feared that they would be ostracized if the others came to know, and even before they could be counselled, both vanished (Patro, 1997).

Johnson *et al.* (1996) assessed HIV risk behaviours in a sample of homeless youth in a large urban area in Chicago and examined factors associated with these behaviours. Overall, 83.7 per cent reported at least one of these risk factors: multiple sex partners; high-risk partners; inconsistent condom use; history of sexually transmitted disease; anal sex; prostitution; and/or intravenous drug use. An index of these behaviours was associated with being male, having unmet personal needs, being interviewed in street locations, and having a history of sexual abuse.

Craig and Hodson (2000) found signs and symptoms of psychiatric disorder among 55 per cent homeless children, associated with adverse childhood experiences and rough sleeping. Sourander (1998) examined the traBharatitic events and behaviour symptoms of 46-unaccompained refugees and found that 'refugee children are more vulnerable to emotional distress than older children'. Senanayake *et al.* (1998) observed that Colombia street children were mostly exposed to road traffic accidents and physical and sexual abuse.

In another study Ayerst (1999) revealed that stress and depression were positively correlated for the street youth, and that these youth had higher levels of stress and depression than that of non-runaways. There were also differences in coping strategies: street youth were more likely to engage in acts of self-harm and to use drugs and alcohol, while non-runaways more frequently resorted to productive problem solving and disclosure/discussion with someone they trust.

Addiction and Gambling Problems

Most children on the streets are exposed to the risks of tobacco, alcohol and substance abuse and the subsequent addiction.

Those who attempt to eke out an honest livelihood by doing odd jobs or rag picking etc. are most of the time underpaid, thus end up being exploited for their vulnerability. Their hard-earned money is also stolen or forcefully taken away. Many children on the streets prefer not to save money for these reasons and therefore spend almost the entire amount of what they earn, mainly on food, gambling and addictions and vices. Children on the streets are also used as drug peddlers and pushers (injectors). The lure of money is high. The drug trade (involving heroin and its derivatives) flourished during the late eighties and the early nineties attracting a number of children and youth to the trade as pushers and consumers. Though the trade still exists, it is not as open, or as flourishing, as it was earlier due to several intervention programmes. Gambling in the form of satta and playing cards is most common among all age groups of males including boys and they can be seen playing cards in the park and on every street of the cities.

A noteworthy feature is that of the majority of children on the street who live alone; most are part of some type of household. Mostly these are incomplete households where the mother is alone with her children, or the father or the children are left to grandparents, aunts, uncles etc. Usually, these are mainly women who are separated from their husbands rather than unmarried females, who have never experienced a stable hBharatin relationship before.

Following is the case study of a child who ran a high risk of abuse found on the streets/platforms of Kolkata city:

> ***Case 3:*** *Ramesh was 4 year-old when his mother eloped with another man. His father unable to bear the stress of bringing up his children took to drinking. In this drunken state he beat the children frequently. Gradually, Ramesh (and his sister) took to staying away from school and stealing money from his father to spend. Ramesh would often run away from home and would be found by the police, wandering about, begging or stealing at various railway stations. Their father had their so-called 'aunt' living in with him. In 1990, when he was twelve, unable to take any more thrashings or humiliations from his father, Ramesh and his sister finally ran away from home for good. He*

was 'pretty' in appearance, enjoyed wearing female apparels and ornaments and hence became a target of sexual abuse for older boys and men.

Another study states the fact that socio-emotional development in early childhood broadly pertains to the quality of children's evolving participation in relationships, with the parent-child relationship serving as a primary focus in early childhood. This article discusses socio-emotional development in early childhood from the vantage point of attachment theory. It was argued that specific threats to the quality of parenting will place young children at risk for insecure attachment and, in turn, for socio-emotional difficulties in the wider world. Socio-emotional risks from the parent, the parent's social-ecological niche, and the child were examined, and it included non-autonomous parental states of mind with regard to attachment, parental psychopathology, marital discord, insufficient parental social supports, and difficult infant temperament. Individual and cumulative effects of risks were addressed, along with suggestions for future directions that included closer examination of the manner in which protective and risk factors interact in predicting children's socio-emotional health- (Teta, 2002).

Occupation of Street Children

For normal, healthy physical and mental development of children minimal facilities like adequate food, safe shelter, basic education, medical care, congenial environment, love affection are the primary needs for survival. But unfortunately street children are deprived of all these basic minimal facilities and moreover they have to struggle every day for earning their bread and butter.

Street children mostly work as petty hawkers, shoeshine boys, scavengers of raw material or even thieves and street prostitution. By the nature of their work and lives, they are on their own, largely unprotected by adults, and become vulnerable to many dangers and abuses. If a street child cannot live on earnings from working or begging, then he or she turns to other means of survival like thefts, acts of violence, prostitution & drug peddling and other vices (Teuns, 1990 and Thilagaraj & Priyamvadha, 2000).

In the eyes of parents, the 'street' affords an environment where it is appropriate for them to send their children to work as a way of contributing to the overall good of the family. Encouraging or sending their children to work on the street was a strategy for dealing with serious economic problems. In some families children were expected to start contributing to the family income once they were judged old enough. A high proportion of the children give their wages to their parents or other relatives with whom they live. Rural children work more than urban children with agricultural work being the main type of rural work.

Stealing food from the roadside shops is a common act indulged in by many young children living on the streets. They often consider it as a sign of being 'smart' under the influence of the peer groups to establish their macho image. As a result, sometimes the people badly and/or mercilessly punish them when they are caught.

In many instances, child street workers and their families can be thought of as winners, losers, and survivors. Street work cannot be evaluated every time in terms of a simplistic dichotomy of 'good' or 'bad' in terms of its effects on children and families. In cases, where street life involvement brings positive benefits to the child and the family, these children can be regarded as winners. For some children, participation in street life brings negative results. This may be due to environmental factors (a child gets knocked down in a traffic accident) or personal characteristics of the child (he/she does not have the cognitive or social skills for the demands of the street work or are unable to restrain themselves from being abused). Many children are unable to develop a street sense because their ability to deal with the demands of the busy street environment, particularly the traffic is not adequate.

As an increasing number of children face severe economic hardship, more and more children become child labourers in whatever occupations are available, including a practice that the Indian government described as, 'decadent social practices like scavenging...' in the form of rag picking, and increasing criminal activity.

The child on the streets must start working as soon as possible, or else perish. Guided by his peers and friends, he drifts into unorganized work like shining shoes, rag picking, massage work, loading and unloading, or doing odd jobs for a contractor in road repairs, construction, catering, in car garages. But these are seasonal or temporary daily-wage jobs of unpredictable nature. The adolescent street child is more preoccupied with thoughts of vocation, skill and long-term survival. Deep down, what he desperately yearns for is a regular job with a steady income.

Some of the children start to work when they are only 5-6 years of age, and by the time they are 20 they are burnt out. They are physically, mentally and emotionally exhausted so that they are no longer able to work and are doomed to unemployment even in cases when employment is available. The vicious cycle restarts when they want their children to work for them.

The worldwide picture shows that the largest numbers of the child labourers are in Asia, 44.6 million; followed by Africa, 23.6 million; and Latin America, 5.1 million. Estimates by country showed even developed European countries are not immune from this. Among the 10-14 year old children the working rate is 41.3 per cent in Kenya, 31.4 per cent in Senegal, 30.1 per cent in Bangladesh, 25.8 per cent in Nigeria, 24 per cent in Turkey, 17.7 per cent in Pakistan, 14.4 per cent in India, 11.6 per cent in China, 11.2 per cent in Egypt, 6.7 per cent in Mexico, 4.5 per cent in Argentina, 1.8 per cent in Portugal and 0.4 per cent in Italy. This is only the tip of the iceberg; no reliable figures for workers under 10 years are available, though the numbers are significant (*The Statesman,* Feb. 4, 2002).

The tragedy is that life on the street does not prepare a child with the discipline or skill required in a formal job. His sense of punctuality is poor, and he is unaccustomed to shouldering duties and responsibilities. Routine bores him, and his language is rough, and peppered with the abusive slang of the streets. Used to daily wages, he finds the monthly salary unfamiliar. No wonder, up to 90 per cent of street youth drops out of formal jobs. The street seems better to them.

Involvement of street girl children as maidservant to supplement the family income is common practice among migrant population in developing countries especially in the SAARC region. India is not an exception to that. Domestic work is one of the largest categories of child labour in the world and often equivalent to slavery, we continue to know very little about this most hidden and marginalized group of mainly girl workers.

Data on child workers especially street child worker is virtually non-existent. A recent survey by the International Labour Organization showed 73 million children aged 10 to 14, works. In Indian context the estimates on the magnitude of child labour falls short of the actual and factual figures for a number of reasons like multiplicity of definitions, different approaches of computation, diverse sources of data, lack of correct information. Still H Bharatin Rights Watch, 1996 estimates that 60 and 115 million working children are in India—the highest number in the world; India is the largest example of a nation plagued by the problem of child workers (Walolkar, 2003).

Almost all street children in Kolkata live with both or single parents and very few (about 3%) live alone on the streets. Almost all (99.92%) street children in Kolkata earn less than Rs. 200 per month and a majority (55.6%) less than Rs. 100. More than 80 per cent of their mothers have low earnings (<Rs. 200 per month) and the majority of fathers earn between Rs. 100 and Rs. 600 per month, with more than 70 per cent earning more than Rs. 200 per month. In Kolkata, Chennai, Mumbai and Bangalore, street children parents belong to the very low-income groups. Most families have an average of five members. Most street children in Kolkata have 1-3 siblings (*Source:* CINI-IPER Report, 1994).

Street Children in Kolkata work in the worst possible conditions. About 20 per cent are exposed to hazardous materials and machinery. In Chennai, Mumbai, and Bangalore, the proportion is much higher at 32.7 per cent, 38.9 per cent and 37.9 per cent respectively. Fifty per cent of working street children in Kolkata are self-employed. Most children employed in the service sector (63.1%), especially girls, work as domestic help. Among the self-employed, rag picking is the most predominant occupation (60.7%). Self-employment predominates among street children in Chennai, Mumbai and Bangalore as well. Household work is the next most prevalent in Kolkata (31.5%) although in other cities, it is employment in shops, establishments and garages. Street Children and other major cities in India are abused in different ways by employers, the most common being overwork and physical abuse. Despite exploitation at work, 60 per cent of working street children in Kolkata and 72.3 per cent in Chennai maintain a positive attitude toward their employer. In Bangalore, however, only 27 per cent love and respect their employers (*Source:* IPER Report, 1992).

The children working on the street are 12 years old or under, working for economic reasons, earning near to the minimum legal wage. They belong to families with many children living in overcrowded conditions. The children generally work at the weekends, during summer vacations and at any time of the day as the need arises. They start working early in the morning and may continue until the late evening. The children experience difficulties due to the kind of work they perform, the weather, the police and municipal people. The majority of them had been taken to a municipal police station at least once. The children quarrel with their friends, for stealing clients, swearing at and making fun of each other. They get angry with, or may be frightened by, other street children adult street workers, clients, gangs and pickpockets.

The Mumbai state government's reaffirmation to eradicate child labour by 2007 is indeed a welcome aspiration. Given at the state alone has around 11 lakh children under the age of 14 working in various sectors, some of which fall under the hazardous category, and also many employed in the domestic sector which is not covered in the Child Labour Prohibition Act, this may prove a tough job. Together, the Child Labour Act, 1986 and the Shops and Commercial Establishments Act passed by the state prohibit employment of children below the age of 14 and slap a fine of Rs. 10,000 and above besides imprisonment. However, that children continued to languish as labour department sources point to the fact that mere legislation cannot solve any problem (Report of *The Deccan Herald,* dated January 10, 2002). No amount of legislation is enough to solve the problems of the street children, nor can any amount of NGO intervention programmes make a significant dent on the iceberg of problems of street children. Nothing short of a Government and NGO people combine movement can root out the most heinous searge of modern civilization—the phenomenon of street children. The sight of the ill-clad starving street children may give you an opportunity to indulge in Wordsworthian poetic sensibility to say in a pseudo-tragic tone: 'see what man has made of man; inhumanity oozing out of humanity' or an opportunity of political speechifying in Churchilian fashion: 'O! Never before in human history has so many been exploited so much by so far for so long.' The spirit of the suffering of street children pricks our conscience and nags us with a queer sense of uneasiness, and with a 'smart' crow-like closing of the eyes, we hide the sight from our conscience and move away from the scene, conveniently rationalizing that it is something else's job to set right what has gone wrong with our society. Modern man lives in his cocoon of 'enlightened self-interest with a dead conscience. The world is not as it could have been made, but it is as it is, not because of the reckless 'action' of the rascals and criminals but because of the 'inaction' of the normally good people like any one of us. The failure of the good people to make their mite of contribution towards the world as it could have been made has turned them into criminals by default. The resurrection of the modern man from the grave of dead conscience alone can bring into existence a 'people's movement' fuelled by passion to clean the society of all crimes, the worst being the phenomenon of street children.

Education of Street Children

Majority of the street children are illiterate. They can neither read nor write their name. But the children who run away from the families they can read and write. Now a days because of intervention programme undertaken by various NGOs for the welfare and rehabilitation of street children, a good number of them have got the opportunity to get basic education and they can at least write their name and read simple things in local language.

Children on the streets generally do not attend any forms of education whatsoever, which in itself almost condemn them to persistent poverty. When asked about the reasons for not going to school, the answers generally relate to three types of factors—

- The requirements of the education bureaucracy (birth certificates, parents documents, parents contribution to the cost of schooling, books and uniforms).
- Discrimination (beggar-children, out cast as they are not easily admitted to any kind of schooling, whether they comply the rules and regulations or not).
- The impossibility of conventional schools to respond to the very peculiar situation in which street children have to study and to adjust their programme accordingly.

This third factor appears as the most serious one. Not surprisingly, attempts to coerce street children to attend school have been largely unsuccessful. The education system, obviously has quite a lot to answer for education, which one hopes as the engine for social mobility of the urban poor, but today's street children remain largely deprived of it. 'Deprivation of' not simply without it, because nearly all will indicate their willingness to go to school, if only it could be made possible. Therefore, to enable them to undergo a form of training appears to be of great importance. Needless to urge that this training should match their possibilities.

The education of children on street get affected because more positive reinforcement they receive from the street work activities than from the school activities because the money they earn has a high positive value for the family. Pedagogies designed for these clients it is nowadays widely agreed upon, calls for a thorough understanding of the child's emotional needs and socio-economic environment.

School dropouts continue to be one of the biggest problems facing primary education in India. It is estimated that nearly 50 per cent children dropout from before completing their V grade. Often it is argued that majority of children leave school for economic reasons, as they have to support their families. However, lack of conclusive evidence fail to determine the degree to which gainful employment result ill school dropout. Nonetheless, it remains a fact that education is yet to reach most of the children living in difficult circumstances. A survey was conducted in 450 villages/urban pockets to examine among other issues, the activity status, type of employment, earning, health, physical condition, aspiration and achievement level of children dropping out from primary schools. The study also explored the reasons of dropout. The findings indicated that, in general, less than 10 per cent dropouts were engaged in gainful employments. However, the chances of dropout due to employment varied from place to place indicating significant linkages with the employment opportunities. The poor quality of education was suggested as the most important reason for dropout. If education is made relevant and meaningful to the economic needs of the community then it has greater chances of attracting and holding children.

About 66 per cent of street children in Kolkata have never attended school. Of those who have received some education, only 18 per cent have completed primary school. Children who do not complete at least Class III (81.7%) have been found to lapse into illiteracy. Thirty-three per cent of the children studied for a maximum of two years, more than 34 per cent for 2-4 years and only 10 per cent and 3.4 per cent for 4-6 years and above six years respectively. More than 78 per cent had discontinued studies and 21 per cent were continuing studies through NGO projects. Dropouts have been attributed to migration, continuous shifting within the city, and lack of proper facilities like school in the vicinity, unsuitable timings and apathy of teachers in that order, accounting for 28 per cent of the dropouts. Thirteen per cent dropped out due to lack of interest, pointing to the inadequacies of the system (*Source:* CINI-IPER Report, 1994).

In Turkey, a great number of children start to work at early ages, either to support themselves or to contribute to the family income. Despite the fact that five year primary school is compulsory, some of these children work on a full time basis, starting at very young ages, and some work, during off hours and vacations on a part-time basis or as seasonal workers. The children work in agriculture, manufacturing industry and service sector jobs such as trade, restaurants and hotels, while a large portion of them work in the marginal sectors. Turkey is in a period of rapid urbanization with a high birth rate. In the urban areas, employment of child labour has, to a great extent, shifted outside, away from the family. The children are mostly found in workplaces where vocational skills are transferred through the master apprentice set up. House work, service sector and to a great extent, in the marginal sector. Starting from 1990s growing numbers of poor marginalized urban children and street children in particular became a matter of public concern.

For the girl child on streets in India victimization is not only in the form of atrocities such as rape or incest. It is often subtle but nevertheless shackling, not allowing her to attain her full potential as an individual. Cultural practices and poverty ensure that the girl child drops out of school at a very young age. Girls form more than half of the illiterate children in the age group 5-9 years and 65 per cent in the 10-14 years age group. Nearly one-third of the number of girls who manage to enter formal education in Class I drop out by Class II. The number of dropouts and stagnation cases in girls is nearly twice than in boys. The dropout rates of rural girls are higher than urban girls. Along with this the dropout rates of street girl child is more than that of non-street ones.

The girl child is the most disadvantaged of all street children, working for an income while being responsible for the care of her siblings and household chores and standing a great risk of being exploited psychologically, emotionally and sexually. Most girl street children surveyed expressed a need for privacy as a majority of them (83%) have attained puberty. Of the girls staying alone, 61 per cent live in the open street. Those staying in hutments also lack adequate protection and privacy. Most girls are harassed by city or government officials during eviction drives. Thirty-six per cent reported of harassment by the police and 56 per cent by local people. Nearly 61 per cent reported that they are subjected to eve teasing. Almost 96 per cent of sample girl street children had no access to toilets or bathing facilities. Girl street children usually get married at an early age. Those (17%) who remain on the streets are exposed to physical and sexual abuse and face the risk of being lured into prostitution (*Source:* CINI-IPER Report, 1994).

The reason is not far to seek. Girls are expected to look after their siblings. Parents are also worried of the girls being sent to far away or co-educational schools after they attain puberty even if the girls are eager to learn. One such case is narrated below:

Case 4: *Rina Pawar is a mere 13 year old but her sights are set on goals that go beyond the narrow confines of her little village, Talegaon, Maharashtra. She studied up to the Standard V. Rina would have loved to continue education but her parents took her out from school. She now cooks and cleans at home and looks after her younger siblings. Says she with stars in her eyes, 'I want to study much further, and I would like to take courses in knitting and sewing'. Will she be able to attain her goals is a mute question? (the girl child oblivion; Nagpur-street adhar Kendra).*

Like Rina there are several such girls who desire to go to school, even if they are in the streets of Kolkata and other cities of India. But the society at large poses a barrier in some form and tries to keep these children in dark. Eventually, 'for every darker side there is a brighter side'.

Reasons for Leaving Home and Accepting Street Life

Children leave home for the most trivial of reasons, such as fear of being scolded or wounded pride at some imagined insult. By the time the harsh reality of street life hits them, fear of rejection or punishment makes it impossible for them to think of returning home. But living on the streets is unthinkable too, for every moment is a threat, every breath a hardship. The streets, however, are not open repository for any child who wants to leave home. Food, employment, income, and dignity—these do not come easy on the streets. Those who thought that leaving home would bring them to a better life are the most disillusioned of all. Their deep need to do better, to prove their worth and to justify their decision to run away from home forces them into a cycle of abuse and exploitation. Frustrated and devastated, such children are easy prey for drug-pushers. Some may turn to petty theft and crime, and a few even attempt suicides. The ideal solution for a street child is re-unification with the family.

'A seven year old boy from Tirupati had run away from home after being burned with cigarette butts by his father'. Should an abusive father be given guardianship? When the case came for hearing in the Juvenile Welfare Board, he was bundled into the next train to Tirupati, Andhra Pradesh as the parents have the right to custody. The law of the land gives custody of children to parents even if they abuse their children regularly. Law doesn't empower children to fight abuse (*Source:* Report of *The New Indian Express,* December 2001).

Deb and Mitra (2002) carried out a study in Kolkata, India with a view to identifying the multi-factorial causes responsible for leading children to accept a street life. A group of 40 children, 18 male and 22 female, in the age group of 9-19 years were covered in the present study. Findings disclosed that the factors which mostly pushed children to street, half-dug pavements, railway platforms include influence of step-parents, death of either or both parents, ill-treatment of grandparents, family disintegration, gender bias of parents, effect of poverty and/or unemployment, deviant behaviour of parents, parental carelessness and environmental influence. From such stressful experience these children also developed some future aspirations like other children living in normal family environment.

In Kenya, Wainaina (1997) found that most of the children are on the street due to family related problems. Author further argues that most of them come from a family background of physical, emotional and/or sexual abuse. Although these findings point to family dysfunction and disintegration as the major reasons why children end up on the streets, it should be noted that most of these family problems are aggravated by poverty.

Abuse/Maltreatment of Street Children

Street children are subjected to all forms of abuse and maltreatment since most of them do not have any guardian and/or safe shelter. People of larger society especially anti-socials, small and petty businessman and even educated people take the full advantage of their helplessness condition. Society has a negative attitude towards them. In fact little sympathy of general population towards street children could be of great help for them to lead a reasonably better life and to get merged into the mainstream of the society.

To understand the effects of violence on children it is important to carry out multidisciplinary research to understand the issue holistically.

There is no security for children on the street. India's antiquated laws are not sensitive at all to their problems and needs, and an overburdened police department views them myopically as a law and order problem.

The following case is of a girl child living on a railway platform:

> ***Case 5:*** *Bharati was nine years old when a gang of homeless boys at the New Delhi railway station, where she also lives, first raped her. She said it happened over and over again after that, until last year she became pregnant and delivered a stillborn child on the platform. The 14-year-old has not been well ever since. A doctor she goes to have told her she has tuberculosis but she has not responded to the treatment. Bharati has not been tested for AIDS, but clinical symptoms point to her having the deadly disease. Bharati collects used plastic water bottles and glasses for a living. She makes about 60 rupees daily (36 rupees to a dollar) from the sales, enough to feed her and pay for her treatment.*

'Not a single girl here is spared,' says Veena Lal of 'Karma Marg', an NGO, which works exclusively with the homeless girls on the station. She said pregnancy rates are high, and the foetus is usually aborted with 'tambi', a traditional method of abortion. Girls are especially vulnerable, points out Devanand Shrivastava of the Salam Balak Trust, as rival gangs rape them to assert their supremacy. 'Rape is a weapon here,' he said.

Sexual abuse is, however, not limited to just girls on the streets. Along with them the boys are also subjected to rape and sexual exploitation and there have been instances of boys getting beaten up if they refused.

A report states that more than intravenous drug use which is another daily habit of the street children; they are at risk from unprotected sex. In a survey carried out by Dr George of the

Salam Balak Trust, an NGO working with street children at the New Delhi railway station, 80 per cent of the street children (mainly boys) interviewed admitted to being homosexuals. 'They know of condoms, but do not want to use them', Dr George said. According to Dr George, the younger boys are abused by those older, and they soon graduate to heterosexual relationships, frequenting the city's red light district, which is next to the railway station.

Street children and youth are ill most of the time. Their disempowerment makes them vulnerable to exploitation, sexual abuse and discrimination. Tuberculosis is known to be among the first symptoms AIDS victims in India display. Twenty per cent of the street children at the New Delhi railway station have TB, says Dr Bitra George, a physician with the 'Salam Balak Trust'. Dr George who carried out the tests says that he cannot say for sure if the other boys were not infected with the virus that causes the deadly AIDS.

In general, girl children are born in India into an inhospitable environment. Discrimination starts right from the birth in case of girl child. Child rape and incest are increasingly being perpetrated on the girl child with the law not adequately protecting her. Every 51 minutes there is a sexual assault on a woman in India, every 26 minutes there is a case of eve-teasing and every 54 minutes there is a rape committed somewhere in India.

This section illustrates numerous incidents a child face worldwide while living on the street, railway platforms, half-dug pavements etc.

A study on street children in Ethiopia was conducted between Latin American and Ethiopian street children particularly to examine the victimization of street children. The study confirms widespread abuse of street children. More than half of the street boys questioned reported being 'regularly' physically attacked. Street life is also highly victimogenic for street girls. Sexual offences, in particular, were widely spread (Lalor, 1999). In another study carried out in Uganda, author found that most children who live and work on the streets had been abused by their step-mothers (Reed, 1996).

The food they eat, frequently outside street-kitchens and shrines that feed the poor as a charitable act, is gruel, stripped of nutrition and barely edible. Food given free by restaurants outside various religious shrines is often demeaning. They are constantly the target of wandering cops, drug peddlers and pimps, prey to violence, drug addiction, sexual abuse and worse. They are easily hauled up for petty crimes and bullied by the so-called law-and-order machinery. As they grow up, their struggle to escape their miserable conditions and create an identity and a living for themselves only binds them tighter to the same tortured lives. Eventually many of them revert to lives of petty crime or become deeply anti-social. Some get drawn into drug-addiction, a few attempt suicides.

The diabolical recurrence of police torture, result/s in a terrible scare in the minds of common citizens that their lives and liberty are under a new peril when the guardians of law gore hBharatin rights to death. The vulnerability of hBharatin rights assumes a traBharatitic, torture some poignancy when the police arm of the state whose function is to protect the citizens and not to commit gruesome offences against them perpetrates the violent violation. The police apparently take the attitude that any child or youth on the street is automatically a delinquent and in their efforts to protect the material belongings of the section of society, which possess them, they take the children into custody.

Indian street children are routinely detained illegally, beaten and tortured and sometimes killed and are viewed as vagrants and criminals by the police. While the extent of juvenile crime is unknown, several factors contribute to this phenomenon: police perceptions of street children, widespread corruption and a culture of police violence, the inadequacy and non-implementation of legal safeguards, and the level of impunity that law enforcement officials enjoy. Police abuse of street children is symptomatic of three problems: the increasing population of street children, the perception of street children as criminals, and the lawlessness of police.

While it is true that street children are sometimes involved in petty theft, drug-trafficking, prostitution and other criminal activities, the police tend to assume that whenever a crime is committed on the street, street children are either involved themselves or know the culprit. Their proximity to a crime is considered reason enough to detain them. This abuse violates both Indian domestic law and international hBharatin rights standards.

Following is the report of a study, which, was conducted, on police personnel's in Delhi in 1992 (*Source:* hBharatin Right Watch, 1992). Five police officials, one at Connaught Place and four at New Delhi railway station, were interviewed to find out their perception of these children and their experiences in dealing with them. The police invariably were quite critical about this children-excepting one officer who was quite sympathetic. According to the three police at the railway station and one at Connaught Place, these children were anti-social elements. They perceive them as thieves, rogues and drug addicts who have to be remanded in institutions and disciplined. They feel there might be only 2 to 3 per cent who are 'honest' and are at the station and street to earn a living.

While working, the children come in contact with the police and municipal officials who object to their work. Many police officials were found to be quite critical about the porter boys who used to work in New Delhi railway stations. They believed that these children were thieves, rouges and drug addicts, who should be put in jail or sent to a remand home (Subrahmanyam and Sondhi, 1990).

Not only, is the situation prevalent in New Delhi station but also innumerable cases are available worldwide. The frequent intervention of the local dada or gang leaders who bully the working child and often ask for a share in their earnings is a regular disturbance on the street.

Street children are the easy targets. They are young, small, poor, and ignorant of their rights and often have no family members who might come to their defense. It does not require much time or effort to detain and beat a child to extract a confession, and the children are unlikely to register formal complaints. When some property (e.g., a bag) belonging to the public is lost/stolen at the station, these children are rounded up and some even framed. To prove that they are not guilty, the children have to do their best to find the culprit and save their skin. Police have financial incentives to resort to violence against children and use street children as a scapegoat for all sorts of things. The most common complaint of street children without families is, to fill the 'quota' which police are expected to do; they were beaten on the street because of money. The prospect of being sent to a remand home, the police station or jail, coupled with the threat of brutal treatment, creates a level of fear and intimidation that forces children or in some cases, their families, to pay the police or suffer the consequences.

Violence is a recurrent event in the daily life of most street children and is caused by misery of an extreme order at his former home. From the recent increasing crime scenario in India it has been observed that most of the crimes are committed by those youths who are neglected, abused and deprived of their basic rights in their formative years of life.

Thilagaraj and Priyamvadha (2000) observed that street children are used as the instruments of professional conmen to evade police and vigilance in a state. To the people of underworld especially those who are involved in organized crime these neglected children are the resources to fulfil their vested interest. Being guided properly these children could be a good resource for the country. There is no reason to believe that these children are less intelligent and less capable compared to children of normal families. These pavement dwellers directly or indirectly are exposed to drug peddling, vandalism, robbery, murdering, sexual commitment, petty theft, addiction, delinquency, bullying, fighting etc.

The street is a place where the children spend a significant part of their time. When families disintegrate, it is usually left to the mother to bring up her (substantial) number of children. The very disadvantaged position of low class women is the next critical factor. In practice, without outside assistance, it is virtually impossible for single women with children to fend for themselves. The widow or divorced wife and her offsprings become then dependent upon series of stepfathers. The sad fact is that males in such a situation occasionally are more interested in the services of their new mate, then in her offspring by a predecessor.

Criminal syndicates, especially for the sale and distribution of illegal drugs, are using more and more children. There is also increasing evidences of children becoming the victims of extortion rackets by slightly older adolescents. A report of the International Confederation of Free Trade Unions discusses 'a new sub-culture of society' involving 'children as young as five years old who live in basements and on the streets of Moscow'. Some of these children work in brothels and use drugs, and suffer horrific psychological damage (*Source: The Statesman,* February 5, 2002).

In one study conducted among African street children in Rwanda, it was found that mostly they were adolescent boys, almost half of whom were homeless (42%), with a high proportion of orphaned children or children who had lost at least one parent. Two variables predicted homelessness: child's guardian and reason for being in street. Qualitative accounts of children conveyed the impact of death of family members, repatriation, imprisonment of parents, and poverty of their lives. The analysis highlighted the need for community-based support for children in alternative guardianship care and for policies to support the reintegration of male youths as prevention strategies for street migration (Veale and Dona, 2003).

The elderly people are mostly abusing street children physically, sexually, and commercially in every moment across the society (Lahor, 1999). As a result, a good number of sexually abused street children have acquired sexually transmitted diseases like HIV/AIDS. Recently in Delhi local Counsellors have taken an initiative to identify the culprits who abused street/working children sexually with the help of sexually abused children to register criminal cases against them (*Source: Times of India,* Jan. 24, 2001). The same initiative should be taken in all the metropolitan cities in India.

The consequences of abuse and exploitation can be devastating. Researchers and clinicians have documented the impact of physical, psychological, sexual abuse and neglect on the children in later life (Helfer, 1975; Sandguard *et al.*, 1974; Ryan *et al.*, 2000; Craig, 2000). Physical damage can range from death, brain damage, and permanent disabilities to minor bruises and scrapes. The psychological consequences can range from lowered sense of self worth to severe psychiatric disorders, including dissociative states. Cognitive problems range from severe organic brain disorders to reduced attention and minor learning disorders. Maltreated children's behavioural problems can include severe, violent and criminal behaviour and suicide as well as inability to relate to peers.

As a result of being abused or neglected, children may also exhibit behaviours such as aggression, provocative behaviour, or withdrawal that could lead to more abuse. Sexually abused children may develop or learn sexualized behaviours that put them at risk of continued abuse by the same perpetrator or new abuse by different perpetrators (Dodge *et al.*, 1990; Friederich, 1988). Ayerst (1999) found that stress and depression were positively correlated for the street children. In another study Vostanis *et al.*, (1998) observed that mothers with a history of abuse and poor social integration were more likely to have children with persistent mental health problems.

So far as intellectual performance and the associations of IQ with the quality of psychosocial functioning of homeless older adolescents are concerned, Rohde *et al.*, (1999) found that the WASE-R scores were comparable to population means, with performance IQ scores tending to be higher than verbal IQ scores.

In India very few studies on street children were completed and reported. For example, Segal and Ashtekar (1994) found that 60 per cent of the children ran away from home to avoid physical abuse and later Segal (1995) observed that 42 per cent of middle class families considered violence as moderate, and 2.9 per cent of these families considered violence in an extreme form. Deb and Senapati (1993) identified four major modes of mal-handling by the parents, viz., physical torture, wilful negligence, exploitation of innocence and dependency of the child and enticement to accept disgraceful life. Deb and Senapati's study further revealed mainly the influences of five aggravating factors for parents' cruelty and socio-pathic family environment, viz., illiteracy, unemployment, conjugal discord, lack of attachment and history of victimization in the early life of parents.

Extensive literature review indicates that no such local study has so far been reported and published revealing street children's creative potentiality, cognitive ability and personality characteristics. Hence, there is a need to carry out study on this issue for developing need-based rehabilitation programme for the street children.

Community Perception about Street Children

The painful fact is that the law lashes the child often but seldom comes to his/her rescue. The Indian mind set strongly believes that any child not living in family is a potential criminal, a threat to society, so keep them in a home or institution or to some place where they can never be seen. The Delhi Corporation passed an order that no child should be seen begging in traffic signals because it is an insult for the city. This is the condition of the street destitute.

All India scenario shows that the place for street dwellers is like jails, where they are treated as 'incorrigible criminals', and remain recipient of some charity. It is found that most street children have more than one instances of mindless police atrocity against them, so much so that they perceive police as the biggest danger. Some of the stories of police atrocities against them are truly heart rending.

In our country several Children's meet are held regularly to make the society aware for their protection and safety. One such 'Girl Child Week' campaigning was organized in New Delhi, during September 18-24, 2001 by Global Movement for Children (GMC) who stated that like adults, children also want to express their feelings. But no one listens them; they came out with a slogan of 'Say yes to Children' (*Source:* Report of *The Pioneer Newspaper,* September 24, 2001).

Prevention, Intervention and Rehabilitation of Street Children

Prevention

For prevention of further growth of street children the following steps could be adopted:

The rapid growth of street children in almost all cities is the result of rapid urbanization through migration. Hence, migration should be checked arranging basic amenities and employment opportunities in the rural areas.

Poverty is one of the main causes behind a large number of children who come to city for finding the means of life. In the rural areas awareness should be generated about the sources of financial support from the banks for cultivation, income-generating activities and/or for small business.

In some families parent-child relationship is not healthy. As a result, a good number of children leave home on account of differences of opinion with the parents. Hence, it is important to launch intervention programme in the rural areas to create awareness about child rearing practices and importance of cordial parent-child relationship. In the urban areas NGO should identify run away children and reintegrate them with the family.

Intervention

For normal and healthy mental and physical development of children basic amenities like adequate nutrition, safe shelter, health care facilities and education should be provided to each and every child. In case of street children more and more NGOs should come forward and provide these facilities.

Non-Formal Education

Basic and/or minimum literacy is needed for each and every child for leading a better, and well-adjusted life. In general, street children do not give importance to education owing to lack of guidance and exposure. For the same some provisions of non-formal education for the street children should be arranged in the form of evening or holiday schools for which infrastructure of Government schools could be utilized with due permission from the authorities of those schools.

In this regard, the Ministry of hBharatin Resource Development, Government of India launched the non-formal education scheme for the street children which was partially successful in the rural areas but in the urban areas it did not get much success owing to lack of infrastructure. NGOs should launch this programme through partnerships approach with the Government and Private schools in the urban areas.

For imparting effective non-formal education to street children services of retired teachers and/or educated people and youths could be utilized. In fact, it would be more beneficial for the NGOs as well as for the needy children. Likewise, a lot of public and private spaces remain vacant/unutilized, which can be utilized for a good cause. For this purpose NGOs should take initiative to explore all these resources and utilize it properly. Sometimes people used to say that shortage of fund is the main barrier to initiate welfare activities. But it is not always correct. NGOs should be innovative enough to generate resources and utilize underutilized resources for the welfare of disadvantaged children.

Vocational Training

It is important to mention that in case of street children emphasis should be given more on vocational training as per the aptitude of the children so that they can find the means of life and lead a better life. But there is one problem. Since these children are occupied in different activities, which are essential for their survival, they can neither afford time nor money for such training. Hence Govt. should introduce a special vocational training programme for the street children and it should be arranged in such a way so that these children can continue their present economic activities if it is not deviant social activity. The street children who are working in automobile or two wheeler repair shops, electrical shops, tailoring shops and the like can be given training in the respective trades to develop specialized skills. The children who work as rag pickers or doing odd jobs with no skill can select a suitable vocation after ascertaining their aptitude.

For the welfare and rehabilitation of street children a number of NGOs are working in different parts of the country and some of them are working effectively while majority of them lack proper planning and do not know how to implement the programme. They also lack basic knowledge and expertise about monitoring and documentation. As a result, it is very difficult to understand the efficacy of the programme.

Special Arrangements and Night Shelter for the Street Children Especially for the Girl Children

Street children are subjected to all forms of abuse and maltreatment in every day life. Besides other harassment girl children are more prone to sexual abuse. Hence, a safe nigh shelter is urgently needed for these children especially girl children to protect them from anti-socials and from pimps.

This apart, an arrangement for keeping the belongings of children is required. So night shelter should have the same arrangements.

Lack of adequate clothing is another problem faced by the street children. In order to solve this problem, NGOs should take initiative to collect used and old cloths from the high and middle class families and distribute the same to the street children.

Resource Generation

For taking up different programmes for the street children resource is required. Besides resources of government and international funding agencies, NGOs should initiate dialogue with the private agencies like industrialists, business houses and trust bodies to motivate them for funding programmes for street children.

Apart from financial resource, students and teachers should be motivated to take up social work programmes both individually and collectively for street and working children like organizing literacy camps, recreational meets, cultural programmes in association with the help of voluntary organizations.

Rehabilitation of Street Children

Now, there is a general feeling among people of all walks of life that street children should be helped and rescued. They should be provided with proper food, clothing and safe shelter in the form of an orphanage. For giving shelter to these neglected, abused children and to take care of their basic needs a lot of national and international funding agencies have come forward with their commitments. Side by side local NGOs are also working for the rehabilitation of these children.

In the recent decade problems of disadvantaged children especially street children drew attention of academicians and researchers. A number of studies on different dimensions of street children especially for rehabilitation of the street children have been carried out in India by the researchers. In this regard, in a follow-up study Deb *et al.* (1997) found that supportive counselling and continuous efforts brought some positive change in the outlook of street children resulting in moderate improvement in interpersonal relationships and some interest in vocational training. The findings of that study suggest detachment of street children from pathogenic parental influence during rehabilitation.

It has also been observed that street children have developed dare devil attitude towards the society because of prolonged deprivation (Deb, 1996a). In another action research study Deb (1996b) observed that seven out of 10 street children were successfully institutionalized and pursuing their studies satisfactorily while the remaining three children were unable to settle down to institution and became dropouts due to certain personal and environmental factors like unfavourable parental influences, pathological and deviant behaviour of either of the parents, low intelligence, organic impairment and uncongenial living environment.

Findings of a study suggest that for merging street children into the mainstream of the society they should be orientated with socialization process first. For bringing positive changes in street children's behaviour encouragement towards their performance and introduction of reward system should be initiated. For facilitation of rehabilitation process cooperation of guardians, if available is urgently needed. The Welfare Agency should hold periodic meetings with the guardians to make them understand about their important role in motivating children towards studies. Feedback about children's performance and conduct should be given to the respective guardian. Linkage should be established with the guardian who does not visit the child at all. Authorities of welfare organizations should initiate dialogue with the authorities of residential schools for facilitating the admission of these children (Deb and Mitra, 2002).

Role of Media

Media can take active role to sensitize the larger society about the problems of disadvantaged children in general and street children in particular which will in turn help in developing a sympathetic attitude towards street children. Media should also encourage issueless parents to adopt street children, which is an alternative approach to rehabilitate the street children.

Socio and Legal Measures for Welfare of Disadvantaged Children

The Juvenile Justice (Care and Protection of Children) Act, 2000

The stated law repealed the previous law meant for juveniles called 'The Juvenile Justice Act', 1986. In this law the issue of childcare and protection has given due importance. The following section has abided prevention of cruelty to juveniles.

> ***Section 23: Punishment for Cruelty to Juvenile or Child:*** *Whoever, having the actual charge of, or control over, a juvenile or the child, assaults, abandons, exposes or wilfully neglects the juvenile or causes or procures him to be assaulted, abandoned, exposed or neglected in a manner likely to cause such juvenile or the child unnecessary mental or physical suffering shall be punishable with imprisonment for a term which may extend to six months, or fine, or with both.*
>
> ***Section 24: Employment of Juvenile or Child for Begging:*** *(i) Whoever employs or uses any juveniles or the child for the purpose or causes any juvenile to beg shall be punishable with imprisonment for a term which may extend to three years and shall also be liable to fine.*
>
> *(ii) Whoever, having the actual charge of, or control over, a juvenile of the child abets the commission of the offence punishable under sub-section (1), shall be punishable with imprisonment for a term which may extend to one year and shall also be liable to fine.*
>
> ***Section 26: Exploitation of Juvenile or Child Employee:*** *Whoever, ostensibly procures a juvenile of the child for the purpose of any hazardous employment keeps him in bondage and with holds his earnings or uses such earning for his own purposes*

shall be punishable with imprisonment for a term which may extend to three years and shall also be liable to fine.

Child Welfare and Juvenile Justice: An Integrated Programme for Street Children under the Ministry of Social Justice and Empowerment, Government of India

Goal: Full and wholesome development of children without homes and family ties.

Aim: Prevention of destitution and withdrawal of children from a life on the street and their placement into national mainstream.

Objective: Provision of shelter, nutrition, health care, sanitation and hygiene, safe drinking water, education and recreational facilities and protection against abuse and exploitation to destitute and neglected street children.

Strategy: Developing awareness and providing support to build capacity of the Government (Central, State and Local), non-Governmental organizations and the community at large to realize the rights of the child enshrined in the Convention on the rights of the Child and in the Juvenile Justice Act, 1986.

Target Group: The programme will endeavour to provide non-institutional support necessary for the wholesome development of street children particularly those without homes and family ties and children especially vulnerable to abuse and exploitation such as children of sex workers and children of pavement dwellers. Children living in slums and with their parents shall be excluded from the coverage of the revised scheme as experience has shown that they tend to dominate the programme at the expense of more vulnerable children such as those without homes and family ties. Also the programme of other Ministries such as hBharatin Resource Development, Urban Areas and Employment and labour already cover children living in urban slums.

Programme Components

- City level surveys to determine the number of destitute and neglected street children.

- Documentation of the existing facilities both governmental as well as non-governmental, available to meet the developmental needs of these children and preparation of city level plans of actions.
- Contact programmers offering counselling, guidance and referral services to destitute and neglected children aimed at their eventual withdrawn from a life on the street.
- Establishment of 24 hours drop-in shelters for children with facilities for night stay, safe drinking water, bathing, latrines, first-aid and recreation.
- Non-formal education programme imparting literacy, numeracy and life education.
- Programme for reintegration of children with their families and placement of destitute and children in foster care homes/hostels and residential schools and their maintenance therein.
- Programmes for enrolment of these children in schools including full support for subsistence, education, nutrition, recreation and their wholesome development.
- Programmes providing facilities for training in meaningful vocations, trades and skills to earning capacity.
- Programmes for occupational placement of destitute and neglected children.
- Programmes aimed at mobilizing preventive health services and providing access to treatment facilities.
- Programme aimed at providing recreational facilities.
- Post ICDS/Anganwadi programmes for children beyond 6 years of age who are not enrolled in schools, providing health care and nutritional supplement as well as special assistance to facilitate enrolment in schools.
- Programmes for capacity building of NGOs, local bodies and State Governments to undertake related responsibility.
- Programme for advocacy and awareness building on Child Rights.
- Any other programme consistent with the Rights of the Child and/or covered under the Juvenile Justice Act, 1986.

Eligibility for Assistance

Under the scheme, grants shall be sanctioned subject to terms and conditions laid down by this Ministry and provided applications for the same is received as per prescribed proforma. The agencies eligible for assistance shall be as follows:

- State Governments and Union Territory Administrations.
- Institutions or organizations set-up by Government as autonomous bodies either under a statue or as a society registered under the Societies Registration Act, 1860 or otherwise.
- Educational and other institutions of the like local bodies and cooperative societies.
- Non-Government Organizations meeting the following requirements:

  (i) It is a registered body under an appropriate Act so that it gets a corporate status and a legal personality and a group liability is for its activities.
  (ii) It has an appropriate administrative structure and a duly constituted managing/executive committee.
  (iii) The aim and objects of the organization and programmes in fulfilment of these aims and objects and preciously laid down; and
  (iv) The organization is initiated and governed by its own members on democratic principles, without any external control.
  (v) The organization shall not run for profit to any individual or a body of individuals and shall take an undertaking to submit periodically and punctually reports and returns as prescribed from time to time by the Government of India (Ministry of Social Justice and Empowerment, Govt. of India).

The concerned organization should have been registered for a period of two years but in case of North-Eastern region, Jammu and Kashmir, desert areas and under-served/represented areas the condition of two years will not be applicable. In any other deserving cases where an individual or a group of individuals has substantial background experience in specific sector and the individual or group of individuals want to work in that area the condition of two years may be relaxed by Secretary of Social Justice and Empowerment.

Funding Pattern

The Government of India will provide up to 90 per cent of the cost of the project and remaining shall be borne by the organization/ institution concerned. In case of State Government/Municipal Bodies undertaking execution of any activity directly the funding pattern will remain 90:10 between the Government of India and the State Government/Municipal Corporation. However, where the Union Territory Administration takes up an activity, 100 per cent of the cost shall be borne by the Government of India. Similarly, if the Ministry of Social Justice and Empowerment itself executes any part of the programme (city-wise enumerations, appointment of lead consultants/Chartered Accountants, advocacy and awareness generation activities, etc.) full cost shall be payable from budgetary allocations made for the programme.

Extent of Support to the Project

Under the programme while no pre-defined cost heads shall be stipulated, at the project formulation stage each implementing agency shall submit a detailed proposal clearly bringing out programme modalities and individual expenditure heads. The Ministry of Social Justice and Empowerment while approving the projects shall indicate the extent of support to the project as a whole as well as to each component of the project, which shall not be variable except by prior approval of the Ministry. The staffing norms and honorarium for full time and part time staff will broadly be on the pattern of the other schemes of the Ministry. Depending upon the type of activity and the nature of service an appropriate amount not exceeding Rs. 15 lakhs per annum will be sanctioned as recurring cost to each project. In exceptional cases, the ceiling may be relaxed by the Secretary of Social Justice and Empowerment.

Application and Sanction

An organization desirous to apply for grant-in-aid under this programme will send its application to an authority or body designated for the purpose by the Ministry of Social Justice and Empowerment.

On receipt of an application for grant-in-aid, inspection will be undertaken by the prescribed agency. On the basis of the inspection report of the prescribed agency, the proposal will duly be processed.

Steps for Effective Implementation of Intervention Programme

The following steps are suggested for effective implementation of intervention programme for the disadvantaged children in general and street children in particular on the basis of author's first hand field and research experience:

- Identification of disadvantaged and/or street children.
- Listen to their problems, basic requirements/needs and try to contact with the family members for reintegration.
- Thorough medical examination should be done and extend medical services, if required.
- Extend individual and group counselling for establishing trust building relationship and to develop fellow feeling and improve group cohesiveness.
- Extend family counselling, if parents or either of the parents are available and seek their cooperation for future career of the child.
- Provide non-formal education to disadvantaged/street children to make them familiar with the socialization process.
- Provide formal education at least up to primary level and more in case of better performance.
- Ascertain the aptitude and interest of the disadvantaged/ street children for providing need-based and potential vocational training.
- Follow-up and monitoring of performance and movement of these children as they are likely to be involved in deviant

activities again under the influence of peer group members and may run away from Home and/or Residential School.

- Organize outings and cultural programmes for the children for recreation and to develop a positive feeling about life.
- Give feedback to the children periodically about their performance, which will motivate them to perform better.
- Reward system should be introduced to reinforce their motivation and active involvement children in various activities of an intervention programme.
- Precautions should be taken while selecting staff/personnel for dealing with disadvantaged/street children. Effort should be made to select personnel with child friendly attitude and preferably female candidate with motivation and interest in this work. Otherwise, despite all other proper arrangements one may not get the better and /or expected results from the programme.
- Monitoring of performance of staff/counsellors who directly deal with the children and to take appropriate measures. In this regard, it is important to speak to the beneficiary children to gauge their perception about the behaviour of the service providers/counsellors/trainers.
- Develop coordination and partnership with other similar agencies/NGOs for sharing of resources and for working together so that basic needs of the children are addressed. One organization may not have all the facilities. So, coordination and partnership with other similar agencies/ NGOs will help to fill up the gaps.
- Periodic evaluation of intervention programme for effective implementation of the same by an out side agency. Evaluation does not necessarily mean to criticize the designer of the programme and/or to find out the faults of a progrmme, rather it helps to understand the shortcomings in service delivery, if any and thereby helps in taking course corrective measures.
- Attend and share your learning experience, whether positive or negative, in a seminar/workshops/conferences so that others can learn from your experience and replicate the positive results, if necessary.

- Dissemination of information and/or outcome of an intervention programme through publication of papers in the journals and in periodicals for wider coverage of audiences.

Latest Selective Study Findings

Roy *et al*. (2003) carried out a study to estimate the incidence rate of injection drug use in the population in North America and to identify predictors of injection drug use. Findings revealed that injection drug use is frequent among street youths, but prevention appears possible. Independent predictors of initiation were recent episode of homelessness; age younger than 18 years; being tattooed; recently using hallucinogens, heroin, and cocaine/crack/freebase; having a friend who injects drugs; and having ever experienced extrafamilial sexual abuse.

Ayuku *et al.* (2003) has applied The Maastricht Social Network Analysis (MSNA) as the core instrument in a battery to measure the health status of the street children. Owing to the absence of census data of street children in Kenya and the difficulty in tracking this mobile population, the authors adopted mixed approach i.e., snowball and convenience sampling techniques to recruit research subjects. Three hundred street and orphanage children, and 100 primary school children as a control group, were included in the study. The MSNA provided a social diagnosis that complements the clinical diagnosis of the health status of the sample. Only one main methodological question is presented: is the MSNA applicable to describe the personal social networks of (1) children and (2) people living in a Kenyan culture? Qualitative field observations, key informant interviews and focus groups inform the adaptation of the MSNA instrument, and improve its face validity. A case series analysis is presented. Findings revealed that the street children population consists of distinct subgroups defined by the UNICEF classification as 'on' and 'of' the street and by gender. Street children networks have some notable deficiencies depending on the subgroup. Constant across the groups is the deficiency of service providers in their networks. The conclusion is that the MSNA is a suitable instrument for obtaining a social diagnosis and gathering other useful information that helps in understanding the social and health backgrounds, status and daily experiences of Kenyan scavenging street children. Applying the MSNA protocol was successful in the diagnosis and interpretation of the findings.

Dekel *et al*. (2003) followed 345 Israeli youngsters who had been residents of two shelters for runaway and homeless youths, 6-12 weeks after their departure. Telephone interviews were conducted with the youngsters, their parents, and social workers in the community. A majority of the youngsters had either returned to their family homes, or had been placed out of home. Their residential stability was found to be low. Post-shelter place of residence was related to length of stay at the shelter, amount of contact with their family while at the shelter, and manner of departure. Findings of the study lead to a typology of shelter uses, and also raise questions about the extent to which shelters achieve their declared goals.

Weber *et al*. (2002) compared human immunodeficiency virus (HIV) risk factors among female street youths involved in prostitution and those with no history of prostitution. Youths aged 14 to 25 years were recruited into the Montreal Street Youth Cohort. Of the girls, 88 (27%) reported involvement in prostitution, and 177 girls reported no history of prostitution at the baseline interview. Girls involved in prostitution were two times and five times more likely to have reported bingeing on alcohol and on drugs, respectively. A history of injection drug use was four times more likely to have been reported by girls involved in prostitution. Further, these girls were 2.5 times more likely to have reported injected cocaine as their drug of choice. Girls involved in prostitution were younger the first time they had consensual sex and were twice as likely to have reported anal sex. Consistent condom use for anal, vaginal, and oral sex was low for all girls. Girls involved in prostitution reported more risky sexual partners. In conclusion, girls involved in prostitution may be at increased risk of HIV infection due to their injection drug use and risky sexual behaviours. Unique intervention strategies are necessary for reducing HIV infection among female street youths involved in prostitution.

Tyler and Cauce (2002) examined abuse specific variables among homeless and runaway adolescents and looked at perpetrators of childhood abuse. A total of 372 homeless and runaway adolescents were interviewed using a systematic sampling strategy in metropolitan Seattle. Young people were interviewed on the streets and in shelters by outreach workers in youth service agencies. Findings revealed that about one-half of these young people reported being physically abused and almost one-third experienced sexual abuse. Females experienced significantly higher rates of sexual abuse compared to males, and sexual minority youth experienced significantly higher rates of physical and sexual abuse compared to heterosexual youth. Average duration of physical and sexual abuse was 5 and 2 years, respectively. Both types of abuse were rated as extremely violent by more than half of those who were abused. The average number of different perpetrators of physical and sexual abuse was four and three, respectively. Biological parents were the majority of perpetrators for physical abuse whereas non-family members most often perpetrated sexual abuse. Average age of perpetrators was late 20s to early 30s and the majority of perpetrators were male for both types of abuse. The pattern of exploitation and victimization within the family may have serious and cumulative developmental consequences for these youth as they enter the street environment. Early intervention programs are needed to break the cycle of exploitation and abuse that adolescents experience within the family. Without intervention, many of these youth may be at risk of future exploitation and re-victimization out on the street.

According to Rew (2002) there is a significant and growing number of adolescents who separate early from their families and become homeless. These youths are heterogeneous in terms of gender, race, ethnicity, and socioeconomic status, but the majority come from families that have been disruptive or dysfunctional in some way. Homeless adolescents are vulnerable to a variety of physical and psychologic problems related not only to their family histories but to the stressful environments in which they try to survive. Although numerous federal, state, and local programs have been developed to meet their needs for shelter, health care, and education, much remains to be done to ensure their healthy development and to prepare them for responsible life in the larger society.

Woods *et al.* (2002) evaluated the factors associated with initiation of services in the Boston HAPPENS Program, which is a collaborative network of care consisting of multi-service outreach agencies, community health centers and hospitals, for human immunodeficiency virus (HIV)-positive. The program served 2116 youth who were 19.8 +/- 2.9 years old; 64 per cent female; 45 per cent youth of colour; 16 per cent gay/lesbian, bisexual, or undecided; and 10 per cent homeless or runaway. At first contact with the program, 56 per cent received outreach services; and 91 per cent received a health intervention. Among those receiving a health intervention, 55 per cent had HIV counselling and testing services, 49 per cent medical care, 24 per cent case management, and 9 per cent mental health services. HIV-positive youth needed more contacts before a first medical visit than those who were HIV-negative or untested ($p < 0.001$). Different kinds of service sites reached different populations of at-risk youth. Logistic regression modeling showed that for young women, older age, lesbian-bisexual orientation, substance use, high-risk sexual behaviours, and receiving outreach services at first contact were independent predictors of initiation of services at outreach agencies; however, unprotected sex with males, and pregnancy were associated with a greater likelihood of care at hospitals or community health centers. For young men, older age, Asian/other ethnicity, and substance abuse were associated with care at outreach agencies; however, positive HIV status and unprotected sex with females were associated with care at hospitals or community health centers. Comprehensive networks of care offering a continuum of services and a variety of entry routes and types of care sites are needed to connect underserved youth to health care.

Morakinyo and Odejide (2002) made an attempt to determine the pattern of psychoactive substance use among street children and also explored those socio-demographic and street factors that could be related to current psychoactive substance use. Using a multistage sampling method in a local government area in Nigeria, 180 children aged 18 years and below who had left the custody of their parents for a period of not less than a month were interviewed. Findings revealed that the most commonly used psychoactive substances were alcohol, kolanut, tobacco and cannabis. None of the respondents reported the use of cocaine, opiates or hallucinogens. Length of stay on the street was found to be significantly predictive of current psychoactive substance use. The readily available and relatively cheap substances were in common use among street children with the length of stay on the street being a significant predictive factor.

Ribeiro and Ciampone (2002) reported experience of homeless children about their living in shelters. The data, gathered by individual interviews, were organized according to the method of the Analysis of Contents and principles of the theory of the Social Representation. The categories detached from the speech transcript, were grouped into meaningful experiences for the children, among which 'the shelters'. The analyses of this category showed clearly that the lack of a personal and affectionate attendance in the shelters contributes to the children choosing to stay in the streets.

The objective of Rew's (2003) study was to explore self-care attitudes and behaviours of homeless adolescents. Individual interviews were conducted with 15 homeless adolescents. Interviews were audiotaped, transcribed verbatim, and analyzed using the constant comparative method of grounded theory. Findings revealed a basic social process of taking care of oneself in a high-risk environment. This basic social process was supported by three categories: Becoming Aware of Oneself, Staying Alive With Limited Resources, and Handling One's Own Health, each including two processes. Findings support Orem's conceptualizations of self-care and self-care agency and suggest the need for programs to support further healthy growth and development among homeless adolescents.

Snell (2002) explored and analyzed the help-seeking and risk-taking behaviour of Black urban street youth in Washington, DC, USA and Cape Town, South Africa. The target population of 100 youths came from the streets of Washington, DC and Cape Town, South Africa. Structured face-to-face interviews and direct observation of informal and formal settings where youths congregated were used to gather data. Major findings indicate that the majority received high levels of support from families and friends.

In terms of formal systems, social and mental health services are viewed as much less accessible or useful. Youths were knowledgeable about HIV/AIDS but did not translate this into safer sexual practices. Implications for health and social policy are outlined.

Ensign (2003) provided an overview of the main ethical challenges of conducting qualitative research with homeless youths and proposed possible solutions to these challenges. This paper was informed by a review of professional guidelines ıor the ethical conduct of adolescent health research, national (US) and international bioethics bibliographical searches, and personal experience with qualitative research with homeless youths. The main ethical challenges of conducting qualitative research with homeless youths include establishing and maintaining healthy researcher roles and boundaries, addressing the risks of researcher burn-out and safety issues, assuring optimal confidentiality, and avoiding sensationalism and voyeurism. It is important for qualitative researchers who work with vulnerable populations to ensure that research is conducted in the most ethical way possible.

Rew and Horner (2003) conducted a secondary research to identify strengths that protect homeless youth. Findings revealed two types of strengths emerged: resources and self-improvement. Resources served as the foundation for survival whereas self-improvement served as a process that enabled youth to consider a more healthy future. By recognizing the many strengths of homeless youth, nurses may develop community-based programs to help this population reenter society.

According to Kidd (2003), the use of inadequate operational definitions of suicidal behaviour is often a limitation of suicide research. In his article, the results of an exploratory qualitative study of street youth suicidality was contrasted with the existing literature to highlight the problems associated with defining suicidal behaviours. It was argued through the use of the case example of street youth that accurate and detailed assessment of suicidal history, context, and intent was necessary to avoid substantial threats to the validity and clinical use of research findings.

Beech *et al*. (2003) conducted a cross-sectional study covering 150 homeless youth to determine the predictors of human immunodeficiency virus (HIV) and hepatitis infections among homeless youth. Venous blood samples were collected as well. Most respondents (95%) had engaged in sexual intercourse, with 13 years as the median age at first coitus. Approximately 36 per cent indicated they had exchanged sex for food, shelter, or drugs. Although youth reported a high rate of consistent condom use, 16 per cent of the sample tested positive for HIV, 17 per cent tested positive for hepatitis B (HBV), and 12 per cent tested positive for hepatitis C (HCV). The positive rates for HIV, HBV, and HCV observed in this study are higher than those of many previous reports among street youth.

Ginzler et al., (2003) examined the sequence of substance-use among 375 street youth (aged between 13-21) who were interviewed from 1994-99 in Seattle, Washington. Based on the "gateway theory," participants were categorized into six profiles to describe the order in which they initiated use of various substances (i.e., alcohol, marijuana, other drugs), or classified as non-progressors if they had not tried all three classes of drugs. Youth progressing in the hypothesized gateway order (i.e., alcohol preceding marijuana, followed by other drugs) initiated their use at an earlier age than youth who had not progressed through all three substance classes. However, there was no relationship between a substance initiation profile and current substance-use. Implications include the recognition that street youth may follow different patterns of use than normative groups, and that interventions geared toward youth who use substances heavily must include contextual factors, in addition to substance-use history.

Paradise and Cauce (2003) conducted a study to find out the relationship between adolescent substance use and delinquent behaviour in a sample of homeless young people. Confirmatory factor analyses indicated that delinquency and substance use are best described as discrete factors, and competing theoretical models of the longitudinal association between these two factors were examined using structural equations modeling techniques. The results suggest that delinquent behaviour is associated with changes in alcohol, marijuana, and drug use across time. This effect was statistically significant over relatively brief lags in time of six months or less. Combined with previous results, these findings challenge the utility of single-factor explanations of adolescent deviance for at-risk populations and suggest that the relationship between substance use and externalizing across time may be more dynamic than previously thought.

Wittig *et al.* (1997) examined whether drug use among Honduran street children is a function of developmental social isolation from cultural and structural influences. Data from 1,244 children working and/or living on the streets of Tegucigalpa are described, separating 'market' children from 'street' children. The latter group is then divided into those who sniff glue and those who do not to identify salient distinguishing factors. An OLS regression of drug usage on these variables results in a model that explains 75 per cent of the variance, where family relations, length of time on the street, and delinquency are the most important factors.

Kidd and Kral (2002) found a history of attempted suicide among 76 per cent of the street youth. Further probing revealed that isolation, rejection/betrayal, lack of control, and most centrally, low self-worth are some of the factors responsible for attempt to commit suicide. Additionally it was found that trading sex, in which most participants had been or were currently involved, was linked with their suicidal experiences and may account for the high attempt rate.

According to Filgueiras (1993) the absence of familial support leads these marginalized adolescents vulnerable to pregnancy and illegal abortion; their illiteracy and non-school attendance isolates them from sources of information about sexuality and birth control. Filgueiras further stated Government agencies must assume responsibility for providing these citizens with shelter, food, access to the public school system with a culturally sensitive curriculum, and health services that address the special needs of this population. Non-governmental organizations, on the other hand, are urged to develop innovative programs for street children, including outreach programs, educational strategies and materials, legal advocacy, hot-lines, and itinerant van units.

Tantoco (1993) stated that almost 2 million of Manila's 2.5 million children younger than 15 years old live on or below the poverty line. 75,000 of these children live on the streets after having run away from home or being abandoned. They beg, steal, scavenge for food, and sell newspapers, cigarettes, and leis. About 20,000 of the street children prostitute themselves. It is these latter children and adolescents who are at particular risk of HIV infection. Studies in the Philippines indicate that 91 per cent of reported HIV infections are among individuals aged 15-44, the male/female infection ratio is one to one, the transmission rate is 45 per cent, and the most common mode of transmission is through heterosexual intercourse. The high incidence of child sexual abuse and child prostitution in the Philippines would suggest that there are a significant number of children and adolescents under age 15 who are infected with HIV.

MacLean *et al.* (1999) assessed three models of adolescent substance use like the deviance-prone, affect-regulation, and normative development models regarding their ability to predict the substance use of a high-risk homeless adolescent sample with high rates of deviance, depression, and substance use. Hierarchical multiple regression analyses that included tests for curvilinear and gender interaction effects were performed. Results supported the deviance-prone model most strongly, with delinquency but not aggressive behaviour predicting substance use. The affect-regulation model received support for females but not for males. With respect to the normative development model, results did not indicate that moderate substance users were better off than abstainers in terms of negative affect or interpersonal relationships.

Adlaf *et al.* (1999) made an attempt to describe the configuration of mental health and substance use outcomes among 211 street youths in Toronto, Ontario, Canada. The revealed that distress, self-esteem, psychotic thoughts, attempted suicide, alcohol problems, drug problems, dual substance problems, and dual disorders varied significantly among the eight clusters. Overall, the findings suggest the need for differential programming. The data showed that risk factors, mental health, and substance use outcomes vary among this population. Also, for some the web of mental health and substance use problems is inseparable.

Booth *et al.* (1999) assessed HIV-related drug and sex risk behaviours and evaluated factors associated with change in risk behaviours among runaway and homeless adolescents. Findings revealed that despite the intervention's success in increasing knowledge of HIV and AIDS, the association between knowledge, perceived likelihood of infection and high risk behaviours suggest that, without other alternatives, runaways will maintain their risks. The association noted between lower concern and high risk behaviours underscores the challenge faced in developing effective interventions with this population.

Ennett *et al.* (1999) made an attempt to understand the personal social networks of runaway and homeless youth and examined network characteristics of these children associated with risky behaviours. Although authors found that most youth reported current social relationships, a significant minority (26%) did not. Youth without a social network were significantly more likely to report current illicit drug use, multiple sex partners, and survival sex than youth with a network. For youth with a network, the networks were small, strong in affective and supportive qualities, comprised primarily of friends, typically included an alcohol or illicit drug user, and usually were not a source of pressure for risky behaviours.

Senanayake *et al.* (1998) studied the background, life styles, health and prevalence of abuse of street children in Colombo. The children were aged between 4 and 17 years. Sixty four per cent were males and 18 per cent belonged to ethnic minorities. The majority (84%) had family ties. Family disintegration was mentioned as the cause for life on the streets by 36 per cent. Child labour was reported in 38 per cent. 16 per cent admitted to being sexually abused. 20 per cent were tobacco smokers. Respiratory and skin infections, and injuries incurred in road traffic accidents were the main causes of morbidity. Street children in Colombo are an abused and exploited group. Road traffic accidents, and physical and sexual abuse are the main hazards of the street they are exposed to.

Greene and Ringwalt (1998) found that youth living on the streets had the highest lifetime rates of pregnancy (48%), followed by youth residing in shelters (33%) and household youth (<10%).

Shelter and street youth were at much greater risk of having ever been pregnant than were youth in households, regardless of whether they had recent runaway or homeless experiences. Such youth need comprehensive services, including pregnancy prevention, family planning, and prenatal and parenting services.

According to Inciardi and Surratt (1998) risk of exposure to HIV is rapidly becoming an area of concern among street youths in Brazil since a large number of them are engaging in unprotected sexual acts, both remunerated and nonremunerated. Moreover, Brazil's street children are targets of fear. Because of their drug use, predatory crimes, and general unacceptability on urban thoroughfares, they are frequently the targets of local vigilante groups, drug gangs, and police 'death squads.'

REFERENCES

Adlaf, E.M., and Zdanowicz, Y.M. (1999). A Cluster-Analytic Study Of Substance Problems And Mental Health Among Street Youths, *American Journal of Drug and Alcohol Abuse,* 25(4):639-60.

Ayerst SL (1999). Depression and Stress in Street Youth. *Adolescence,* 34 (135), 567-75.

Ayuku, D., Odero, W., Kaplan, C., De Bruyn, R., and De Vries, M. (2003). Social Network Analysis For Health And Social Interventions Among Kenyan Scavenging Street Children. *Health Policy Plan,* 18(1):109-18.

Beech, B.M., Myers, L., Beech, D.J., and Kernick, N.S. (2003). Human Immunodeficiency Syndrome And Hepatitis B And C Infections Among Homeless Adolescents. *Semin Pediatr Infect Dis.,*14(1):12-9.

Blanc, C. *et al.*, (1994). *Urban Children in Distress: Global Predicaments and Innovative Strategies.* Gordon and Breach, New York and UNICEF.

Bosco Institute of Social Work (1989). Situation Analysis of Street Children in Madras City. Sacted Heart College. Tirupattur.

Booth, R.E., Zhang, Y., and Kwiatkowski, C.F. (1999). The Challenge Of Changing Drug And Sex Risk Behaviours Of Runaway And Homeless Adolescents. *Child Abuse & Neglect,* 23(12):1295-306.

Craig, T. K., and Hodson S. (2000). Homeless Youth in London: II. Accommodation, Employment and Health Outcomes at 1 Year. *Psychological-Medicine,* 30, (1): 187-94.

Deb, Sibnath and Senapati, Shishir (1993). Safety Needs of Abused Proletarian Bengalee Children (Major Modes of Causal Factors). *Indian Journal of Psychological Issues,* 1 (1): 1-9.

Deb, Sibnath, Datta K. and Ghosh M. (1997). Modification of a Deviant Street Children's Behaviour: An In-depth Case Study. *Indian Journal of Criminology,* 25 (1): 15-22.

Deb, Sibnath (1996a). Perception of Juvenile Delinquents Towards the Society. Paper presented in the *4th Asian Conference on Child Abuse & Neglect,* organized by the Indian Institute of Psychological and Educational Research, Calcutta, India held between 25-27 Nov. 1996.

Deb, Sibnath (1996b). Institutionalization of Abused Street Children: An In-depth Study. Paper presented in the *11th International Congress on Child Abuse and Neglect,* organized by the University of Dublin, Ireland between August. 18-21.

Deb, Sibnath and Mitra, Kathakali (2002a). Deviance Among Disadvantaged Children in Kolkata and Reasons Thereof. *Indian Journal of Criminology and Criminalistics,* XXII, 1: 41-59.

Deb, Sibnath and Mitra, Kathakali (2002b). Lost Childhood - Unraveling the Story Behind the Street Life. The 26th International Conference of Cross-cultural Psychology held in Yogyakarta, Indonesia between July 15-19, 2002.

Dekel, R., Peled, E., and Spiro, S.E. (2003). Shelters For Houseless Youth: A Follow-Up Evaluation. *J Adolesc.,* 26(2):201-12.

Dodge, K.A., Bates, J. E., and Pettit, G.S. (1990). Mechanisms in the Cycle of Violence. *Science,* 250, 1678-1683.

EASCAP - HRD, United Nations, NY (2002). Training Manual on Psychosocial and Medical Services for Sexually Abused and Sexually Exploited Children and Youth.

Ensign, J. (2003). Ethical Issues In Qualitative Health Research With Homeless Youths. *J Adv Nurs.,* 43(1):43-50.

Ennett, S.T., Bailey, S.L., and Federman, E.B. (1999). Social Network Characteristics Associated With Risky Behaviours Among Runaway And Homeless Youth. *J Health Soc Behav.,* 40(1):63-78.

Filgueiras, A. (1993). Needs of Rio Street Children. *Plan Parent Chall,* 2:22-4.

Ginzler, J.A., Cochran, B.N., Domenech-Rodriguez, M., Cauce, A.M., and Whitbeck, L.B. (2003). Sequential Progression Of Substance Use Among Homeless Youth: An Empirical Investigation Of The Gateway Theory. *Subst Use Misuse,* 38(3-6):725-58.

Ghosh, A. (1992). *Street Children of Calcutta - A Situational Analysis.* National Labour Institute, Noida, UP.

Glauser, B., (1990). *Street Children: Deconstructing a Construct: Contemporary Issues Temporary Issues in Sociological Study of Childhood,* London, New York, Philadelphia, The Freeman Press.

Greene, J.M., and Ringwalt, C.L. (1998). Pregnancy Among Three National Samples Of Runaway And Homeless Youth. *Journal of Adolescent Health,* 23 (6):370-7.

Helfer, R.E. (1975). Why Most Physicians Don't Get Involved in Child Abuse Cases and What To Do About it. *Children Today,* 4, 29-32.

Johnson, T.P., Aschkenasy, J.R., Herbers, M.R., and Gillenwater, S.A. (1996). Self-Reported Risk Factors For AIDS Among Homeless Youth. AIDS *Educ Prev.*, 8(4):308-22.

Kidd, S.A., and Kral, M.J. (2002). Suicide And Prostitution Among Street Youth: A Qualitative Analysis. *Adolescence,*37(146):411-30.

Koller, S.H., and Hutz, C.S (2002). Street Children: Psychological Perspectives; University of Rio Grande do Sul Porto Alegre; Brazil.

Lalor, K.J. (1999). Street Children: A Comparative Perspective. *Child Abuse and Neglect,* 23(8), 759-70.

MacLean, M.G., Paradise, M.J., and Cauce, A.M. (1999). Substance Use And Psychological Adjustment In Homeless Adolescents: A Test Of Three Models. *Am J Community Psychol.,*27(3):405-27.

Morakinyo, J., and Odejide, A.O. (2002). A Community Based Study Of Patterns Of Psychoactive Substance Use Among Street Children In A Local Government Area Of Nigeria. *Drug Alcohol Depend,* 20;71(2):109-16.

Paradise, M.J., and Cauce, A.M. (2003). Substance Use And Delinquency During Adolescence: A Prospective Look At An At-Risk Sample. Subst Use *Misuse,* 38(3-6):701-23.

Patro, Bijoy Basant (1997). INDIA-AIDS: *Street Children Are Most Vulnerable; Inter Press News Service (IPS); Wednesday, 3 September 1997,* New Delhi.

Pinto, Gerry (1990). Street Children-An Urban Phenomenon. *PROCEDINGS: Ist Asian Regional Conference,* Calcutta, 23-24.

Pinto, Rita, P. and Nangia, Parveen (1988). Children in Specially Difficult Circumstances in Delhi. Focus on working and Street Children. UNICEF Report.

Redd, Barna (1996). *New Uganda: Able and Aspiring,* Ready to Compete. Redd Barna, Kempala, Uganda.

Rew, L., and Horner, S.D. (2003). Personal Strengths Of Homeless Adolescents Living In A High-Risk Environment. *ANS Adv Nurs Sci.,* 26(2):90-101.

Rew, L. (2002). Characteristics And Health Care Needs Of Homeless Adolescents. *Nurs Clin North Am.,* 37(3):423-31.

Rew, L. (2003). A Theory Of Taking Care Of Oneself Grounded In Experiences Of Homeless Youth. *Nurs Res.* ,52(4):234-41.

Ribeiro, M.O., and Ciampone, M.H. (2002). Street Children Talk About Shelters. *Rev Esc Enferm USP.,* 36(4):309-16.

Rizzini, I. et al., (1994). Brazil: A New Concept in Childhood, in Cristine Blanc (ed.) *Urban Children in Distress: Global Predicaments and Innovative Strategies.* Gordon and Breach, New York and UNICEF.

Rohde P, Noell J., and Ochs L (1999). IQ Scores Among Homeless Older Adolescents: Characteristics of Intellectual Performance and Associations with Psychosocial Functioning. *Journal of Adolescent;* 22 (3): 319-28.

Roy, E., Haley, N., Leclerc, P., Cedras, L., Blais, L., and Boivin, J.F. (2003). Drug Injection Among Street Youths In Montreal: Predictors Of Initiation. *J Urban Health,* 80(1):92-105.

Ryan, K.D., Kilmer R.P., Cauce A.M., Watanabe H., and Hoyt D.R., (2000). Psychological Consequences of Child Maltreatment in Homeless Adolescents: Untangling the Unique Effects of Maltreatment and Family Environment, *Child Abuse and Neglect,* 24(3): 333-52.

Sandguard, A., Gaines. R.W., and Green, A.H. (1974). Child Abuse and Mental Retardation: A Problem of Cause and Effect. *American Journal of Mental Deficiency,* 79, 327-330.

Segal, U.A. and Ashtekar, A. (1994). Detection of Intrafamilial Child Abuse: Children at Intake it a Children's Observation Home in India. *Child Abuse & Neglect,* 18: 957-969.

Segal, U.A. (1995). Child Abuse by the Middle Class? A Study of Professionals in India. *Child Abuse & Neglect,* 19, 217-233.

Senanayake, M.P., Ranasinghe A., and Balasuriya C. (1998). Street Children--A Preliminary Study. *Ceylon Medical Journal,* 43 (4), 191-3.

Snell, C.L. (2002). Help-Seeking And Risk-Taking Behaviour Among Black Street Youth: Implications For HIV/AIDS Prevention And Social Policy. *J Health Soc Policy,* 16(1-2):21-32.

Sourander, A. (1998). Behaviour Problems and TraBharatitic Events of Unaccompanied Refugee Minors. *Child Abuse and Neglect,* 22 (7):719-27.

Tantoco, F.G (1993). Philippines: Street Children, Children At Risk. *Child World.,* 20(2-3):35-7.

Teta, D.M. (2002). *Early Childhood: Socio-emotional Risks.* University of Maryland,Baltimore,USA.

Teuns, Sjef (1990). Right of the Child *How to go on?* Report of Asian Conference on Child Exploitation and Abuse, 9.

Thilagaraj, R., and Priyamvadha, M. (2000). Deviance Among Street Children. *Indian Journal of Criminology,* 28 (1), 41-44.

Times of India (2001). Abused Children to Help Trace Culprits, 7.

Tyler, K.A., and Cauce, A.M. (2002). Perpetrators Of Early Physical And Sexual Abuse Among Homeless And Runaway Adolescents. Child Abuse & Neglect, 26(12):1261-74.

Veale, A., and Dona, G (2003). Street Children And Political Violence: A Socio-Demographic Analysis Of Street Children In Rwanda. *Child Abuse & Neglect,* 27(3):253-69.

Vostanis, P., Grattan E., and Cumella S. (1998). Mental Health Problems of Homeless Children and Families: Longitudinal Study. *BMJ;* 316(7135): 899-902.

Walolkar, D. (2003). Child Labour In India. Lecture delivered in the Ist Multidisciplinary Training Programme on Child Abuse and Neglect, jointly organized by the Government Medical College, Nagpur and MIDSW-Metropolitn (Bypass) Institute for Developmental Studies and Welfare, Kolkata during Feb.3-4, 2003 and sponsored by ISPCAN, USA.

Weber, A.E., Boivin, J.F., Blais, L., Haley, N., and Roy, E. (2002). HIV Risk Profile And Prostitution Among Female Street Youths. *J Urban Health.* 79(4):525-35.

Woods, E.R., Samples, C.L., Melchiono, M.W., Keenan, P.M., Fox, D.J., and Harris, S.K. (2002). Initiation Of Services In The Boston HAPPENS Program: Human Immunodeficiency Virus-Positive, Homeless, And At-Risk Youth Can Access Services. *AIDS Patient Care-STDS,* 16(10):497-510.

Wainaina, Joseph (1997). Street Children: The Christian Approach. Christian Living, 1, Kenya.

Wittig, M.C., Wright, J.D., and Kaminsky, D.C. (1997). Substance Use Among Street Children In Honduras. *Subst Use Misuse,* 32(7-8):805-27.

4

Child Trafficking and Child Prostitution

Introduction

Child trafficking is a major problem of South East Asia, African continent and to some extent of Europe. In this part of the world innocent children who are the future of the nation are trafficked for various purposes for the vested interest of some anti-socials and criminals. It is really a shame for human civilization that even in the 21st century one group of children plays in the computer and surf internet while another group of disadvantaged children work as bonded labour and/or child prostitute against their will. The small children of economically disadvantaged families do not know when they are sold to some middle men and/or for what purpose they are shifted from one place to another place. Finally, they land up in some unknown place and grow up in an uncongenial, unhealthy and criminogenic environment far away from their home and accept the deviant life and/or life of bonded labour under compulsion. Since they do not get the opportunity of study through out their lives they are exploited and abused. While these children work as domestic servant they are badly treated across the social strata. Educated and moneyed masters do not treat them as human being and take them granted to carry over their orders, right or wrong. If they forget to perform any duty/task by mistake, they are subjected to physical and mental torture. In some families they are also abused sexually. As there is no intervention agency in most of the developing countries they do not get justice for being abused and manhandled (Deb, 1997).

Even the educated people of the larger society treat these disadvantaged and unfortunate children as something nasty and problem creators. But in the truest sense these disadvantaged children are not the problem creators, they are the victims of differential social treatment and/or inaction of policy makers and powerful persons in the society who could, perhaps, provide safe shelter and other basic minimal facilities to these children. These children are totally deprived from parental love and affection and very few of them get the adequate opportunity to meet their family members.

Trafficking is on the rise across the globe although there is no accurate estimation about the magnitude of the problem. However, the UN estimates that around four million people a year are traded against their will to work in some form of slavery like either as domestic servant, or to work in construction sites, or begging, and/ or to work as child prostitute. In India, especially in the middle and upper middle class families there is a need for small girl children to work as domestic servant and to look after small babies in absence of parents especially during office hours. In order to meet this need every year a large number of rural children are traded to urban areas through some channels for domestic work. This apart, a large number of girls from very poor families are traded to brothels for prostitution.

Children are also trafficked to work market stalls or as shop assistants. Children are trafficked from South Asia to the Gulf to meet the demand for camel jockeys. One recent press report from the *Times* claimed children were being smuggled from Africa and Latin America by European football clubs in search of the next Ronaldo. In South East Asia, most of the victims are girls, trafficked for the purposes of prostitution (David, 1998).

The release and repatriation of the Vietnamese twins unfortunately continues to reflect the exception rather than the rule, and many young girls continue to be condemned to a life of sexual slavery, cut off from their own culture and from the protection of the law.

Prostitution has become a very profitable trade and there is a global market for the same which involves millions of children, particularly girls, and which generates billions of dollars profit for the traffickers involved. The demand by wealthier countries for cheap sex workers is a major motivating factor in the recruitment by various means of women and children for the extensive and lucrative sex industries of cities such as Bombay, Karachi and Bangkok. Brothels in these cities are playing host to an increasing number of women and children from countries such as Nepal and Bangladesh, Burma, Laos and Cambodia, where poverty and income disparity, and lack of economic opportunities render many women and families vulnerable to deception (David, 1998).

Women and children from countries other than India, Pakistan and Thailand are also involved, but still constitute a minority of the total number of sex workers. They are, however, considered potentially more profitable because of their (usually) low level of literacy, and their ignorance of the law, culture and often the language of the countries to which they are taken. These factors not only weaken their physical and psychological independence, but also increase the ease with which this modern form of slavery is perpetuated. Another notion working behind recruitment of children from poor neighbouring countries is that they are less likely to carry sexually transmitted diseases, especially HIV/AIDS.

The UNICEF's East Asia and Pacific Regional Office report (2001) entitled 'Children on the Edge' notes that while some girls and women may be seen to be entering the sex trade 'voluntarily' because 'they simply hunger for the bright lights of big cities', most of them are fleeing poverty or physical, sexual, and mental abuse at home.

'Many have been raped or abandoned by a boyfriend or husband. Given the cultural, economic and individual complexities of their situation, it is hard to suggest that these women and children have any real freedom of choice. The sex trade feeds on the despair, ignorance and poverty of those it seeks to exploit', the UNICEF report says.

Definition

Commercial Sexual Exploitation of Children

It is defined by the United Nations as the use of a child for sexual purposes in exchange for cash or in-kind, favours between the customer, intermediary or agent and others who profit from the trade in children for these purposes (parent, family member, procurer, teacher etc.).

There are three forms of commercial sexual exploitation of children, which have already been defined by the United Nations: child prostitution, trafficking and sale of children across boarders with within countries for sexual purposes and pornography.

Definition of Child Prostitution

According to UN Convention on the Rights of the Child (1990), child prostitution means sexual exploitation of a child below the age of 18 for remuneration in cash or kind.

In other words 'child prostitution' refers to the sexual exploitation of a child for remuneration in cash or kind, usually but not always organized by an intermediary like parents, family members and/or procurer etc. (Gathia, 1998).

Child prostitution is a term in popular usage but this terminology is inaccurate because it implies consent. And a child does not give any consent. H/she is rather victimized into sexual slavery (Tandon and Sudarshan, 1997). Hence sexual exploitation of children is the better terminology.

'Sexual abuse' becomes 'sexual exploitation' when a second party benefits—through a profit or through a *quid pro quo* (exchange) or perceived exchange—through sexual activity involving a child. This can include child prostitution and child pornography.

The child knows the 'organisers' (i.e. the madams or pimp) but the 'customers' (at least in the beginning) are strangers.

'Sexual exploitation' includes trafficking in children for purposes of sexual exploitation, child sex tourism, distribution of pornographic material featuring children, exploitative use of children in prostitution (*Source:* UNICEF).

Definition of Child Trafficking

'Trafficking in persons' shall mean the recruitment, transportation, transfer, harbouring or receipt of persons, by means of the threat or use of force or other forms of coercion, of abduction, of fraud, of deception, of the abuse of power or of a position of vulnerability or of the giving or receiving of payments or benefits to achieve the consent of a person having control over another person, for the purpose of exploitation.

Definition of Child Pornography

Child prostitution is closely connected with child pornography. It refers to the visual or audio depiction of a child for the sexual gratification of the use, and involves the production, distribution and/or use of such materials (Gathia, 1998).

Definition of Devadasi

In India there is one category of religious prostitutes. They are known as 'devadasi'. Though the term 'devadasi' did not figure earlier than Chola times (850 to 1280 AD), it is largely believed that the practice started about the third century AD.

The term '*devadasi*' means servant. Her duties mainly include ritual, entertainment to assert positive fertility and prosperity. They on account of being married to god or goddess, such as Yellamma or Mathamma were called 'Nitya Sumangali'. This system presently exists in Andhra Pradesh, Maharashtra and Karnataka and some parts of Goa. A girl whose mother is 'devadasi' usually becomes a 'devadasi' (Gathia, 1998).

In this chapter two types of commercial sexual exploitation of children have been discussed which are interlined.

Genesis of Trafficking in South East Asia

The trafficking of women and children has largely followed the route established by economic migrants back in the 1960s when Thai women began travelling from Thailand to Europe in search of a better future. In the 1980s, Malaysia and Singapore also became significant destinations, and served as transit centres for women who then moved on to Japan, Taiwan, and Hong Kong (David, 1998).

There is clear evidence of new migratory flows developing in the region, as more and more women seek out 'opportunities' abroad. Initially, the main flow was into Thailand from its neighbouring countries. The pattern is, however, constantly evolving. The Mekong sub region as a whole has since become a focal point for the traffic in women and children, and the flow has increased rapidly in the past few years.

There are reports of Burmese women, for example, being smuggled across the border into Ranong Province. There is no evidence as to what age of these cross voluntarily—on a day-to-day basis to work in bars, massage parlours and brothels in different parts of South East Asia. However, it is estimated that sixty of these women are under the age of 18. ECPAT reports that the number of Burmese women and girls in Thai brothels has soared in recent years. Similarly, there are Chinese women across the borders from Yunnan, for prostitution in Bangkok, Chiang Rai in the north, and Singaikolok in the south.

Thailand, however, is not the only destination. There is growing evidence that the trafficking of children across the Vietnam-Cambodia border is widespread. The age of Vietnamese girls working in prostitution is estimated at between 35 and 40 per cent of the approximately 20,000 commercial sex workers working in Phnom Penh alone. The average age of these girls, according to major surveys, has dropped from 17 to 15 years over the last couple of years.

In Laos, while there is little hard data available, there are many stories of children being taken over to Thailand, especially from the north and south of the country, where families are duped into letting their children go in the promise of jobs and money. There are also fears that trafficking within the country will increase with the rise in tourism. As awareness of the issue is only just beginning to emerge, there has been little action taken as yet to address the problem.

World Vision workers in the west zone of India have also reported trafficking of girls between Nepal and Bombay—it is estimated that between 20 and 30 per cent of sex workers in Pune and Bombay are from Nepal. The NGO 'Child Workers in Nepal' (CWIN) were recently involved in the repatriation of 71 girls from Bombay, and their experience supports this evidence.

It should be noted that, along with trafficking across the borders within South East Asia itself, there is evidence of trafficking of children from the region to other parts of the world. At a meeting of the ministers of the EU last year it was conceded that Western Europe illegally imports 500,000 prostitutes a year. Mostly from Eastern Europe (ex Soviet Union), but also from Asia and other parts of the world. Similarly, women are trafficked into the USA; the Filipino American Service Group is currently carrying out a study into the growing numbers of young women from Thailand, Laos and China trafficked into California for prostitution.

In India, massage parlours and Resorts are the flourishing business in which a good number of disadvantaged children are employed. In the massage parlours small children are utilized otherwise in the name of massage. In the recent past, there have been many such rackets identified by the local Police leading to the arrest of the owners.

Commercial sexual exploitation of children refers to the sexual exploitation of children, which is organized, and benefits a section of people commercially. Child prostitution, child pornography, child sex trafficking and child marriage are the four faces of commercial sexual exploitation of children (*Source:* Red Alert: Combat Commercial Sexual Exploitation of Children, produced by Sanlaap—an NGO).

As per Article 35 of the UN Conventions on Rights of the Child, sale, trafficking and abduction it is the state's obligation to make every effort to prevent the sale, trafficking and abduction of children. But unfortunately most of the states in the developing world have failed to protect the children from being trafficked.

Severity of the Problem of Child Trafficking and Prostitution

Unfortunately there is no accurate estimation of the number of children trafficked annually and the number of children in prostitution owing to the covert nature of the child sex trade. But different agencies like the governments, the United Nations and various non-governmental organizations estimated the number of children trafficked and in prostitution based on available data and their experience. Some of the estimation of different agencies is given below:

- The International Organization for Migration (IOM) estimates that 175,000 people are trafficked from Central and Eastern Europe and the CIS each year—roughly one quarter of the estimated 700,000 to 2 million people trafficked around the world annually.
- Brazil has 250,000-500,000 children in the sex trade and the number of children involved in Colombia, Russia, and Benin is growing rapidly. Asia is the center of child prostitution with an estimated 60,000 child prostitutes in the Philippines, 400,000 in India, and 800,000 in Thailand. Most of the sex workers are under 16 years old and most are female, although some parts of the world offer almost exclusively young male prostitutes. Indeed, almost all of Sri Lanka's 20,000-30,000 child prostitutes are boys (Sachs, 1994).
- The Thai Government estimates that there are between 12,000-18,000 child sex workers in Thailand, but some NGOs estimate that the number of children involved in the sex trade is actually in the hundreds of thousands.
- About 60 of the 71,000 sex workers registered in Indonesia, where the sex industry is found in two thirds of the country, are between 15 to 20 years of age.
- In Taiwan, an estimated 40,000-60,000 children are involved in the commercial sex industry.
- Estimates on the number of child sex workers in China range between 200,000 to 500,000.
- Bangladesh Government estimates that several thousand women and children have fallen victim to trafficking for work, including prostitution, in south Asia and the Middle East. Other reports suggest that the problem may also exist in Pakistan and Sri Lanka, among others; child prostitution

in Sri Lanka, mostly of boys, has also emerged as a serious problem (ILO - World of Work, No. 19, March 1997).

- As many as one third of sex workers in Cambodia are children under 18 years of age.
- The number of child prostitutes in the Mekong Sub-region (Thailand) now constitutes one third of all sex workers plying the trade here, and the younger the children are the more likely it is that they have entered the trade against their will, according to a new report from the United Nations Children's Fund (UNICEF, 2001).
- The UNICEF report (2001) entitled 'Children on the Edge: Protecting Children from Sexual Exploitation and Trafficking in East Asia and the Pacific', further says that surveys indicate 30-35 per cent of all sex workers in the Mekong Sub-region (Thailand, Cambodia, Viet nam, Myanmar, Lao PDR, and Yunan and Guangxi in southern China) are between the 12-17 years of age.
- Another estimates states that India is home to an estimated 4,00,000 children who are sexually exploited in the red light areas of Kolkata, Mumbai, Delhi and even small districts towns of the various states while Kolkata itself alone having 40,000 child sex workers (*Source:* Red Alert: Combat Commercial Sexual Exploitation of Children, produced by Sanlaap—an NGO).
- In south Asia, thousands of Nepali and Bangladeshi girls and women are reportedly sold every year to brothels in Calcutta, Bombay and Delhi. The Government of Nepal estimates that in 1992, at least 200,000 Nepalese women and girls were working as prostitutes in India. In fact, the governments of both of these countries acknowledge the problem.
- According to the National Institute of Public Cooperation and Child Development (NIPCCD), child prostitution is increasing by 10 per cent annually in India. NIPCCD estimates that there are four lakhs child prostitutes in the country. Child prostitutes earn around Rs.11,000 crore, and some communities have 'traditionally accepted prostitution

as their profession' (*Source:* Child prostitution in increasing, Indian Express New Delhi 16th August, 1999).

- Another current estimation says that 90 million people in India are involved in prostitution, a third of them below 14 years i.e., about 30 million children in prostitution. It is also reported that young students and housewives getting involved in prostitution to make a quick buck (*Source*: Sex Trade Stats Shock. *Sunday Times,* Aug.31, 2003, p.4).

Asian countries are prosecuting more offenders, but actual convictions are negligible, often because police are in collusion with the syndicates. One factor sustaining the child prostitution industry is the belief that the children are free of AIDS (McIntosh, 1995).

It also comes at a time of growing concern about the number of women and children being moved across the borders of Western Europe, Central, and Eastern Europe (CEE), the Commonwealth of Independent States (CIS) and Baltic States (all loosely grouped as 'Europe and Central Asia).

Factors Responsible Behind Trafficking and Prostitution

There are many causes of trafficking. But the most important cause is poverty. Poverty has long been the reason behind the migration of workers from rural to urban areas. Other causes include increasing income disparity, improved communications and unkept promises. In addition, adventurous mind of some section of people have added momentum in trafficking (Deb, 2004).

All over the world, the child's vulnerability to commercial sexual exploitation lies in his or her family circumstances. The majority of sexually exploited children are either from marginalized families, and destitute families, or children of women already in the sex industry.

In India, systems of child prostitution as varied as the Devadasi or the Jogini, and the trafficking system that moves young girls across south Asia and into urban centers, reveal the active exploitation and the socio-economic realities that make such exploitation possible. In the last few years, some instances of sexual abuse of children have also come to light in popular tourist destinations (Tandon and Sudarshan, 1997).

The demand for child prostitutes encouraged middlemen and anti-socials to look for supply. On the demand side, market forces have been at play too. Urban migration by men has increased the demand for sexual services. Economic and social development, which brings greater opportunities for local women but the social stigma, inhibits the supply of local prostitutes, and increases the demand for foreign women. This demand further has become lucrative because of the lower rates of migrant women and children.

Child prostitution is the largest form of commercial sexual exploitation of children. The business of trafficking and prostitution is the third largest and the most profitable organized crime, commonly referred to as the 'dry dollars business'. The common targets of such exploitation are children from poor families, living in rural or semi-urban areas, where the traffickers trap them into prostitution either with the lure of 'jobs' or marry them with little or no dowry and then sell them to madams and brothel owners in red light areas (*Source:* Red Alert: Combat Commercial Sexual Exploitation of Children, produced by Sanlaap—an NGO). The hard reality in life i.e. poverty does not allow curious mind of parents to ask the middlemen and the exploiters whether their girl child will be safe in the city and/or in the working place.

The lack of enforcement of legal measures, lack of political will, and inaction of the various state and civil society agencies are responsible for the continuance, and in fact, proliferation of child prostitution (*Source:* Red Alert: Combat Commercial Sexual Exploitation of Children, produced by Sanlaap—an NGO).

Globalisation has added an international dimension. The desire of families to break out of their cycle of poverty has made them increasingly receptive to 'opportunities' abroad. Options for women are, however, limited largely to domestic service, offers of marriage by wealthy outsiders, or prostitution. The apparent lack of alternative options for self-improvement mean that it continues to be relatively easy to trick women into 'migrating' for employment overseas, or into selling their children to a broker for a cash advance of money the child will be able to 'earn' in their 'care' (David, 1998).

It is believed that younger girls are less likely to have HIV/AIDS. As a result, there is a great demand for younger children in the sex industry, as they are perceived to be less likely to carry sexually transmitted diseases like HIV/AIDS.

In India there is another myth that make men to have sex with young girls, believing that with that sex with virgins can cure sexually transmitted diseases. As a result, a good number of sexually victimized girls get sexually transmitted diseases like HIV/AIDS.

In spite of the increasing number of stories involving the trafficking of women and children, it is worrying that many are still willing to take a chance to explore the new world in life for better future.

Many of the countries in the European region are in the phase of transition. Their proximity to societies perceived, particularly by young people, to offer more stable and prosperous lifestyles is an important factor in this movement. Increasingly open borders between Member States of the European Union facilitate movement into and through Western Europe.

In the region, too, there exist a number of factors that increase the vulnerability of children to exploitation: In Western Europe, a growth in the commercial sex sector and growing consumerism put pressure on children to earn money in a situation of unmet demand for commercial sex. Poverty and discrimination based on gender, ethnicity, disability and citizenship status are all important vulnerability factors. In many of the transition countries, high levels of unemployment, inadequate skills and training for available employment opportunities, and poor preparation of children and young people for work and social integration, all increase pressures on children to seek alternative ways to earn money for their family or their future. This may make them more vulnerable to pimps and recruiters seeking to exploit them in commercial sex work or encourage them -or indeed force them—to move within the country or across borders where perceived returns are greater. In the transition countries, too, the more than 1 million children who are growing up in institutions, rather than with their families, are at particular risk as they exit unprepared into societies that are equally unprepared to integrate them (*Source:* UNICEF Report, 2001, Geneva).

The human rights organisation Asia Watch has documented a considerable amount of evidence that indicates that young women and children as young as 9 or 10—mostly girls but also boys—are deceived into leaving their home towns or villages by the promise of well paid work elsewhere such as working a laundry. Similarly, families may be encouraged to persuade their daughters to travel abroad to work as domestic helps. High wages and an initial down payment—often amounting to several hundred US dollars—may be used as an incentive. The promises of opportunities are often made by brothel agents—who could be family members or friends —or by prostitutes whose freedom to leave a brothel may be contingent on securing a replacement. They also target families who are especially poor or which are experiencing financial hardship due to the seasonal impact on employment.

So deceived, young women and girls are taken to brothels, when they eventually realize the deception or that they have been sold. The money paid for them forms the basis of that person's debt to, and subsequent control by the brothel owner (this is known as debt bondage). They are then left with little choice but to prostitute herself/himself in order to pay off the debt. They are rarely told the size of the debt, which is usually doubled with interest payments and the provision of daily expenses for clothing, toiletries, doctors' visits and medicines, or the conditions of its repayment, are additional methods used by brothel owners to maintain control of those in their service. Force, including beatings and rape, is also often applied to further deny them any element of choice.

The young women and children are also frequently sold by one brothel to another, which further compounds their confusion as to their geographical location and their knowledge of what they owe, to whom, and how much longer they will be forced to prostitute themselves. Brothel owners exploit their frequent inability to speak the local dialect or language, and the likelihood that young and inexperienced individuals will be easily intimidated, to ensure that they perform the sexual acts requested by their clients. The lack of freedom to negotiate the terms of the sexual service they are required to provide means that women and children have little or no opportunity to protect themselves from abuse and infection (David, 1998).

In Asia, child prostitution, and prostitution in general, is deeply embedded in many local and national cultures. For example, a Harvard University researcher has determined that 75 per cent of all men in Thailand have had sex with a prostitute. While nationals frequent and effectively support the prostitution industry, many foreign travellers also visit countries in search of sex. Young prostitutes are in particular demand due to the myth that youngsters are somehow relatively virgin and bereft of infection with sexually transmitted diseases. The author discusses the causes of rural poverty, the growth of sex tourism in Asia during the Vietnam War, government complicity in the industry, and the need to develop political will to end child prostitution (Sachs, 1994).

In West Bengal (India) there are villages like Madhusudanpur and Jyotishpur in South 24 parganas district of West Bengal where from almost each house one-girl child work in Sonagachi red light area as child prostitute. The economic background of most of the families is not good. Hence, to supplement the family income girl children are sent to Sonagachi red light area. In the village people usually say that their girl child is working as maidservant in Kolkata. One NGO called Sanlaap has started working in that village to sensitize people about the negative impact of sending children to Kolkata to work as maidservant.

In a recently conducted study covering 35 rescued girls in a Rehabilitation Home in Kolkata, it was found that that the main factors behind trafficking of these children include poverty and illiteracy, followed by influence of external agents, promise of job, lack of supervision, immaturity, family crisis, uncongenial family environment, love for adventure, helplessness, kidnapping, addiction, environmental crisis, running away from home, false promise of marriage and mother being a prostitute (Deb and Gunguly, 2004).

There are a number of factors works together behind child trafficking. Following are the examples of correlation of poverty, wrong promise of job, hard reality and child trafficking/prostitution.

Case 1: *Rina, 14 years, just literate, was born and brought up in a red light area in Rambagan, Kolkata (India). Her mother and grandmother were working as commercial sex worker. She had five siblings. Suddenly, her mother became physically sick and was unable to run the business. During this crisis period, author of this book and his colleagues wanted to include her in an action research project as one of the study subject's, which was funded by the Save the Children Fund, U.K. Since she was the only source of income for survival of seven members family, she could be drifted into this profession any time. Because of the said reason the study team wanted to remove her from the locality to a Halfway House. In this regard, the study team members discussed the issue with her, her mother and both of them replied that her grandmother is the decision maker in the family and so the study team members were advised to speak to grandmother. Next day when the study members discussed the issue with the grandmother, she had given an ambivalent response regarding replacement of Rina in a Halfway House. Very next day the study again visited the area again and enquired about Rina to convince her grandmother, but Rina disappeared. Later on, it was found out that the Rina has been moved to Mubmai Brothel against a handsome amount of money. Unfortunately after six months Rina came back to Rambagan with HIV positive.*

Case 2: *Anima, 17 years, six siblings was born and brought up in a very poor family in a remote village. Father was working as petty businessmen while mother was making 'bedi'. It was very difficult to have two meals a day. Anima studied up to class IV in a village school. At the age of 12 years a tout offered her a job in Mumbai. Utter poverty encouraged her to visit Mumbai to explore an opportunity. In Mumbai she* *was landed in a red light area. When she realized and wanted to come back by this time the middlemen disappeared. Since then she was in Mumbai red light area for two years in this commercial sex trade. She did not receive a single paise and she had to work without money as her contact person has taken the money on behalf of her. After two years of service she was arrested by the Police and was sent back to Kolkata. Through Juvenile Court she was forwarded to Liluah Observation for female juvenile delinquents. There her blood was tested for ascertaining HIV status and she was found to be HIV positive. After ascertaining the status of HIV she was subjected to social discrimination. Currently, she is in a shelter home run by an NGO where she is getting vocational training. She visits her family in the village during vacations. Her parents came to know about the disease and they extended mental support. Counselling and group activities of the Shelter Home and family support helped her to over come depression and she has developed a positive outlook about life.*

Case 3: *Farida, 20 years of age was trafficked two years back. She was born in a farmer's family in Bangladesh and had four siblings. She had never been to school. Farida got married and had a daughter. But as her husband was mentally ill and she used to stay with her father, mother and siblings. Farida's family was very supportive regarding her unfortunate marriage. But they were in a very wretched condition and it was becoming difficult for her to run the family and look after her child. A woman from her village promised her work at Kolkata. But instead handed Farida over to a dalal who sold her in Bombay at a beer bar. She was there for 1 year. She used to be beaten when unable to dance as expected. She was rescued in a police raid and sent to 'Sanlaap'— an NGO working for the rehabilitation of trafficked* *children and women. She has been staying in 'Sanlaap Home' for past 5-6 months. She wants to go back home as soon as possible to her one son. She feels depressed most of the time and is anxious about her son's well-being. She does not have any apparent physical anomaly but occasionally suffers from headache and insomnia.*

Case 4: *Dolly, aged 24 years, was trafficked when she was barely four years old. She was born in U.P but her mother now stays at Khidderpore. She is in touch with her mother. Her father was a magazine seller and she had four siblings. Dolly's father was a drug addict. He sold her when she was not even four years old. Then the person to whom he had sold Dolly, he took her to Bombay and sold her to one of the beer bars over there. The 'Seth' and 'malkin' of the bar brought her up. When she started growing up she was made to learn dance so that she got prepared for the work. Gradually she became one of the several dancers out there. The moment she stepped into her puberty she was transferred to the 'bazaar' (red light area). She then once again became one of the thousands CSW's working in Bombay. She used to take customers out of the city to various states. She continued like this for 5-6 years. Then once when she was in Andhra Pradesh with one of her customers, she was caught in a police raid. Then she was sent to Liluah Observation Home for female juvenile delinquest in West Bengal where she stayed for one year. For the past 10 years she has been staying in 'Sanlaap'—an NGO working for trafficked children. Currently she is getting vocational training in embroidery and stitching there in 'Sanlaap'. She is found to be HIV positive.*

Case 5: *Khushboo is 17 years old. She was born in Bhopal. She was trafficked three years back. She has* *three siblings. She used to stay with her mother and younger brothers. Her elder sister was married a year before her father expired. After her father's death they had a severe financial crisis leading to a state of begging. Khushboo was totally fed up with this wretched condition and started looking for an opportunity to get some work. She then came to Kolkata with an unknown person, who promised her job and took her to Sonagachi (Red Light Area) and sexually abused her. He left her over there. Then she thought of starting to earn by selling herself for the reason, she had already been spoilt. She hired a room and started the so-called 'dhanda'. She used to send some money to her home to support her family. After continuing for almost two years she was caught by the police and sent to Liluah Observation Home for female juvenile delinquent where she stayed for six months and after that to 'Sanlaap'—an NGO working for trafficked children. Here she is the vice head girl. And is learning karate, English, dancing and block printing. She wants to stay here forever and earn her livelihood well. She is suffering from a skin problem and has headaches frequently.*

Case 6: *Padma belongs from Kolkata, is 17 years of age, was trafficked two years back and has no contact with family. Her parents had died when she was small. Her mashi (Aunti) and mama (Uncle) brought her up. They didn't used to treat her very well. One day her mama sold her to a brothel keeper in Sonagachi. There she stayed for 2 weeks and then was rescued by the police and was sent to Liluah Observation Home for juvenile delinquents, stayed there for one year and then sent to 'Sanlaap'. She is learning embroidery and block printing over here. She wants to spend her life here and doesn't want to look back to her past life ever.*

> ***Case 7:*** *Sister to three other siblings, 17 years old Swapna was trafficked a year ago. She was born to a farmer's family in Orissa and never got a chance to go to school. Her husband, an alcoholic left her. Poverty compelled her to look for work. Her uncle assured her job and brought her to Sonagachchi and sold her. The police rescued her from there after 10 days. She is worried about her future and also feels restless. Now her father comes to meet her often in 'Sanlaap'.*

The Consequences of Trafficking and Child Prostitution

Commercial sexual exploitation endangers children's mental and physical health and impairs their development. The most common physical health problems are related to injury resulting from accidents and physical conditions in the working environment, long working hours, lack of sleep and substance use. The common symptoms of psychosocial disorders manifested by most of the children engaged in commercial sex are severe depression, guilt, powerlessness, deflated self-esteem and self love, escapism through dissociation, distorted perceptions of sex, inability to trust others, excessive emotional attachment, multiple phobias, loneliness, isolation, impaired ability to learn, poor memory and concentration span (*Source:* ESCAP HRD, United Nations, 2002).

The consequences of trafficking of children and child prostitution on health and society are in the form of irreparable damage to the society. Society and nation lose potential human resource, which is required for building a healthy and economically strong society. Very little systematic study has been carried out on long-term effects and/or consequences of child prostitution.

However, from available data it is clear that they are vulnerable to sexually transmitted disease, and some of them get HIV/AIDS as they do not have any control over the sexual acts they are required to perform for clients (Deb *et al.*, 2005). Poor, unhealthy and unhygienic working conditions, low education or no education about sexually transmitted diseases increases the vulnerability of getting HIV/AIDS more. This is especially the case for younger girls who may be at a higher risk of infection due to an immature reproductive system and inadequate immunity more likely. After getting the disease they are unable to bear the expenditure treatment costs and face the consequences of the diseases. More so they are subjected to social discrimination owing to their profession and disease. Hence, majority of them remain untreated.

While many commercial sex clients believe that having sex with so-called 'virgins' or children with reportedly few sex partners will help protect them from HIV/AIDS, the report says they are badly mistaken. Surveys show that some girls are forced to serve an average of 5 to 10 customers a day. In addition, the report notes that child sex workers are themselves often ignorant of HIV/AIDS and how to prevent it, powerless to insist on condom use with clients, and extremely vulnerable to not only HIV/AIDS but other sexually transmitted diseases such as syphilis and herpes (*Source:* UNICEF's East Asia and Pacific Regional Office report, 2001). While sex tourism has been a highly visible problem in Thailand for many years and is becoming an increasing problem in countries such as Cambodia and Viet nam, the aid UNICEF report notes that the sex trade and the demand for underage sex is still largely driven by local clients.

Strong social stigma discourages trafficked women and child prostitutes to get merged into the family in future. As a result, in later life they lead a lonely life and no body is there to take care of their basic needs. Economically they are in miserable condition in old age as there is a negative correlation of age with this profession of prostitution.

Recently Deb and Chatterjee (2004) conducted a study in Kolkata covering 35 rescued trafficked children. The problems encountered by the trafficked children may be categorized into four groups like mental, physical, social and economic. HIV/AIDS is the most prevalent physical health problem among of trafficked children. Among the mental problems depression is most common, followed by loneliness and loss of interest towards life. Finally, social discrimination i.e., rejection by the family members after rescue from the red light areas, shatter their last hope of living in this world.

While HIV testing is carried out in many brothels, the results are shared with the brothel owners, and are frequently not confidential although they are often withheld from the individuals tested. The frequency of HIV testing is thought to be responsible for creating the false impression that risk of infection is minimized because infected women and children have been identified. In reality, infected individuals are usually made to continue to work, though at a reduced price to clients.

Young women and children who have been forced to work as prostitutes are likely to continue to experience the physical and psychological consequences of their entrapment, repeated physical and sexual abuse, uncertainty and fear and the absence of personal control, poor health care and working conditions, and infection from STDs including HIV/AIDS. Consequences include anxiety and depressive states including trauma, an attitude of hopelessness and helplessness in relation to future decisions, social stigma and discrimination especially if HIV positive, sterility, physical illness including terminal illness. Compounding the original abuse, a proportion of girls may feel compelled to return to or stay in prostitution because the shame of having worked as a prostitute, regardless of the deception perpetrated against them; their marriage prospects are very low and the likelihood of discrimination is high in cultures where virginity and sexual inexperience is prized (David, 1998).

A more disturbing possibility is that young women and children in forced prostitution may be experiencing an increasingly more extreme and risky range of sexual acts, risky in terms of their potential for serious abuse (especially of children) and infection. Fear of HIV infection may be influencing the membership, character and preferences of a population who formerly used prostitutes on a casual basis. This may be encouraging the current client population to become increasingly more exclusive in its interest in children and deviant and dangerous acts.

Following are the two bright examples of consequences of child trafficking and finally child prostitution:

Case 1: *Rani is 18 years old girl from Bonga, West Bengal. She comes from a poor family and her father is a lorry driver by profession. Her mother does not work and looks after the household. She has a younger brother. Rani had a quarrel at home with her mother. Being fed up with her mother she decided to leave home and find out some work for herself. Rani discussed her family problems with a local dada. The dada promised her to give a domestic job. The dada took Rani to Bombay. There she was kept in a 'jhoparpatti' for 2-3 days. Then Rani was sold to a kothi. But Rani was not told that. There were many more girls in the kothi and they only told Rani that she had been sold for Rs. 10,000. Rani stayed there for 2 months and she began with prostitution. At the beginning she was not ready to take up the profession but soon she realized that she had no other way out. While the kothi was raided Rani told entire story to the police. Rani still hoped for being rescued. The police took Rani to a home in Bombay. From there she was sent to 'Sanlaap'—an NGO working for rehabilitation of trafficked children through Liluah Observation Home for female juvenile delinquents. Rani says, 'I have lost everything from my life, I don't have a family now, I know nobody at home will accept me. Nobody can marry me even. Still I want to go home, but I have got HIV positive. A small trust on the dada has taken away everything from my life... don't know how can people do this type of things to girls... Wherever I go I will be known as a dhandawali only (prostitute)...'*

Case 2: *Shilpa is 18 years old girl from Kakdwip, West Bengal. She came out of home at the age of twelve. She has no siblings. Her father works as fishermen. At present Shilpa has no attachment with the family. She had received education till class V. Shilpa's mother expired and the father married again.*

The stepmother treated her very badly. She received thrashing from her. A man from the local village promised to give her a job in the city. She left with that person for good. This man sold her in Bombay for Rs. 1,500. She was put into prostitution with several other girls like her. She was doing quite well in the profession. She used to get Rs. 4000-5000 per month. Shilpa became ill suddenly and the 'malkin' found her of no further use. Forcefully she was put into train. She landed up in Kolkata. She knew nobody out there. In the Howrah station the police caught only her. She was sent to Liluah home. There she stayed for 2 yeas. From there she has been sent to Sanlaap, Narendrapur.

Combating the Problem of Child Trafficking and Rescue of Child Prostitutes

For combating child trafficking and prostitution steps at the local, regional, state, international and bi-lateral level are required. Despite the severity and magnitude of the problem, some progress has been made at all levels in the recent past to tackle this problem. For example:

- According to the Thai Police Crime Suppression Bureau, more than half of the girls and young women removed from brothels in Thailand over the last few years were from Myanmar and China.
- In October 1994, 80 out of 152 girls removed from brothels in Bangkok were from Myanmar.
- In February 1995, 10 out of 23 rescued in Khon Khaen Province came from Myanmar and China.
- So did 17 of 19 girls brought out of brothels in Chiang Mai Province in March 1995. Aside from prostitution, children from Myanmar are also commonly found in Thailand near the border with Myanmar working in construction sites, gas stations, and restaurant and on fishing boats (ILO Report—World of Work, No. 19, March 1997).

- In 2002-2001, Sanlaap—an NGO based in Kolkata has received and provided services to over 300 children and minors who were rescued from prostitution. Forty per cent of them were HIV positive.

However, it requires a continuous and coordinated effort to tackle this problem. In this regard, state and central government should take keen interest to solve this problem through holistic and bi-lateral approaches. In the third world countries this problem is directly linked with poverty. Hence, it is not possible for any government or NGO to improve the economic condition of disadvantaged families overnight. However, with the active cooperation from government, non-government organizations and international agencies some strategies can be formulated for identification of families living below poverty line and they can be offered alternative options for income as per their aptitude. What is most important to achieve some realistic progress in this regard is political will. The World Congress Against the Commercial Sexual Exploitation of Children, which took place in August 1996 in Stockholm, has served as a catalyst, mobilizing greater international support. While the focus of the Congress and the resulting Agenda for Action is upon the wider issue of commercial sexual exploitation of children, trafficking is an increasingly important part of the follow-up (David, 1998).

A recent report from ECPAT International details the progress made to date by countries, intergovernmental agencies and NGOs since the Congress.

At the State Level

In 1994, Deb and Gunguly carried out a study to understand the causes of child trafficking. On the basis of the findings authors suggested a number of steps for prevention of child trafficking. First, a survey should be carried out in the high-risk villages to identify the families living below the poverty line and some income generating programmes should be undertaken for those families. Second, information should be provided to the villagers about the rural development programmes including programmes available for welfare of women. Community mobilization is urgently required especially in the villages from where children are being trafficked. Third, awareness generation about magnitude and severity of this problem is also needed along with awareness about the discriminatory attitude of guardians towards girl child. Parents send their children to Anganwadi Centre and/or to School. Fourth, Village Development Forum (VDF) should also be developed for prevention of the problem. Community leaders like school teachers, Panchayat members, health workers, Block Development Officer, Child Development Project Officer, Police Personnel, senior and youth members of the village should be included in the VDF. Fifth, the issue of cross-boarder trafficking should be taken up at the bilateral level between the neighbouring countries and stringent legal measures should be adopted to stop the same. Sixth, efforts should also be made by the welfare agencies to contact the family members who do not visit their girl child in welfare home rescued from 'Red Light Areas' and counsel them so that they take their child back home. Authorities of welfare organizations should work hand in hand with the legal agencies to deal with the problem of child trafficking effectively. Media should also be sensitized about the issue so that they take interest and in turn take the lead role to sensitize the policy makers to take proper measures for combating the problem of child trafficking. For implementation of all these programmes NGO should come forward and take the lead role.

At the National Level

Nearly twenty countries have now developed National Plans of Action as well as created national focal points for tackling the sexual exploitation of children. The Vietnamese Government, for example, has developed a National Plan of Action between the various Ministries involved—in particular the Committee for the Protection and Care of Children (CPCC), and the Ministry of Labour, Invalids and Social Affairs (MOLISA). The key elements of this National Plan are international co-operation, multi-lateral and regional co-operation.

Over twenty countries have carried out legislative reforms; Thailand, for example, has two new laws against child prostitution and trafficking in children under 18 years of age. In Nepal they have also created special police units to specifically combat the trafficking of girls. Several western countries, such as the UK and Sweden, now have extra-territorial legislation, which enables the prosecution of their nationals for offences carried out overseas.

There is also strong evidence that Governments have been establishing new partnerships. In Cambodia, for example, government officials have been holding meetings with NGOs to look at ways of tackling the problem. NGOs, such as the Cambodian Center for the Protection of Child Rights (CPCCR), which have established an investigation unit, and the Cambodian Women's Association, who have become involved in rescues, have also become more proactive in dealing with the problem.

NGOs have been broadly supportive of the National Plans and are willing to assist in the implementation of the Plan, having a strong role to play in the training of national counterparts (World Vision in Vietnam, for example, has been active in training social workers in recognizing families at risk). Most NGOs have tended to concentrate primarily on the provision of services to those who have been trafficked, in preventive activities to vulnerable communities, and, increasingly, in advocacy. While in some cases NGOs are now getting involved more directly in the rescue of trafficked children, these cases are still rare.

At a Regional Level

Asia

The 1998 ECPAT International report on the implementation of the Agenda for Action notes the fact that the major concern amongst the countries of the developing world is the trafficking of women and children. This concern is reflected in the number of recent initiatives in the Asia Region, which seek to address the issue.

A number of Regional seminars and conferences have been held over the past two years, such as:

- The seminar on 'Illegal Labour Movements: the Case of Trafficking in Women and Children', held in Bangkok;

- The 'Regional Conference on Trafficking in the Mekong Region', also in Bangkok;
- The 'Asia and Pacific Conference on Trafficking in the Philippines';
- The regional conference on 'Society's Responsibility Against Sexual Exploitation' in Bombay;
- The Asian Lawyers for Human Rights Meeting in Karachi on 'Trafficking in Women and Children' organized in collaboration with UNESCO.

Several large research projects have also recently been carried out in order to determine with more precision the issues involved. The Center for Advanced Studies in Cambodia, for example, has recently completed two studies on the Trafficking of Cambodian Women and Children to Thailand, in partnership with the IOM, World Vision and CRS. There has also been a recent Needs Assessment on Cross Border Trafficking in Women and Children in the Mekong Sub-Region prepared for the UN Working Group on Trafficking in the Sub Region.

Increasingly, therefore, a regional perspective is being developed based on research into the patterns and methods of trafficking. The ILO International Programme for the Elimination of Child Labour has established a programme to stop child trafficking in South Asia and the Mekong Basin countries, which also captures most of the NGO experience and concerns. The programme aims to increase awareness of the issues at all levels of society, improve law enforcement, carry out preventive and rehabilitation measures, as well as aid in the repatriation of the victims of trafficking.

Europe

Focus within Europe has been on the issues of trafficking within Europe, and the sexual exploitation of children over the Internet, building upon the concerns over sex tourism and paedophilia.

A legislative framework exists within which trafficking issues can be tackled, for example:

- The Council of Europe Recommendation R (91) 11 on 'Sexual Exploitation, Pornography and Prostitution of, and Trafficking in, Children and Young Adults' (1991), reinforced by the 1996 Consultation, the 1997 Council of Europe Summit, and the 1998 European follow-up Conference to the World Congress.
- The 1996-97 EU Parliament resolution/paper on trafficking of children and youth.
- Joint Action 96/748/JHA which extended the mandate given to the Europe Drugs Unit to include trafficking in human beings.

On a practical level, the European Commission has initiated the STOP programme, a multi-year programme against the trafficking in human beings and sexual exploitation of children, and funds exchanges for those involved in working in the area.

Cross Regional Co-operation

With regards to assisting in the fight against the trafficking in women and children in Asia, the EU has certain provisions under its external programmes to promote human rights, in particular under the ASEAN and Asian agreements.

The UK has, however, played an important role in developing a more practical, proactive approach to the issue through its Memorandum of Understanding with the Philippines to combat child sexual abuse, which has enabled the development of formal and informal links between the countries, which are vital to the investigation of offences and to strengthening child protection measures. Similar initiatives have been initiated with Thailand and Sri Lanka.

The recent ASEM Child Welfare Initiative (1998) proposed jointly by the UK and the Philippines seeks to move forward the implementation of the Stockholm Agenda for Action amongst member countries, looking at improving practical co-operation, identifying good practice models in training, assistance and develop/strengthen links between states, NGOs and international agencies. This widely supported initiative provides the perfect opportunity to increase attention and focus on the cross border trafficking issue.

At the International Level

The Declaration from the 1990 World Summit for Children (the World Declaration on the Survival, Protection and Development of Children, and Plan of Action), and the Stockholm Agenda for Action serve as key reference points for international action on this issue.

The creation of the Focal Point for the Agenda for Action within the NGO Group for the Convention on the Rights of the Child to monitor the implementation of the Stockholm Agenda for Action reflects a determination internationally to address the area of commercial sexual exploitation of children. It is itself an innovative partnership between UN agencies, the Office of the High Commissioner on Human Rights, governments, ECPAT, and a vast NGO network.

Similarly, a comprehensive legislative framework exists at this level to ensure the issues are addressed. Amongst the key documents are:

(a) The 1950 UN Convention for the Suppression of the Traffic in Persons and the Exploitation of the Prostitution of Others, together with the 1996 Programme of Action.
(b) The 1979 Convention on the Elimination of all Forms of Discrimination Against Women—Article 6 calls on government to take all appropriate measures to suppress all forms of trafficking of women, and the exploitation of the prostitution of others.
(c) The 1989 UN Convention on the Rights of the Child (CRC) which is explicit in its reference to the trafficking of children—Article 35 reads "States parties shall take all appropriate national, bilateral and multilateral measures to prevent the abduction, the sale of or traffic in children for any purpose or form".
(d) The 1992 UN Programme of Action for the Prevention of sale of Children, Child Prostitution and Child Pornography —Article 10 states "The sale of children...cannot be justified by reason of poverty or underdevelopment… it is essential

that States take urgent and immediate measures to reduce the dangers that children face." (Article 38 places particular emphasis on child abduction.)

Important Issues Require Attention

There has clearly been progress made in addressing the wider issue of the commercial sexual exploitation of children, most notably at the national level where many countries seem to be taking clear steps forwards. As the recent ECPAT International report points out, however, while there is evidence of a drop in the number of children from some groups being exploited by the sex trade, children from other groups are now being lured or tricked into the trade from neighbouring countries.

Action is needed on two fronts: (1) to address the cross border issues, an area in which progress has, to date, been far less marked; and (2) greater consistency in responses at the national level (David, 1998).

Cross Border Issues

There is no lack of applicable legislation. World Vision, as a member of the NGO Group for the Convention on the Rights of the Child, believes that 'priority should be given to urgent and co-coordinated implementation of existing instruments at national and international levels'.

Consideration should be given to a central co-ordination unit, which looks specifically at establishing inter-country mechanisms to prevent the trafficking problem in both sending and receiving countries, including the provision of safe and protective repatriation programmes. There is a need to harmonise approaches and procedures, and to work towards the standardization of practices. Particular attention is needed for determining regional standards in treatment of victims, and for ensuring child sensitive procedures. (The need for a central co-ordination unit has been recognized on other issues, which have cross-border implications, such as trafficking in drugs and small arms).

Consistency of Approach

The reports of the Special Reporter on the Sale of Children, Child Prostitution and Pornography have consistently highlighted the need for attention to be paid to the demand and supply sides, to tackling the root causes, and the need for a proactive multifaceted approach. While progress has been made in taking measures to address these issues individually, there is a need for greater co-ordination/ consistency in their application at the national level.

While, for example, positive steps are being taken at the national and city levels, these continue to be undermined by illegal organized activities at the street level. There is therefore a need for better law enforcement at the street level, and at border crossings, to ensure that trafficking activities are stopped. In general, there has been little action to address the problem, and it is disturbing that there is involvement of local police officers and political figures in profiteering from this lucrative 'trade'. There is a need therefore to improve law enforcement at the local level, through better procedures and training of law enforcement personnel.

Prevention work is being carried out through the targeting of awareness raising activities (for example, providing communities with information on the process of abduction/duping, and on the realities of life abroad) and development work at vulnerable communities from which children have been trafficked. In particular, educational and income generating activities aimed at girls. In Thailand, for example, World Vision has been working on providing relevant education and vocational training in the vulnerable north.

A similar level of attention has however yet to be paid to the recovery and reintegration of victims, helping them, their families and their communities come to terms with the experience (psycho-social recovery) and also the empowerment of girls through skills training, coupled with initiatives which help the families better provide for themselves.

Awareness campaigns need to work at local, national and regional levels to highlight the problem and mobilize action by concerned parties from the community up to policy making bodies; create the environment for a social movement at national regional and international levels to stop child trafficking. As well as increasing the awareness of the local/affected populations, their participation in the devising and implementation of measures is vital, as is the establishment of rural support networks.

The UK Response

As a signatory of the Convention on the Rights of the Child, the UK has a commitment to promote the Convention not only within the UK but also internationally. This is reflected by the inclusion, in the recent White Paper on Development, of a section on child rights, and similarly, through the stated commitment of the Foreign and Commonwealth Office to place human rights—including child rights—at the heart of the UK's foreign policy.

The UK has, as a signatory of the Stockholm Agenda for Action, increasingly played a positive role in addressing the commercial sexual exploitation of children abroad.

As previously mentioned, the recent ASEM Child Welfare Initiative (1998) proposed by the UK together with the Philippines seeks to move forward the implementation of the Stockholm Agenda for Action amongst member countries.

Role of the International Labour Organization (ILO) to Tackle the Problem of Child Trafficking and Prostitution

In order to tackle the problem of child trafficking and child prostitution and other intolerable forms of child labour in ten Asian countries, the International Labour Organization (ILO) launched a new programme, which specifically targets children under 18 who are at risk and are victims of trafficking in the Mekong Basin and in South Asia. Priority was given to girls, children from ethnic minorities and tribal populations, and to children under 12 years of age. The programme, carried out by the ILO's International Programme on the Elimination of Child Labour (IPEC) covering Cambodia, China, Thailand and its neighbouring countries and Vietnam, as well as Bangladesh, Nepal, Pakistan and Sri Lanka. The aim of the ILO-IPEC programme was to develop and strengthen special task forces on child trafficking at the national and provincial levels in each of the participating countries. These task forces were composed of governmental and non-governmental organizations, and the ILO assisted in the formulation and adoption of national plans of action. All aspects of the issue were covered, including prevention, monitoring and enforcement, the provision of assistance to potential victims and their families, awareness-raising campaigns, and the social protection, rehabilitation and repatriation of the exploited children. IPEC initiated several activities in the field, which was the basis for this programme. A 1995 child labour workshop in Nepal included child trafficking in the national framework of action, and assistance was provided to NGOs in undertaking preventive measures against such trafficking in follow-up action on the Stockholm Congress Against Commercial Sexual Exploitation of Children (August 1996) and in the formulation of a draft national plan of action. In Bangladesh, IPEC prepared a project document for joint activities with the Government and UNICEF.

The problem of child prostitution was highlighted at a national workshop on child labour held in Sri-Lanka in September 1996. The ILO considers child trafficking to be a form of forced labour, in flagrant violation of the ILO's Forced Labour Convention, 1930 (No. 29). This international standard calls for countries to 'suppress the use of forced or compulsory labour in all its forms within the shortest possible period'. All of the countries covered by the new ILO-IPEC programme, except China, have ratified this Convention and are bound by its terms. The ILO is also calling for the adoption of a new international convention focusing on the most intolerable forms of child labour, including hazardous occupations, slavery, servitude, forced labour, bonded labour, serfdom and prostitution.

Recommendations: World Vision calls upon the UK Government to take a firm lead in issues relating specifically on the issue of trafficking of children. In particular by Development Assistance:

Providing increased development assistance, which targets the current weaknesses in the response to the problem:

- The recovery and reintegration of victims, helping them and their families process the experience and develop initiatives which enable families to better provide for themselves; and

- Raising the awareness of local/affected populations and the level of participation in the devising and implementation of appropriate responses.

To tackle the problem of child trafficking and prostitution at the global level due consideration should be given to the key issue of establishing a central co-ordination unit to look specifically at establishing inter-country mechanisms, harmonizing approaches and procedures, and working towards the standardization of practices in relation to the issue of child trafficking.

Role of UNICEF to Combat Child Trafficking and Child Prostitution

The United Nations Children's Fund, UNICEF, is calling on governments in Europe and Central Asia to ratify three international instruments that are vital to efforts to combat trafficking in children, a growing problem in the region: the 2000 Optional Protocol to the Convention on the Rights of the Child on the Sale of Children, Child Prostitution and Child Pornography; the Protocol to Prevent, Suppress, and Punish Trafficking in Persons, Especially Women and Children, supplementing the UN Convention against Transnational Organized Crime (2000); and ILO Convention 182 on the Worst Forms of Child Labour (1999).

UNICEF Regional Director for Europe, Stephen Woodhouse said that, 'we must not underestimate the use of international conventions in our work to end the heinous trade in children for sexual purposes and exploitative labour. These are not just vague promises; they provide frameworks that, among other things, smooth out differences between national laws'.

The call for ratification comes one week before the opening of the European and Central Asian Preparatory Conference to the Second World Congress against Commercial Sexual Exploitation of Children held in Yokohama, Japan. This meeting, held in Budapest on November 20-21, brought together 52 countries of Europe and Central Asia to discuss progress since the first World Congress in

Stockholm in 1996, to share experiences and lessons learned, and to develop a regional strategy for accelerated implementation of the Stockholm Agenda for Action (UNICEF, 2001, Geneva).

The Budapest meeting will hear that these disturbing challenges will nevertheless be met by some positive developments since the first World Congress in 1996:

- Increased public awareness of commercial sexual exploitation of children (CSEC), and decreased tolerance of those who exploit or abuse;
- An increased knowledge base and, importantly, better and more detailed understanding of both the demand and supply sides of CSEC;
- Improved effectiveness and professionalism built on this knowledge base and supported by better information sharing, good practice formulation, strategic planning, and consultation;
- Better cooperation across borders, within countries and regions, and among the different sectors involved in combating this multi-faceted phenomenon - child protection agencies, governments, intergovernmental bodies, law enforcement, social services;
- New laws in many countries, including the introduction of extraterritorial jurisdiction provisions, and some national plans of action against CSEC.

Prevention

A number of actions have emerged at the national and local levels to prevent or combat the commercial sexual exploitation of children in the developing countries. However, these activities remain limited and not well established at the community level.

Primary prevention programmes focus on awareness creation regarding the causes, the exploiters and methods of recruitment, the effect on the children and appropriate ways of intervening (*Source:* EASCAP-HRD, United Nations, NY, 2002).

Preventive Measures Through Community Mobilization, Training and Advocacy:

Trafficking in children is the burning example of one of the deep rooted-problems of a society that has lost the ability to care and protection of the children. The people of larger society are either ignorant of the exploitation of children and/or indifferent about the issue.

First, it is important to understand why and how innocent children are trafficked and finally, land up in prostitution. From the available data and various reports it is clear that poverty is one of the root causes of this social problem. There are backward villages and districts that are the source areas for the traffickers. That is where the real problem lies. The brothels in the cities are a symptom of the problem. NGOs working towards rural development should target such poor families that are forced to send their children to earn. The poverty alleviation and development programmes should target such families that are at risk (Tandon and Sudarshan, 1997).

Two levels of prevention are aimed at parents who have not yet maltreated i.e., primary prevention and secondary prevention.

Primary prevention includes activities that exert a positive influence on the whole system, thereby increasing healthy family functioning and eliminating some of the risk conditions that contribute to maltreatment. Included in the scope of primary prevention are policies that improve educational and employment opportunities for parent, the promotion of family planning in order to avoid unwanted births or births that are too closely spaced, parental care for pregnant women in order to reduce the number of premature and low birth weight babies, policies which support new parents during the parental period such as 'rooming in' during the hospital stay and parental leave with job security, economic improvements such as reduction of unemployment through job training programmes and placement services efforts to reduce the overall level of violence in the society such as the promotion of violence-free problem solving in general, alternatives to corporal punishment in schools and in homes. More specifically the primary preventive measures, which could be beneficial include:

- Opportunities of primary education to all children free of cost.
- Arrangement of safe shelter for displaced, homeless, orphan and run away children.
- Promotion of child rights in family and school education programme to sensitize parents that it is the responsibility of both the parents to care and protect children from any sort of maltreatment and abuse.
- Advocacy for effective implementation of existing laws for protection of child trafficking and sexual exploitation of children.
- Mobilization of business/corporate sector to come forward and to take up programmes for child protection activities.

Secondary prevention refers to efforts aimed at identified high-risk populations e.g., families living in poverty, single parents, parents dealing with unexpected or unwanted pregnancies, parents with impulse control problems, depression, or substance abuse, and families in economic or emotional crisis. Specific approaches include parents in stressful situation, other forms of crisis support such as crisis nurseries in hospitals, ongoing family support services such as assistance with day care, medical care etc., and self-help support groups such as Parents Anonymous, which provide social support and some specific behavioural management techniques to address anger that threatens to go out of control.

Treating victimized children is another approach to secondary prevention. Providing an opportunity to acknowledge past suffering, teaching effective interpersonal problem solving and planning strategies and offering situations in which abused and neglected children can increase their self-esteem, can serve to reduce the probability of maltreatment in the next generation. Considerable research has been directed at refining methods of assessing adults child abuse potentials in order that direct prevention services could be directed to the individuals in most need (Tandon and Sudarshan, 1997).

However, there are models on prevention approaches to combat trafficking. In 1999, a programme on Campaign, Awareness

Generation, Training and Networking aiming at building awareness in an indicated source area (through earlier research done in red light areas which provided information on where the women, all of who were minors at the time of being trafficked, were trafficked from). The programmes were initiated with a stipulated awareness generation capsule with inbuilt components to measure the changes in levels of information, as well as gather information to learn more on the sort of peculiarity that leads to trafficking in that particular area. This programme served the dual purpose of the intended awareness generation thereby building the base for any conscious intervention that could be initiated by the community or the local authorities to combat trafficking. Secondly, and more importantly, it provides information on a whole lot of other factors that have caused the children and women to be trafficked and how the system has been socialized into it. Any approaches that are built from this realization will then address the root problems through whatever programmes are introduced to address the manifestations. Prevention models need to address root problems in the area of trafficking. All interventionists—programme support, designers and implementers and the target community, need to understand the real reason for a community targeting violence on its children, girl children in particular. They need to look at reasons beyond poverty, for every poverty stricken community does not find its children dispensable nor disposable to violence and discrimination. The perfect example to illustrate this incidence is Purulia in West Bengal. While almost all other states, in some degree, is affected by trafficking, the incidence of trafficking in Purulia is almost negligible. Thus, programme interventions need to identify the peculiar and crucial factors that lead to trafficking. Instances where a poor family grabs the chance of marrying off their teenage daughter to a trader from the city who does not ask for dowry leads us to the broader issues of child marriage, dowry and discrimination against the girl child which leaves her without an education or a means of supporting herself. It is not a feasible objective to set up organizations in each of these areas to work on trafficking and then diversify to all other areas to address root problems. An inter-sect oral approach to integrate consciousness amongst all existing NGOs who work with the vulnerable groups of women and children on issues of health and education and sensitizing them to address issues of gender inequity, violence against women, discrimination against the girl child, and role of Panchayat and Police in ensuring protection to all children vulnerable to trafficking is a better approach (Sen and Sinha, 2003).

There is a need to integrate all these initiatives and link it up with an advocacy network to lobby with the police and Panchayat to ensure prosecution of traffickers as well as those who perpetrate violence against women and children. To reiterate, one has to focus on continuing child marriage and the deprivation of education to girl children, preventing them to grow into self-reliant individuals who have the option of living a dignified life.

It is important to organize multidisciplinary training programme for the law enforcement agencies like police officers and NGO personnel with a view to sensitizing them about the severity of the problem child maltreatment and how come they can enforce the existing laws strictly to penalize the perpetrators. In this regard, ISPCAN and ECPAT has taken active initiative to train the professionals to curb the problem of child abuse and neglect in general and child trafficking and prostitution in particular.

MIDSW-Metropolitan (Bypass) Institute for Developmental Studies and Welfare, an NGO involved in child protection activities organized the first multidisciplinary training programme in India in 2003 for the NGO and Police personnel in Kolkata and in Nagpur in association with the Government Medical College with a view to achieving the following objectives:

- To sensitize Police Personnel about the severity and magnitude of child abuse and neglect in India.
- To provide basic information about this issue i.e., types of child abuse and neglect, causes and consequences.
- To provide information about existing legal measures available in the country in regard to child abuse and neglect.
- To provide information about current CAN activities in India undertaken by various Government and non-government organizations.

It is believed that one can gain additional knowledge attending any workshop and training. The sole objective of this training programme was to sensitize the Police and NGO Personnel about this social problem and also to provide them detailed information about various laws available in the country, which could be applied to penalize the perpetrators. On the other hand, in turn trainees would be able to disseminate the same information with their colleagues. Hence, it was expected that when they will come across any child abuse case special attention would be paid to them. On the other hand, security issue of the victims will also be taken care of.

The training programmes were sponsored by the International Society for Prevention of Child Abuse and Neglect, USA. The programmes were highly successful and created good interest among the participants about the issue. Thereafter a national society called Indian National Society for Prevention of Child Abuse and Neglect has been formed in India to address the problem of child maltreatment holistically through partnership approach.

In addition, cross border trafficking remains an issue that has not been addressed adequately. However, there are directions towards the development of a holistic alliance between sending, receiving and transit countries as set by informal initiatives. Organizations like STOP, SANLAAP and PRAAJAK though its experience in repatriation partnership with BNWLA (Bangladesh), DHAKA AHSANIA MISSION (Bangladesh), ACD (Bangladesh) is extending its alliance to cover preventive and advocacy initiatives to combat trafficking focused interventions in identified vulnerable areas and transit routes and consequent unified advocacy with border police and respective governments can increase monitoring and put a check to corruption within the State Agencies (Sen and Sinha, 2003).

For prevention of child trafficking and child prostitution the role of media is very important. Within a short time span media can sensitize the larger society about the issue.

Intervention

For combating child trafficking and prostitution, multi-level steps—local, regional, state, international and bilateral—are required. Despite the severity and magnitude of the problem, some progress has been made at all levels in the recent past. However, continuous and coordinated efforts are needed, and State and Central governments must adopt holistic and bilateral approaches. In third-world countries, this problem is directly linked to poverty. Hence, it is not possible for any government or NGO to improve the economic condition of disadvantaged families overnight. With active cooperation from government, NGOs and international agencies, however, some strategies can be formulated for identification of families living below poverty line and they can be offered alternative earning options as per their aptitude. Progress in this regard will depend on political will, however (Deb, 2005).

A similar level of attention is required for the recovery and reintegration of victims, helping them, their families and their communities cope with the experience (psychosocial recovery) and also the empowerment of girls through skills training, coupled with initiatives to help families better provide for themselves (Deb, 2005).

Very few NGOs have been involved in residential rehabilitation including treatment of sexually exploited children. Due to their small size and limited budget, the number of children reached with services is often a fraction of those needing care.

However, given the overall trafficking scenario, various models have been developed by various agencies for intervention. However, by and large most of the models cover following aspects for intervention.

- Psychosocial re-integration of trafficked children and children rescued from prostitution.
- Child Protection Programme.

Psycho-social Re-integration of Trafficked Children Rescued from Prostitution

Rescue: First it is important to rescue a trafficked child for re-integration. Rescue operation, of minors in prostitution, is primarily a State responsibility, which is to be carried out by the State Police. The role that an NGO solely depends upon the nature of the interventions carried out by that NGO. Organizations like STOP (Delhi) and Maiti (India) specialize on rescue operations in India. Such organizations play a more active role in the identification and rescue of minors using their own strategies in obtaining the information and working in partnership with the police.

Sometimes NGOs play a role of being key informant to Police for rescue of a trafficked child. There is the danger of key informants within the red light areas and people, who accompany the police during the rescue operations, of being identified and later attacked. Incidents of such identified people being injured, or killed, might be demoralizing to other people and scare them off. One must be aware of the fact that the Mafia controls all forms of institutionalized and street prostitution. And it is this Mafia that extorts the women and co-ordinates the balance between supply and demand of prostitution—madams, brothel owners, pimps and brothel keepers amongst others.

There are organizations that work in the red-light area providing services to the children of women in prostitution as well as the women themselves. It is not possible for them to take such a direct role in rescue operations. There are models (Sanlaap, Prerana) in which organizations have facilitated a process whereby the youth and women in prostitution have organized to resist sale of children and women into the red light areas. There are examples set where the youth groups or the women have reported a case to the police or the 'link NGO' as soon as a new girl or woman is brought to the area by a trafficker for sale. These have been met with varying degrees of success. There have been instances where the reporting has resulted in the rescue of the girl or the woman by the police through an immediate raid. In other cases, where the joint adventure with the police has not been as successful, the raid has not ended in the rescue of the girl. The nexus of corrupt officials and the people who control the movement of the trafficked girl have been the prime hindrance to the process.

Some rescue operations carried out in the past have been often ill planned and hasty. There had been no planning or co-ordination between the police and the shelter homes or NGOs who run shelter homes to ensure sensitive handling of the rescued children. Reflection on the 1996 raids in Bombay bear testimony to the claim that children go through victimization at the hands of the State when rescued without adequate arrangements of their shelter and custody. Thus, there need to be a constant process of sensitization of the law enforcing agents who carry out the rescue operations. Agencies that initiate rescue operations need to network with Government remand homes, or shelter homes run by NGOs recognized by the Juvenile Justice Board to run a home under the J.J. Act authorized to take custody of the child. Such collaborations and partnership ensure sensitive handling of the rescued child and minimize the trauma that the child is subjected to during the operation.

Recovery: So far as recovery of rescued children is concerned, it is the State's responsibility to keep a child in remand homes till the court files against the identified criminal—trafficker, madam, brothel owner or keeper, is dismissed. Bureaucratic red tape and slack investigation and judicial processes keep the cases running for years at the end. It is the classic example of lack of State accountability and irresponsibility where children live in the remand home for years after years. There are Model Interventions that include the State Remand Home in Liluah (West Bengal) where NGOs work inside the remand home with programmes for the children—on education, mental health recovery and vocational training programmes. The NGO interventions inside the shelter home also aids indirect monitoring of the staff inside the remand home. The NGO staff also assists in sensitization of the government staff who can be ignorant in handling children and are, thereby, insensitive. Certain changes in the structure and processes in preparation, which are insensitive to children and violate their rights, can also be changed through advocacy. Such examples can be found in changes that have been brought in the State Remand Home, at Liluah, with regard to forced HIV testing and breach of confidentiality and of sero-positive children rescued from prostitution.

Very few systematic study has been conducted on problems of trafficked children and that too most of the study findings are not reported in the standard journals. Hence, there is an urgent need to carry study to understand the psychological as well as physical health problems encountered by the trafficked children engaged in different professions. However, personal experience of the author and other NGOs in dealing with trafficked children engaged in domestic work and in prostitution reveal that these children mostly suffer from severe stress disorder and behavioural problems like poor self-esteem, poor self-concept, disturbance in sleep, depression, anxiety, frustration and so on. This apart, they also suffer from adjustment problems owing to loss of trust and, prolonged isolation. Substance abuse is very common among a good number of such children. The individual counselling of such children is found to be very much effective in helping them to overcome psychological problems like depression, inferiority complex, adjustment problems and to regain confidence in developing positive outlook towards life. Practical experience of author's recent visit to an NGO in West Bengal called 'Sanlaap' is a bright example of how a group of motivated and dedicated people can bring smile in the face of helpless/rescued trafficked children.

Repatriation, Restoration and Re-integration: The best practice in repatriation has been set by Sanlaap in 1997 (with Nepal) and 1998 (with Bangladesh) when for the first time it set the officially recognized repatriation process in motion, with the NGO role set to linking and speeding up of procedures. This was particularly important with regard to Bangladeshi victims who were, until then, 'pushed back', which put the victims in grave danger during and after the push back. The Repatriation Process that involved the Consulate/High Commission of both countries along with the NGOs who facilitates the process (especially from the sending country) and takes custody and initiates restoration (receiving country) . The model has, since then, been replicated by other NGOs dealing with the same target group as well as other groups, Prajaak, an NGO dealing with destitute boys, some of whom have been trafficked from Bangladesh and Nepal, has since January 2001, repatriated 16 boys to Bangladesh following that set process (Sen and Sinha, 2003).

Effective restoration of children rescued from prostitution need to consider a host of issues:

- Ensuring the consent and participation of the child about to be restored.
- Sensitization of the family of the survivor to be restored.
- Sensitization of the community, especially community leaders like the Panchayat members, school teachers and the Police, who are likely to be responsible for the child and her welfare and safety.
- Addressing the vulnerability of the situation, which led to the trafficking of the child in the first place.
- Identifying local agents/agencies they will be entrusted with the follow-up reporting of the restored child.
- Assessing the viability and exploring options of the child to be restored if s/he is sero-positive and taking possible safeguards without the breach of confidentiality of the status of the child.
- Ensuring that the child has a contact to turn for help in crises.

Restoration processes, which have adhered to the necessary considerations, have been few. There needs to be greater linkage and collaboration between rural and urban NGOs, rescuing and restoring NGOs with organizations/agencies in the location of the family of the survivor for such processes to be regularized. Existent networks of NGOs working on the issue of trafficking have been urban and most of the agencies/NGOs who work on rescue and recovery and not been able to build networks with organizations/agencies in the rural districts where the children are trafficked from.

Finally, it is important to give the child training in some vocational trade considering the aptitude, interest and future prospect of that vocational training so that the child can be economically independent and also help the family members. In addition, NGOs in association with Government and other international agencies should identify the pockets or areas from where children are mostly trafficked and they should concentrate in those areas and sensitize people about the negative consequences of trafficking. It is also necessary to address the basic problems which lead trafficking.

Child Protection Programme

Trafficked children are subjected to all forms of abuse, violence and discrimination. Basic rights of the children belonging to socio-economically backward families like adequate food, clothing, safe shelter, health and education remain unmet. Panchayat is also ignorant and careless about this issue. However, upcoming Child Protection Units in 3 source areas of West Bengal (Matia—North 24 Parganas, Madhusudanpur and Jyotishpur—South 24 Parganas) are models of what could become, with inclusion of such units in the State Government/Panchayat schemes, a sustainable initiative to address the protection of children vulnerable to trafficking through setting up of a time bound process aiming at providing basic education and vocational skills could break socialized processes of violence of trafficking. The Child Protection Units also aim at advocating for adoption of responsibility of these children by the Panchayat and the Police. Increasing accountability, responsibility and democratic and co-ordinated functioning of the Panchayats hold the key to such action. UNICEF attempts at creating model Panchayats could be trail blazing in re-framing the role and responsibility of the Panchayat (Sen and Sinha, 2003).

Interventions in disaster-prone and disaster affected areas need to be sensitive to the vulnerability that is exploited by traffickers who poach on women and children in the guise of recruitment for jobs, marriage or other forms of aid. Classic examples of such traffic are found in Orissa and West Bengal after recent floods, The trafficking that happens in the river of migration is invisible and remains undetected. This is a new area of intervention which requires urgent attention of policy makers.

Very little studies have been undertaken with a view to understanding the phenomenon and evolving strategies to prevent and combat sexual exploitation of children. Moreover, caregivers have not received adequate training to enable them to address the needs of the victims of sexual exploitation and their families. This means that care is often provided on a trial and error basis (*Source*: EASCAP-HRD, United Nations, NY, 2002). Hence, there is a need to carry out systematic study to understand the efficacy of various preventive measures/strategies.

Latest Selective Study Findings

Deb *et al*. (2005) carried out a study to understand how children and young women are trafficked in West Bengal. A study of 35 trafficked children and young women found that trafficking is usually conducted through offers of false marriages and jobs, or through outright abduction and sale. In almost all districts and even some villages, the traffickers, who have a strong network, engage agents, who include: another person who herself is a victim of trafficking, unemployed persons, drug addicts/alcoholics or aged women with no income. Sometimes, these agents work under compulsion and/or are blackmailed into abetment. Since poverty and illiteracy are the prime factors contributing to trafficking, income-generating and literacy programmes should be arranged for needy families. Local NGOs also need to take the initiative to raise awareness levels in panchayats in order to check trafficking. Training programmes and workshops need to be organised too, for the local administration, panchayat members and police officers.

Deb and Sen (2005) made an attempt to understand the extent of psychological trauma experienced by the young trafficked women. A group of 35 young trafficked women aged between 14 - 22 and working as prostitutes were covered in the study. Data were collected by the TSI (Trauma Symptom Inventory by John Briere). The study was carried out in West Bengal, India in December, 2004. Analysis of the background data pointed toward low literacy, large family size, low family income, low general awareness level and young age as vulnerability factors for trafficking. The TSI results indicated that close to half the sample (42.9%) experienced post-traumatic stress, sexual difficulties and self-dysfunction, while 29.0 per cent experienced dysphoric mood. A significant difference was found between the trafficked and the non-trafficked sample on the clinical scales of depression, intrusive experiences, sexual concerns and dysfunctional sexual behaviour ($p<.01$). The findings suggest comprehensive rehabilitation of the trafficked women with special emphasis on need of mental health.

Deb *et al*. (2005) remarked that child trafficking is on the rise in the Asian countries. In India, West Bengal is also badly affected by this social problem. Child trafficking and sexual exploitation of children is the result of traditional class system, in equal distribution of national resources and lack of proper child protection services in India. The broad objective of the study of Deb *et al*. (2005) was to understand the socio-economic profile of the young trafficked women in West Bengal, substance abuse among them and their HIV status as very few studies were carried out on this issue. A group of 35 young trafficked women were covered in the study and they were interviewed by a semi-structured questionnaire. Findings revealed that majority of the young trafficked women (82.9%), mostly illiterate (57.1%) and semi-literate (42.9%) with more than two siblings (91.4%), were aged between 18-20 years. Parents' mostly illiterate and very poor were involved in agriculture as a labourer and some of them work as vegetable seller. After trafficking only 28.6 per cent have contact with their family and occasionally parents visit them in the rehabilitation homes. However, most of the parents did not know that their girl child was involved in prostitution after trafficking. About 89.0 per cent of the trafficked women had a history of sexual abuse in early life. After coming into flesh trade about 80.0 per cent became dependent on different types of substances while 20.0 per cent became pregnant accidentally. Four of them (11.4%) were also tested HIV positive. Findings suggest awareness campaign about the child trafficking in the rural areas and in this process all the Panchayat Members and senior community leaders like school teachers, Police and local administrators should be involved. In addition, for improving the rural economy awareness about government welfare programmes should be created and NGO should come forward to help poor people to enjoy the benefits of the government programmes.

Deb (2005) stated that child trafficking has become a serious social problem in some parts of India. West Bengal is one of the badly affected States. Especially at risk are the girl children of rural areas from poor and poorly connected families. Improvement of the rural economy (to lessen the lure of monetary inducement that poor families face) and creating awareness in rural areas, along with the involvement of panchayat members and the local administration as well as NGOs, are preventive measures that need to be urgently promoted. In addition, awareness about the issue should be created among the law enforcement agencies and legal measures enacted to prosecute perpetrators.

Chatterjee *et al.* (2005) carried out a study with a view to investigating the short and long term problems faced by the trafficked children. A group of 41 female trafficked children, in the age group of 10-18 years was covered in the present study and they were selected following incidental sampling technique from the rehabilitation Home of 'Sanlaap' (an NGO) and from the Observation Home for Girls. Data were collected from the trafficked children following an in-depth interview method. Further for better realization of the objective detailed case studies have been developed. Findings highlighted the problems encountered by the trafficked children, which can be broadly categorized as mental, physical and social. HIV/AIDS—the dreaded disease was found out among 6 out of 41 trafficked children covered in the study. Among the mental dispositions depression, loneliness and loss of interest disturb nearly every child. To top it all they feel the discrimination in the social sphere which encompasses two broad areas, namely stigmatization and family rejection. A further analysis of the after effects were clubbed into two dimensions namely short term and long term problems of which minor health problems and settlement in future are the dominant ones respectively. Findings also revealed that family members had developed a negative attitude towards these children and generally do not come to visit them. Authorities of the welfare agencies should initiate dialogue with the family members of all trafficked children for merger with the family.

Identified parents of the trafficked children should be counselled to change their neglecting attitude towards these children. So far as rehabilitation is concerned, trafficked children are receiving some vocational training in Sanlaap. However, in the Government Observation Home similar activities should be arranged after identification of their skills, interest and demand of the market.

Bennett (1999) discussed the issues and options in the prevention of trafficking of women and children in Asia. Studies revealed a higher prevalence of trafficking in Asian countries such as Nepal, India, Bangladesh, Philippines, Cambodia and Thailand. This is due to a huge population, growing urbanization, and poverty. Several programmes by the government and non-government organizations have been developed to address the trafficking problem. In Nepal, the Maiti programme was organized to help trafficking victims return to their home country, while occupational alternatives and awareness campaigns were organized for young women vulnerable to trafficking. In Thailand, greater penalties were imposed to customers as compared to the sellers so as to discourage the continuance and decrease the prevalence of trafficking. Other strategies have also been identified, such as prosecution of procurers, community awareness through campaigns, poverty alleviation, and gender equalization to address the trafficking problem.

Sivaraman (1998) discussed the weakness and/or helplessness condition of children. According to the author, the inability to resist the ease with which they can be enticed and the absence of possible pregnancy complications make children easy targets for sexual assaults in India. According to the Indian crime statistics, 25 per cent of the 10,000 reported rape cases in 1990 involve children under 16 years old. During a public hearing on minor rape conducted by the India Democratic Women's Association, several incidents of child rape came into the open as parents recalled the incidents before the jury and the public. Commenting on the common trends observed on the revealed cases, the district secretary, Sarasam Jayaraj, noted that the rapist was invariably a familiar person and that the defenceless daily wage earners were the common targets. Considering the seriousness of this problem, the issue has to be a priority in welfare and women's organizations in their national campaigns. This crime also demands an urgent response from the government and socio-political systems.

In a study Debabrata (1998) found that 28 out of 86 brothels along the G.B. Road in India revealed that almost 60 per cent of the prostitutes were children. The law does not punish prostitutes who are older than 18 and do not solicit business publicly, but it does punish running a brothel, living on the earnings of prostitutes, procuring or inducing people to become prostitutes, and soliciting in public places. The law, which is mostly used to harass prostitutes, invokes penalties of imprisonment for procuring or trafficking and for forcible detention for the purpose of prostitution while creating a special police force to stop trafficking, special courts to deal with cases, and protective homes for "rescued" girls. The law fails to punish clients or make provisions for the rehabilitation of rescued women. Offenses rarely end in convictions. In fact, police officers extort money from traffickers, prostitutes, and madams and abet the system of prostitution through a scheme of false registration of the girls that creates the fiction that they are not minors and creates a debt paid by the madams that places the girls in virtual bondage. There is a set of rate for police bribes, depending upon the size of the brothel. Police also are clients themselves and/or extort money from clients. When arrests are made (to make police records look good), police deliberately target adult prostitutes instead of the minors because it is harder to get the minors released back into prostitution. The police are reluctant to release records about prostitution and are complicit when madams present false affirmations that they are relatives of minor girls to get them released from juvenile remand homes. The girls are recruited from impoverished families in the countryside who are paid for giving their daughters in false marriages.

Krishna (1995) offers 12 suggestions for improving the protection of sexually victimized children and discusses the extent, form, causes, and consequences of sexual victimization of female children in India. Female victimization includes child marriage, polygamy, rape, incest, and kidnapping for immoral purposes. A female child is victimized from birth to maturity. Girls are born into a secondary status and married off. If her dowry is meagre, a girl is subjected to ridicules, criticism, or denigration. The number of prosecuted sex offenses against girls and the number of reported sex offenses increased during 1980-89. However, most sex offenses are unreported. About 63 per cent of rape cases pertain to girls 16-30 years old. Only 18 per cent of rape cases occur among women over age 30. During 1971-89, kidnapping increased by over 79 per cent. Most kidnapping involves girls 3-16 years old and is connected with prostitution, begging, sexual gratification, unemployment, extreme poverty, broken homes, and antisocial surroundings. One study in 1991 found that 48 per cent of adolescent schoolgirls had been molested. Another study in 1985 found that 54.29 per cent of rape victims were 7-16 years old, and 3.27 per cent were under 7 years old. 53.88 per cent were unmarried, and 45.32 per cent were married. Most of the victims were unemployed, dependents, or students. The victims know most rapists. The rapist and the victims tend to come from middle or lower socioeconomic classes. Brother-sister incest is about 5 times more common than father-daughter incest. The literature suggests that children are sexually abused for pleasure or material gain. A current city study found that 15 per cent of prostitutes were less than 15 years old; 24.5 per cent were 16-18 years old. Girls enter prostitution through a temple devdasi life, abduction, regular employment, and initiation by parents and brothel keepers. Marriage victimizes girls who marry at an early age or with a poor dowry.

Purewal (1995) discusses the forms of sexual abuse of female children and the psychosocial impact on the well-being of girls in India. Child sexual abuse statistics reveal an estimated 50 per cent of girls being sexually abused before the age of 15 years. Girl children are abused and then are made to feel personally responsible, guilty, or persecuted. Girls are threatened with violence if they tell about the sexual abuse. Pregnancies arising from sexual abuse result in shame and early márriage. Male children are also abused but they are not made to feel punished. Child sexual abuse is technically sexual activity (rape, fondling of genitalia, masturbation, forced oral sex, sodomy, or vaginal penetration) that is committed by someone in a position of authority, power, or trust over the child or by a stranger. The World Health Organization estimates that 1 in 10 child worldwide is sexually abused. Rape within the family is particularly difficult for the victim. In almost 60 per cent of rape cases, the victim was unwilling to report the name of the abuser. Families remain silent about sexual offenses in order to protect the family image. Mothers remain silent if the abuser is the father, which interferes with a child's relationship to both parents. Sexual abuse can result in bed wetting, nightmares, sleep disorders, depression, anxiety, running away from home, multiple personality disorders, precocious sexual behaviour, or sexual inhibition and low self-esteem. Parental responses tend to inappropriate discipline or ignoring it. Children may experience flashbacks or other long-term effects. Girls who experience sexual abuse once tend to be more vulnerable to abuse in adult life. Healing is a slow and systematic process. The first aim is to restore a girl's ability to say no and to teach her to protect herself. Healing is about removing guilt and resolution of the conflict between blame and the grossness of the violation.

Marozzi (1998) reviewed the background of the street children. 'Tuloy sa Don Bosco', one of the programmes supported by the Children and Youth Foundation of the Philippines (CYFP), gives a number of Filipino street children the chance to escape a life of exploitation. The project covers 118 boys between the ages of 8 and 18 years, with a further 100 that arrive for their classes daily. These children come from a variety of problem backgrounds, including domestic violence and abuse. CYFP operates by identifying effective partners such as the "Tuloy sa Don Bosco" project, arranging funds, and enhancing the partner's capabilities to implement programmes. In northern Luzon, CYFP supports projects dealing with child labour, prostitution, out-of-school girls, and entrepreneurial training. CYFP aims to place children and youth on the government agenda, international funding institutions, the private sector, and nongovernmental organizations.

O'grady (1993) stated that fear of acquired immunodeficiency syndrome (AIDS) has resulted in a demand for young, healthy prostitutes in Thailand. Girls, as young as 10 or 11, are often kept in a separate room; their health is guaranteed and their price is higher. Since the children are considered less likely to have AIDS, the customers are less likely to wear condoms. However, the tissues of young boys and girls are thinner than in adults and rupture easily, allowing direct passage of the human immunodeficiency virus (HIV) into the bloodstream. Medical examinations have shown that sex between an adult and a child usually results in tearing. A female child subjected to sex with several men a day has internal injuries, including bleeding and abrasions, which are never allowed to heal. Because of the high incidence of sexually transmitted diseases (STDs), there are many open sores. These internal injuries and open sores provide portals for the virus. This information needs to reach those adults who use children as sex partners. Sex with children is not safe; it is a risk behaviour that increases a person's chance of contracting HIV.

The article of Poudel and Carryer (2002) focused on trafficking of young Nepalese girls and women. Trafficking is an integral part of the social and economic fabric of Nepal, as in other parts of the world. The practice causes intolerable degradation and suffering for the girls and young women involved, who are treated as a commodity. It presents a risk to their physical and mental health, and in particular to their sexual health. The article examines the connections between coercive sex work and HIV infection, and community and government responses to HIV infection among trafficked sex workers. In particular, it considers the current AIDS prevention and control program in Nepal, and criticizes it from the feminist perspective of the authors, who are a Nepalese nurse who has undertaken academic work in New Zealand related to women's health, and a New Zealand feminist academic, who is also a nurse.

According to Reinfeld (1993), 200,000 Nepali women are believed to have been sold into prostitution in India, some at the age of 11, by their families. Since Nepali women are considered more beautiful and very young ones are considered virginal and free of human immunodeficiency virus (HIV) and other sexually transmitted diseases (STDs), the girls command a higher price. However, one survey in Bombay indicated that 50 per cent of female prostitutes were infected with HIV. Caste prostitution also exists; among the Bhadi, the women are traditionally sex workers whose earnings support the whole community. The girls (usually the daughters of clients, raised by their single mothers), after being trained by their mothers, begin work at menarche with great ceremony, suffer no social isolation, and retire back into the community. Few marry because men outside the caste do not marry former sex workers and men inside the caste only marry girls from families with at least 3 daughters in order to protect the income to the community. 70 per cent of these Bhadi workers are infected with STDs, but HIV has not made significant inroads. The Nepali prostitutes returning from Indian brothels and the seasonal migrant workers who use their services introduce HIV to a broader range of communities in Nepal. Conventional prevention programmes that focus on teaching prostitutes to tell clients to use condoms and how to negotiate this, will fail; the children are in no position to do so. They are considered free of disease by clients who see no need to use condoms and command too high a price as "virgins" for brothel owners to disturb the situation by requiring condom use. Control efforts to stop trafficking have not been successful and do not have priority among the country's many survival needs. A comprehensive, culturally specific approach to HIV prevention is needed that includes education of clients and brothel owners about condom use, and community-based residential facilities for daughters of caste workers so that they may attend school and delay entry into sex work. Finally, the status of women must change, so that they are considered autonomous individuals who can make their own decisions.

In an article Seth (1995) discussed the state of social change and the disparity between India's Constitutional aims and actual practice in addressing gender inequality and the special risks of female children in India. The second part of this article summarizes Constitutional articles and laws relating to protection of women and a girl child. Before birth, a female child is at risk of fetal death. A woman is at risk of poorly performed abortions and maternal mortality. After birth, a girl child is at risk of child care of younger siblings, housework, lack of education, wage work for the household, sexual abuse, vulnerability at work or school or on the street, murder by her parents, abuse, malnutrition, and desertion. The SAARC summit declared 1990 as the Year of the Girl Child. UN conventions and a world summit focused on the Rights of the Child. A child has a right to freedom from exploitation, neglect and abuse, and access to food, health care, and education. Articles 14, 15, and 16 of India's Constitution guarantee protection from discrimination on grounds of religion, race, caste, sex, or place of birth and equality of opportunity in public employment. Article 23 prohibits trafficking in humans and forced labour. Article 24 prohibits child labour under the age of 14 years. Article 39 assures an adequate means of livelihood, equal pay, and protection from child abuse and economic pressure to work in jobs unsuitable to a child's age and strength. Article 45 provides for free and compulsory education up to 14 years of age. Articles 51 prohibits derogatory practices against women. Article 325 and 326 prohibits sex discrimination. Other laws pertain to dowry, marriage age, prostitution, abortion, juvenile justice, kidnapping, obscenity, procurement of a minor, sexual offenses, divorce and child support, child care, maternity benefits, and cruelty by a husband or relatives. The girl child in India continues to live in perpetual threat, both physiologically and psychologically.

Pedersen and Hegna (2003) investigated adolescents who reported to have given sexual favours for payment. The sample consisted of all adolescents in the public and private school systems in Oslo, the capital in Norway (age group 14-17, response rate 94.3%, N=10,828). Adolescents who had sold sex form 1.4 per cent, three times as many boys as girls. Half the group had done it more than 10 times. Most were under the legal age of sex in Norway (16 years) when this first happened. We found no associations with socio-demographic variables or residential area in Oslo. However, sex sale was associated with low intercourse debut age, conduct problems, alcohol problems, use of drugs (including heroin) and violent victimization.The conclusion is that a small group in the general adolescent population sells sex, and many of the clients are assumed to be homosexual or bisexual men. Adolescents who take part in these activities are often heavily involved in delinquent behaviours and use of drugs, and many probably are in a risk zone for sexually transmitted diseases (including HIV), drug abuse and a delinquent and criminal development.

According to Anti-Slavery International (1993) in Para and Maranhao States in Brazil, women and young girls are enticed from their towns by the promise of jobs in mining encampments and near large civil construction sites only to be sold into servitude in brothels. The women are virtually slaves who are told they must work as prostitutes to pay their transportation costs and other debts incurred (such as the purchase of medicine to treat malaria). Once this is done, the women must reimburse the brothel owners for the price paid for them. Since the brothel owners collect the client's money directly and transportation costs out of the area are high, few women can leave. Those who try to escape are beaten, tortured, or even killed. The local police are alleged party to this situation. After publication of this situation in 1992, federal police raided a number of brothels, released more than 70 prostitutes, including many minors, and arrested 10 brothel owners. There is evidence that this problem is widespread in Amazonia, despite the fact that Brazil has ratified several international conventions designed to outlaw slavery and forced prostitution and to protect children.

Archavanitkul (1999) estimated the number of child prostitutes (CPs) in Thailand. It is estimated by Mahidol University that CPs amounted to about 36,000 children out of 150,000-200,000 prostitutes. The Center for the Protection of Children's Rights estimates that Thai and foreign child prostitutes aged under 11 years, in 1996, amounted to about 800,000 out of a total 2 million prostitutes. An estimated 20,000 establishments employed about 700,000 sex workers. About 30,000 underground sex establishments registered about 1.3 million sex workers. The Ministry of Public Health estimates that CPs amounted to about 16,276 in 1995. The 3 different estimates vary widely. This study estimates the number of CPs aged under 18 years of age, differentiates between Thai and foreign prostitutes, and accounts for those who entered prostitution prior to the age of 18 years. 16 per cent of the total number of prostitutes may be Thai CPs; 50 per cent may have begun their work under the age of 18. About 30 per cent of total foreign prostitutes may be children; 75 per cent may have entered prostitution as minors. A 1997 census of establishments indicates 7816 sex establishments. Based on field research on underestimation, it is estimated that 18,248 were foreign sex workers in Thailand in 1997, or 20 per cent of the total of 90,915 sex workers. 90 per cent of the foreign sex workers were estimated to be from the Mekong subregion of Myanmar, Laos, Cambodia, and Vietnam. An estimated 4927 (30%) were CPs. During 1990-97, an estimated minimum 80,000 children and women from the Mekong subregion entered the sex trade. An estimated 18,000 were Thai CPs.

Das (1991) made critical comments concerning the plight of prostitutes children in India. Little attention has been paid to these children who are victims of their circumstances from birth, denied the opportunity to be free of their background, and deprived of an environment conducive to healthy physical and psychological development. The children suffer from nutritional deficiencies, minimal health care, non-availability of basic needs, and social handicaps. Although government has initiated measures to improve conditions for these children, their status isolated them from the mainstream and places them on the lowest social ring. They are also likely to follow in their mothers' footsteps, and eventually engage in procurement or pimping. Discrimination among the children is exhibited in education where boys are given priority, in denial of choice in joining a trade for self-development, and/or in inheritance where prostitution earnings accrue to sons. The estimate 5,000,000 children of prostitutes in India deserve priority treatment. The mothers' backgrounds divide the children into several categories. Prostitutes bear children out of a desire to enter into a tangible human relationship that is genuine, meaningful, and lasting. Sometimes children are economic and emotional necessities to their mothers.

Walker (2002) stated that the numbers of children in contemporary society involved in prostitution is still largely unknown. However, there are multiple factors, which leave children vulnerable and involved in prostitution. This article aims to explore the historical context of child prostitution, factors which may predispose an adolescent engaging in prostitution, and the role that professionals within the healthcare settings can offer.

Mukhopadhyay (1995) discussed the nature, magnitude, causes, and consequences of female child prostitution in India and offers measures for control and prevention of girl prostitution. Data are obtained from the 6-city study of prostitution and the author's own research. An estimated 85 per cent of all prostitutes in Kolkata and

Delhi entered the work at an early age. The numbers are rising. The promotion of tourism is linked with prostitution. Girl prostitutes are primarily located in low-middle income areas and business districts and are known by officials. Brothel keepers regularly recruit young girls. An estimated 33 per cent of prostitutes are young girls. In Bangalore, Kolkata, Delhi, and Hyderabad, there are an estimated 10,000 girl prostitutes. UNICEF estimates about 300,000 child prostitutes. Girl prostitutes are grouped as common prostitutes, singers and dancers, call girls, religious prostitutes or devdasi, and caged brothel prostitutes. Religious prostitutes are mainly found in the South. Caged ones are found in Mumbai. A little over 50 per cent of prostitutes come from other countries, such as Nepal and Bangladesh. The girls tend to come from urban slums and poor rural areas. High prostitute supply regions include Andhra Pradesh, Karnataka, Maharashtra, Uttar Pradesh, Tamil Nadu, and West Bengel states. About 85 per cent are Hindus, and about 66 per cent are from scheduled castes and tribes. Bangalore and Mumbai have a higher proportion of girl prostitutes. The causes of prostitution include ill-treatment by parents, bad company, family prostitutes, social customs, inability to arrange marriage, lack of sex education, media, prior incest and rape, early marriage and desertion, lack of recreational facilities, ignorance, and acceptance of prostitution. Economic causes include poverty and economic distress. Psychological causes include desire for physical pleasure, greed, and dejection. Most enter involuntarily. A brief profile is given of the life of a prostitute.

Willis and Levy (2002) stated that child prostitution is a significant global problem that has yet to receive appropriate medical and public health attention. Worldwide, an estimated 1 million children are forced into prostitution every year and the total number of prostituted children could be as high as 10 million. Inadequate data exist on the health problems faced by prostituted children, who are at high risk of infectious disease, pregnancy, mental illness, substance abuse, and violence. Child prostitution, like other forms of child sexual abuse, is not only a cause of death and high morbidity in millions of children, but also a gross violation of their rights and dignity. In this article we estimate morbidity and mortality among prostituted children, and propose research strategies and interventions to mitigate such health consequences. Our estimates underscore the need for health professionals to collaborate with individuals and organisations that provide direct services to prostituted children. Health professionals can help efforts to prevent child prostitution through identifying contributing factors, recording the magnitude and health effects of the problem, and assisting children who have escaped prostitution. They can also help governments, UN agencies, and non-governmental organisations (NGOs) to implement policies, laws, and programmes to prevent child prostitution and mitigate its effects on children's health.

Harcourt *et al.* (2001) determined the health and welfare status of female and transgender street sex workers and their work-related experiences. And also estimated population numbers, determined work locations, and identified the most appropriate education, health and welfare services for this group. Forty-eight street sex workers completed a questionnaire, mainly at their place of work. Demographic and sexual health profiles of sex workers attending the Sydney Sexual Health Centre and the Kirketon Road Centre in 1997 were compared with the street sample. Up to 120 female and transgender sex workers worked on the streets in Sydney, Newcastle, Wollongong and surrounding areas in any one night: more than 80 per cent of these were female. Of those sampled, fewer street workers than brothel sex workers (6% vs. 41%; $p<0.001$) were from non-English speaking backgrounds, and more (77% vs. 7%; $p<0.0001$) were currently injecting drugs. The street workers reported lower rates of condom use at work than local brothel workers (91.7% vs. 98.8%; $p<0.016$) and high rates of hepatitis B and C infection. Seventy-five per cent had experienced violence at work. Child care, lack of supportive relationships, community intolerance and low self-esteem were important problems for the street workers. While the police were frequently required by the community to move the street workers on, there were no reports of corrupt behaviour by police. Health services need to specifically target this group with particular attention to the prevention of blood-borne virus infections, contraception, drug dependency and transgender issues. Consideration should be given to developing a network of safe houses to reduce community pressure and violence.

Ayalew and Berhane (2000) reported that very little is known about prostitution in general and about child prostitution in particular in Ethiopia. Hence authors carried out a study to determine the magnitude of child prostitution and to identify problems associated with it. A cross-sectional study design was utilized. Data were collected using structured questionnaire. A total of 650 commercial sex workers were interviewed. Eighty-eight (13.5%) were below the age of 18 years at the time of data collection. At the time of joining prostitution 268 (41.2%) were under 18 years of age. Poverty, disagreement with family, and peer influence were the major reasons leading to prostitution. Child prostitutes were likely to be victim of physical violence [OR = (95% C.I.) = 1.93(1.18,3.15)] and sexual violence [OR = (95% C.I.) = 2.20(1.36,3.35)] compared to adult prostitutes. Child prostitutes were about five times more likely to desire rejoining their family than the adult prostitutes [OR = (95% C.I) = 5.47(3.01;9.93)]. Strategies need to be developed to rescue child prostitutes from on-job violence, and to establish a rehabilitation programme for those interested to discontinue prostitution along with efforts to minimize entry into prostitution.

Brannigan and Brunschot (1997) examined research that attempts to explain entry to prostitution in terms of the family experiences of young prostitutes. Though there is some evidence of rape, incest, and other kinds of sexual trauma in these backgrounds, this evidence is inconsistent and contradictory. A more plausible approach to the question is based on general control theories. Any traumas or conflicts that unattach children and youth from their families make youngsters highly vulnerable to delinquency. In the case of adolescent females, breach of family attachments appears to heighten the risk of early sexual involvements that, in the context of gender differences in sexual development, expose them to partners significantly older than themselves, and in significantly larger numbers than would otherwise be the case. These factors help explain the role of dysfunctional backgrounds in entry to prostitution without presupposing a role for unobservable traumas and psychiatric disturbances. They likewise recognize a role for the interaction between social control factors and the normal process of sexual development.

REFERENCES

Anti-Slavery International (1993). Forced Prostitution Of Women And Girls In Brazil. *Focus-Gend.*,1(2):40-1.

Archavanitkul, K. (1999). What Is The Number Of Child Prostitutes In Thailand? *Warasan Prachakon Lae Sangkhom,* 7(2):1-9.

Ayalew T, Berhane Y. Child prostitution: magnitude and related problems. *Ethiop Med.J.*,38(3):153-63.

Bennett, T. (1999). Preventing Trafficking In Women And Children In Asia: Issues And Options. *Impact HIV,* 1(2):9-13.

Brannigan, A., Van Brunschot, E.G. (1997). Youthful Prostitution And Child Sexual *Trauma. Int J Law Psychiatry,* 20(3):337-54.

Chatterjee Pooja, Chakraborty Tanusree, Srivastava Neerajakshi, and Deb Sibnath (2005). Short And Long-Term Problems Faced By The Trafficked Children: A Qualitative Study. *Social Science International (accepted)*.

Das, D. (1991). Giving The Children Of Prostitutes Their Due. *ICCW News Bull.,* 39(3-4):31-7.

David, Westwood (1998). Child Trafficking In Asia - Child Rights and The UK Promoting The Convention On The Rights Of The Child World-Wide, Briefing Paper No. 4 - November 1998.

Deb, Sibnath, Chakraborty Tanusree, Chatterjee Pooja, and Srivastava Neerajakshi (2005). Processes of Child Trafficking in West Bengal: A Qualitative Study. *Social Change* 35(2): 112-123.

Deb, Sibnath (2005). Child Trafficking In South Asia: Dimensions, Roots, Facets and Interventions. *Social Change,* 35(2): 143-155.

Deb, Sibnath, Sen, Purba and Roy, Sahana (2005). A Study on Socio-Economic Profile Of The Young Trafficked Women in West Bengal, Substance Abuse and Their HIV Status. Presented in the European Conference on Child Abuse and Neglect, held during Sept. 11-14, 2005, Berlin, Germany.

Deb, Sibnath and Sen, Purba (2005). A Study On Psychological Trauma Of Young Trafficked Women. Presented in the 6th ISPCAN Asian Regional Conference on Child Abuse and Neglect, held during Nov.16-18, 2005 in Singapore.

Deb, Sibnath (2004). Dynamics, Causes And Consequences Of Child Trafficking In South Asia With Special Reference To Prevention And Intervention. Lecture delivered in the ISPCAN Global Institute in San Diego, California, USA on Jan.25, 2004 as Visiting Faculty of ISPCAN Global Institute.

Deb, Sibnath (1997). Harassment of Urban Girl Children Engaged in Domestic Work. Presented in an International - Interdisciplinary Conference on the Urban Childhood, Organized by the Institute of Child Research, Trondheim, Norway between 9 -12 June, 1997.

Deb, Sibnath and Gunguly, Sohinee (2004). Causes of Child Trafficking, *Social* Defence (accepted).

Debabrata, R. (1998). When Police Act As Pimps: Glimpses Into Child Prostitution In India. *Manushi,* 105:27-31.

EASCAP - HRD, United Nations, NY (2002). Training Manual on Psychosocial and Medical Services for Sexually Abused and Sexually Exploited Children and Youth.

Gathia, Joseph (1998). *Child Prostitution in India.* Concept Publishing Company, New Delhi.

Harcourt, C., Van-Beek, I., Heslop, J., McMahon, M., and Donovan, B. (2001). The Health And Welfare Needs Of Female And Transgender Street Sex Workers In New South Wales. *Aust N Z J Public Health,* 25(1):84-9.

Krishna, K.P. (1995). Girl Child And Sexual Victimization. *Soc Change.,* 25(2-3):124-32.

Marozzi, J. (1998). Aiding the poorest. The Philippines: Children and Youth Foundation. *Financ Times,* 30,4.

McIntosh, A. (1995). Asian Child Prostitution on Rise Despite New Laws. *J Int Assoc Physicians AIDS Care,* 1(10), 46.

Mukhopadhyay, K.K. (1995). Girl Prostitution In India. *Soc Change,*25(2-3): 143-53.

O'grady, R. (1993). Thailand Sexually exploited children: receivers and transmitters of HIV. *Child World,* 20(2-3):43.

Pedersen, W., and Hegna, K. (2003). Children And Adolescents Who Sell Sex: A Community Study. *Soc Sci Med.,* 56(1):135-47.

Purewal, J. (1995). Sexual Violence And The Girl Child. *Soc Change,* 25(2-3): 154-60.

Poudel, P., and Carryer, J. Girl-Trafficking, HIV/AIDS, And The Position Of Women In Nepal. *Gend* Dev., 8(2):74-9.

Reinfeld, M.R. (1993). Nepal: A Cultural Prostitution. *Child World* 1993:20(2-3):45-6.

Sachs, A. (1994). The Last Commodity: Child Prostitution in the Developing World. *World-Watch,* 7(4),24-30.

Sen, Roop and Sinha, Indrani (2003). *Trafficking in Children: An Overview.* Lecture delivered in the Multidisciplinary Training Programme on Child Abuse and Neglect for NGO and Police Personnel in Koikata, Conducted by MIDSW in association with the Government Medical College and sponsored by the ISPCAN, USA, held in Feb. and June, 2003.

Seth, P. (1995). Girl Child And Social Change. Soc Change, 25(2-3):107-15.

Sivaraman, M. (1998). Children: A Soft Target. *Hindu,* 8:28.

Tandon, R.K. and Sudarshan, K.N. (1997). *Child Prostitution.* APH Publishing Corporation, New Delhi.

Walker, K.E. (2002). Exploitation Of Children And Young People Through Prostitution. *J Child Health Care,* 6(3):182-8.

Willis, B.M., and Levy, B.S. (2002). Child Prostitution: Global Health Burden, Research Needs, And Interventions. *Lancet,* 20:359(9315):1417-22.

[5]

Child Labour

Introduction

Children are the future of the nation. During childhood they should receive adequate nutrition, education, health care services, love and affection, proper guidance and congenial living environment for normal mental and physical development and for cultivation of their inherent potentials. But unfortunately a large number of children in our country and across the globe are deprived from the said basic minimal facilities and work as child labour owing to various factors.

Child labour in ancient India existed in the form of child slaves. From the very beginning children have been participating in both inside and outside household activities. In the earliest times children used to be engaged in the work relating to agriculture and grazing of animals. In the medieval period they used to be involved in various types of crafts and trades, besides the agricultural activities. In the current century children can be seen performing a number of odd jobs, which are hazardous to their physical and mental growth and development. Agriculture continues to be the most dominant occupation, engaging an overwhelming majority of the working population in this country. Nowadays children perform different types of repetitive, monotonous, unpromising, boring and hazardous jobs and are maltreated and exploited.

India has the second largest child population in the world. Hence, India is very rich in terms of human resource if properly utilized. But in reality a large number of children are compelled to work for survival and for giving support to their family. In fact, child labour is one of the oldest professions of the world, which remained as the most neglected phenomenon for the last few centuries.

The International Year of the Child was celebrated in 1979 and since then working children and their problems have been receiving the attention of researchers, voluntary organizations, social activists and the media. The Government of India, however, has shown serious concern over this problem and taken several measures. The constitutional provisions and the several legislative measures resorted to by both the State and Central Government, constitutes of several enquiry commissions, committee to look into the problem and suggested measures to government to ameliorate the suffering of working children bear the testimony to this. One estimate suggests that there were roughly about 300 legislations in India in 1982, which were concerned with children in general and many of them dealt with working children.

The term 'Child Labour' refers to those who are engaged in gainful work. Therefore, children working in all forms of industrial or non-industrial occupations, which are not healthy to their physical, mental, moral and social development is covered under the definition of 'Child Labour' (Kulshreshtha, 1978).

Regarding age limit different laws set varying age limits for the determination of what is a child. In conjunction with 'labour' ILO Convention No. 138 places the general limit at 15 years or, under special national circumstances, 14 years.

Definition of Child Labour

There are different definitions of child labour given by various agencies. According to National Institute of Public Cooperation and Child Development (*Source:* NIPCCD, 1994), 'child labour includes children leading prematurely adult lives working for long hours for low wages under conditions damaging to their health and to their physical and mental development, sometimes separated from their families, frequently deprived of meaningful educational and training opportunities that could open for them a better future'.

Bonded child labour is any individual under 18 years of age providing services arising out of a loan/debt/advance. Bonded labour 'refers to the phenomenon of children working in conditions of servitude in order to pay off a debt' (*Source:* Human Rights Watch, 1996). According to ILO (1992), there are about one million bonded child labourers in India.

Child labourers are divided almost equally between boys and girls, with boys making up a slight majority. Among children engaged in hazardous work, boys hold a majority of 55 per cent.

The largest numbers—127 million—of working children age 14 and under are in the Asia-Pacific region. Roughly 2.5 million children are economically active in the developed economies, 2.4 million in the transition countries, over 17 million in Latin America and the Caribbean, 48 million in Sub-Saharan Africa and more than 13 million in the Middle East and North Africa (*Source:* ILO Report 2002).

Extent and Dimensions of Child Labour in India

India has the largest number of child labourers in the world. According to ILO and UNICEF (1996), the number of child labourers in India can be anywhere between 14 -100 million while Human Rights Watch (1996) estimates that figures could be between 60 and 115 million—the highest number in the world.

However, regarding the total number of child labourers in India various figures have been projected by different agencies. Other estimates on the magnitude of child labour in India include:

- 13.6 million—The 1981 Census
- 17.36 million—The Planning Commission, 1983
- 44 million—The Operation Research Group, Baroda, 1983.
- 20 million—Labour Minister, August 1994, at the time of announcing a plan to liberate 20 million children working in hazardous employment.
- 60 to 115 million working children in India—the highest number in the world. India is the largest example of a nation plagued by the problem of child labour (*Source:* Human Rights Watch, 1996).

All these estimates are fall short of the actual figure for a number of reasons like multiplicity of definitions, different methods of computation, diverse sources of data, lack of information on the vast unorganized sector of the economy which, in fact, employs most children and non-inclusion of domestic workers.

There are some recent estimates, which are based on the number of families living below the poverty line:

- 111 million—The Balai Data Bank, Manila. If nearly half of the India's over 800 million population lives in poverty, the number of working children in India is likely to be over 100 million.
- 77 million—Commission on Labour Standards and International Trade, Government of India, 1995. Estimate computed on the basis of families living below the poverty line. Campaign Against Child Labour, based on the number of non-school going children and families living in destitution.
- 70-80 million—Campaign Against Child Labour, based on the number of non-school going children and families living in destitution.

Although the figure for the number of child labourers varies, they are all significantly high when considering that the Child Economic Activity Rate for 1980-1991 was 13.5 per cent for males and 10.3 per cent for females (International Labour Organization, 1995, 113). In comparison, other developing countries such as Sri Lanka and Malaysia (where data is available), have lower activity rates: 5.3 per cent for males and 4.6 per cent for females in Sri Lanka, and 8.8 per cent for males and 6.5 per cent for females in Malaysia (*Source:* International Labour Organization, 1995, 113).

The National Sample Survey Organization (NSSO) estimated that there were 16.6 million child workers in India in 1979 of which 10.4 million were boys and 6.2 million were girls. Another study commissioned by the Labour Ministry and conducted by the Operation Research Group of Baroda (1980) estimated that about 44 million children in India participate in work. Among them 79 per cent are found in the rural areas and 21 per cent in the urban areas. Two-third of the child workers in India are in the age group of 12-15 years. Out of the remaining one-third 33 per cent are below the age of 10 years. This wide variation in the estimates says the problem of conceptualizing, defining and measuring child work but confirm the fact that the number of working children in India is indeed very large.

In all, if children under 14 who are economically active were included, the figure would rise to around 250 million. And if those who carry water for the family were counted, the total would jump to 400 million. Other child workers are hidden from the statistician's view, particularly girls doing domestic work; their numbers would push the total still higher.

These children work in industries, such as cracker making, diamond polishing, glass, brass-ware, carpet weaving, bangle making, lock making and mica cutting to name a few. And a large number of them work as domestic servants.

Industry-wise total number of male and female child workers in India is given in Tables 3.1 and 3.1A. This is not the exhaustive list of industries in India where children are working. There are so many other industries across the country where children are employed. However, the above tables give some idea about the magnitude of child labour in each industry. Definitely the actual number would be more.

Table 3.1: Number Of Male Child Labour By Industrial Category In India 1961-2001 (Index Base: 1961=1000)

Male Child Workers#	1961	1971	1981	1991*	1996*	2001*
Total	869045	780222	743784	832876	838118	725032
Cultivators	422526	304222	290397	321396	319297	275496
Agricultural Labourers	175247	300427	280152	310932	309734	267392
Mining Quarrying etc.	837340	758050	586209	652700	651558	562730
Household Industry	927740	199263	234372	267018	274760	238744
Manufacturing other than household Industry	185649	240735	396500	471731	506400	443600
Construction	44011	42304	54381	64701	68334	59677
Trade and Commerce	129052	197380	228416	273080	295738	259486
Transport Storage & Communication	21190	35662	32424	39174	42656	37465
Other Services	567738	282388	200049	237067	251416	219734
Non-Workers	506585	709657	860950	972307	915714	916061
Students (Fulltime)	236410	325103	490867	573846	545376	527488
Non-Workers Non-Students (Nowhere Children)	270174	384554	370082	398461	370337	388573

Table 3.1A: Number Of Female Child Labour By Industrial Category In India 1961-2001 (Index Base: 1961=1000)

Female Child Workers	*1961#*	*1971*	*1981*	*1991**	*1996**	*2001**
Total	57793	28617	37576	43411	43643	37365
As Cultivators	31709	75406	10957	12518	12418	10666
As Agricultural Labourers	14383	15821	19860	22771	22662	19479
Household Industry	555171	139070	198611	233980	239982	207523
Manufacturing other than household Industry	55313	74465	147790	183801	187042	162366
Construction	22524	17371	31033	36088	37287	32290
Trade and Commerce	24555	13966	20789	24171	25313	21978
Transport Storage & Communication	2248	5991	3124	6043	6328	5494
Mining Quarring etc.@	202706	151115	153750	178242	177573	152663
Other Services	307493	123553	120777	149770	182743	139628

Source: Census of India 1961,1971,1981 and 1991
CMIE Basic Statistics Relating to the Indian Economy Vol. 2 States Sept. 1984
Note: * Projections Using Metagraphics Software Corporation's People and Workers projection modules 1987-88 (1981 Participation rates Assumed)
Census data not give breakdown for age group 0-14 NSS estimates suggest that the core of labour is in age group 10-14. Hence projection for 1996 & 2001 is for 10-14.
Chaudhri, D.P. (1995) Dynamic Profile of Child Labour in India 1961-1991, p. 95.

Extent and Dimension of Child Labour Worldwide

Around the world, some 246 million children between 5 and 17 years old are working instead of attending school - a number nearly as large as the entire population of the United States (280 million). That is one out of every six children in the world work today. Nearly three-quarters of these children are exposed to work that is hazardous for their health and safety. That equals one out of every eight children around the world (*Source:* ILO Report, 2002).

Nearly three-quarters of the world's child labourers, about 180 million children, are exposed to the worst forms of child labour - that is, work that is hazardous for children. That equals one out of every eight children around the world.

The International Labour Organization estimates that worldwide 110 million children aged 5-14 years are engaged in labour that can be described as hazardous or intolerable. Most of this takes place in Asia and the Pacific, although the highest prevalence is in Africa, where children younger than 14 years make up a third of the total workforce (*Source:* ILO Report, 2002).

Some estimated 8.4 million children are trapped in the most abhorrent forms of child labour—slavery, trafficking, debt bondage, prostitution, pornography and other such activities. These forms are by their nature totally unacceptable for children under any circumstances and should be outlawed immediately.

More than 10,000 boys and girls were forcibly recruited in the conflict in Sierra Leone as soldiers, cooks, porters, and sexual partners for male combatants (*Source:* UNICEF, 1999).

The bulk of child labourers work in agriculture and industry, often in hazardous environments. In 1992 in Pakistan, over two-thirds of the estimated 1.5 million people employed in the carpet industry were children (*Source:* UNICEF, 1992). Among all of the world's working children, most are in the informal sector where they do not have legal or regulatory protection...

- Most work on farms and plantations. 70 per cent are in agriculture, commercial hunting and fishing or forestry.
- 8 per cent are in manufacturing.
- 8 per cent are in wholesale and retail trade, restaurants and hotels.
- 7 per cent are in community, social and personal service, like domestic work.
- 4 per cent are in transport, storage and communication.
- 2 per cent are in construction.
- 1 per cent in mining and quarrying.

Findings of ILO Recent Study

Ten years after launching a worldwide campaign against child labour, the International Labour Office (ILO) issued a landmark global study showing that despite 'significant progress' in efforts to abolish child labour, an alarming number of children are trapped in its worst forms (*Source:* ILO Global Report on Child Labour, 2002).

"Despite the increasing commitment by governments and their partners to tackle child labour worldwide, it remains a problem on a massive scale," said Juan Somavia, Director-General of the ILO.

"While there has been significant progress towards the effective abolition of child labour, the international community still faces a major uphill struggle against this stubbornly pervasive form of work that takes a tragic toll on millions of children around the world".

The ILO's most comprehensive study on the subject, notes that there has been a worldwide response to calls for abolishing child labour, especially in its worst forms, through direct action at the local, national and international levels.

The report found that 246 million children—one in every six children aged 5 to 17—are involved in child labour. Among its startling new findings, the report also says that one in every eight children in the world—some 179 million children aged 5-17—is still exposed to the worst forms of child labour which endanger the child's physical, mental or moral well-being.

The report also says that of these children:

- About 111 million in hazardous works who are under 15 and should be 'immediately withdrawn from this work'.
- An additional 59 million youths aged 15-17 should receive urgent and immediate protection from hazards at work, or also be withdrawn from such work.
- Some 8.4 million children are caught in 'unconditional' worst forms of child labour including slavery, trafficking, debt bondage and other forms of forced labour, forced recruitment for armed conflict, prostitution, pornography and other illicit activities.

Child labour continues to be a global phenomenon—no country or region is immune, the report says. A wide range of crises—including natural disasters, sharp economic downturns, the HIV/AIDS pandemic and armed conflicts—increasingly draws the young into debilitating child labour, including illegal and clandestine forms such as prostitution, drug trafficking, pornography and other illicit activities.

The Shape of the Problem

The figures in the new report differ from the previously accepted estimate of some 250 million working children aged 5-14 in developing countries—the best estimate possible in 1996. The report notes that the latest methods to gather data provide a more precise picture of the problem of child labour, its distribution among regions and between age groups, and therefore provide figures that are not open to simple comparison with the original estimate.

The report describes child labour at the start of the 21st century as 'endlessly varied and infinitely volatile'. Drawing on recent survey data, it says an estimated 352 million children aged 5 to 17 are currently engaged in economic activity of some kind.

Of these, some 106 million are engaged in types of work acceptable for children who have reached the minimum age for employment (usually 15 years) or in light work such as household chores or work undertaken as part of a child's education (see ILO Minimum Age Convention No. 138 adopted in 1973).

The remaining 246 million children are involved in child labour, which the ILO says should be abolished. These forms include:

- Work performed by a child under the minimum age specified for a particular kind of work by national legislation or international standards;
- Hazardous work that jeopardizes the physical, mental or moral well-being of a child, either because of its nature or the conditions in which it is performed; and
- 'Unconditional' worst forms of child labour as defined in the ILO Worst Forms of Child Labour Convention, No. 182.

In terms of geographical distribution, the Asia-Pacific region harbours the largest absolute number of working children between the ages of 5 and 14, with some 127 million or 60 per cent of the world total. Sub-Saharan Africa is second with 48 million, or 23 per cent of the total, followed by Latin America and the Caribbean with 17.4 million or 8 per cent, and Middle East and North Africa with 13.4 million or 6 per cent.

The report says about 2.5 million, or 1 per cent of the world's child labourers, are in the industrialized countries, while another 2.4 million are found in transition economies.

Surveys in developing countries indicate that the vast majority (70 per cent) of children who work are engaged in such primary sectors as agriculture, fishing, hunting and forestry. Some 8 per cent are involved in manufacturing and wholesale and retail trade, restaurants and hotels; 7 per cent in domestic work and services; 4 per cent in transport, storage and communication; and 3 per cent in construction, mining and quarrying.

Child labour often assumes serious proportions in commercial agriculture associated with global markets for cocoa, coffee, cotton, rubber, sisal, tea and other commodities. Studies in Brazil, Kenya and Mexico have shown that children under 15 make up between 25 and 30 per cent of the total labour force in the production of various commodities. The report notes that "in many developed countries, agriculture is also the sector in which most children work" and that "family farms are a common exemption from minimum age legislation."

The informal economy, in which workers are not recognized or protected under the legal and regulatory frameworks of the labour market, is where by far the most child labourers are found.

According to the ILO analysis: "The preponderance of child labour in the informal economy, beyond the reach of most formal institutions in countries at all levels of income, represents one of the principal challenges to its effective abolition."

Some work, such as mining and deep-sea fishing, is obviously dangerous, while other work, which at first sight may appear harmless, may be similarly hazardous especially for young, undernourished and otherwise vulnerable children.

Classification of Child Labour

The 1981 Census of India divided child labour into nine industrial divisions i.e., (i) Cultivation, (ii) Agricultural labour, (iii) Livestock, Forestry, Fishing, and Plantation, (iv) Mining and Quarrying,

(v) Manufacturing, Processing, Servicing and Repairs, (vi) Construction, (vii) Trade and Commerce, and (viii) Transport, Storage and Communication, and (ix) Other Services.

UNICEF classifies the hazards of child labour into three categories: (i) Physical (ii) Cognitive (iii) Emotional, Social and Moral.

Physical Hazards

There are jobs that are hazardous in themselves and affect child labourers immediately. They affect the overall health condition, strength, vision and hearing of children. One study indicates that hard physical labour over a period of years stunts a child's physical stature by up to 30 per cent of their biological potential. Working in mines, quarries construction sites, and carrying heavy loads are some of the activities that put children directly at risk physically. Jobs in the glass and brassware industry in India, where children are exposed to high temperatures while rotating the wheel furnace and heavy and sharp tools, are clearly physically hazardous to them (*Source:* UNICEF, 1997).

Cognitive Hazards

Education helps a child to develop cognitively, emotionally and socially, and needless to say, education is often gravely reduced by child labour. Cognitive development includes literacy, numeric and the acquisition of knowledge necessary to normal life work may take so much of a child's time that it becomes impossible for them to attend school, even if they do attend, they may be too tired to be attentive and follow the lessons.

Emotional, Social and Moral Hazards

There are jobs that may jeopardize a child's psychological and social growth more than physical growth. For example, a domestic job can involve relatively light work. However long hours of work, and the physical, psychological and sexual abuse to which the child domestic labourers are exposed make the work hazardous. Studies show that several domestic servants in India on average work for twenty hours a day with small intervals. According to a UNICEF survey, about 90 per cent of employers of domestic workers in

India preferred children of 12 to 15 years of age. This is mostly because they can be easily dominated and obliged to work for long hours and can be paid less than what would have to be paid to an adult worker. Moral hazards generally refer dangers arising for children in activities in which they are used for illegal activities, such as trafficking of drugs, the sex trade, and for the production of pornographic materials (*Source:* UNICEF, 1997).

Causes of Child Labour

The available data on the causes of child labour are normally related to the phenomenon in general, and a great deal remains to be learnt about the causes of child labour in hazardous work as distinct from non-hazardous occupations. However, poverty is the most important reason why children work. This apart, demands for child labour, illiteracy, unemployment, death of parents, helplessness condition of the children are some of the contributory factors of child labour in India. It has been officially stated that 'child labour is no longer a medium of economic exploitation but is necessitated by economic necessity of the parents and in many cases that of the child himself' (Government of India Report on Child Labour in India (1954, 2).

Unfortunately a large number of children in India are deprived from their childhood. When children are supposed to enjoy their childhood and attend the school a large number of them work in the most unhygienic and unhealthy condition against minimum wage to supplement family work and/or for their own survival, which is more applicable in case of orphan and destitute children.

In the urban Metropolitan Cities of the developing countries there is a good market for disadvantaged children to work as maidservant and as a casual worker in tea stalls, shops, hotels, markets, and garages. In the Metropolitan Cities where both the family members work there is an urgent need for maidservant for household works. Besides elderly men and women, a large of families employ minor aged migrant children for the same with minimum wage. These children mostly come from the rural areas and from the neighbouring states because of utter poverty. Unfortunate parents send their children to Metropolitan Cities through some channels with a hope that at least their children will get two meals a day and some money at the end of month since parents are unable to feed their children. These small children work from early in the morning till owners go to bed at night. Very few children get sympathetic and good employers. In most of the cases these disadvantaged children are not only treated as bonded labourers, but are also abused and maltreated. They have to digest all agonies silently since they are the poorest of the poor and have nowhere to go.

There are many causes of child labour and it varies from child to child. Broadly, the causes of child labour are as follows:

Poverty

The main cause of child labour in India is poverty. Poor households need the money, which their children can earn, and children commonly contribute around 20-25 per cent of family income (Anker and Melkas, 1996). According to Naidu (1985), working children contribute up to almost 90 per cent of the family income. Because of utter poverty a large number of parents in India send their children to seek employment instead of sending them to school. Sometimes parents they themselves engage their children in family profession as an assistant or take their children in the working place to assist them.

The National Institute of Public Cooperation and Child Development, New Delhi conducted a seminar during Nov. 25-28, 1975 on this issue. At the end of the seminar participants concluded that millions of families of child labour were below the poverty line and they had to deploy their children in the labour market in order to eke out a bare subsistence (*Source:* NIPCCD Seminar Recommendations, 1975).

A study conducted by the ILO Bureau of Statistics found that 'Children's work was considered essential to maintaining the economic level of households, either in the form of work for wages, of help in household enterprises or of household chores in order to free adult household members for economic activity elsewhere' (Mehra-Kerpelman 1996). In some cases, the study found that a child's income accounted for between 34 and 37 per cent of the total household income. This study concludes that a child labourer's income is important to the livelihood of a poor family.

The percentage of the population of India living in poverty is high. In 1990, 37 per cent of the urban population and 39 per cent of the rural population was living in poverty (*Source:* International Labour Organization 1995). Poverty has an obvious relationship with child labour, and studies have 'revealed a positive correlation—in some instances a strong one—between child labour and such factors as poverty' (Mehra-Kerpelman 1996). Families need money to survive, and children are a source of additional income. Poverty itself has underlying determinants, one such determinant being caste. When analyzing the caste composition of child labourers Nangia (1987) observes that, "if these figures are compared with the caste structure of the country, it would be realized that a comparatively higher proportion of scheduled caste children work at a younger age for their own and their families' economic support". Scheduled caste (lower caste) children tend to be pushed into child labour because of their family's poverty. Nangia (1987) goes on to state that in his study 63.74 per cent of child labourers said that poverty was the reason they worked.

The combination of poverty and the lack of a social security network form the basis of the even harsher type of child labour—bonded child labour. For the poor, there are few sources of bank loans, governmental loans or other credit sources, and even if there are sources available, few Indians living in poverty qualify. Here enters the local moneylender; for an average of two thousand rupees, parents exchange their child's labour to local moneylenders (Human Rights Watch, 1996, 17).

Even though poverty is cited as the major cause of child labour, it is not the only determinant. Inadequate schools, a lack of schools, or even the expense of schooling leaves some children with little else to do but work. The attitudes of parents also contribute to child labour; some parents feel that children should work in order to develop skills useful in the job market, instead of taking advantage of a formal education.

Demand for Child Labour

Research on the causes of child labour tend to concentrate on the supply factors, both because of a justifiable preoccupation with the victims, the children, and because of the commonly shared view that poverty is the driving force. But the demand for child labour plays a critical role in determining the involvement of children in hazardous work.

There are a number of reasons why employers hire child labour, commonest explanations that are given, being the lowest cost and the irreplaceable skills afforded by children. In fact, however, these two claims are often unsustainable, and there are many others and more telling reasons why children are hired (*Source:* ILO, 1996).

Large Family and Wrong Notion of Future Security of Parents

In the rural areas there is a notion among poor parents that if they have a large family their future will be secured. Driven by this perception of future security, a large of parents opt for more number of children and they engage them in economic activities in early age instead of getting their children admitted in school. This is one of the major causes of child labour among poor families.

Alcoholism and Irresponsible Parents

There are parents especially fathers who are dependent on alcohol and they are mostly involved in casual work like rickshaw pullers, vendors, drivers, helpers and other daily wage earners. Everyday after working hours they take country made alcohol for which they spend a big portion of their daily income. As a result, they cannot take care of the basic minimal needs of their families and children. This sort of situation compels some children to work to run the family.

Child Condition i.e., Orphan and Destitute Children

At the beginning of life, orphans and destitute children survive eating leftovers. Since nobody is there to give them shelter and take care of them they live on their own on the street. They are deprived from basic child rights and remain illiterate. Later on, they accept odd jobs with minimum wage for survival and are subjected to all forms of abuse and exploitation.

Lack of Interest in Studies

After attending primary school a good number of children become school dropouts in India especially in the rural areas because of disinterest in studies and/or lack of guidance and care both in the school and in the family. During this time parents try to engage their children in some activity so that they develop some skills and at the same time they can earn some money, which is needed for the family.

Illiteracy and Wrong Perception of the Parents About Value of Education

In India, still about 40 per cent of the population are illiterate they mostly live in the rural areas and in urban slum areas. They are mainly concerned about their present and hardly think about their future because of illiteracy and wrong perception about the value of education. Most of the illiterate parents think that there is no point of sending children to school. It will be wastage of time as well as deprivation from child contribution and/or assistance. Thus, illiteracy and wrong perception about the value of education are the important causes of child labour in India.

Easy Availability and Cheap Labour

In order to maximize the profit in a business employer of some of the unorganized industries always has a tendency to recruit children because they are easily available. Employer's think that the children in their workplaces can do a lot of work and this labour of children is very cheap in comparison to that of men. It ensures employers more margin of profit over less investment.

Death or Illness of Main Earning Member in the Family

Sometimes sudden death or chronic illness of main earning member in the family compels small children to engage themselves in economic activities to run the family and discontinue education. It happens mostly because of break down of joint family system in

India. Earlier in the joint family in sort of situation other family used to extend support and children could continue their studies. This is the disadvantage of single-family concept.

Nature of Job

In carpet industry children are suitable for doing the job. Easy availability of job in the carpet industry encourages some parents to engage their children in those activities especially in case of school dropout children and the children who do not have any interest in study.

Bonded Labour System

Since the earnings of bonded child labourers are less than the interest on the loans, these bonded children are forced to work, while interest on their loans accumulates. A bonded child can only be released after his/her parents make a lump sum payment, which is extremely difficult for the poor (*Source:* Human Rights Watch, 1996). Even if bonded child labourers are released the same conditions of poverty that caused the initial debt can cause people to slip back into bondage labourers because they are given to the loom owners on the false promise of an education or good wages to be sent back home to help the family. Others are simply sold to loom owners because their families cannot afford to feed them. Even more children are simply kidnapped and sold into slavery. In each case, children are enslaved and typically live at the looms where they work.

Lack of Education Facilities and Its Impact on Child Labour

In the remote rural villages in India there is no education facility and even if there is a primary school but there is no teacher or teacher does not attend the school for a long time. This is the common scenario in the remote villages in India. As a result children hardly get any opportunity for education and in the development process they are engaged in cultivation and collection of wood from the forest and sale in the market.

India's state of education lacks effectiveness in yielding basic literacy in the population. It has been observed that 'the overall condition of the education system can be a powerful influence on the supply of child labour' (Grootaert and Kanbur 1995, 193). The 1991 Census of India shows that 64 per cent of males and 39 per cent of females are literate (The World Bank 1995, 113)—an increase of 17 per cent and 14 per cent respectively from the 1981 census (Census of India 1981 cited in Weiner 1991, 11). These increases seem significant, but India's overall literacy rate lags behind other developing countries such as China (72.6%), Sri Lanka (86.1%), and Indonesia (74.1%), all of which have Per Capita Incomes comparable to India's (Weiner 1991, 161). India's primary-school survival rate of 38.0 per cent is also lower than China's rate of 70 per cent and Sri Lanka's rate of 90.8 per cent (United Nations Educational, Scientific, and Cultural Organization cited in Weiner 1991, 159). This indicates that few students are reaching fifth or sixth grade, and dropout rates support this conclusion. Dropout rates measured by the Department of Education show that 35 per cent of males and 39 per cent of female's dropout (Government of India cited in The World Bank 1995, 113). What is the reason for these high dropout rates and poor school survival rates? One possible argument given by Nangia (1987) is that 'the pressing need for the child's earnings as well as low perceived advantages of school' cause parents to withdraw children from school and deposit them in the labour force. In this case, poverty and the inadequacy of the school system play significant roles in causing child labour, but also affect each other. Poverty forces high dropout rates, and thus no matter how good schools are, school survival rates and literacy rates will still remain low.

The concept of compulsory education, where all school-aged children are required to attend school, combats the force of poverty that pulls children out of school. Policies relating to compulsory education not only force children to attend school, but also contribute appropriate funds to the primary education system, instead of higher education.

The Indian state of Kerala distinguishes itself from the rest of India with its educational system. The government of Kerala allocates more funds to education than any other state, with a per capita expenditure of 11.5 rupees compared to the Indian average of 7.8 rupees (Weiner 1991). It is not only the expenditure of more funds, but also where the funds are used that makes the difference. Kerala spends more money on 'mass education than colleges and universities' (Weiner 1991). No correlation exists between expenditure on education and literacy when comparing different countries because some countries, such as India, spend more funds on higher education than primary education (Weiner 1991). Kerala's emphasis on primary education has lead to a dropout rate of close to 0 per cent, a literacy rate of 94 per cent for males and 86 per cent for females (*Source*: The World Bank 1995), and a low child work participation rate of 1.9 per cent (in 1971) compared to the Indian average of 7.1 per cent in 1971 (Weiner 1991). Weiner (1991) points out that 'The Kerala government has made no special effort to end child labour. It is the expansion of the school system rather than the enforcement of labour legislation that has reduced the amount of child labour.'

Ineffective Implementation of Legislation

There are a number legislation's in India to stop child labour like articles 24 and 39(e) of the Constitution of India and Bonded Laour System Act, 1976 and so on. Since these legislations are not properly implemented the number of child labourers is increasing day by day. What is needed at this hour is strong political will and support and cooperation of people of all walks of life to stop further recruitment of child labour and improvement of existing working condition of child labour.

ILO Global Report on Child Labour (2002) lists the many causes of child labour, all of which must be addressed. While poverty is a major factor, there are many other related causes such as economic and political instability, discrimination, migration, criminal exploitation, traditional cultural practices, and a lack of decent work for adults, inadequate social protection, a lack of schools and the desire for consumer goods.

On the demand side, factors include a lack of law enforcement, the desire on the part of some employers for a cheap and flexible workforce and the low profitability and productivity of small-scale, family enterprises, which cannot afford adult, paid labour.

In spite of the difficulty of addressing all these causes, the ILO report insists that "the campaign for universal ratification of Convention No. 182 has given the general fight against child labour a new urgency and scope, by focusing world attention on its worst forms". Since its unanimous adoption by the International Labour Conference in 1999, Convention No. 182 has been ratified by nearly 120 of the ILO's 175 member States. In addition, the ILO Minimum Age Convention No. 138, adopted in 1973, has been ratified by 116 member States as of 25 April.

'The world is increasingly aware of child labour and is demanding action to stop it. In this regard one social activist said that a majority of governments across the world now acknowledge the existence of the problem—on greater or smaller scales and in different forms. Many have already set out to measure and understand it, and are taking action against it.'

Social Aspects of Child Labour

Mainly the economic backwardness pushes the child to the world of child begging, juvenile delinquency, vagrancy, truancy, etc. Thus, they are thrown into a situation physically and morally polluted. The various causes may be summarized as follows (Patel, 1990):

- The emotional ties between children and their parents are disturbed.
- As a result of such interactional distortion, the children slip off from the family bondage and step into the world of disorganization.
- The emotionally affectionate relation between parent and child turns into commercial interaction.
- The parents who live below the poverty line are compelled to sell the labour of their children, which results in exploitation of child, through demand of maximum turnover at minimum wages.
- Many of the problems created by working children are economic in nature. Child labour involves the use of labour at its point of lowest productivity and is, therefore, an inefficient utilization of labour power. It frequently precludes

the most productive adulthood by distributing child workers in blind alley occupations thereby causing economic loss to the country.

- Child workers are necessarily handicapped by limitations of physical strength and experience so that they are not so productive as the adults.

Consequences of Child Labour

Child labour has negative impact on overall socio-economic development of the country. There is no doubt that in most of the cases children are forced by circumstances to work in tender age when they are supposed to go to school and enjoy their childhood. In the following section the adverse affect of child labour has been discussed:

Retards Normal Growth of the Child

Engagement of children in economic activities at an early age retards the normal mental and physical growth of the children and they become more prone to exploitation and abuse. As a result the mental and physical strength of the children are burned in their early age of life.

Deprivation from Child Rights (as per the UN Convention on the Rights of the Child)

Involvement of children in economic activities at an early age means deprivation from child rights like the right to survival (i.e., adequate nutrition and adequate standard of living), the right to protection (i.e., freedom from all forms of exploitation, abuse, and inhuman or degrading treatment), the right to development (i.e., the right to be educated, to receive support for development and care and social security, play, practice own religion and culture), and the right to participation (i.e., access to appropriate information freedom of thought and expression, conscience and religion).

Academic Backwardness

Because of involvement in economic activities working children remain deprived from education and thereby their inner potentials remain under utilized. Hence, nation loses a good amount of good human resource. As a result of massive carpet training programme, thousands of school-going children were diverted towards carpet weaving activity from their studies. The early age at which children are taught to weave, results in cutting them off from the educational system, or just one or two years schooling or without that. In this way a large number of future generation is deliberately pushed into darkness and illiteracy in utter disregard of the canons of law.

Deviation from the Mainstream of the Society

The children who are involved in economic activities in early age are deprived from basic minimal education and as a result in later life they do not find good job. After some years of work if they lose their job or the company is closed down where they used to work, no option is left to them to survive following honest and/or normal means. As a result, during unemployment period a good number of them involve themselves in antisocial activities under slightest provocation and gradually a large number of them deviate from the mainstream of the society. Hence, it is a great loss for a society.

Economic Exploitation

A number of factors encourage employers to recruit children in the unorganized and small-scale industries. The factors include:

- Less developed ego and status of consciousness;
- Lesser affection by feeling of guilt and shame;
- No hesitation to do non-status, even demanding jobs;
- Activeness, agility and quickness and lesser feeling of tiredness;
- Greater discipline and control;
- Less expensive to maintain;
- Superior adaptive abilities;
- Lack of organization; and
- Acquisition of fitness through initiation in the early age.

Thus, for maximization of profit the general tendency of employers to exploit children to fullest extent possible.

Working Conditions and Health Hazards

Owing to nature of different kinds of work and work environment children are victims of different forms of health problems, both physical and mental. Children starting work at an early age have a longer period of exposure to cumulative hazards. In certain enterprises, children are hired because adult health has already been compromised as for example in limestone, slate and glass industries. Exposure in early life to substances with long latency periods such as asbestos increase the possibility of contacting chronic diseases such lung cancer in young adulthood instead of at a later age. Children have a lower heat tolerance than adults and are therefore much more subject to heat stress, just as young workers are more susceptible to induced hearing loss from noise exposure. For these reasons, maximum permitted heat and noise levels for adults may not be stringent enough for children. Ionizing radiation, too, is likely to be particularly harmful for children since their injurious effects on growing tissues are well known and the risk is cumulative.

Following are some of the examples of working conditions and health problem children suffer from, which sometime causes permanent damage:

Agriculture

Children work in agriculture throughout the world and are subjected to occupational hazards such as exposure to machinery, biological and chemical agents. In the agricultural sector, children have to work in the fields in the scorching heat of summer (which causes headache or sunburns), biting cold of winter (which develops fissures in their hands and feet), penetrating dust storms and/or pouring waters. They are also exposed to poisonous animals like snakes and scorpions.

They can be found mixing, loading and applying pesticides, fertilizers or herbicides, some of which are highly toxic and potentially carcinogenic. Pesticides exposure poses a considerably higher risk to children than adults and has been linked to an increased risk of cancer, neuropathy, neurobehavioural effects and immune system abnormalities (*Source:* ILO, 1996).

Matches and Fireworks Industry

The production of matches normally takes place in small cottage units or in small-scale village factories where the risk of fire and explosion is present all the time. Children as young as 3 years of age are reported to be involved in the production of matches in unventilated rooms where they are exposed to dust, fumes, vapours and airborne concentrations of hazardous substances—asbestos, potassium chlorate, antimony trisulphide, amorphous red phosphorous mixed with sand or powdered glass, tetra phosphorus trisulphide. Intoxication and dermatitis from these substances are frequent (*Source:* ILO, 1996).

In India children in match and fireworks factories at Sivakasi work in the dark and dingy sheds, handling dangerous and poisonous chemicals such as potassium chlorate, phosphorous and zinc oxide. Most the children working in match and fireworks factories are aged between 4-15 years. They leave their villages for their work sites between 3-5 a.m. and return home between 6-9 p.m. In spite of over 12 hours of work a day with little relaxation, the younger children earn an average of Rs. 2 per day, whereas, the older ones are able to earn Rs. 6-7 in the same period. These children develop skin and eye diseases and occasional explosions in the factories prove to be fatal to them (Kothari, 1983).

In September 1995, a blaze had charred 23 children at Haturia village, three km north of Bagnan—district town of West Bengal. They were all working at a cracker factory. The accident had jolted the administration and like after any such calamity, pious resolutions were made. That was all. Things are no different now. Little hand still makes firecrackers in the small, dark rooms that flank the muddy footpath snaking through the Haturia village. The factory that was gutted seven years back never reopened, but three new units have come up. Most of the factories are not licensed. They are still raking in profits and the villagers who work there have remained poor as ever.

Stone Quarries and Slate Industries

Children working in stone quarries and slate industries inhale silicon dust, which forms patches of silica in the lungs, thereby reducing their capacity to absorb oxygen. Lack of oxygen may suffocate the patient do death. Mitra (1986) observed that in Multanpura village of Mandsaur, there are hardly any old person. Nearly one-third of the married people were widowed. Young children were forced to work in the slate industry to sustain the lives of their dying parents and kin. In the process, they themselves became the victims of dust (silicosis), fatigue and inhumanity. Most of the workers in this industry choke to death before reaching the age of 40.

Bidi Industry

In the bidi industry, workers are paid low wages for their dawn to dusk drudgery. Contractors invariably reject, at least, 10 per cent of workers' output as sub-standard thus depriving them of full payment for their labour. Children in bidi industry basically work as helpers to adult workers and their daily payments range from Rs.1.5—Rs. 5. They are exposed to tobacco fumes throughout the day, which leads to tuberculosis and asthma. Continuous cold, backache, body-ache, gas trouble, piles and rheumatic complaints are quite common in the industry because workers have to sit in the crouched positions in the over-crowded places which lack ventilation (Mohandas, 1980).

Carpet Industry

In the carpet industry, most of the children work on the looms located in dingy and dark sheds, which lack proper ventilation and seating capacity. They develop common diseases with breathing problems such as tuberculosis and asthma. Children also suffer from body-ache and joint and finger pains. Lack of exercise and constant sitting in one posture also results in loss of appetite. A bent posture adversely affects the reproductive capacity of the female children (Nangia, 1988).

Lock Industries

The lock industry is mostly concentrated in the Aligarh district of Uttar Pradesh. In the lock industries of Aligarh, and metal industries of Moradabad, Varanasi and Delhi, children work on hand presses, buffing machines, electroplating and spray-painting units. The chemical fumes emitted during the process affects their respiratory system and white-hot flames damage their vision. Children also complain of giddiness, tiredness and burning sensation. Also the children are at risk for work place accidents due to exhaustion; many also lose the tips of their fingers, which get caught in the machines.

Brassware Industry

In the brassware industry of Moradabad, children remove the earthenware crucibles full of molten brass from the underground furnace and pass it to the adult workers. The life span of children employed in the brass industry is quite short. The hazards of the job also include the inhaling of metal dust, which leads to tuberculosis and premature death (Nangia, 1987).

Glass Bangle and Glass Blowing Industry

In the glass bangle and glass blowing industry, children work close to the furnaces, where temperature ranges from 700 to 1800 degrees Celsius. Children work with cyanide and silica, some of them for 24 hours at a stretch, because the employers do not want the furnace heat to go to waste. Due to extreme heat and chemical fumes, tuberculosis is widespread and the life span is short. Most of the children are unable to work after they reach the age of 35 (Burra, 1986).

Retarded Mental and Physical Growth

Early employment retards the development of a child. Majority of the child workers suffers from malnutrition. Poor nutrition coupled with manual work affects normal physical growth of the children. Malnutrition, anaemia, hard work and fatigue increase the susceptibility of child labourers to communicable diseases (Naidu, 1985).

Child Domestic Workers

Violence and sexual abuse are among the most serious and frightening hazards facing children at work. It is of course almost inevitable that children growing up in such an environment will be permanently damaged both psychologically and emotionally.

Among the groups subject to such abuse are child domestic workers. Child domestic workers service is a widespread practice in the developing countries like India where employers in urban areas often recruit children from rural villages through some personal contacts and/or channels i.e., through other domestic workers. While most of the domestic workers come from extremely poor families, many have been abandoned, are orphaned or come from single parent families.

Deb (1997) made an attempt to investigate the nature and workload of girl children engaged in domestic work, their wage package and the kind of problems faced by them. A group of 180 girl children of 10-18 years' age group working in middle and upper income group of families in Kolkata. Surprisingly, truths disclosed are far from satisfactory. The significant majority of the girl children are found to have been receiving wages too low (ranging from 1 to 10 US $ p.m.) compared to the nature and volume of work performed by them (i.e., cleaning utensils, clothes, rooms, taking care of younger children, cooking and shopping), not to mention untold psychological (i.e., threatened to dismiss from the work, not allowed to enter into the house, withdrawal of food, confinement in a room) and even physical torments (i.e., being beaten up by stick, utensils, iron rod and hot iron) inflicted upon them for minor mistakes. Not infrequently these girls become victims of sexual harassment particularly in the upper class families. Almost in all cases they are treated no better than slaves and are forced to feed on leftovers of the meals served to the concerned household members. Well or unwell, they are compelled to do all types of household chores, because they are altogether deprived of medical attention. While reality stands as observed above, it is of utmost importance of the hour to create widespread social awareness in order to change the lots of countless neglected and abused girl children for the better which they rightly deserve.

In the urban Metropolitan Cities of the developing countries there is a good market for disadvantaged children to work as maidservant and as a casual worker in tea stalls, shops, hotels, markets, and garages. In Metropolitan Cities in India where both the couples work an urgent need for maidservant for managing household works has been felt. Besides elderly men and women, a large number of families recruits minor children for the same on a minimum wage package. These children mostly come from the rural areas and/or from the neighbouring states. Unfortunate parents send their children to Metropolitan Cities like Kolkata through some channels with a hope that at least their children will get two meals a day and some money at the end of month. In another study Deb and Mitra (2002) attempted to understand the nature and types of abuse and neglect among migrant child labour in South Kolkata and its consequences. A group of 120 migrant child labour working in households, tea-stalls, garages and shops were covered in the present study following snowball technique and data were collected through informal interview method. This apart, observation method was also employed to have first hand experience about the behaviour of the employer towards these children and nature of workload taken by the disadvantaged children.

Findings of Deb and Mitra's study disclosed that a large number of the children are either abused physically, mentally, sexually and/or in combination. In case of health problems, a good number of them remain untreated. In most of the cases these children are treated as a bonded labour. As a result of abuse and neglect most of the children have developed negative attitude towards the authority figures and society. Authors suggested that law enforcement agencies should be very strict against the perpetrators and the children should be given justice. Otherwise in future these children may be drifted into a negative direction.

Slavery and Forced Child Labour

Slavery is not dead. Societies are loath to admit to still harbouring it but, as can be surmised from cases reported to the ILO Committee of Experts on the Application of Conventions and Recommendations, numerous children are trapped in slavery in many parts of the world (*Source:* ILO, 1996). India is not exception to that. Of all working children, surely these are the most imperiled. One of the most common forms of bondage is family bondage, where children work to help pay off a loan or other obligation incurred by the family. The lenders, who are often landlords, usually manipulate the situation in such a way that it is difficult or impossible for the family to pay off it debt, thereby assuring essentially free labour indefinitely. A family may thus remain bonded through generations, with children replacing their aged or infirm parents in an inter-generational bondage arrangement (*Source:* ILO, 1996).

A large number of child labours are badly treated by the employers and sometimes they are forced to work for a long period. The following case will illustrate how child labours are treated. This is not an isolated case. There are thousands of such children who become the victim of vicious cycle and for which they have to work for a long period as bonded labour.

> ***Case 1:*** *A 16-year-old boy was chained and made to work for 16 days by his former employer at a small leather factory in Tiljala, Kolkata. The boy was rescued by Tiljala Police. According to Police, he took a loan of Rs. 1,600 from his past employer. As he could not repay it, former employer kept him confined in a style reminiscent of medieval barbarism. Both his legs were tied with long iron shackles, which were tethered to the window-bar so he could not get away without delivering work Rs.1,600. For 16 days, he was made to toil this way. He was only released to attend nature's call and to take a bath (Source:* Boy chained at work for 16 days, *Sunday Times,* Aug. 31, 2003).

Street Work

There are thousands of children who live and work in the city streets of India. According to a study conducted among the street children in the city of Chennai (Madras) about 90 per cent of them live with their parents in the streets (*Source:* National Labour Institute, 1992) Contrary to the general conception that many street children are delinquents the study revealed that only 6.6 per cent of the total sample had served time in juvenile homes or correctional institutions.

Studies in a few other India cities showed that the majority of the street children were doing rag picking for their living. Usually, these children are unable to submit references or pay deposits to their employers to obtain any work.

Scavenging is the work that faces children with the most extreme risk. As many of them work with bare feet, they get dust they are also exposed to extreme weather conditions, sunstroke, pneumonia, influenza and malaria. They have to carry heavy loads, which stunts their physical growth. They suffer from digestive disorders and food poisoning as they eat thrown away or left over food. A recent study conducted in Delhi found they were at risk of catching AIDS, as they may accidentally come into contact with infected needles deposited in the refuse. Since animals scavenge in the same heaps of refuse, dog bites are quite common among these children. The local police and even the municipal cleaners create great difficulties for the street children in India. For any petty thefts they are the first ones to be accused by the police. It is observed that the police extort about half the earnings of the rag pickers as commission. The children also had to pay some staff members of the municipally to ease the way for rag picking (*Source:* National Labour Institute, 1992)

Prostitution and Trafficking of Children

The commercial sexual exploitation of children has in recent years become an issue of global concern, and the indications are that it is on the rise. Children are increasingly being bought and sold across national borders by organized networks. For example, every year large number of children from the rural areas, from the hill stations and from the neighbouring countries like Nepal and Bangladesh are coming to different red-light areas in Kolkata and Mumbai.

At the root of the commercial sexual exploitation of children in many countries lies poverty, the inability of rural and urban families to support and educate their children. In some cases ethnic origin, cultural practices and social discrimination render children from indigenous population, minority groups and the lower castes are especially vulnerable. Commercial sexual exploitation is one of the most brutal forms of violence against children. Child victims suffer extreme physical, psychosocial and emotional abuse, which have lifelong and life-threatening consequences. With the advent of HIV/AIDS these girl children are exposed to this disease because of lack of knowledge about the mode of transmission (*Source:* ILO, 1996).

Some factory owners employ children to earn more profit. As many as 150 of them could be spending long hours in these death traps (*Source: The Times of India*, Nov. 5, 2002).

The carpet-weaving children are exposed to several health hazards and are not covered by health insurance and are seldom visited by a physician. According to a news Correspondent (*The Times of India,* 1979) a boy, whom the Correspondent met in a carpet-weaving center, had already become 'mentally and physically handicapped'.

Given the above health hazards scenario, it is the job of the respective state governments to implement the laws in this regard very strictly and ensure safety and security of children health.

Prevention of Child Labour

Total eradication of child labour in India in the present context may not be possible, but government can evolve a strong national machinery to ensure that the child workers are not exploited. Besides taking steps to enforce existing legislations it will have to see that children work in jobs, which are safe, secure and free from health hazards. It should also ensure that child labourers are given a proper wage. According to Srivastava (1986) the total eradication of child labour is neither feasible nor desirable in the foreseeable future, unless basic minimal facilities like food; shelter clothing, health and educational facilities are provided for all. To tackle the problem of child labour, long term as well as short-term policies should be formulated. In the long-term policy it is necessary to create conditions by providing a proper climate and social security, educational training and other facilities in order to gradually eradicate child labour. In the short-term policy it is necessary to eliminate and minimize the impact of adverse conditions affecting child labour. This can be done by regulating hours of work, weekly holidays, leave, health services, safety, and welfare and among others, social security (Pande, 1979).

Social Awareness

Social awareness is urgently needed to sensitize people of cross-section of the society about the negative aspects of child labour and its consequent long-term impact on over all socio-economic development of the country. The awareness programmes need to be organized separately for different target groups. For creating social awareness mass media especially through television show, non-government welfare organizations, trade union, government and various political parties can play an important role in creating awareness about the dire consequences of child labour and its negative effect on child and in the society by changing the attitude of employers, police and general population.

In this regard concerned government officials should be targeted first. If the willingness prevails, concerned government officials can curb the menace of child exploitation to a great extent. If the provisions made in various Acts regarding minimum age at employment, wages, working hours, rest interval, type of work etc. are strictly adhered to, the working environment of children can be improved and their working life can turn out to a rewarding experience instead of exploitative.

Constitutional Safeguards Against Child Labour in India

The constitution carries important expression of the government policies against the abuse of child labour. Fundamentally the Constitution provides that 'no child below the age of fourteen (as against the UN Declaration of fifteen) years shall be employed to work in any factory or mines or engaged in any hazardous employment (Article 24). It further proclaims that the State shall, in particular, direct its policy towards securing that the health and strength of the tender age of children are not forced by economic necessity to enter avocations unsuited to their age or strength (Article 39e). Apart from that the Constitution also endeavours to provide free and compulsory education for all children until they compete the age of fourteen age (Article 45).

This apart, there are also certain other provisions contained in Part IV dealing with the Directive Principles of State Policy, which although do not lay emphasis on the child welfare directly, yet the children are bound to be the beneficiaries if these provisions are implemented. Articles 38, 41, 42, 43, 46 and 47 contain such provisions, which *inter alia* provides strategy for indirectly promoting the welfare of the children.

Article 38 (1) provides that State shall strive to promote the welfare of the people by securing and protecting as effectively as it may secure a social order in which justice, social, economic and political shall inform all institutions of national life. Naturally, an effective implementation of this principle resulting in promoting the welfare of the people through social, economic and political justice is expected to promote proportionately the child welfare.

Article 41 says that the State shall within the limits of its economic capacity and development; make effective provision for securing, *inter alia,* the right to education and to public assistance in cases of unemployment and other cases of underserved want. Implementation of such provision is expected to promote the welfare of the children proportionately.

According to the provisions of Article 42 of the Constitution the State is required to secure just and humane conditions of work besides some maternity benefit. This provision envisages a healthy psychological environment to the child particularly during the significant period when the child requires a normal bringing-up.

Article 43 of the Constitution lays emphasis that the State shall endeavour to secure, by suitable legislation, to all workers, agricultural, industrial or otherwise; not only work but also living wage with specified conditions of work ensuring a decent standard of life and full enjoyment of leisure and social and cultural opportunities. This provision also includes child labourers in its widest interpretation.

Article 46 of the Constitution, similarly lays down that the State shall promote with special care the educational and economic interests of the Scheduled Castes and Scheduled Tribes and other weaker sections of the society. The children belonging to such category are the worst affected and need to be constitutionally protected.

Similarly, Article 47 of the Constitution lays emphasis that it shall be the primary duty of the State to raise the standard of living of its people, which includes children.

Legal Measures Adopted by the Government of India

In regard to child employment several laws were passed with an objective of improving working conditions and for protecting children against abuse, exploitation, and health hazards. Following are some of the important legislations providing legal protection to child labour in India:

- *The Child (Pledging of Labour) Act, 1933:* The main purpose of this Act is to prohibit the pledging of labour of children. Here child means a person who has not completed the age of 15 years according to Section 2 of this Act. The Act lays down that an agreement, oral or written, expressed or implied, made by parent or guardian of a child in consideration of some payment or benefit for causing or allowing the services of a child to be utilized in any employment, shall be void (Section 3). The Act makes provision for fine up to Rs.50 in case of parent or guardian if found guilty of making an agreement to pledge the labour of the child (Section 4), up to Rs. 200 for making with parent or guardian agreement to pledge the labour of the child (Section 5) and up to Rs.200 for employing a child whose labour has been pledged (Section 6) from September 1971, this act has been extended to whole of India.
- *The Employment of Children Act, 1938:* This Act extends to whole of India and aims at regulating the employment of children in certain establishments. The Act prohibits employment of children who have not completed 15 years of age in any occupation connected with the transport of passengers, goods or mails by sail ways etc [Section 3 (1)]. The Act permits the employment of child of more than 15 years and less than 17 years in any of the above mentioned occupations on the conditions that the child is allowed a rest interval of at least 12 consecutive hours in a

day which shall include at least 7 consecutive hours between 10 p.m. and 7 a.m. [Section 3(2)]. The penalty for the preach of the provisions of Act is simple imprisonment up to one month or fine up to Rs.500 or both (Section 4).

- *The Minimum Wages Act, 1948:* This Act makes provisions for fixation of minimum rates of wages in certain employment's, which have been specified by appropriate government in the schedule of the Act. The Minimum Wages Act provides for a four and half hours and differential rates of minimum for child workers.
- *The Factories Act, 1948:* This Act extends to whole of India and applies to establishment employing 10 or more workers with power [Section 2 (m)]. Under this Act, 'child' means a person who has not completed the fifteenth year of age [Section 2 (c)]. Hour of work of the child workers shall be in accordance with the period of work of children displayed in the notice. A register of child workers shall be maintained by employer (Section 73). Employment of children in any part of the factory for pressing cotton, in which cotton opener is at work, is normally prohibited (Section 27). The State Government is empowered under this Act to make rules regarding maximum weights, which they may lift, by adolescent and children [Section 34 (2)]. The Act prescribes penalty of imprisonment of two months or fine up to Rs. 1000 or both in case of using false certificate of fitness (Section 98) and of a fine up to Rs. 1000 on parent or guardian in case of double employment of children (Section 99).
- *The Plantation Labour Act, 1951:* This Act extends to whole of India except the State of Jammu and Kashmir. All tea, coffee, rubber, cinnamon and cardamom plantations measuring five hectares or more and employing 15 or more persons are covered under this Act [Section 1 (4a)]. A child (below 14 years) cannot be employed for work unless he is certified fit for work by a surgeon (Section 26). Use of a false certificate of fitness is punishable by imprisonment,

which may be extended to one month or with fine up to Rs.50 or both (Section 34).

- *The Mines Act, 1952:* This Act covers whole of India. For the purpose of the Act, mine includes all excavations where any operation for the purpose of searching for or obtaining minerals is carried out. The Act prohibits employment of person below 18 years in any mine or part there of (Section 40) and also there presence in any part of the mine above ground where any operation connected with or incidental to any mining operation is being carried out (Section 45). The Act prescribes punishment of fine up to Rs.500 in case of employment of persons below 18 years (*Section* 68).
- *The Merchant Shipping Act, 1961:* This Act applies to sea going ships registered in India. This Act prohibits employment of children less than 15 years in a ship, except in a school ship or training ship (Section 109). The Act restricts employment of a person below the age of 18 years as trimmers or stockers in any ship.
- *The Motor Transport Workers Act, 1951:* The Act extends to whole of India and covers every motor transport undertakings employing five or more persons. The State Government is authorized to apply all or any of the provisions of this Act to any motor transport undertakings employing less than five workers (Section 1). The law prohibits employment of persons under 14 years of age in any capacity in the motor transport undertaking (Section 21). The contravention of the provisions of the Act shall be punishable with imprisonment up to three months or fine up to five hundred rupees or both (Section 31).
- The Apprentices Act, 1961: This Act extends to whole of India (Section 1) and applies to any area or to any industry in any area notified by the central government [Section 1(4)]. The Act lays down that a person shall not be qualified for being engaged as an apprentice to undergo apprenticeship training in any designated Trade unless he is not less than 14 years of age; and satisfied such standards

of education and physical fitness as may be prescribed (Section 3). The Act prescribes that in case of minors the contract of apprenticeship has to be entered into by guardian [Section 4(1)] and it should be registered with the Apprenticeship Adviser [Section 4(2)].

- *The Atomic Energy Act, 1962:* In 1971 the Radiation Protection Rules have been framed under Section 30 of this Act. Rules 5 prohibits the employment of persons who have not completed 18 years as radiation workers except with the prior written permission of the competent authority.
- *The Bidi and Cigar Workers Act, 1966:* The Act extends to whole of India except the state of Jammu and Kashmir (Section 1). It covers all industrial premises where in any manufacturing process connected with making of bedi or cigar or both is being, or is ordinarily, carried on with or without the aid power [Section 2 (1)]. The Act prohibits the employment of children below 14 years in any such premises (Section 24). The Act provides penalties for breach, which may be for the first offence with fine which may extend to Rs. 250 and for a second or any subsequent offence with imprisonment for a term which shall not be less than one month or more than six months or with fine which shall not be less than Rs.100 or more than Rs.500 or with both [Section 33 (1)].
- *State Shops and Establishment Acts:* These Acts were passed with a view to regulating the conditions of work of workers in shops and commercial establishments. These Acts prohibit the employment of children in shops, commercial establishments like hotels and restaurants. Night employment of children in shops and commercial establishments is prohibited and the daily working hours are generally up to 5 hours with half an hour or one-hour break after 3-4 hours of work.

Government of India's Policies and Actions

The National Child Labour Policy

Increasing attention is now being paid to strengthening the enforcement machinery related to child labour. Soon after the enactment of the comprehensive Child Labour (Prohibition & Regulation) Act, 1986, the Government of India adopted a National Child Labour Policy in 1987, in accordance with the constitutional provisions and various legislation on child labour. The idea of adopting a separate policy on child labor was not only to place the issue on the nation's agenda, but also to formulate a specific programme of action to initiate the process of progressive elimination of child labour. The policy consists of three complementary measures:

- *Legal action plan:* This policy envisages strict enforcement of the provisions of the Child Labour (Prohibition and Regulation) Act, 1986 and other child-related legislation.
- Focus on general development programmes benefiting children wherever possible: The policy envisages the development of an extensive system of non-formal education for working children withdrawn from work and increasing the provision for employment and income generating schemes meant for their parents. A special cell —Child Labour Cell—was constituted to encourage voluntary organizations to take up activities like non-formal education,—vocational training, provisions of health care, nutrition and education for working children.

Area specific projects: To focus on areas known to have high concentration of child labour and to adopt a project approach for identification, withdrawal and rehabilitation of working children.

National Child Labour Projects (NCLP)

Under the action plan of the National Policy on Child Labour, there have been National Child Labour Projects (NCLP) sets up in different areas to rehabilitate child labour. A major activity undertaken under the NCLP is the establishment of special schools to provide non-formal education, vocational training, supplementary nutrition etc. to children withdrawn from employment. Under the project based action plan of the policy, 12 NCLPs were started in the States of Andhra Pradesh (Jaggampet and Markapur), Bihar (Garwah), Madhya Pradesh (Mandsaur), Maharashtra (Thane), Orissa (Sambalpur), Rajasthan (Jaipur), Tamil Nadu (Sivakasi) and Uttar Pradesh (Varanasi-Mirzapur-Bhadohi, Moradabad, Aligarh and Ferozabad).

Rehabilitation of Children Working in Hazardous Occupations

A major programme was launched on 15th August, 1994 for withdrawing child labour working in hazardous occupations and for rehabilitating them through special schools. Under the programme a total of two million children are sought to be brought out of work and put in special schools where they will be provided with education, vocational training, monthly stipends, nutrition and health-checks. As a follow-up, a high-powered body, the National Authority for the Elimination of Child Labour (NAECL) was constituted on 26th September, 1994 under the Chairmanship of the Minister for Labour, Government of India. The functions of NAECL are:

- To lay down policies and programs for the elimination of child labour, particularly in hazardous employment;
- To monitor the progress of the implementation of programmes, projects and schemes for the elimination of child labour;
- To coordinate the implementation of child labour related projects of the various sister Ministries of Government of India (to ensure convergence of services for the benefit of the families of child labour).

Secretaries to Government of India in the Ministries of Labour, Information and Broadcasting, Welfare, Rural Development, Textiles and the Departments of Expenditure, Education, Health, Family Welfare and Women and Child Development are members of the National Authority for the Elimination of Child Labor. The NAECL has already met five times on October 1, 1994, November 1, 1994, and January 1, 1995, July 10,1995 and December 31, 1996.

Present Coverage Under National Child Labour Project

So far 76 child labour projects have been sanctioned under the National Child Labour Project Scheme for covering 150,000 children. Around 105,000 children are already enrolled in the special schools. The following Table 3.2 gives the figures of the state-wise coverage of children under the National Child Labour Project.

Table 3.2: Coverage under National Child Labour Project

State	*Districts*	*Sanctioned Schools*	*Coverage Children*	*Actual School*	*Coverage Children*
Andhra Pradesh	20	807	43550	610	36249
Bihar	08	174	12200	173	10094
Gujarat	02	040	2000	023	1254
Karnataka	03	100	5000	024	1200
Madhya Pradesh	05	138	9800	087	6524
Maharashtra	02	074	3700	024	1200
Orissa	16	430	33000	239	14972
Rajasthan	02	060	3000	054	2700
Tamil Nadu	08	379	19500	307	14684
Uttar Pradesh	04	150	11500	105	7488
West Bengal	04	219	12000	164	8250
Total	76	2571	155250	1810	104615

Budgetary Support to Child Labour Programme

A plan provision of Rs. 150 million was made for child labour elimination programme in India's Eighth Five-Year Plan (1992-93 and 1996-97). The budgetary allocation was substantially stepped up after the launching of programme in August 1994 for the rehabilitation of child labour working in hazardous occupations. The allocation during 1995-96 and 1996-97 was of the order of Rs.344 million and Rs.560 million. As against this, the actual expenditure for these two years was of the order of Rs.343 million and Rs.338

million respectively. The allocation for 1997-98 is Rs.784 million. (In 1995-96 and 1996-97, $1=Rs.35 approximately. In 1997-98, $1 = Rs. 37 approximately).

Status of Free and Compulsory Education

India's National Policy on Education, 1986 gives the highest priority to the programme of universal elementary education, and recommends that free and compulsory education of sufficient quality be provided to all children up to the age of 14 years before we enter the 21st century. The present thrust is on three aspects, namely, universal access and enrolment, universal retention of children up to 14 years of age, and substantial improvement in the quality of education to enable all children to achieve essential levels of learning. All these aspects have been incorporated in the various initiatives taken up by the Ministry of Human Resource Development.

All the State Governments have abolished tuition fees in government schools up to the upper primary level education. In schools run by local bodies and private-aided institutions is almost free. However, unaided institutions (3 to 7%) do charge fees. Compulsory Education Acts have been enacted in 14 states and 4 Union Territories viz. Assam, Andhra Pradesh, Bihar, Delhi, Gujarat, Haryana, Jammu & Kashmir, Karnataka, Madhya Pradesh, Maharashtra, Punjab, Rajasthan, Tamil Nadu, Kerala, West Bengal, Chandigarh, Pondicherry and Andaman and Nicobar Islands.

Assistance to Voluntary Organizations

Under the grant-in-aid scheme, voluntary organizations are being financially assisted to the extent of 75 per cent of the project cost for taking up welfare projects for working children where the children are provided with education, supplementary nutrition, health care and vocational/skill training.

The government needs to take concrete steps, such as a well-planned job creation system to address this problem. This would ensure that the adults in the family get jobs and are able to support their families. The education system does not prepare the child for work and fails to benefit the child in the long run. It is a failure on the part of the state not to make education attractive enough for the child too long to go to school. 6-11 years is a very important period for the development and intellectual growth of a child. So the state should have a legal obligation to provide compulsory primary education to all. After the age of 14, the child should have an option to go in for vocational training, which will be useful for him in the long run. Education needs to undergo a total revamp in order to make it useful for the child to go to a school.

Supreme Court Directions on Child Labour

The Supreme Court of India, in its judgement dated 10th December, 1996 in Writ Petition (Civil) Number 465/1986, has given certain directions regarding the manner in which children working in the hazardous occupations are to be withdrawn from work and rehabilitated, and the manner in which the working conditions of children working in non-hazardous occupations are to be regulated and improved. The judgement of the Supreme Court envisages:

- Simultaneous action in all districts of the country;
- Survey for identification of working children (to be completed by June 10, 1997);
- Withdrawal of children working in hazardous industries and ensuring their education in appropriate institutions;
- Contribution of Rs. 20,000 per child to be paid by the offending employers of children to a welfare fund to be established for this purpose;
- Employment to one adult member of the family of the child so withdrawn from work, and if that is not possible a contribution of Rs.5000 to the welfare fund to be made by the State Government;
- Financial assistance to the families of the children so withdrawn to be paid out of the interest earnings on the corpus of Rs. 20,000/25,000 deposited in the welfare fund as long as the child is actually sent to the schools;
- Regulating hours of work for children working in non-hazardous occupations so that their working hours do not exceed six hours per day and education for at least two

hours is ensured. The entire expenditure on education is to be borne by the concerned employer;

- Planning and preparedness on the part of Central and State Governments in terms of strengthening of the existing administrative/regulatory/enforcement framework (covering cost of additional manpower, training, mobility, computerization etc.) implying additional requirement of funds.

Follow-up Action on the Directions of the Supreme Court

As a follow up of the directions of the Supreme Court, all the State Governments were sent detailed guidelines on December 26, 1996 indicating the manner in which the directions of the Supreme Court were to be implemented. A meeting of the NAECL was convened on 31st December, 1996 to discuss the directions of the Supreme Court on child labour. It was decided in the meeting that the Ministry of Labor should immediately release funds to the State Governments so as to enable them to conduct surveys of working children before June 10, 1997. A conference of the Labour Ministers of State/Union Territories was convened on January 22,1997 to finalize an action plan for the implementation of the directions of the Supreme Court on withdrawal and rehabilitation of working children. In the conference, all the participating States and Union Territories welcomed the judgement and demonstrated their political will to eliminate child labour. However, all the States pleaded for additional and liberal financial assistance from the Central Government for implementing the judgement of the Supreme Court. The following significant recommendations were made in the Conference:

- The survey envisaged in the judgment of the Supreme Court would be in two phases. In the first phase the survey would be conducted in all industries, establishments, shops, work places in urban and semi-urban catchments areas where hazardous processes will be identified. In the event of any child labour being found employed in any such process, simultaneous action would be taken to recover an amount of Rs. 20,000 from the offending employer.

Hazardous establishments in the rural areas would also be fully covered by the survey in the first phase. The door-to-door survey for the purpose of identification and enumeration of working children will be taken up in the second phase.

- While primarily it is the responsibility of the State Governments to provide necessary funds for taking up activities in compliance of the directions of the Supreme Court, funds for conducting the survey will be released by the Central Government to the agencies at the district level immediately. If the funds released for the first phase of survey fall short of the actual requirement in any district, the State Governments will provide the additional funds for this purpose. Since this first phase of the survey is concentrated on industrial establishments, the requirement of funds would be worked out by the Central Government and the same would be released immediately.
- Immediate action will be initiated by the State Governments for strengthening the enforcement machinery at various levels and for creation of a separate cell at the State level to monitor and coordinate the activities to be taken up in compliance of the directions of the Supreme Court. They will also send their requirements of funds in this regard, if any, to the Planning Commission at the earliest.
- If the State Governments are not in a position to complete the survey by 10th June, they will apprise the Hon'ble Supreme Court about the reasons for delay and seek extension of time from the Hon'ble Supreme Court well in advance.
- If for some reason, the State Governments find it difficult to give effect to any one or more directions of the Supreme Court, they will seek necessary clarification/directions from the Hon'ble Supreme Court well in time.

As a follow-up of the decision taken in the State Labour Ministers' Conference, the Chief Secretaries of State and Union

Territories have been sent detailed guidelines for carrying out the survey as per the directions of the Supreme Court. A copy of the child labour survey form has also been sent to the Governments of State and Union Territories. Funds have been released to all the State and Union Territories governments for the purpose of conducting the surveys. The Chief Secretaries were specifically instructed that if the State Governments could not complete the surveys in time, they should apprise the Supreme Court through an affidavit about the reasons for delay and seek extension of time from the Supreme Court well in advance.

Global Approach to Combat this Social Problem

ILO Conventions and Recommendations

The ILO adopted its first Convention on child labour in 1919, the year of its foundation. The Minimum Age (Industry) Convention, 1919 (No.5), prohibits the work of children under the age of 14 in industrial establishments. Subsequently, nine sectoral Conventions on the minimum age of admission to employment were adopted applying to industry, agriculture, trimmers and stockers, maritime work, non-industrial employment, fishing and underground work. Numerous other ILO standards contain provisions setting minimum ages for various activities.

The recent and comprehensive ILO instruments on child labour are the Minimum Age Convention, 1973 (No.138), and Recommendation (No.146). Convention No.138 is a consolidation of principles that had been gradually established in various earlier instruments and applies to all sectors of economic activity, whether or not the children are employed for wages.

The Convention obliges ratifying States to fix a minimum age for admission to employment or work and undertakes to pursue a national policy designed to ensure the effective abolition of child labour and to rise progressively the minimum age for admission to employment or work to a level consistent with the fullest physical and mental development of young persons. The Convention was not intended as a static instrument prescribing a fixed minimum standard but as a dynamic one aimed at encouraging the progressive improvement of standards and of promoting sustained action to attain the objectives.

A Recommendation No. 146, which supplements Convention No.138, provides the broad framework and essential policy measures for both the prevention of child labour and its elimination (*Source:* ILO, 1996).

IPEC: ILO's International Program for the Elimination of Child Labour

The International Program on the Elimination of Child Labour is a global programme launched by the International Labour Organization in December 1991. India was the first country to join it in 1992 when it signed a Memorandum of Understanding with the ILO. The long-term objective of IPEC is to contribute to the effective abolition of child labour. Its immediate objectives are:

- Elimination of the capability of ILO constituents and Non-Government Organizations to design, implement and evaluate programmes for Child Labor Elimination;
- To identity interventions at community and national levels which could serve as models for replication; and
- Creation of awareness and social mobilization for securing elimination of child labour.

At the international level, IPEC has a Programme Steering Committee consisting of representatives of the ILO, the donors and participating countries. At the national level in India, there is a National Steering Committee of which the Labour Secretary is the Chairman. This is tripartite in its composition with representation from NGOs as well. There is a National Programme Coordinator based at New Delhi who coordinates IPEC work between the Ministry of Labour, the agencies receiving assistance and ILO Headquarters. ILO has made an allocation of $4.15 million between 1992 and 1996 for the IPEC programme in India.

As per the Memorandum of Understanding between the Government of India and the ILO, the IPEC programme was to continue till December 31, 1996. The MOU was extended on

Table 3.3: State-wise Projects Under IPEC and Number of Children Covered (1992-1997)

State	*Project Approved*	*No. Children*	*State*	*Projects Approved*	*No. Children*
Andhra Pradesh	15	15455	Bihar	3	1340
Delhi	6	4200	Gujarat	5	1350
Haryana	1	300	Karnataka	2	1320
Kerala	2	2000	Madhya Pradesh	6	2050
Manipur	1	500	Maharashtra	7	1750
Orissa	4	1500	Rajasthan	7	5800
Tamil Nadu	17	6710	Uttar Pradesh	11	13939
West Bengal	19	22890	Regional	2	NA
All India Institutions	11	NA			

Total Projects Approved: 120
Total Number of Children Covered Under the Projects: 81154

January 28, 1997, until December 31, 1997 in the first instance. Thereafter, the MOU continues with mutual agreement.

Other International Treaties

A good number of international treaties are relevant to child labour and the protection of children from its most intolerable forms. Foremost among these is the United Nations Conventions on the Rights of the Child, 1989 (entry into force on September 2, 1990; 187 ratifications as at July 31, 1996). This Convention is the most comprehensive treaty on the rights of children, whom it defines as persons under the age of 18, unless the age of majority is attained earlier. It seeks to protect a wide range of children's rights, including the right to be protected from economic exploitation and from performing any work that is likely to be hazardous or to interfere with their education, or to be harmful to their health or physical, mental, spiritual, moral or social development. It requires state parties to take legislative, administrative, social and educational measures to ensure implementation and, in particular, to provide for (a) a minimum age or minimum ages for admission to employment, (b) appropriate regulation of the hours and conditions of employment, and (c) appropriate penalties or other sanctions to ensure the effective enforcement of its provisions (*Source*: ILO, 1996).

Latest Selective Study Findings

Weller *et al.* (2003) made an attempt to understand the nature of injuries among high school students who work long hours during the school year in South Texas. Anonymous surveys were collected from 3565 secondary students in 23 schools. Self-reported data included weekly work hours and type of injury and job when injured. A dose-response effect was observed: increasing weekly work hours were related to injury (1-10 hours, adjusted odds ratio [AOR] = 1.0; 11-20 hours, 1.4; 21+ hours, 1.5), P < .000. The AOR for restaurant work was 3.2; for construction, 3.0; for factory, office, or skilled labour, 2.9; for agriculture, 2.8; for yard work, 2.0; and for baby sitting (1.0). Males (OR = 1.5) were more prone to injury. High-intensity weekly work increased the likelihood of injury. Prevention efforts should be targeted to youth to reduce work injuries.

Probabilistic migration models assume that search for urban jobs is entirely an urban-based activity and that employment in free-entry activities is a transitional phase during which migrants are actively searching for formal sector employment. In this regard Banerjee (1984) tested the empirical validity of these assumptions using data, collected by the author in a sample survey in Delhi [India] in 1975-76, on 1,400 migrants from rural areas. Evidence is presented that the migration process postulated in probabilistic models is not realistic in the case of Delhi. Over one-half of the sample had moved to Delhi after lining up specific jobs; a sizeable proportion expected to enter on arrival activities generally considered to be characterized by freedom of entry; and the majority of entrants into free-activities did not search for alternative employment and were engaged in the same activities at the time of the survey.

Mathews *et al.* (2003) reported that despite the existence of laws in India that prohibit the labour of children under age 14, 70 to 115 million children between the ages of 5 and 14 are estimated to be part of India's labour force. Child labour in the agriculture sector accounts for 80 per cent of child labourers in India and 70 per cent of working children globally. From May 2001 to July 2001, Physicians for Human Rights (PHR) investigated the health experiences of 100 children in hybrid cottonseed production in rural Andhra Pradesh. Eighty-eight per cent of the survey participants were girls, ages 7 to 14. PHR found that children worked on average 12 hours a day, were frequently exposed to pesticides, and were not provided with safety equipment, not even shoes or water to wash their hands and clothes. Children reported having frequent headaches and dizziness and skin and eye irritations after pesticide spraying. All 100 children reported that they were unable to go to school during the hybrid cottonseed season due to work demands. Ninety-four children reported to PHR that they would rather be in school. In addition, a majority of child workers interviewed by PHR reported physical and/or verbal abuse by their employers. Moreover, PHR interviews with representatives of multinational and national companies revealed knowledge of child labour practices for up to 10 years. Child labour is a significant health and human rights problem for children in India. The progressive elimination of child labour practices will require the support of a wide cross-section of civil society.

In a study Price (2003) made an attempt to understand the volume of recruitment of children in nursing profession. The survey was initially undertaken in 1998 and repeated in 2002. A letter requesting an application pack for 'a position as a D grade staff nurse on your children's ward/s' was sent to English NHS trusts identified as having a children's service. In 1998, 28 out of 47 (56 per cent) of the trusts appeared willing to employ nurses without a children's nursing qualification, indicating that a registered general nurse (RGN) or enrolled nurse qualification (EN) would be acceptable. In 2002, 12 of the trusts had changed their registration requirements for the D grade post since 1998 but four (out of 19 that provided data) were still apparently willing to employ non-children's nurses on children's wards. The size of the sample makes it inappropriate to generalize the results across all acute NHS trusts but there are indications that in spite of government policy and recommendations, some trusts appear willing to consider employing nurses without a children's qualification on children's wards.

Wu *et al.* (2003) examined the association between employment status and substance use among students aged 12 to 17 years. Secondary analysis of data from the 1995 and 1996 National Household Surveys on Drug Abuse was conducted. The survey was a primary source of data on licit and illicit drug use among non-institutionalized Americans aged 12 years or older. Participants were interviewed at their places of residence. Multiple logistic regression procedures yielded estimated associations. About one in six adolescents reported both going to school and holding a job. Approximately one-fourth of students smoked cigarettes, and one-third consumed alcohol in the past year. An estimated 1.6 per cent of students were current heavy cigarette smokers, and 2.6 per cent were current heavy alcohol users. One-year prevalence estimates of any illicit drug use and heavy illicit drug use were 16.7 per cent and 1.8 per cent, respectively. Among students employed full time, prevalence estimates increased to 9.7 per cent for heavy cigarette smoking, 13.1 per cent for heavy alcohol use, 38.1 per cent for any illicit drug use, and 5.0 per cent for heavy illicit drug use. Logistic regression analyses supported relatively high rates of cigarette use, alcohol use, illicit drug use, and heavy substance use among working students. Mental health problems, especially externalizing behavioural syndromes, were found to coexist with the use and heavy use of substances. The observed associations varied somewhat by gender. CONCLUSIONS: The workplace may be an appropriate venue for establishing substance use prevention and early intervention programmes focused on younger workers, including adolescents who work part-time.

Using the data of the Indian Census of 1961, Prabhakara (1984) examined the rate of child migration to the cities of India and the proportion of the migrant children who were engaged in the labour force. The volume of child migration is found to be positively associated with total migration. Just over a fifth of the urban children were migrants but nearly forty per cent of the child labourers were migrant children who were found to be concentrated in a few occupational divisions. Rural migrant children were short distance migrants while urban migrant children made long distance moves.

Oberai *et al.* (1984) made an attempt to understand the migration, employment and the urban labour market in Punjab, India. Fears are often expressed that migration to the towns is a cause of surplus labour, increased unemployment, and the general decline in the quality of life in urban areas. In a detailed study of the interaction between migration and the urban labour market in an Indian city, the authors investigate these questions and show how the migrants fare as compared with the urban natives. They find no evidence that migrants are confined to marginal employment or contribute disproportionately to urban underemployment. Policy-makers are cautioned against adopting measures to curb migration, which is part of the process of economic growth and social advance, without first making a detailed assessment of its effects.

REFERENCES

Anker, R. and Melkas, H. (1996). Economic Incentives for Children and Families to Eliminate or Reduce Child Labour (Geneva, ILO).

Banerjee, B. (1984). Information Flow, Expectations And Job Search: Rural-To-Urban Migration Process In India. *J Dev Econ.,* 15(1-3):239-57.

Burra, Neera (1986). 'Glass Factories of Firozabad-I, Plight of Workers, Economic and Political Weekly, XXI (46), Nov. 15: 1983-1985.

Child Labour at Cracker Units Still a Reality, *The Times of India,* Nov. 5, 2002.

Deb, Sibnath (1997). Harassment of Urban Girl Children Engaged in Domestic Work. Presented in the International, Interdisciplinary Conference entitled 'Urban Childhood', organized by The Norwegian Center for Child Research, Trondheim, Norway between June 9-12, 1997.

Deb, Sibnath and Mitra, Kathakali (2002). Nature and Types of Abuse and Neglect Among Migrant Child Labour: A Qualitative Study. Presented in the International Conference on Child Abuse and Neglect held in Denver, USA in June 2002.

Human Rights Watch, The Small Hands of Slavery - Bounded Child Labour in India, Human Rights Watch, New York, 1996, p. 122.

International Labour Organisation (1996). Child Labour - Targeting the Intolerable, Geneva, 86, VI (1).

International Labour Organisation Global Report on Child Labour Cites 'Alarming' Extent of Its Worst Forms Monday 6, May, 2002.

International Labour Organisation (1993). World Labour Report. Geneva, ILO.

International Labour Organisation (1995). World Labour Report. Geneva, ILO.

International Labour Organisation Report (1992).
International Labour Organisation Report (1978).
Kothari, Smithu (1983). 'Child Labour in Sivakasi', *Economic and Political Weekly*, July 2, 1983.
Kulshreshtha, J.C. (1978). Child Labour in India, Ashish Publishing House, New Delhi.
Mathews, R,, Reis, C., and Iacopino, V. (2003). Child Labor. A Matter Of Health And Human Rights. *J Ambul Care Manage,* 26(2):181-2.
Mehra-Kerpelman, K. 1996. Children At Work: How Many And Where? *World of Work* 15:8-9.
Mitra, Nirmal (1986). 'Slave Children of Mandsaur'. Sunday, June 15-21, 1986, p.100.
Mohandas, M. (1980). 'Bidi Workers in Kerela: Conditions of Life and Work', *Economic and Political Weekely,* Sept. 6, 1980, p. 1522.
Nangia, Sudesh (1988). 'Child Workers in Carpet Weaving Industry in Jammu and Kashmir', UNICEF-ROSCA, New Delhi, Memeographed, pp. 160-161.
Naidu, Usha and Kamini, Kapadia (Eds.) (1985). *Child Labour and Health: Problems and Prospects,* Tata Institute of Social Sciences, Mumbai.
Naidu US, Parasuraman S. Health situation of working children in Greater Bombay. A report of the World Health Organization. Bombay: Tata Institute of Social Sciences, 1985.
Nangia, P. (1987). *Child Labour: cause-effect syndrome*. New Delhi: Janak Publishers.
Oberai, A.S., Manmohan, and Singh, H.K. (1984). Migration, Employment And The Urban Labour Market: A Study In The Indian Punjab. *Int Labour Rev.,* 123(4):507-23.
Patel, S. (1990). *Concepts and Measures of Child Labour in Rehabilitation of Child Labourers in India,* Ashish Publishing House, New Delhi, 43-55.
Pande, B.B. (Ed.) (1979). See the Recommendations of the National Seminar on 'Employment of Children' (Nov. 25-28, 1975, Delhi) Quoted in Edited Book, '*Child and the Law*'.
Prabhakara, N.R. (1984). Patterns Of Child Migration And Child Migrant Labour In The Cities Of India. *Janasamkhya,* 2(1):19-28.
Price, S. (2003). Employing Children's Nurses? *Paediatr Nurs.,* 15(3):24-7.
Report of the Committee on Child Labour, Government of India, 1980 (11-12).
Report of National Sample Survey Organisation (1979).
Report of National Labour Insitute, 1992.
Srivastava, S.C. (1986). 'Role of Law Towards Prevention of Exploitation of Child Labour', in the Edited book of D.N. Saraf, '*Social Policy, Law and Protection of Weaker Sections of Society*', Eastern Book Company, New Delhi.
The World Bank. 1995. *Economic Developments in India: Achievements and Challenges.* Washington: The World Bank.

UNICEF. Action to assist war-affected children in Sierra Leone proposed by special representative for children in armed conflict. Press release HR/4432, 14 September 1999, Francesca Scanlon, *acting consultant in child psychiatry.*

UNICEF, The State of the World's Children 1997, p.25.

UNICEF. *Child labour in the carpet weaving industry in Punjab.* Punjab: UNICEF, 1992.

International Labour Organization. 1993. *World Labour Report.* Geneva: International Labour Organization.

International Labour Organization. 1995. *World Labour Report.* Geneva: International Labour Organization.

Weiner, M. 1991. *The Child and the State in India.* Princeton: Princeton University Press.

Weller, N.F., Cooper, S.P., Basen-Engquist, K., Kelder, S.H., and Tortolero, S.R. (2003). The Prevalence And Patterns Of Occupational Injury Among South Texas High School Students. *Tex Med.*, 99(8):52-7.

Wu, L.T., Schlenger, W.E., and Galvin, D.M. (2003). The Relationship Between Employment And Substance Use Among Students Aged 12 To 17. *J Adolesc Health,* 32(1):5-15.

[6]

Juvenile Delinquency

Introduction

Juvenile delinquency may be described as a universal social problem. On the other hand, it may be described as a complex psychosocial problem whose growth speaks for a slow but steady rate (*Source:* Crime in India, 1981). The element of atrocity varies in nature and degree in different parts of teenagers' population of the globe. In India, a large majority of the labelled juvenile delinquent reveals antecedents of their inability to keep pace with the demands of their social and cultural realities due to personal lapses or unresolved misunderstanding with social agents. Behaviour of Indian juvenile delinquents generally reflects their inadequacies of socialization and acculturation processes—in their nature of waywardness, incorrigibility and contra-cultural reactions (Bose, 1980; Nagla, 1981; Ferdinand, 1986).

Lowrey (1928), possibly first, drew the attention of researchers about the basic psychodynamics of juvenile delinquency in the light of his propositions 'conflict over difference'. Healy and Bronner (1936) confirmed the assumptions of Lowrey in their studies with the delinquent cases. Lowrey (1944) further remarked in that the said 'conflict over difference' 'may rise with respect to any attribute to the individual physical abilities and appearance, intellectual abilities, emotional and behaviour characteristics, economic and social status of the family or self, race, religion, vocation (specially where there is a difference between vocational interests and the vocation actually engaged in) etc. The mechanism of the conflict is related to the ego ideals, real or imagined, of the individual and the group or groups in which he wishes to be accepted and valued and, perhaps, be a leader. Anything, at all which happens in group's relationships to indicate that the individual is not accepted or is actually regarded with hostility, may activate the mechanism'. By examining the self-descriptions of actual and ideal personality of delinquents, Witte and Witte (1974) ascertained that the differences between real and ideal self, were smallest for the juvenile delinquency. Many delinquents are emotionally disturbed or have personality disorders (Glueck and Glueck, 1974). Socio-economically middle-class offender is more likely to be an emotionally disturbed person than the socio-economically lower class offender. The violent behaviour of restive youth indicates the emergence of a new clustering to express a radical contra-cultural outlook (Bose, 1980). Singh (1979) found that the offenders with minor crimes show a significantly better home, social and emotional adjustment than the major crimes offenders who are better adjusted to health occupation. But, with reference to overall total adjustment scores minor crime offenders are better adjusted than the major crime offenders. Shanmugam (1988) found that neuroticism scores of the delinquent boys are higher than non-delinquent. Hartjen and Priyadarshini (1984) observed that those young people who are arrested, as offenders appear to be those who for one reason or other have lost a family network or supportive kin. In a Calcutta-based study Deb (1995) explored the personality characteristics of the teenage student population with reference to their covert cognitive impressions about self-identity, masculine adequacy, direction of person-specific aggression and communication habit. Findings revealed that 85.30 per cent of the students were free from the possibility of being drifted into delinquent practices, because of their moral and cultural values. Contradictory views and attitudes regarding the existing social and cultural norms were found present in 14.70 per cent students. Findings give a hint of poor intra-parental and parent-child relation and a tendency of parents to ignore the personal choice and likings of their children with regard to their future career, which made them unhappy and disgusted with regimented life. As a result, gradually these teenage children are becoming more dependent on peers in order to get recognition. Moreover, Deb observed that the 'risk group' students are suffering from some conflicts and confusions with regard to decision-making process and their exact role and status in the society. As a result, a hidden hostility flared up aggression and compelled the teenage students to commit delinquent acts in school and community in order to prove their masculine worth, or in pursuit of 'ego-autonomy' their aggressiveness turned them a wayward in social life (Lowrey, 1944). In another study Deb (1993) found that about 14.7 per cent teenage student population in Calcutta with predisposition conducive to delinquency while 15.6 per cent were identified as risk group. Further probing revealed that 38.4 per cent of the risk group students possessed antisocial attitude and the remaining 61.6 per cent possessed asocial attitude. Qualitatively their responses indicated an attitude favouring waywardness, incorrigibility and contra-cultural behaviour. These students badly need immediate psychological attention.

Self-concept is one of the indicators to understand whether a teenager has a possibility of being drifted into a negative direction. In this regard, one study was carried out by Deb (1993-94) in Calcutta. Findings revealed that the majority of the student population in Calcutta possessed positive self-concept i.e., free from the possibility of becoming delinquent whereas only 13.27 per cent possessed negative self-concept i.e., predisposition of becoming a delinquent. Findings suggested an early intervention programme through community approach like student counselling and periodic meeting of parents in schools and in the community.

Delinquent behaviour signifies the legally deviant behaviour of a teenager. Accordingly, it is the prototype of criminal behaviour. From sociological point of view juvenile delinquency may be described as behaviour that violets the legal norms, understanding about legally permissible behaviour and law-bound expectations of a society. Normative roles are inherent in the nature of the societal systems involving different organizations and institutions. It ranges from waywardness to serious behaviour disorders, from minor infractions to blatant violations of law.

Psychologically speaking it is a mode of responding of a particular individual to his social situations and to his organizational life. It speaks more of its subjective decisions and strategy to interact with others for the exclusion satisfaction of self in a self-centered narrow world. It involves the whole biological make-up, psychological make-up and personal, social relation of him with others around him to take law in his own hand to other obey norms of life and he thinks best and to regard that culture which his self recognizes only.

Definition

Juvenile delinquency may be referred as any behaviour of children below 18 years which disturb others and/or the community and for which legal intervention is solicited.

In other word, juvenile delinquency refers to conduct by children or youths that is either violative of the prohibitions of the criminal law or is otherwise regarded as deviant and inappropriate. The subject is treated in a variety of entries and articles (*Source:* Encyclopedia of Crime and Justice, The Free Press, NY, Vol.2, 1983).

In fact, juvenile delinquency may be regarded as a complex psychosocial problem and shoes growth speaks for a slow but steady rate. In today's context the concept of delinquency may be considered with reference to three characteristics behaviour of the teenagers viz., waywardness, incorrigibility and contra-cultural views and attitudes and with reference to 'interpersonal response trait' viz., aggression -hostility (Krech *et al*., 1962).

Profile of Juvenile Delinquents and Their Activities

Findings of a recent study revealed the profile of the deviant children. It has been observed that more than two third of the-children (67.9%) were from 12—16 years age group while about-half of them were illiterate (50.9%). It indicates that the children of higher age group are more prone to deviant activities and illiteracy is one the attributable factors behind deviancy. Out of 112 children studied, less than half (52) was selected from the street. The income of the children varies from time to time, as reported. However, the majority of them earn more than Rs. 600 per month (Table 6.1).

The children of disadvantaged families are involved in a variety of deviant activities. Stealing vegetables and fruits from the local market is the main source of earning to most of the children (25%)

Table 6.1: Profile of the Deviant Children

Profile	*Respondents (N=112)*	
	Frequency	*Percentage*
• *Age Group:*		
6 - 8 years	8	7.1
9 - 11 years	28	25.0
12 -16 years	76	67.9
• *Education:*		
Illiterate	57	50.9
Studied up to Primary Level	40	35.7
Primary and above	15	13.4
• Family Type:		
Single-parent family/orphan	42	37.5
Joint Family	14	12.5
Nuclear Family	56	50.0
• *Monthly Income of Children from Deviant Activities (Approx):*		
Below Rs. 200	10	8.9
Rs. 201 - 400	21	18.6
Rs. 401 - 600	37	33.1
Rs. 601 and above	44	39.3

Source: Deb and Mitra (2001).

concentrated in the railway station platform, followed by alcohol selling and drug peddling (20.5%), pick-pocketing in bus and local trains and dacoity (13.4%), selling stolen goods (10.7%) and gambling and begging (8.9% each). Remaining 7.1 and 5.4 per cent of the children selling pornography books and working as carrier of smuggled goods respectively.

Interestingly, street children concentrating in the railway platforms mostly survive by stealing vegetables and fruits coming to local market from the districts through local trains (Deb and Mitra, 2001). Street children are involved in deviant activities mostly under the influence of deviant peer group and for survival (Thilagaraj and Priyamvadha, 2000).

On the other hand, slum children are involved in a variety of deviant activities like selling alcohol and drugs, pick-pocketing in bus and local trains, selling stolen goods, gambling, begging, selling pornography books and working as carrier of smuggled goods. A

Table 6.2: Nature of Deviant Activities of the Disadvantaged Children

Nature of Deviant Activities	*Respondents (N=112)*	
	Frequency	*Percentage*
• Stealing vegetables and fruits from the market	28	25.0
• Alcohol selling and drug peddling	23	20.5
• Pick-pocketing in bus and local trains and dacoity	15	13.4
• Activities connected with gambling	10	8.9
• Begging pretending blind and or sick	10	8.9
• Selling stolen goods	12	10.7
• Working as carrier of smuggled goods	6	5.4
• Selling pornography books and or working in video parlor showing adult movies	8	7.1

Source: Deb and Mitra (2001).

small number of them were even found to be associated with a gang involved in criminal offence like dacoity. A variety of factors that work in combination are found to be responsible for deviant activities of the children. These are poverty, illiteracy, and deviant activities of parents, unhealthy and criminogenic environment, influence of peer group and anti-socials. Lack of parental care and guidance and sudden crisis in the family act as attributing factors in this regard. To a good number of disadvantaged children deviant activities are regarded as normal as they have been observing these activities done by their parents or seniors in the community.

Deb's study further revealed that an overwhelming number of the parents were abused and neglected in early childhood and also they experienced family disruption. In this regard, Kayfman and Zigler (1987) revealed that the parents, who experienced family disruption and were abused in childhood, tend to abuse and neglect their own children. This observation corroborates with our findings. The most damaging aspect of continuous exposure to hostile and criminogenic environment is that it develops a dare devil attitude among the children (Deb, 1996a). On the contrary, these children could be a good resource, if guided properly. Given the above scenario, there is an urgent need to develop comprehensive development and welfare plan of action for the children in need and it should be implemented through participatory approach. Although few NGOs are working for the welfare of slum children in different parts of the country, but their effort is still inadequate compared to the extent of the problem. For delivering better services NGO should have proper coordination and collaboration amongst themselves.

Classification of Juvenile Delinquents

Different academicians and researchers on the basis of their logic have classified juvenile delinquents. In the following section views of some of the researchers are given in this regard:

Psychologists have classified juvenile delinquents on the basis of their individual traits or the psychological dynamics of their personality into five groups viz., mentally defective, psychotic, neurotic, situational and cultural.

Trojanowicz (1973) has classified them as accidental, unsocialized, aggressive, occasional, professional and gang-organized.

Incidence and Nature of Crime Committed by Juvenile Delinquent in India

Reported data in regard to incidence of juvenile crimes as compared to total cognizable crime of the last ten years are depicted in Table 6.1. It may be stated without any hesitation that the reported data with regard to number of juvenile crimes in each year is far below the actual incidence owing to so many unforeseen reasons. However, this reported data may be considered as baseline information to have some idea about the situation in regard to juvenile crimes in India.

From the Table 6.1 it has been observed that incidence of juvenile crimes as compared to total cognizable crimes in the last ten years reduced gradually as in 1990 the percentage of juvenile crimes to total crimes was 0.9 per cent, which has come down to 0.5 per cent in 2000. In the last four years i.e., from 1997 to 2000 the incidence of juvenile crimes to total cognizable crime in India remained same and/or steady.

Table 6.3: Incidence and Rate of Juvenile Delinquency Under IPC (1999-2000)

Year	*Incidence of*		*% of Juvenile Crimes to Total Crimes*	*Estimated* Mid-Year Population (in lakh)*	*Rate (Incident of Crime per lakh of Population)*
	Juvenile Crimes	*Total Cog. Crimes*			
1990	15230	1604449	0.9	8270	1.8
1991	12588	1678375	0.8	8496	1.5
1992	11100	1689341	0.7	8677	1.3
1993	9465	1629936	0.6	8838	1.1
1994	8561	1635251	0.5	8999	1.0
1995	9766	1695696	0.6	9160	1.1
1996	10024	1709576	0.6	9319	1.1
1997	7909	1719820	0.5	9552	0.8
1998	9352	1778815	0.5	9709	1.0
1999	8888	1764629	0.5	9866	0.9
2000	9267	1771084	0.5	10021	0.9

**Source:* The Registrar General of India.

Further reported data in regard to nature of crimes committed by juveniles in 1990, 1995, 1996, 1996, 1997, 1998, 1999 and in 2000 are provided in Table 6.2. It has been observed that juveniles were mostly involved in crimes like theft followed by burglary, riots, hurting people, murder and attempt to commit murder, rape, robbery, dacoity, kidnapping/abduction, dowry deaths, molestation, sexual harassment and others.

Further analysis of data in regard to various categories of juvenile crime it has been observed that over the period of time over all juvenile crimes reduced significantly but certain categories of crimes committed by juveniles has increased like rape, hurting people, dowry deaths, molestation and sexual harassment. It indicates that a good number of adolescents of current generations are sexually very active and/or perverted. It could be because of influence of media and lack of guidance and supervision in the family. Lack of role model in the family and in the society is another important factor behind drifting of adolescents in a negative direction.

Table 6.4: Juvenile Delinquency (IPC) Under Different Crime Heads and Percentage Changes in 2000 Over 1990, Quinquennial Average (Q.A.) and 1999

Sl. No.	*Crime Head*	*1990*	*1995*	*1996*	*1997*	*1998*	*1999*	*Quinquennial Avg. (1995-19 QA)*	*2000*	*% Change in 2000[(+) increase/(-) decrease] over*		
										1990	*Q.A*	*1999*
1	2	3	4	5	6	7	8	9	10	11	12	13
1	Murder	377	253	270	316	253	250	**268**	**267**	**-29.2**	**-0.5**	**6.8**
2	Attempt to Commit Murder	218	208	202	147	163	179	180	196	-10.1	9.0	9.5
3	C.H. not Amounting Murder	38	23	21	25	22	21	22	27	-28.9	20.5	28.6
4	Rape	184	174	157	163	199	159	170	198	7.6	16.2	24.5
5	Kidnapping & Abduction	92	152	132	72	153	83	118	83	-9.8	-29.9	0.0
	(i) Of Women & Girls	83	66	43	48	134	66	71	54	-34.9	-24.4	-18.2
	(ii) Of Others	9	86	89	24	19	17	47	29	222.2	-38.3	70.6
6	Dacoity	116	56	44	20	35	25	36	33	-71.6	-8.3	32.0
7	Preparation & Assembly for Dacoity	9	3	0	1	2	2	2	7	-22.2	337.5	250.0
8	Robbery	185	76	87	50	52	68	67	79	-57.3	18.6	16.2
9	Burglary	1764	1285	1315	1162	1294	1344	1280	1241	-29.6	-3.0	-7.7
10	Theft	3778	2835	2356	1975	2143	2172	2296	2388	-36.8	4.0	9.9
	(i) Auto Theft	*	*	*	*	*	158	*	256	-	-	62.0
	(ii) Other Theft	*	*	*	*	*	2010	*	2132	-	-	6.1
11	Riots	1525	955	856	513	574	509	681	532	-65.1	-21.9	4.5
12	Criminal Breach of Trust	104	33	18	16	19	13	20	24	-76.9	21.2	84.6

Table 6.4: Contd...

Sl. No.	*Crime Head*	*1990*	*1995*	*1996*	*1997*	*1998*	*1999*	*Quinquenial Avg. (1995-19 QA)*	*2000*	*% Change in 2000[(+) increase/(-) decrease] over*		
										1990	*Q.A*	*1999*
13	Cheating	47	54	60	43	32	31	44	37	-21.3	-15.9	19.4
14	Counter feiting	0	1	0	1	0	7	2	3	0.0	66.7	-57.1
15	Arson	*	8	33	40	24	40	29	29	-	0.0	-27.5
16	Hurt	*	791	1395	1242	1645	1472	1309	1497	-	14.4	1.7
17	Dowry Deaths	*	27	42	49	77	52	49	78	-	57.9	50.0
18	Molestation	*	86	117	131	136	116	117	151	-	28.8	30.2
19	Sexual Harassment	*	27	13	25	37	27	26	41	-	58.9	51.9
20	Cruelty by Husband and Relatives	*	192	166	154	249	273	207	334	-	61.5	22.3
21	Importation of Girls	*	*	*	*	*	0	*	0	-	-	0.0
22	Other IPC Crimes	6793	2527	2740	1764	2243	2045	2264	2022	-70.2	-10.7	-1.1
23	**Total Cognizable Crimes Under IPC**	**15230**	**9766**	**10024**	**7909**	**9352**	**8888**	**9188**	**9267**	**-39.2**	**0.9**	**4.3**

*Indicates that the Crime Head was not introduced till that year, Calculation in Col. 12 is based on actual figures averaged

Source: National Crime Record Bureau, New Delhi

In 1999 and 2000 juveniles were mostly booked under other SLL crimes followed by Prohibition Act, Gambling Act, Indian Railway Act, Excise Act, Immoral Traffic Act, Arms Act, Prevention of Atrocities Act, Indecent Representation for Women Act, NDPS Act and other Acts (Table 6.3). As compared to 1999, in 2000 juvenile crimes were booked more under Indecent Representation for Women Act, Excise Act, Gambling Act, Protection of Civil Rights Act, NDPS Act, Essential Commodities Act, Child Marriage Restraint Act, Prevention of Atrocities Act, Immoral Traffic (P) Act and Copyrights Act.

Table 6.6: Juvenile Delinquency (SLL) Under Different Crime, Heads/Acts and Percentage Variation in 2000 Over 1999

Sl. No.	*Crime Head*	*No. of Cases Report During*		*% Change 2000 Over 1999*
		1999	*2000*	
1	Arms Act	40	35	-12.5
2	Narcotic Drugs & Psychotropic Substances Act	9	16	77.8
3	Gambling Act	113	131	15.9
4	Excise Act	75	113	50.7
5	Prohibition Act	733	519	-29.2
6	Explosive & Explosive Substances Act	7	3	-57.1
7	Immoral Traffic (P) Act	75	82	9.3
8	Indian Railways Act	105	78	-25.7
9	Registration of Foreigners Act	14	10	-28.6
10	Protection of Civil Rights Act	1	5	400.0
11	Indian Passport Act	16	4	-75.0
12	Essential Commodities Act	2	4	100.0
13	Terrorist & Disruptive Activities Act	0	0	-
14	Antiquity & Art Treasure Act	0	0	-
15	Dowry Prohibition Act	3	3	0.0
16	Child Marriage Restraint Act	1	5	400.0
17	Indecent Representation of Women (P) Act	1	25	2400.0
18	Copyrights Act	2	4	100.0
19	Sati Prevention Act	0	0	-
20	SC/ST (Prevention of Atrocities) Act	18	25	38.9
21	Forest Act	73	2	-97.3
22	Other SLL Crimes	4281	4090	-4.5
23	Total Cognizable Crimes under SLL	5569	5154	-7.5

Source: The Registrar General of India.

Causes and Dynamics of Juvenile Delinquency

The causes of deviant behaviour among children of different social and economic strata are different. The various factors single and/or in combination are responsible for delinquent behaviour among juveniles. In general, however, the causes of deviant behavour of children are categorized into three broad groups viz., (i) socio-economic, cultural and environmental factors, (ii) pathogenic family pattern, and (iii) personal pathology.

Socio-economic, Cultural and Environmental Factors

Poverty: In the third world countries like India, poverty is one of the main causes of deviant behaviour among disadvantaged children. For example, the street/destitute children mostly survive eating leftovers and stealing vegetables from the market. In the eyes of law these activities are regarded as deviant activities and are punishable. According to UN Convention on the Rights of the Child, it is the duty of the respective State Governments to provide the basic minimal facilities to the street/destitute children. But in reality most of the State Governments in India do not have any such facilities for street/destitute children. Hence, street/destitute children will survive stealing vegetables from the local trains and from the markets and/or doing deviant activities.

Since most of the street children are on their own, they mostly survive stealing vegetables and fruits from the local markets and railway station platforms. The following case study is about a street child who lives in the railway platform:

> ***Case 1:*** *KM, aged 12 years, male, never been to school, was living at Sealdah Railway Station Platform. He has no knowledge about his parents. Initially he survived eating leftovers. After sometime he developed friendship with other children in the platform. Under the influence of peer group now a day he survive stealing vegetables and fruits from the local trains and nearby wholesale market. Once he was caught for stealing and beaten up badly. But still he does the same activity for survival.*

This apart, every year a good number of poor children from Bangladesh cross the border and come to India without any valid passport. When they cross the border without valid document they are arrested by the personnel of Border Security Force and produced to Juvenile Court. Finally, Juvenile Court forwards these children to the Observation Homes for juvenile delinquents for committing the said offence. First-hand experience of author says that these children voluntarily cross the India-Bangladesh border without valid document just to be arrested by the personnel of Border Security Force, which would help them to survive. As long as they will be in the Juvenile Observation Home they will get at least two meals a day. In Bangladesh these children suffer from starvation. Whatever may be the case these disadvantaged children are regarded as juvenile delinquents according to The Juvenile Justice (Care and Protection of Children) Act, 2000. In the Observation Homes of West Bengal, the number of such category of juvenile delinquents is not insignificant.

Illiteracy: The disadvantaged children living in the rural areas and in the urban slum areas are deprived from minimum level of education. Some of them are admitted to school. But after sometime they lose interest in studies and become school drop out solely because of lack of guidance, supervision and or improper functioning of school. As a result, they have nothing to do but to engage in some deviant activities directly or indirectly encouraged by the guardians to supplement the family income.

Low Social Network: From various studies it has been observed that the people who have low social network with poor socio-economic background are prone to deviant social activities. People with high social network normally think twice before indulging themselves in deviant social activities out of a fear of being judged by people who know them. Fear of social criticism discourages children to commit deviant activities.

Academic Stress: This is experienced by growing population of tender age who lacks the ability or motivation to do well in school and are unable to find acceptable jobs in the community. Owing to the unemployment scenario in India and over competition academic pressure has become intolerable to them. The academic performance of children who cannot cope up with academic stress gradually deteriorates. As a result a large number of parents feel frustrated and never try to understand the child's capacity which in turn causes serious psychological stress among children. Finally, these children develop a feeling of rejection and under situational adversities and/or slightest provocation they involve themselves in deviant activities. The following case will illustrate the influence of academic stress in developing deviant activities among children:

> ***Case 2:*** *SD, aged 16 years, school dropout, started stealing things from homes along with his friends. He was living in a locality, where a fairly large number of adolescent boys were engaged in criminal activities like wagon breaking, stealing etc. He gave up studies after a beating by his teacher for not having prepared his lessons. After dropping out from school SD made friends with boys involved in the above activities. They often scolded and beat him. However, his mother was very affectionate to him and he used to pay her around Rs.350/ a week secretly. Environmental influence coupled with parental negligence and inappropriate corrective measures, resulted in his deviation from normal life. Due to these factors he had earlier run away from home and began to stay at Howrah Railway Station.*

Influence of Anti-socials and/or Deviant Peer Group Members

A large number of disadvantaged children without any guidance and care become the victim of circumstances and involve themselves in deviant activities under the influence of anti-socials and/or deviant peer group members knowingly or unknowingly. The following case study is an example of how anti-socials recruit innocent children to fulfil their vested interest:

> ***Case 3:*** *BD, aged 12, only child of his parents, never been to school, lives in Tiljala Bustee, lost his father while he was very young. His mother works as maidservant and somehow manages the family of two members. Owing*

to lack of guidance and care BD used to loiter here and there whole day. Two years back an anti-social involved in different criminal activities noticed BD while he was in the look out for a work. That anti-social had given him ten rupees for doing some work and asked to see him if he needs more money. That was the beginning of BD association with criminals in Kolkata. After a short period, BD became trained in different criminal activities. BD used to work as informer during dacoity and robbery and carrier of arms and bomb. Since he was minor he could easily escape attention of police. He was wanted for a long time. Finally police caught him on March 3, 2001 in the Baishali Crossing, Tangra, Kolkata. His mother visited him in the Police Station but did not urge the Police Officer to release her son.

This is not a single case. There are so many such cases of disadvantaged children in the developing countries. In fact, children of disadvantaged families mostly become victims of such circumstances.

Stressful Situation/Sudden Crisis in the Family

Although poverty is one of the prime factors responsible for leading children into deviant activities, stressful situation or sudden crisis in the family (like discordant intra-parental or parent-child relationship, problem due to second marriage) sometimes compels children to accept deviant activities. The effect of stressful situation which create crises in the family are exemplified in the following case:

Case 4: *MG, aged 15 years, was earning about Rs. 350 per month selling smuggled goods. His father, an alcoholic, worked in a restaurant at a very poor salary. He took a second wife. The stepmother started ill-treating MG, his mother and his younger sister. As a result, they had to leave the home and went to his uncle's house, where they were also ill-treated. Thus, under severe socio-*

economic distress, they came back to Calcutta and MG got involved in the said work in a bid to survive with his mother and younger sister.

Alienation and Rebellion

Feeling of unrelatedness and alienation are common to many young people today especially among the children of middle and upper class societies. Feeling of alienation develops among children who are confused about their own values and sense of identity. Often they view the world as a hostile and artificial place, inhabited by 'squares' who make unfair distinctions and discriminations about race and class, who work at useless jobs that they pompously assume are meaningful, and who try to 'sell' the younger generation on a fraudulent and inevitably disappointing way of life. Outwardly the youths may passively submit to their elders' demands, but they may find it easier to do so with the use of drugs; or they may rebel, 'drop-out', leave home, and drift into groups in which drug usage and other behaviour—considered delinquent by established social standards—is more or less the normal way of life (Coleman and Broen, 1975).

Environmental Influence

The role of environmental influence in prompting children to take deviant activities is common among the children who live in criminogenic environment. There are some localities where elderly people are involved in deviant social activities like alcohol selling, drug peddling, flesh trade, stealing etc. for survival and children have been observing these activities from the beginning of their lives. The children who live in criminogenic environment the said deviant activities are considered as normal economic activities. In some cases parents involve their children in the said activities to assist them and gradually they take up the responsibility to run the business, as their parents grow older.

So far as etiological factors with regard to deviant behaviour of the disadvantaged children are concerned, some studies have been carried out in different parts of the country. In this regard, Bose (1980, 1988) stated that faulty socialization process breads in deviant children a desire in achieving goals of life by ignoring ethics, norms and legal directives. Deb (1992) found that children in the slum and red-light areas in Kolkata are in a distressed condition and at high risk solely because of adverse social as well as physical environment where a lot of illegal activities are carried out on by the elders. Social isolation due to the parent's unlawful activities, financial hardship, psychological trauma and unhealthy living environment children of disadvantaged families are compelled to follow the family tradition in near future. In another study on socio-economically disadvantaged children Deb and Senapati (1993) identified four major modes of mal-handling by the parent's viz., physical torture, wilful negligence, exploitation of innocence and dependency of the child and enticement to accept disgraceful life.

Influence of Mass Media

With the advancement of science and technology, television (TV) programme has become very popular source of entertainment to people of all age groups. It is very informative. At the same time sometimes some of the TV programmes like violent and adult movies misguide adolescents and children and indulge them in negative directions. Influenced by some of the violent and adult movies adolescents involve themselves in deviant activities and ultimately are labelled as juvenile delinquents.

Personal Pathology

Brain Damage and Mentally Retarded

A small number of children and adolescent with brain pathology show lower inhibitory controls and a tendency toward violent behaviour (Caputo and Mandell, 1970; Loomis *et al.*, 1967). These adolescents are often hyperactive, impulsive, emotionally unstable, and unable to inhibit themselves when strongly stimulated, but typically their inner controls appear to improve with age. Often acceptance or rejection by families and peers has a marked influence on their behaviour, as does the presence or absence of opportunities to learn aggressive acts (Coleman and Broen, 1975). This apart, children and adolescents with low intelligence are unable to foresee the probable consequences of his/her actions or to understand their significance. This is particularly true in case of mentally retarded and sexually delinquent girls (Wirt *et al.*, 1962).

Neurotic and Psychotic Delinquents

About 10-15 per cent of delinquent behaviour appears to be directly associated with neurotic disorders. Here the delinquent act often takes the form of a compulsion such as 'peeping', stealing things that are not needed, or setting fires. Such compulsions often seem related to deviant sexual gratification in over inhibited adolescents who have been indoctrinated in the belief that masturbation and other overt forms of sexual discharge are terribly evil and sinful. Often such adolescents fight their inner impulses before committing the delinquent act, and then feel extremely guilty afterward (Coleman and Broen, 1975).

About 3-5 per cent of delinquent behaviour is associated with a psychotic disorder. In such cases there is often a pattern of prolonged emotional and social withdrawal, culminating, after long frustration, in an outburst of violent behaviour (Bandura and Walters, 1959). Wirt *et al.*, (1962) found a number of delinquents in this category to be descriptively schizoid rather than actually schizophrenic i.e., distant from others, eccentric in their thoughts, and showing a flatness of affect but lacking delusions, hallucinations, and other symptoms of a full-blown psychosis.

Psychopathic Delinquents

A large number of persistent delinquents appear to share the traits typical of the antisocial or psychopathic personality—they are impulsive, defiant, resentful, devoid of the feelings of remorse or guilt, incapable of establishing and maintaining close interpersonal ties, and unable to profit from experience (Coleman and Broen, 1975). Because they lack conscience and reality controls, they often engage in seemingly 'senseless' acts that are not planned but occur on the 'spur of the moment'. These adolescents may steal a small amount of money that they do not need. In essence, these adolescents are 'unsocialized delinquents' who are largely at the mercy of their inner impulses, seek stimulation and excitement, and live in the present with little thought of the future (Skrzypek, 1969).

Drug Dependent Delinquents

Nowadays an increasing number of delinquent acts—particularly acts involving stealing and prostitution—are directly related to drug problems. Most of the adolescents who are dependent on heroin must steal in order to maintain their habit, which is highly expensive. Initially drug dependent juveniles arrange money for getting drugs selling household goods. Later on they start stealing outside the home. Some of them also start peddling drugs in a condition if they can sale 10 purias (local name of heroin) they will get two purias free of cost.

Pathogenic Family Pattern

Broken Homes and Family Violence

A number of studies have found positive relationship between history of broken family as well as family violence and delinquent behaviour of the children. In a study of institutionalized delinquents, Barker and Adams (1962) found that only about a third of them came from complete home settings—in the sense that they lived with both of their original parents. More than a fourth of them lived only with the mother. Similarly, in another study Anderson (1968) observed that well over half of them came from homes lacking a father—with the incidence being higher for blacks than for whites. Since mothers or mother subordinates were almost uniformly present, Anderson concluded that the loss of the father and lack of a father surrogate was of crucial importance in the socialization failure of these delinquent youths—the youths being particularly vulnerable to parental loss from the ages of 4 - 7.

Orphan/Destitute Children

The number of street children is increasing day by day in all the Metropolitans cities in India. Since nobody is there in the street to look after street/destitute children, they live on their own and survive eating leftovers and/or stealing. In a Calcutta-based study Deb and Mitra (2001) found that most of the street/destitute children were involved in deviant activities for survival.

Influence of Deviant Activities/Habits of the Parents

Lack of ideal role model is one of the main reasons of children involved in deviant activities. Furthermore, if parents are involved in deviant activities and children observe their parent's activities from the early days of their life they accept these activities as normal. Later on, they also accept these activities in their life, directly or indirectly encouraged by their parents. Scharfman and Clark (1967) found evidence of serious psychopathology in one or both parents of 22 of the girls, including 3 cases of incest and many other types of early sexual experience. These researchers concluded that the key factors in the girls' delinquent behaviour were broken homes, combined with early affective or maternal deprivation, patterns of early sexual and aggressive over stimulation and irrational, harsh and inconsistent parental discipline. Influence of deviant occupation/habit of the parents in their children's life can be well understood by the following case study:

> **Case 5:** *PP, aged 16 years, had never been to school, eldest son, was earning money by selling alcohol. His parents were involved in this profession for a long time and this was the main source of earning. His chronic alcoholic father did not feel like admitting PP to school, rather he encouraged PP to help him in running the family business. As a result, PP was not admitted to school. For the last three years PP is running the family business, as his father is physically unfit.*

Lack of Parental Care and Negligence

Lack of parental care and negligence is one of the main factors, which draw children into negative activities. The following case excerpt is an example of linkage between parental negligence and children's deviancy:

> **Case 6**: *AH, aged 12 years, school drop-out, first child out of three, was involved in gambling, selling alcohol and stealing of petty things like bricks, iron rods, copper/aluminium wires etc. AH's father worked as a*

sweeper with the Calcutta Municipality Corporation. He was an alcoholic like AH's grandfather, due to which he was unable to maintain the family. This was stated to be the main reason for AH remaining illiterate. Rather, the father persuaded his son to take up a job instead of going to school. After sometime AH managed a job at a local shop with the help of some local boys. AH job was to sell country made liquor which helped his parents financially. Knowing the nature of AH's job his father did not object, rather he encouraged him. Later on, AH was involved in other deviant activities as mentioned above.

Juvenile delinquency is always an individual problem of the child as perceived by the interacting individuals. According to Bhattacharyya (1990), 'the important factors which are mainly responsible for delinquency are emotional, economic, environmental, and personality factors. Generally, unhappy home, uncongenial environment and social disorganization affect the juveniles—conduct, ideals, attitudes, interests, emotions and physical and mental health. Poverty may not be a direct cause of deviance or delinquency, but its unwholesome impact on the child may be disastrous. Moreover, the concomitant factors like feeling of inadequacy, frustration and emotional insecurity play a dominant role in giving rise to anti-social feelings in the child'.

In India, juvenile delinquency is gradually becoming acute in the wake of industrialization and urbanization in the country. At the same time, cities have grown with their heterogeneous population, high mobility, disrupted relationships, loss of extended family bonds and overcrowded conditions which have a beneficial effect on the prevailing value-system and of some of the established social institutions. People especially juveniles are largely affected by these changing conditions. They have been socially maladjusted and psychologically disturbed in this pool of changing values. In view of such conditions, the problem of deviance or anti-social tendencies is rearing its ugly head.

For normal physical and mental development of children minimal facilities like adequate food, safe shelter, basic education, medical care, congenial environment and love and affection are necessary. Unfortunately, disadvantaged children are deprived of all these minimal facilities and brought up in a hostile environment.

No child is born deviant. Deviant children are the products of differential social treatment. A child who receives proper care and guidance has less chance of becoming deviant. Unfortunately, in the developing countries there is a wide class difference. As a result, a child who is born in a well-to-do family enjoys all sorts of facilities while another child who is born in a poor family or on the street is deprived of minimum facilities. This sort of differential social treatment makes few children socially deviant especially the children who live in helpless condition.

Now-a-days involvement of disadvantaged children in deviant/criminal activities has increased in the metropolitan cities in India. In daily newspaper there are reports regarding dacoity, theft, stealing and pick pocketing in which disadvantaged children are involved either as an informer or active member of a group. The causes and forms of deviance among disadvantaged children may differ from locality to locality, but their direct or indirect involvement in those activities has become a regular affair. If no preventive steps are taken in future these children will become hardcore criminals. In a study carried out among teen-age student population in Kolkata, Deb (1993-1994) found that 13.27 per cent of the teen-age students possessed negative self-concept i.e., a predisposition of becoming a deviant or delinquent. The negative self-concept of the said students is expected to bear the influence of role-confusion in social life, unhealthy social and family climate and defective interpersonal relationships with family members and kin's.

Problems Created by Juvenile Delinquents

Juvenile delinquents are of two categories. Juvenile delinquents of first category are those who are already exposed and labelled as juvenile delinquents in the eyes of law. The second category of juvenile delinquents are those who are not exposed in the eyes of law and labelled as juvenile delinquents by the law. The juvenile delinquents of second category create more problems in the society than that of juvenile delinquent of first category. Most of the juvenile delinquents of first category i.e., the children who are regarded as juvenile delinquents by the law are involved in delinquent activities because of their basic needs i.e., for survival and for food. They are mostly orphan and/or destitute children and the children of very poor families. The following case studies developed on the basis of author's firsthand experience will describe the background, activities and nature of problems created by the juvenile delinquents of first category:

Case *7* (a child crossed the boarder for survival): *Ram, 13 years, male, never been to school, third child of his parents was found in a Observation Home for Juvenile Delinquents in Kolkata. Originally he was from Bangladesh. His illiterate parents working as casual labours were unable to feed their three children two meals a day. One day Ram came to know from one of his friends that if they cross the Bangladesh and India border police will arrest him for crossing the border and finally, for this crime he will be forwarded to Observation Home for Juvenile Delinquents in Kolkata where he will get at least two meals a day. Very next day he exactly did the same thing and caught by the Personnel of Border Security Force and was produced in the local Police Station and finally he was produced in the Juvenile Court. From the Juvenile Court he came to Observation Home. Replying to a question whether he is willing to study after release from the Observation Home he replied affirmative but given one condition i.e., one has to ensure that he will get two meals a day. Is he a juvenile delinquent? Perhaps in the eyes of law he is a juvenile delinquent. But for his present condition our social system is responsible.*

Case 8 (a street child was caught for stealing vegetable from the market for survival): *Shyam, 14 years, male, an orphan child, never been to school was living on the Sealdah Station. He survived by stealing vegetables from the local trains and selling it in the local market. Sealdah is a place where vegetables* *come from the neighbouring districts through local trains. Hence this is the easiest way to survive for street children living on the station. He was caught for his activities a number of times and was mercilessly physically punished. Last time when he was caught he was handed over to local Police Station and from there he was forwarded to Observation Home through Juvenile Court for his behaviour modification. The sad part of this case is that instead of behaviour modification what is required is fulfilment of his basic needs, i.e., safe shelter, food and education, which our social system is unable to provide.*

In our society and in daily life major and serious problems are created by juvenile delinquents of the second category who normally come from well off families where both the parents are not so caring about the future of their children and/or giving maximum indulgence. They form a large group. They never come in the light of law because of the contacts and resources of their family members.

Eve teasing is one of the common problems faced by the schoolgirls in our society, which is created by the second category of juvenile delinquents i.e., the children who are yet to be labelled as juvenile delinquents. During school hour they loiter in the city and in front of the girls schools with a motor cycle and disturb pretty girls either by passing bad remarks and/or trying to make friendship with them forcefully. It is really a major problem for school girls in the metropolitan cities in India.

The second major problem created by the second category of drug dependent juvenile delinquents include stealing household goods and selling it in the market for meeting the expenses of drug addiction. Initially they steal household objects and later on start stealing goods from the neighbour's house, which become a major cause of disturbance for the neighbours. They have a tendency to involve peer group members in addiction so that they can maintain their addiction habit and can have group strength. As a result, sometimes some innocent children become the victim of such peer group influence.

Since adolescence is a period of exploration and experimentation, some of the children of second category visit commercial sex workers. Sometimes they also convince other innocent children to visit the red light areas. Hence there is chance of getting HIV/AIDS and other innocent children could also be the victims of HIV/AIDS under the influence of peer group members.

Initially the children of second category are involved in the above types of unsocial activities. When they are caught by the police for some of the above activities and are exposed to their parents and parents become very much strict. As a result, there is chance of these children to be involved in major criminal activities with hardcore criminals. Thereby they become a cause of regular disturbance in the locality.

When the children of second category are exposed to law their family members feel very embarrassed and gradually the family members alienate themselves from social interaction and stop attending social occasions.

In most of the cases of the second category of juvenile delinquents parents are mostly responsible because of their over indulgence and/or over regimented attitude and their personal life style. Once the child is out of control it is very difficult for the parents to discipline him. Hence it is always advisable to develop proper friendship with the children, try to understand their psychology and need, give them some time from the busy schedule and supervise their social interaction, school performance and keep contact with the school authorities to have an up dated information about children academic performance and attendance in school.

Prevention

No single agency can stop deviant activities in the society. It requires joint effort and cooperation and support from the community people. If the personnel of Police Department receive cooperation and support from the community members it would be possible for them to maintain law and order in the society and create a healthy and congenial atmosphere which is required for leading a stress free life. Following are some of the suggested measures to prevent juvenile delinquency in the community:

- In school, students counselling programme should be introduced to deal with the problems of deviant children and help them in improving their academic performance.
- Periodic guardians meeting should be conducted in schools to give feedback to the parents about the interpersonal relationship and academic performance of the children and guide parents to develop healthy parent-child relationship.
- Strict legal measure should be taken in case of any offence committed by any juvenile regardless of their social background and this information should be circulated so that other juveniles think twice before committing any offence and/or creating any problem in the community.
- NGO should be active in providing basic minimal facilities to disadvantaged children including vocational training programme for adolescents and youths so that school drop-outs find a job/work for leading an independent life.
- In the community local youth club members should play an active role in involving children and adolescents in different community-based cultural and welfare activities which would in turn help in developing a good relationship among adolescents and bringing a healthy atmosphere in the locality.
- Local Police authorities should come forward to work together with the community members for a better social life and they should also participate in different community based programmes to gain faith and trust of common people on police and for developing good understanding about the law enforcement agencies and public.
- Community people should extend their cooperation to police for maintaining law and order in the locality providing information about criminal conspiracy and about any culprits, if known to the people.

Role of NGO

So far as welfare of street children and children in need in general is concerned, a lot of NGOs have come forward. The role of NGOs is really appreciable. For rehabilitation of the street and disadvantaged children NGOs are involved in a variety of activities like literacy programme, income generating programme, night shelter, vocational training and/or capacity building programmes.

However, a good number of NGOs lack professional expertise and lack of proper planning. First-hand experience of author says that a good number of NGOs are very serious in paper work particularly in maintaining files, but not so serious in monitoring the activities in the field. As a result, officially, perhaps, they are doing a lot for the welfare of the children in need. There is a wide gap between what NGO proposes to do in their proposal and what exactly they deliver in the field. It happens mostly because of communication gap between policy makers of an NGO and grass-roots level workers. The views of grassroots level workers are not given due importance resulting in demotivation/grievances against authorities and thereby negligence in service delivery. Hence, it is extremely necessary to develop proper communication linkage, not in paper but in practice, with the grassroots level workers, and to monitor their programme activities periodically. On the other hand, funding agencies must monitor and evaluate the activities of NGOs by an outside professional agency with a view to strengthening the future service delivery of the NGOs.

Intervention

A number of steps should be adopted to bring positive change in the behaviour, attitude and outlook of the children who have already drifted into a negative direction and are involved in delinquent activities whether legally they are stamped as juvenile delinquent or not. First, it is important to find out why a particular child is involved in delinquent activities so that need based measures could be provided to them for bringing him/her back in the mainstream of the society. This apart, the following steps should be followed:

- Providing safe shelter to orphan and destitute children so that they do not mix up with the children of deviant groups.
- Periodic counselling of the juvenile delinquents to understand their mental dynamics and to bring positive change in his/her outlook.

- Establishment of linkage of the children with their family members.
- Periodic counselling of parents who are available so that they take the child back home and for improvement of parent-child relationship.
- Vocational training of juvenile delinquents as per their aptitude and interest so that they can be self-reliant.
- Helping the children to get job and/or arrangement of loan facilities so that they can do something on their own.
- Follow-up of behaviour of the children after release from the Observation Home.

Behaviour Modification of Juvenile Delinquents

With regard to behaviour modification of deviant children several studies have been carried out in different parts of the world. These have had moderately satisfactory results. For example, La Vietes *et al*. (1965) and Weinstein (1969) observed significant improvement in the behaviour and emotional dimensions of the concerned children but noted there was no change in their academic performance. In an Indian study by Deb *et al*. (1997) found the supportive counselling and continuous efforts brought some positive change in the outlook of study subject resulting in moderate improvement in interpersonal relationships and some interest in vocational training. The findings of that study suggest detachment of children from pathogenic parental influence during rehabilitation.

In an action research, it has been observed that seven out of 10 children were successfully institutionalized and pursuing their studies satisfactorily while the remaining three children were unable to settle down to institution and became dropouts due to certain personal and environmental factors like unfavourable parental influences, pathological and deviant behaviour of either of the parents, low intelligence, organic impairment and uncongenial living environment (Deb, 1996b).

Findings of previous studies indicate some factors, which are responsible for deviant behaviour of disadvantaged children and positive benefits of behaviour modification programme for deviant children. Recent media reports indicate that crime is on the rise in the metropolitan cities in India in which children of disadvantaged families are involved either directly or indirectly.

Legal Measures

The Juvenile Justice (Care and Protection of Children) Act, 2000: See Chapter 2.

Latest Selective Study Findings

Beyers and Loeber (2003) investigated the relations between depressed mood and delinquency in a longitudinal sample of 506 urban adolescent males across ages 13.5-17.5. Adolescents provided yearly reports of their delinquent activities and depressed mood, as well as reports of peer delinquency at age 13.5 (i.e., baseline). Primary caregivers and teachers provided reports of risk factors for depressed mood and delinquency such as aggressive behaviour problems and low academic achievement. Two-level hierarchical generalized linear models of concurrent relations indicated that depressed mood predicted concurrent variety of delinquent acts, and more variety of delinquent acts predicted concurrent depressed mood, even after controlling common risk factors. Longitudinal analyses indicated that after controlling for common risk factors, depressed mood had a more robust effect on delinquency variety trajectories than delinquency variety had on depressed mood trajectories. Time-averaged depressed mood significantly predicted a more positive rate of change in delinquency variety across time. Baseline delinquency variety predicted baseline depressed mood and time-averaged delinquency variety predicted a more positive rate of change in depressed mood; however, both effects were marginally significant. Implications of the results for theory and intervention are discussed.

In a study Peters *et al.* (2003) collected self-report drug use data from 282 female alternative school students in Houston, Texas. Logistic regression analyses indicated that sexual abuse history was significantly associated with lifetime use (OR = 1.9, p < or = 0.05). While the relationships tested in this study are exploratory, they provide evidence for an important connection between sexual abuse and substance use among female alternative school students.

In a study conduced by Pevalin *et al.* (2003) found that antisocial behaviour is more stable in boys and older children. Structural factors—age of the mother, number of children in the household, and having a single parent—along with family factors—hostile parenting and maternal depression—raise the likelihood of increases in and lower the likelihood of decreases in antisocial behaviour, although there are notable differences by gender of the child and initial level of antisocial behaviour. Consequences of change in antisocial behaviour include scholastic performance, high levels of school mobility, school-parent contacts, and health perceptions.

Paradise and Cauce (2003) focused on the relationship between adolescent substance use and delinquent behaviour in a sample of homeless young people. Confirmatory factor analyses indicated that delinquency and substance use are best described as discrete factors, and competing theoretical models of the longitudinal association between these two factors were examined using structural equations modeling techniques. The results suggest that delinquent behaviour is associated with changes in alcohol, marijuana, and drug use across time. This effect was statistically significant over relatively brief lags in time of six months or less. Combined with previous results, these findings challenge the utility of single-factor explanations of adolescent deviance for at-risk populations and suggest that the relationship between substance use and externalizing across time may be more dynamic than previously thought. Implications for intervention are also discussed.

Chicago Child-Parent Centers provide comprehensive education and family support services to young, low-income children. Using data from 1,539 children in the Chicago Longitudinal Study, preschool participation was associated with significantly higher levels of school readiness, achievement, and educational attainment, and with lower rates of child maltreatment, juvenile delinquency, special education placement, and grade retention. Every dollar invested in the preschool program returned 7.14 dollars to society at large as sated by Reynolds (2003). School-age intervention also provided economic returns that exceeded costs. Findings provided strong evidence that large-scale, public, early interventions can enhance children's well-being. The authors recommend greater investments in programmes with elements similar to the Child-Parent Centers.

Ruchkin *et al.* (2003) conducted a study with a view to assessing psychopathology among incarcerated Russian juvenile delinquents in relation to the onset of conduct problems. 358 male juvenile delinquents were interviewed from January to September 1999, using the Schedule for Affective Disorders and Schizophrenia for School-Age Children-Present and Lifetime Version. Early behaviour problems, current antisocial behaviour, and psychopathology were also assessed through self-reports. The presence of conduct disorder (CD) and other diagnoses was determined according to DSM-IV criteria. About 73 per cent of the incarcerated youths met criteria for CD. About 24 per cent of the total sample reported at least one criterion for CD being present before the age of 10 years. All participants from this early-onset group fulfilled the criteria for CD. This group also had significantly higher rates of psychopathology, and particularly of externalizing behaviours, as compared with youths whose conduct problems began at or after the age of 10 years. Poor psychosocial adaptation and future prognosis in juvenile delinquents with early-onset conduct problems may be related to their greater degree of psychiatric disturbance compared with later-onset delinquent youths. Need for psychiatric treatment should be carefully considered in prevention and rehabilitation efforts for troubled youths.

Grisso *et al.* (2003) assessed the abilities associated with adjudicative competence among 927 adolescents in juvenile detention facilities and community settings. Adolescents' abilities were compared to those of 466 young adults in jails and in the community. Youths aged 15 and younger performed more poorly than young adults, with a greater proportion manifesting a level of impairment consistent with that of persons found incompetent to stand trial. Adolescents also tended more often than young adults to make choices (e.g., about plea agreements) that reflected compliance with authority, as well as influences of psychosocial immaturity. Implications of these results for policy and practice are discussed, with an emphasis on the development of legal standards that recognize immaturity as a potential predicate of incompetence to stand trial.

Penn *et al*. (2003) made an attempt to determine the lifetime history of suicide attempts in incarcerated youths and psychological factors related to suicidal and self-mutilative behaviours during incarceration. Of the 289 adolescents, 12.4 per cent reported a prior suicide attempt. Almost 60 per cent of these attempts were made using violent methods (e.g., cutting). Of the 78 clinically referred subjects, 30 per cent reported suicidal ideation/behaviour and 30 per cent reported self-mutilative behaviour while incarcerated. Suicidal clinically referred adolescents reported more depression, anxiety, and anger than non-suicidal youths. Adolescents who reported self-mutilative behaviour had higher anxiety, anger, and substance use than non-self-mutilative adolescents. Results suggest that incarcerated adolescents have higher rates of suicide attempts and use more violent methods of attempt than adolescents in the general population. Furthermore, incarcerated clinically referred suicidal and self-mutilative youths report more severe affective symptoms than their non-suicidal and non-self-mutilative counterparts, suggesting a need for mental health treatment.

Kerns and Prinz (2002) reviewed a broad range of programmes involving youth, families, or systems that aimed to prevent or reduce violence-related behaviour. The purpose of the review was to address critical issues concerning (1) target level of programming, (2) theory-driven versus problem-driven conceptualization, (3) cultural considerations, (4) developmental considerations, (5) intervention fidelity, and (6) outcome and impact assessment. Conclusions about these issues, address tendencies and trends across programmes.

The mental health needs of children and adolescents in secure care are a matter of concern, but little systematic research has been done. In this regard, Kroll (2002) found that 26 (27%) boys had an intelligence quotient (IQ) of less than 70. The need for psychiatric help was high on admission to a secure unit, with the most frequent disorders being depression and anxiety. There were high rates of aggression, substance misuse, self-harm, and social, family, and educational problems, and associated needs. Areas in which needs were mostly met included education, substance misuse, self care, and diet. Areas where the frequency of need fell substantially, but remained high, were social and family problems, and aggressive behaviours. Psychological needs persisted, with new onsets of depression, anxiety problems, and post-traumatic-stress symptoms shortly after admission. The most frequently required interventions were psychological assessment and cognitive behavioural work. Finally it may be stated boys in secure care have many needs and a high rate of psychiatric morbidity. During the admission period, secure care units address some domains of need, but others remain unchanged or get worse. Psychological and psychiatric provision in secure units need to be improved.

Bynum and Weiner (2002) examined the self-concept and violent delinquency within a group of 155 urban African-American adolescent males. Quantitative measurments of self-concept and delinquency were obtained. In general, the findings did not support containment theory. However, the study does present new data regarding serious violent delinquency.

Blomberg and Waldo (2002) provides an overview of the history and context leading to Florida's efforts to implement an evaluation-driven research and associated quality assurance system for its juvenile justice education policies and practices. The Juvenile Justice Educational Enhancement Programme began implementing Florida's evaluation research and quality assurançe system to juvenile justice education in 1998. The article includes a brief summary of articles comprising this special issue of Evaluation Review that address the Juvenile Justice Educational Enhancement Programme's various functions, methodological components, data, preliminary findings, continuing evaluation research efforts, and impediments.

Canada has no standards, procedural guidelines, or protocols for best practices in the care of youths in custody. Hence, Cesaroni (2001) argues that clear, enforceable standards are important in defining a benchmark of acceptable practice. It argues that without standards, issues may arise which can create further difficulty for youths who are under the care of the state. It suggests that the current legal framework for standards is insufficient in its enforceability and its clarity. The new Youth Criminal Justice Act (YCJA) provides the Canadian government with a timely and much-needed opportunity to establish standards of care for youths in custody.

Indeed, the YCJA contains specific, comprehensive, and relevant provisions that can be seen as laying a firm foundation for standards of care.

A meta-analysis of 51 twin and adoption studies was conducted by Rhee and Waldman (2002) to estimate the magnitude of genetic and environmental influences on antisocial behaviour. The best fitting model included moderate proportions of variance due to additive genetic influences (.32), non-additive genetic influences (.09), shared environmental influences (.16), and non-shared environmental influences (.43). The magnitude of familial influences (i.e., both genetic and shared environmental influences) was lower in parent-offspring adoption studies than in both twin studies and sibling adoption studies. Operationalization, assessment method, zygosity determination method, and age were significant moderators of the magnitude of genetic and environmental influences on antisocial behaviour, but there were no significant differences in the magnitude of genetic and environmental influences for males and females.

Richter *et al.* (2002) performed a cross-validation of results from investigations in juvenile delinquents in Russia and Germany concerning relationships of personality characteristics in terms of temperament and character with parental rearing. Both studies used the Temperament and Character Inventory (TCI) based on Cloninger's psychobiological theory, and the Own Memories on Parenting (Egna Minnen Betraffande Uppfostran-Swedish [EMBU]) questionnaire on parental rearing based on Perris' vulnerability model. The inter-relatedness of parental rearing, temperament, and character traits in socially normally integrated adolescents, as well as in delinquent adolescents, implying direct and indirect pathways from personality and parental rearing to delinquency, could be cross-validated. Differences between delinquents and socially normally integrated adolescents are rather based on different levels of expressions of various temperament traits, harm avoidance and novelty seeking in particular, and the character trait self-directedness, as well as on parental rearing behaviour (predominantly parental rejection and emotional warmth) than on different structures within related developmental processes. Copyright 2002, Elsevier Science (USA).

Ingoldsby and Shaw (2002) examined the effects of neighbourhood context on the onset and persistence of early-starting antisocial pathways across middle and late childhood. Finally, authors suggested that middle childhood may represent a critical developmental period during which children are at heightened risk for neighbourhood-based effects on antisocial behaviour problems.

Pierce and Brodsky (2002) investigated whether court-experienced juveniles differ from court-experienced adults in their understanding of the defense counsel role and their trust in attorneys. Court-experienced juveniles and young adults, ages 12 to 20, were compared on measures of trust, attitudes towards authority, understanding about the role of defense counsel, trial-related knowledge, and the Trust in My Lawyer Scale. The findings showed that court-related knowledge is associated with both level of intellectual functioning and age and that court-related misunderstandings are associated with mistrust in attorneys. The findings did not support the assertion that there are significant differences between juveniles and young adults in their trust of their attorneys. Results regarding parental involvement, attorney characteristics, and interaction effects of race and intellectual functioning in relation to trust are also discussed.

Webster *et al.* (2002) made an attempt to describe how a group of criminally involved youths obtained guns. Youths were randomly selected from a juvenile justice facility to participate in a semistructured, anonymous interview. Transcripts were coded and analyzed with the aid of textual analysis software. Of the 45 participants, 30 had acquired at least 1 gun prior to their most recent incarceration, and 22 had acquired multiple guns. About half of the first gun acquisitions were gifts or finds. The first guns youths acquired were usually obtained from friends or family. The most recent acquisitions were often new, high-caliber guns, and they came from acquaintances or drug addicts. New guns often came from high-volume traffickers. Gun acquisitions from strangers or through "straw purchases" were rare. Though few obtained guns directly through theft, some youths believed their supplier had stolen guns. Youths rarely left their community to obtain a gun.

Conclusions: Guns were readily available to this sample of criminally involved youths through their social networks. Efforts to curtail high-volume, illegal gun traffickers and to recover discarded guns from areas in which illicit drug sales take place could potentially reduce gun availability to high-risk youth.

Chae *et al.* (2001) conducted to identify attention deficit hyperactivity disorder (ADHD) in Korean juvenile delinquents. Intelligence tests (KEDI-WISC, K-WAIS), the Test of Variables of Attention (TOVA), the Teacher Report Form (TRF), the Youth Self-Report (YSR), and the Rosenberg Self-Esteem Scale were administered to 98 incarcerated Korean adolescents (the delinquent group) and 84 adolescent non-delinquents (the control group). The groups were compared, and significant differences were found for ADHD; 42.4 per cent of the adolescents in the delinquent group were identified as having ADHD, in comparison to 11.9 per cent of the adolescents in the control group. Delinquent adolescents and adolescents with ADHD were found to have lower IQ scores, poorer TOVA performance, more severe problem behaviours, and lower self-esteem than non-delinquent adolescents and adolescents without ADHD. Delinquent adolescents with ADHD consistently fared the worst on assessments of intelligence, TOVA performance, problem behaviours, and self-esteem.

Matherne and Thomas (2001) investigated the relationship between family environment and delinquency. One hundred twenty-seven 9th-grade students completed the Family Adaptability and Cohesion Evaluation Scales (FACES III; Olson, Portner, & Lavee, 1985) and a modified version of Elliot and Ageton's (1980) Self-Report Delinquency Scale. Results indicated that the relationship between the two scales was moderated by family status (traditional *versus* nontraditional). The cohesiveness of the family successfully predicted the frequency of delinquent acts for non-traditional families, but failed to predict delinquency for traditional families. Implications for counsellors, educators, and parents are discussed.

Moss *et al.* (2002) examined associations between the child's psychopathology, paternal substance dependence/antisocial personality disorder status, and measures of family and peer environments. Families with the presence or absence of paternal substance dependence were subdivided into those with and without paternal antisocial personality disorder. Grouped families were contrasted on measures of family functioning, the child's peer affiliation, and the child's problem behaviours. Regression analysis determined the influence of these factors on the child's psychopathology. Findings revealed that families with paternal substance dependence functioned worse than normal comparison families. However, families with paternal substance dependence and antisocial personality disorder (N=34) did not differ markedly from those with substance dependence without antisocial personality disorder (N=84). The children of fathers with both substance dependence and antisocial personality disorder had greater affiliation with deviant peers than those with substance dependence without antisocial personality disorder and comparison families (N=104). Children of fathers with substance dependence and antisocial personality disorder demonstrated higher externalizing and internalizing psychopathology than those with substance dependence but not antisocial personality disorder and those without either condition. Paternal substance dependence/ antisocial personality disorder status and the child's affiliation with deviant peers were most robustly associated with the child's psychopathology. Research is needed to develop interventions that effectively address parental risk and healthy peer relations.

Woodward *et al.* (2002) examined the effects of deviant and non-deviant partner involvement at age 21 on patterns of continuity and change in offending between the ages of 18 and 21 years in a birth cohort of 983 young men and women. Findings revealed that those involved with a non-deviant partner had lower rates of offending at age 21 than those with no partner, whilst those without a partner had lower rates of offending at age 21 than those involved with a deviant partner. Associations between deviant/non-deviant partner involvement and offending risk best fitted a main effects model in which both offending at age 18 and young people's partnership choices at age 21 made independent and additive contributions to the prediction of offending at age 21. There was no interaction between offending at age 18 and partner choice at age 21 in determining offending risk in early adulthood. In addition, the effects of deviant/non-deviant partner involvement on patterns of offending were the same for men and women, and were found to persist even after extensive control for the confounding effects of a wide range of selection factors measured during childhood and adolescence. These results highlight the importance of partnership choices during early adulthood in determining young people's risk of offending as adults.

Ruchkin *et al*. (2002) assessed the posttraumatic stress and its relationship to comorbid psychopathology, violence exposure, and personality traits in Russian male juvenile delinquents. Post-traumatic stress and comorbid psychopathology were assessed by a semistructured psychiatric interview (Schedule for Affective Disorders and Schizophrenia for School-Age Children-Present and Lifetime Version) in 370 delinquent youths during winter-spring of 1999. In addition, violence exposure, personality, and psychopathology were assessed by self-reports. Most delinquents reported some degree of posttraumatic stress: 156 subjects (42%) fulfilled partial criteria and 87 (25%) fulfilled full DSM-IV criteria for posttraumatic stress disorder (PTSD). Violence-related experiences (witnessing and victimization) were the most common types of trauma. Higher levels of posttraumatic stress were accompanied by higher rates of comorbid psychopathology, with the most striking differences occurring between the groups with full versus partial PTSD criteria. Violence exposure was related to temperamental behaviour activation (novelty seeking), whereas PTSD symptom scores were predominantly related to behaviour inhibition and poor coping (high harm avoidance and low self-directedness). Similar to findings from American samples, Russian juvenile delinquents represent a severely traumatized population, mainly due to high levels of violence exposure. Those with full PTSD are the most severely traumatized and have highest rates of psychopathology, as compared to those with no or partial PTSD, and they require the most clinical attention and rehabilitation. Both exposure to violence and levels of post-traumatic stress are related to personality traits, which influence degree of exposure and individual perception of stress. The latter should be considered in individualized approaches to rehabilitation.

Holt (2001) investigated the issues specific to the provision of effective mental health treatment for juvenile offenders within juvenile justice departments. A multifaceted treatment approach in this setting should include security officers as well as the customary mental health and medical professionals. Confidentiality issues direct correctional policies that require medical, mental health and security records to remain separate. Such limitations in the exchange of information reduce the likelihood that correctional officers would be considered as part of the treatment team. With high inmate to professional staff ratio and the growing attention to outcomes, this approach needs to be considered.

Stouthamer-Loeber *et al.* (2002) investigated risk and promotive effects as predictors of persistent serious delinquency in male participants of the Pittsburgh Youth Study living in different neighbourhoods. Participants were studied over ages 13-19 years for the oldest sample and 7-13 years for the youngest sample. Risk and promotive effects were studied in 6 domains: child behaviour, child attitudes, school and leisure activities, peer behaviors, family functioning, and demographics. Regression models improved when promotive effects were included with risk effects in predicting persistent serious delinquency. Disadvantaged neighbourhoods, compared with better neighbourhoods, had a higher prevalence of risk effects and a lower prevalence of promotive effects. However, predictive relations between risk and promotive effects and persistent serious delinquency were linear and similar across neighbourhood socio-economic status.

McGee *et al.* (2001) examined gender differences in exposure to violence, coping strategies and problem behaviour among 306 African-American middle and high school students in the state of Virginia. Gender differences in problem behaviours among youth exposed to violence as either victims or witnesses are examined in addition to variations in coping strategies. Relying on recent research examining violent behaviour and victimization events, the study focuses on the internalizing and externalizing behavioural characteristics (i.e., academic achievement, anxiety, depression, negative self-esteem, and delinquency) of urban students exposed to violence and the extent to which coping strategies differ. Results show specific gender differences with regard to problem behaviour and coping strategy among African-American youth exposed to violence. For adolescent males, exposure to violence and victimization is strongly associated with externalizing problem behaviours such as delinquency, while adolescent females exposed to violence and victimization are more likely to exhibit internalizing symptoms indicative of post-traumatic stress disorder. Among students exposed to violence and victimization, females are more likely to use problem-focused coping (i.e., social support) as an adaptive strategy in comparison to males.

REFERENCES

Anderson, R.E. (1968). Where's Dad? Parental Deprivation and Delinquency. *Arch. Gen. Psychiat,* 18 (6): 641-649.

Barker, G.H. and Adams, W.R. (1962). Comparison of the Delinquencies of Boys and Girls. *J. Crim. Law,* 53: 470-475.

Bandura, A., and Walters, R.H. (1959). *Adolescent Aggression.* New York: Ronald.

Beyers, J.M., and Loeber, R. (2003). Untangling Developmental Relations Between Depressed Mood And Delinquency In Male Adolescents. *J Abnorm Child Psychol.,* 31(3):247-66.

Bhattacharyya, S.K. (1990). Deviance and Social Control. *Employment News (Weekly),* XV (29): 48, Government of India Publication.

Blomberg, T.G., and Waldo, G.P. (2002). Integrating Research, Policy, And Practice In Juvenile Justice Education. *Eval Rev.,* 26(3):241-50.

Bose, Sukumar (1980). Etiology of Violent Behaviour of Restive Youth. *Social Defence,* XX, 79: 5-10.

Bose, Sukumar (1988). Juvenile Delinquency. *Social Defence,* XXVI, 95: 67-72.

Bynum, E.G., and Weiner, R.I. (2002). Self-Concept And Violent Delinquency In Urban African-American Adolescent Males. *Psychol Rep.,* 90(2):477-86.

Caputo, D.V. and Mandell, W. (1970). Consequences of Low Birth Weight. *Develop. Psychol.* 3 (3), 363-383.

Cesaroni, C. (2001). The Case For Standards For Youth In Custody In Canada. *Can J Commun Ment Health,* 20(2):107-23.

Chae, P.K., Jung, H.O., and Noh, K.S. (2001). Attention Deficit Hyperactivty Disorder In Korean Juvenile Delinquents. *Adolescence,* 36(144):707-25.

Coleman, J.C. and Broen, W.E. (1975). *Abnormal Psychology and Modern Life.* D.B. Taraporevala Sons and Co. Private Ltd. Bombay.

Deb, Sibnath (1995). Teenagers Morality: Its Structure and Relation to Delinquent Conduct. Research *Bi-annual for Movement,* 12(3): 15-21.

Deb, Sibnath (1993). A Study on The Cognitive Dispositions of School Students of Calcutta Conducive to Delinquency. *Indian Journal of Criminology and Criminalistics,* XIV,1-2: 27-37.

Deb, Sibnath (1993-1994). Identification of Predisposition towards Delinquency in the Self-concept Measures of High School Students. *Bangladesh Journal of Psychology,* 14: 11-16.

Deb, Sibnath (1996a). Perception of Juvenile Delinquents about the Society. Presented in the *4th Asian Conference on Child Abuse & Neglect,* organized by Indian Institute of Psychological and Educational Research, Calcutta, India held between 25-27 Nov. 1996.

Deb, Sibnath, Datta K. and Ghosh M. (1997). Modification of a Deviant Street Children's Behaviour: An In-depth Case Study. *Indian Journal of Criminology,* 25, 1: 15-22.

Deb, Sibnath (1996b). Institutionalization of Abused Street Children- an In-depth Study. Presented in *11th International Congress on Child Abuse & Neglect,* organized by the University College of Dublin, Dublin, Ireland held between 18-21 Aug. 1996.

Deb, Sibnath and Mitra, Kathakali (2001). Deviance Among Disadvantaged Children in Kolkata and Reasons Thereof. *Indian Journal of Criminology and Criminalistics* xxii (1): 41-53.

Deb, Sibnath and Senapati Shishir (1993b). Safety Needs of Abused Proletarian Bengalee Children (Major Modes of Causal Factors). *Indian Journal of Psychological Issues,* 1,(1):1-9.

Deb, Sibnath (1992) The Existential Crisis of the Children of Calcutta Slums and Red-light Areas. *Journal of Behavioural Research,* 3 (2): 5-14.

Ferdinand, T.N. (1986). A Brief History of Juvenile Delinquency in Bonson and a Comparative Interpretation. *International Annals of Criminology,* 24,1-2: 59-73.

Glueck and Guleck (1974). Delinquency and Crime, Thomas, Springfield III.

Grisso, T., Steinberg, L., Woolard, J., Cauffman, E., Scott, E., Graham, S., Lexcen, F., Reppucci, N.D., and Schwartz, R. (2003). Juveniles' Competence To Stand Trial: A Comparison Of Adolescents' And Adults' Capacities As Trial Defendants. *Law Hum Behav.,* 27(4):333-63.

Hartzen, C.A. and Priyardarshini, S. (1984). *Delinquency in India: A Comparative Analysis.* Rutger University Press, New Jersey.

Healy, W. and Bronner, A. (1936). Delinquents and Criminals. Three Making and Upmaking. New York: Macmillan.

Holt, C. (2001). The Correctional Officer's Role In Mental Health Treatment Of Youthful Offenders. *Issues Ment Health Nurs.*, 22(2):173-80.

Ingoldsby, E.M., and Shaw, D.S. (2002). Neighbourhood Contextual Factors And Early-Starting Antisocial Pathways. *Clin Child Fam Psychol Rev.*,5(1): 21-55.

Kaufman Joan and Zigler Edward (1987). Do Abused Children Become Abusive Parents? *American Journal of Orthopsychiatry,* 57,2:186-192.

Kerns, S.E., and Prinz, R.J. (2002). Critical Issues In The Prevention Of Violence-Related Behavior In Youth. *Clin Child Fam Psychol Rev.,* 5(2):133-60.

Krech, D., Crutchfield, R.S., and Ballachey, A. (1962). Individual in Society. McGrow Hill. Kogakusha, Tokyo.

Kroll, L., Rothwell, J., Bradley, D., Shah, P., Bailey, S., and Harrington, R.C. (2002). Mental Health Needs Of Boys In Secure Care For Serious Or Persistent Offending: A Prospective, Longitudinal Study. *Lancet,* 359(9322):1975-9.

La Vietes R., Cohen R. and Ronall R. (1965). Day Treatment Centre and School: Seven Years Experience. *American Journal of Orthopsychiatry,* 30: 468-482.

Lowery, L.G. (1928). Competitions and the Conflict Over Difference, *Mental Hygiene,* New York, 12: 316.

Lowery, L.G. (1944). Delinquent and Criminal Personalities. *Personality and the Behaviour Disorders.* The Ronald Press Company, New York, Ch.26.

Loomis, S., Robert, P.J., and Hunche, S. (1967). Prediction of EEG Abnormalities in Adolescent Delinquents. Arch. Gen. Psychiat., 17 (4): 494-497.

Matherne, M.M., and Thomas, A. (2001). Family Environment As A Predictor Of Adolescent Delinquency. *Adolescence,* 36(144):655-64.

McGee, Z.T., Davis, B.L., Brisbane, T., Collins, N., Nuriddin, T., Irving, S., Mutakkabir, Y., and Martin, K. (2001). Urban Stress And Mental Health Among African-American Youth: Assessing The Link Between Exposure To Violence, Problem Behaviour, And Coping Strategies. *J Cult Divers,* 8(3):94-104.

Moss, H.B., Lynch, K.G., Hardie, T.L., and Baron, D.A. (2002). Family Functioning And Peer Affiliation In Children Of Fathers With Antisocial Personality Disorder And Substance Dependence: Associations With Problem Behaviours. *Am J Psychiatry,* 159(4):607-14.

Nagla (1981). The Juvenile Delinquents in Society. *Indian Journal of Criminology and Criminalistics,* 9, 1: 44-50.

Paradise, M.J., and Cauce, A.M. (2003). Substance Use And Delinquency During Adolescence: A Prospective Look At An At-Risk Sample. *Subst Use Misuse,* 38(3-6):701-23.

Penn, J.V., Esposito, C.L., Schaeffer, L.E., Fritz, G.K., and Spirito, A. (2003). Suicide Attempts And Self-Mutilative Behavior In A Juvenile Correctional Facility. *J Am Acad Child Adolesc Psychiatry,* 42(7):762-9.

Pierce, C.S., and Brodsky, S.L. (2002). Trust And Understanding In The Attorney-Juvenile Relationship. *Behav Sci Law,* 20(1-2):89-107.

Peters, R.J. Jr, Tortolero, S.R., Addy, R.C., Markham, C., Escobar-Chaves, S.L., Fernandez-Esquer, M., and Yacoubian, G.S. Jr. (2003). The Relationship Between Sexual Abuse And Drug Use: Findings From Houston's Safer Choices 2 Program. *J Drug Educ.,* 33(1):49-59.

Pevalin, D.J., Wade, T.J., and Brannigan, A. (2003). Precursors, Consequences And Implications For Stability And Change In Pre-Adolescent Antisocial Behaviours. *Prev Sci.*, 4(2):123-36.

Reynolds, A.J., Temple, J.A., and Ou, S.R. (2003). School-Based Early Intervention And Child Well-Being In The Chicago Longitudinal Study. *Child Welfare,* 82(5):633-56.

Rhee, S.H., and Waldman. I.D. (2002). Genetic And Environmental Influences On Antisocial Behaviour: A Meta-Analysis Of Twin And Adoption Studies. *Psychol Bull.*, 128(3):490-529.

Richter, J., Krecklow, B., and Eisemann, M. (2002). Interrelations Between Temperament, Character, And Parental Rearing Among Delinquent Adolescents: A Cross-Validation. *Compr Psychiatry.,* 43(3):210-4.

Ruchkin, V., Koposov, R., Vermeiren, R., and Schwab-Stone, M. (2003). Psychopathology And Age At Onset Of Conduct Problems In Juvenile Delinquents. *J Clin Psychiatry,* 64(8):913-20.

Ruchkin, V.V., Schwab-Stone, M., Koposov, R., Vermeiren, R., ande Steiner, H. (2002). Violence Exposure, Posttraumatic Stress, And Personality In Juvenile Delinquents. *J Am Acad Child Adolesc Psychiatry,* 41(3):322-9.

Scharfman, M., and Clark, R.W. (1967). Delinquent Adolescent Girls: Residential Tretment in a Municipal Hospital Setting. *Arch. Gen. Psychiat.,* 17 (4): 442-447.

Shanmugam, T.E. (1988). *Psycho-social Factors Underlying Juvenile Delinquency.* University of Madras Publication, Madras.

Singh, A. (1979). A Study of Personality and Adjustment of Criminals Committing Major Crimes, *Indian Journal of Criminology,* 7, 1.

Skrzypek, G.J. (1969). Effect of Perceptual Isolation on Anxiety, Complexity Preference, and Novelty Preference in Psychopathic and Neurotic *Delinquents, J. Abnorm. Psychol.,* 74: 321-329.

Stouthamer-Loeber, M., Loeber, R., Wei, E., Farrington, D.P., and Wikstrorm, P.O. (2002). Risk And Promotive Effects In The Explanation Of Persistent Serious Delinquency In Boys. *J Consult Clin Psychol.,* 70(1):111-23.

Trojanowicz, Robert C. (1973). *Juvenile Delinquency: Concepts and Control,* Prentice Hall Inc., Englewood Cliffs, N.J.

Thilagaraj, R. and Priyamvadha M. (2000). Deviance among Street Children. *Indian Journal of Criminology,* 28,1: 41-44.

Webster, D.W., Freed, L.H., Frattaroli. S., and Wilson, M.H. (2002). How Delinquent Youths Acquire Guns: Initial Versus Most Recent Gun Acquisitions. *J Urban Health,* 79(1):60-9.

Weinstein, L. (1969). The Project Re-Ed Schools for Emotionally disturbed Children: Effectiveness as Viewed by Referring Agencies, Parents and Teachers. *Exceptional Children,* 35: 703-711.

Wirt, R.D., Briggs, P.F., and Golden, J. (1962). Delinquency Prone Personalities. III. The Sociopathic Personality: Treatment. *Minnesota Med.,* 45: 289-295.

Witte, H. and Witte, E.H. (1974). Self Descriptions of Actual and Ideal Personality by Juveniles From different Social Strata and by Juvenile Delinquents, *Zeitschrift for Social Psychologic,* 5 (3).

Woodward, L.J., Fergusson, D.M., and Horwood, L.J. (2002). Deviant Partner Involvement And Offending Risk In Early Adulthood. *J Child Psychol Psychiatry,* 43(2):177-90.

INDEX